FINANCIAL MANAGEMENT FROM AN EMERGING MARKET PERSPECTIVE

Edited by **Guray Kucukkocaoglu**
and **Soner Gokten**

Financial Management from an Emerging Market Perspective
http://dx.doi.org/10.5772/67898
Edited by Guray Kucukkocaoglu and Soner Gokten

Contributors

Eyyüp Ensari Şahin, Ceyda Aktan, İlhan Küçükkaplan, Asma Salman, Muthanna G. Abdul Razzaq, Razali Haron, Yaşar Erdinç, Bilge Canbaloglu, Gozde Gurgun, Samet Evci, Nazan Şak, Beáta Gavurová, Viliam Kováč, Martin Užík, Wladimir Schubert, Adina Turcu-Stiolica, Mihaela-Simona Subtirelu, Adriana-Elena Taerel, Anamaria Boboia, Anca Berbecaru-Iovan, Başaran Öztürk, Gizem Vergili, İrem Sevindik, Fazıl Gökgöz, Maria Kovacova, Boris Kollar, Tomas Kliestik, Lucia Michalkova, Nizamettin Başaran, Okyay Uçan, Mehmet Kenan Terzioğlu, Sema Bayraktar, Naz Sayari, Bill Marcum, Burcu Dincergok

Published by InTech
Janeza Trdine 9, 51000 Rijeka, Croatia

Publishing Process Manager Dajana Pemac
Technical Editor SPi Global
Cover InTech Design team

First published January, 2018
Printed in Croatia
Legal deposit, Croatia: National and University Library in Zagreb

Additional hard copies can be obtained from orders@intechopen.com

Financial Management from an Emerging Market Perspective, Edited by Guray Kucukkocaoglu and Soner Gokten
p. cm.
Print ISBN 978-953-51-3736-8
Online ISBN 978-953-51-3737-5

For EU product safety concerns:
IN TECH d.o.o., Prolaz Marije Krucifikse Kozulić 3, 51000 Rijeka, Croatia,
info@intechopen.com or visit our website at intechopen.com.

Meet the editor

Editor, Dr. Guray Kucukkocaoglu is a professor and chairman of the Management Department, Faculty of Economics and Administrative Sciences at Başkent University, Ankara, Turkey. He is a part-time instructor at the Turkish Military Academy, Defense Sciences Institute, and Ankara Yıldırım Beyazıt University. Dr. Kucukkocaoglu received his BSBA and MBA Finance degrees from Harmon College of Business Administration, Central Missouri State University, USA, and PhD degree from the Faculty of Political Science, Ankara University, Ankara, Turkey. He has published several books and is serving as a referee to national and international journals. Dr. Kucukkocaoglu has investment advisory, project finance, and corporate valuation experience in several national and international projects.

Co-Editor, Dr. Soner Gokten is an assistant professor at the Department of Management, Faculty of Economics and Administrative Sciences, Başkent University, Ankara, Turkey. He received his BSBA degree from the Faculty of Economics and Administrative Sciences, Başkent University, Ankara, Turkey, and his MBA in Finance and PhD in Accounting and Finance degrees from the Graduate School of Social Sciences, Gazi University, Ankara, Turkey. He has published several articles, books, book chapters, and conference proceedings. Dr. Gokten is serving as a referee to national and international journals and has investment advisory, project finance, and corporate valuation experience in several national and international projects.

Contents

Preface

One of the main reasons to name this book as *Financial Management from an Emerging Market Perspective* is to show the main differences of financial theory and practice in emerging markets other than the developed ones. Our many years of learning, teaching, and consulting experience have taught us that the theory of finance differs in developed and emerging markets. It is a well-known fact that emerging markets do not always share the same financial management problems with the developed ones. This book intends to show these differences, which could be traced to several characteristics unique to emerging markets, and these unique characteristics could generate a different view of finance theory in a different manner. As a consequence, different financial decisions, arrangements, institutions, and practices may evolve in emerging markets over time.

The purpose of this book is to provide practitioners and academicians with a working knowledge of the different financial management applications and their use in an emerging market setting. Six main topics regarding the financial management applications in emerging markets are covered, and the context of these topics are "Capital Structure," "Market Efficiency and Market Models," "Merger and Acquisitions and Corporate Governance," "Working Capital Management," "Financial Economics and Digital Currency," and "Real Estate Finance and Health Finance."

Under the "Capital Structure" topic, Razali Haron examines the ownership concentration and its influences on debt financing in Indonesia.Haron offers insights into how ownership concentration and family-owned firms decide on their capital structure and how certain distinctive characteristics of the firms influence the financing decision in an emerging market setting. Tomas Kliestik and Lucia Michalkova focus on the identification and analysis of selected methods for measuring the value of tax shield with an emphasis on the interest tax shield. As addressed by the authors, theories are based on the premise of the perfect capital market and a clearly defined corporate debt policy. However, both assumptions cannot be met in the realistic conditions of emerging markets; many businesses in emerging markets are not listed, and debt policy is determined based on the book value of debt and not on the basis of a fixed market value of debt or market leverage.

Under the "Market Efficiency and Market Models" topic, Ceyda Aktan, Eyyüp Ensari Şahin, and İlhan Küçükkaplan discuss the implications of market information efficiency on developed and emerging market economies. As majority of the studies about informational efficiency are conducted on developed markets and the interest in emerging economies began to arise, the authors try to solve the market information efficiency phenomena by analyzing the stock prices of 24 emerging economies. Yaşar Erdinç tests the CAPM and Fama-French three-factor and five-factor model with an emerging market data and shows that the five-factor model explains better the common variation in stock returns than the three-factor model and capital asset pricing model. Beáta Gavurová, Viliam Kováč, Wladimir Schubert, and Martin Užík compare the selected market indicators from North America, Europe, and Asia during the dot-com bubble. Even though the study finds similarities in developed and emerging market data, the rise in indices in both markets does not qualify for an asset price bubble. Mária Kováčová and Boris Kollár, with a goal of adjusting credit risk model to real market data, focus on the structural models of credit risk as well as models and different options for credit risk quantification. Furthermore, they tested selected structural models, namely Merton model, KMV model, Black-Cox model, and CreditGrades model, under the conditions of an emerging market.

Under the "Merger and Acquisitions and Corporate Governance" topic, İrem Sevindik and Fazıl Gökgöz analyze the M&A activities in BRICS-T countries (namely, Brazil, Russia, India, China, South Africa, and Turkey) to capture the effect of financial crises in banking sector of M&As. Their results show that Brazil, India, and Russia yield negative mean cumulative abnormal returns, and China, South Africa, and Turkey yield positive mean cumulative abnormal returns in precrisis period. In addition, South Africa, Brazil, and China yield negative mean cumulative abnormal returns, and Russia, Turkey, and India yield positive mean cumulative abnormal returns in postcrisis period. Naz Sayari and Bill Marcum's chapter is on "Corporate Governance and Financial Performance in the Emerging Markets"; they ask whether American depositary receipts (ADRs) perform any better than non–cross-listed emerging market firms. Authors examine the performance of non–cross-listed emerging market firms that implement corporate governance standards similar to those mandated of firms listed in US exchanges. Their main finding is cross-listed firms, whose common stock trades as American depositary receipts (ADRs) and who are subject to the same listing requirements as domestic US firms exhibit no evidence of improved performance.

"Working Capital Management" topic has three chapters. Burcu Dinçergök investigates the relationship between the maturity of debt used to finance working capital requirement and profitability and shows that working capital management financed with short-term financial debt has a positive effect on profitability up to a breakpoint. Above this point, the effect on profitability is found to be negative.Mutlu Başaran Öztürk and Gizem Vergili examine the relation between the components of working capital and profitability under a panel data analysis. The empirical findings of the study show that growth in sales and inventory period has a positive effect on return on assets; however, leverage, cash conversion cycle, and account receivables period have no statistically significant effects on firm profitability. Samet Evci and Nazan Şak's approach to the same topic is from a trade-off point. The authors aim to reveal the trade-off between working capital components and firm's profitability. The working capital component-firm's profitability trade-off was examined via the fixed-effects panel regression model. Findings show the existence of trade-off working capital management-profitability. A negative relationship exists between the return on assets and payables deferral period, the cash conversion cycle, the ratio of short-term financial debts to short-term debts, and the ratio of fixed assets to total assets, while return on assets is positively related to inventory conversion period and sales growth.

"Financial Economics and Digital Currency" topic covers four chapters. Bilge Canbaloglu and Gozde Gurgun study the impact of exchange rate uncertainty on the domestic investment for 25 emerging and developing economies. The empirical results show that the impact of exchange rate uncertainty on domestic investment for emerging markets and developing economies is found to be positive and significant, which may indicate the existence of risk-neutral or insensitive domestic investors to exchange rate uncertainty in these countries. Mehmet Kenan Terzioğlu discusses the importance of inflation from an emerging market perspective. Within the scope of the study, the effect of inflation uncertainty on inflation, economic growth, and selected monetary-fiscal policy variables was examined using multivariate generalized autoregressive conditional heteroscedasticity models. The dynamic conditional covariance model is designed to reflect the strong time-dependent correlation structure. While the inflation-targeting regime studies in developing countries focus on either the adoption or nonadoption of such a regime and its feasibility, this study evaluates the success of the regime in Turkey as an emerging economy. Okyay Ucan and Nizamettin Basaran suggest new policy tools for emerging countries about exchange rate management and exchange rate regimes. The authors discuss the concept and measurement of real exchange rates as well as exchange rate misalignment and its impact upon economic growth. They explain the factors that are important on the selection of an exchange rate regime and the exchange rate determinants for an emerging market and, finally, show the dilemma problem of policy, in the face of sustained capital inflows. Asma Salman and Muthanna G. Abdul Razzaq analyze the historical data of cryptocurrency Bitcoin to understand the market size, market capitalization, and price volatility of the digital currency. Time series data and financial model are applied to realize the shocks, and Monte Carlo simulation is applied to assess the dynamic structure of Bitcoin. As pointed out by the authors, with greater volume and activity, the banks and financial intermediaries may become a history of the past, and the middle man will have no place. It seems like a distant thought, but the facts are pointing toward its reality.

"Real Estate Finance and Health Finance" topic has two chapters; one of which analyses the performance stability of REIT Index and individual REITs over different subperiods and the other one analyses the impact of financial losses due to poor adherence of patients with chronic diseases on health economics. Sema Bayraktar uses three different risk adjusted measures, namely, Sharpe ratio, Treynor ratio, and Jensen's alpha, to analyze the performance stability of REITs under important regulatory changes. The results show that Treynor and Sharpe ratios rank the REITs consistently for the high growth periods. The results also show us that regulatory changes almost have no impact on the performances of the REITs. Adina Turcu-Stiolica, Mihaela-Simona Subtirelu, Adriana-Elena Taerel, Anamaria Boboia, and Anca Berbecaru-Iovan's chapter is about financial economics of health care. Authors state that financial losses due to poor adherence are the result of unnecessary time-consuming work and costs for potential harm to patients. Hospitalization rates are reduced at higher levels of medication adherence. There are two types of financial losses due to poor treatment adherence: medical costs (measured by hospitalization risk) and drug costs (without patient copayments). This financial loss analysis is an underlining to promote medication adherence by patients. National programs combining patient education with behavioral intervention strategies could decrease the financial losses due to poor adherence. To ascertain the true extent of financial losses due to low adherence in emerging countries, more studies are urgently required. The absence of national policies in these countries makes the financial losses grow due to poor adherence.

Academicians in emerging markets have been testing the field of financial management theory by adapting but mostly modifying it to the basic needs of managers, and financial managers have been applying these modified theories and sometimes developing new approaches to the discipline of finance. This book borrows from both academic and professional views of different financial management applications to provide readers with the best possible knowledge about the different applications of financial management in emerging markets.

We would like to express our sincere gratitude to all the authors for their high-quality contributions. The successful completion of this book has been the result of the cooperation of many people. In the end, we would like to thank the Publishing Process Manager Ms. Dajana Pemac for her support during the publishing process as well as the Commissioning Editor Ms. Ana Pantar for inviting us to be the editors of this book.

Professor Guray Kucukkocaoglu
Chairman, Department of Management,
Faculty of Economics and Administrative Sciences,
Başkent University,
Turkey

Assistant Professor Soner Gokten
Department of Management,
Faculty of Economics and Administrative Sciences,
Başkent University,
Turkey

Section 1

Capital Structure

Chapter 1

Ownership and Debt Financing: Indonesia Evidence

Razali Haron

Additional information is available at the end of the chapter

http://dx.doi.org/10.5772/intechopen.70618

Abstract

This study examines whether ownership concentration influences debt financing of firms in Indonesia. Known to be dominated by family owned, firms in Indonesia seem to have certain distinctive characteristics that are evidenced to have significant impact on their debt financing. Apart from the common firm-level determinants, ownership concentration does play an important role in determining the level of debt consumption of the firms. It is revealed that ownership concentration impacts the debt financing positively, reflecting the power and authority of the large controlling shareholders in using debt as controlling mechanism on the entrenched managers. The positive relationship may also be explained by the reluctance of large shareholders to engage with equity financing as to avoid ownership dilution and thus can maintain the control of the firms. In terms of ownership identity, however, family firms in Indonesia seem to consume much lesser debt level due to the alignment of interest between shareholders and managers, which makes issuing debts as manager's disciplinary tool less crucial for family-owned firms. This study contributes to the literature by offering insights on how ownership concentration and family-owned firms decide on their capital structure and how certain distinctive characteristics of the firms influence the financing decision.

Keywords: ownership, ownership identity, family owned, debt financing, emerging, Indonesia

1. Introduction

Ownership structure, an element in corporate governance, is an important mechanism in mitigating the agency problems as evidenced in many capital structure studies. Literature of corporate financing documents that agency problem in ownership structure impacts firm performance significantly. Nevertheless, not many studies tackle the issue of how concentrated ownership structure, particularly family-owned firms, impacts capital structure by taking into account the agency problem especially on emerging markets. [1] argues that the agency conflicts between the owner and the manager occur when the manager manipulates the capital structure decisions to reap wealth through activities that do not lead to value maximization. When other capital structure theories assume that managers always act in the best interests of shareholders, agency theory is focusing on the agency conflict that may arise when managers pursue their self-serving interests at the expense of the value-maximizing activities of the firm [1]. In this case, debt acts as a disciplinary tool to mitigate such agency conflict by curbing manager's self-interest management and investment decisions [2]. Entrenched managers on the other hand, who have discretion over capital structure choice, may opt to lower debt levels to avoid the disciplining role of debt. These are the most common situations investigated and explored on in the literature relating to the agency conflict when examining the impact of ownership structure on capital structure decision.

Focusing on the emerging market in the East Asian region, these markets were badly hit by the 1997 Asian financial crisis. This turmoil has been frequently documented to be attributed by a very poor corporate governance system [3]. The need for a more strategic and effective corporate governance becomes vital over the years, and ownership structure is one of the crucial mechanisms that need to be scrutinized and studied. As documented by [4], East Asian markets are known with the reputation of having a high level of ownership concentration and family control. In such an environment where high ownership concentration and family control are prevalent, the agency problems may arise between the controlling shareholders and minority shareholders and can consequently give a significant impact on the financial decision of the firms.

Firms with highly concentrated ownership, particularly family owned, have specific goals and visions comparative to nonfamily or firms with diverse ownership. Value maximization is not the only vision as they also strive for non-economic goals too, like continuous control over the firm without any interference from outside [5]. Undiversified portfolios normally carry exaggerated risks. This then cautions them over unnecessary risks that may come with debt employment in capital structure [6]. Anderson and Reeb [7] on the other hand state that family firms would opt to debt over equity to avoid dilution of control over the firm. These specific characteristics and aims of the family owned will definitely affect the financing decisions and thus require further investigation, especially on the emerging market.

Therefore, this study sets out to examine the impact of family-owned structure plus firm-level determinants on capital structure of Indonesian firms, being an emerging market to fill the gap in the literature. By using a set of recent data from the year 2000–2014 extracted from the Datastream database and annual reports over 402 firms with the employment of the Generalized Method of Moment (GMM) technique, this study seeks to examine the impact of family-owned structure plus firm-level determinants on the financing decision of the Indonesian firms. Like her other regional neighbors, Indonesia's capital market is featured by higher ownership concentration and family control [3, 4], weaker legal system and investor protection, and weaker disclosure requirements [8] and thus offers a unique case for this study to examine the impact of concentrated ownership on the financing decisions of the firms. Besides that this study also looks at the influence of the commonly cited firm-level determinants on the financing choices of firms in Indonesia. Finally, to analyze which capital structure theories are able to explain the financing decisions of the firms in Indonesia. These objectives shine out this study from the existing one and offer policy implication to not just Indonesia but also the rest of other economies as well.

The rest of the study proceeds as follows. The next section deals with capital structure theories through the lens of family-owned firms, a literature review of past studies on related issue, brief explanation of the determinants examined with the development of hypotheses and follows by the data and methodology employed for the purpose of this study. Later comes the analysis of the findings, discussion, and the last section concludes the study.

2. Capital structure theories and family-owned ownership

The most common capital structure theories which are the pecking order theory, the trade-off theory, and the agency theory are mainly originated from the seminal work of [9]. Since then, extensive studies, investigations, and examinations have been carried out throughout the decades as to determine the capability of the theories in explaining the financing decisions of firms regardless of the economic landscapes. The pecking order theory [10] explains that firm adopts a hierarchical order of financing where internal resources are the most preferred source and follows by debt then outside equity as the last resort if an external financing is required. Information asymmetry issues that occur between managers and potential outside financiers can well explain this financing preference and thus limit the firm's choice to external financing. In the context of family-owned firms, this type of ownership concentration is often characterized by informational opacity [11]; thus, asymmetric information problems are more serious. Another distinctive characteristic of family-owned firms is that they have full control over the firm's asset portfolio and thus are able to channel funds to themselves and the family [12]. In this scenario, the financing decisions of these family-owned firms will be solely motivated by the interest to preserve this privilege and minimize any possible interferences from outside via external sources of financing. The preference of internal financing with regard to the information asymmetry issues reinforces the importance of the pecking order theory in this particular framework. Moreover, Thiele and Wendt [13] state that succession is the priority of concerns in family-owned firms. Therefore, dilution of control is very much a worry and seeking external financing is not the main agenda in the financing decision [11]. The concern over the dilution of control over the firms leads managers to focus on internal financing, and should they need external financing debt will be the option comparative to outside equity since debt means a minimum level of intrusion which is then translated into lower risk of dilution of power over the firm.

The agency theory [1] states that an optimal capital structure can be achieved when the agency conflicts between shareholders, managers, and debt holders are mitigated by using debt as disciplinary mechanism. Looking in the context of family-owned firms, the conflict between shareholders and managers can be regarded as minimal since family owned can naturally align both shareholders' and managers' interests with regard to growth opportunities and risks [1] for the sake of the family as the large shareholders as well as the managers are normally among the family members. In this case, the alignment of interest between shareholders and managers makes issuing debts as manager's disciplinary tool less crucial for family-owned firms. It is expected that family-owned firms do not suffer from agency cost considering that the owner and the management of firms are the same people, and hence no issue of diverging interests is between the two parties [7]. However, expropriation of wealth at the expense of the minority shareholders still exists which literature considers it as the great disadvantage of concentrated ownership, particularly in family-owned firms [6]. Although debt does not act so much as disciplinary tool in a family-owned firm, it does help to discipline the expropriation of wealth in the firm itself [14].

Looking at the trade-off theory, its main aspect is that firms will strive for optimal debt equity ratio by maximizing benefits that come with debt employment but at the same time minimizing the cost of debt which includes bankruptcy risk and insolvency. The balanced and the equilibrium between benefits of debt and the cost of debts will ensure optimum performance of firms which will then increase firm value. From the lens of family-owned firms by controlling the firms, family gains private benefits. As documented in the body of knowledge, family owned normally pursues lower investment or undiversified due to limited use of debt to finance their operations and investment [15]. The bankruptcy risk and insolvency will also be high due to the lower investment and thus may jeopardize the private benefits. Being undiversified, bankruptcy in the firm means bankruptcy for the family too; thus, family-owned firm would try to lessen the risk by lessening the engagement of debt in their capital structure even though that means that they may sacrifice profitable projects [15]. Family-owned firms are expected to employ less debt in their capital structure. Nevertheless, being a family owned with several particular characteristics like undiversified portfolios, concern with firm and family reputation, longer investment horizons, and desire to pass the firm onto their descendent may modify the negative effect of family owned on the employment of debt. These characteristics of family owned may be translated into a reduction of monitoring cost, thus adding to a more favorable lending condition which then leads to higher level of debt use in the financing decision [11]. This notion is confirmed by [16] with evidence that family ownership is associated with greater availability of credit and a lower cost of debt financing for family firms. The concern over power dilution and control of the firm with the intrusion of outsiders drive these family-owned to engage with higher level of debt if they need to employ external financing over equity and thus follow strategies that are focusing on the survival of the company in the long run rather than pursuing value maximization [13].

3. Past studies on capital structure and ownership concentration

Margaritis and Psillaki [17] investigate the connection between capital structure and ownership structure of a firm. They anticipate that family-owned firms can affect leverage either positively or negatively, depending on the firm's risk level. A more risky firm will employ less debt, whereas a less risky firm will engage on more debt to act as monitoring measure. Anderson and Reeb [7] confirm this argument. Nevertheless, [17] document a significant positive relationship between family firm and debt ratio, indicating that the benefit of debt outweighs the cost of debt. Anderson et al. [18] postulate that family firm focuses more on long-term firm survival rather than value maximization as their main concerns are family reputation and long-term survival. As discussed earlier, debt financing is very much avoided as family-owned firms tend to be risk averse as confirmed by [19]. Family firms are argued to have a long-term commitment where succession is a vital aim and thus influences their capital structure. All the findings above illustrate the influence of the pecking order theory of capital structure in family-owned firms.

Thiele and Wendt [13] state that family-owned firms tend to use their voting power to monitor the management of the firm as they have sufficient rights to interfere in the decision making. This active monitoring can avoid managerial opportunism and can exercise their power to replace underperforming managers and cut unnecessary managers' self-interest expenditure [6]. A strong controlling power in family-owned firm acts as a signal of good performance of the firm and thus elevates value of the firm. Consequently, as explained by the signaling theory, debt is then seen as a less reliable signaling tool and hence, rationalizes the negative relationship between family-owned and capital structure as reported by [19]. On another strand, [20] in his study on publicly listed firms in Indonesia find that agency problem is very minimal in family-controlled firms, state-owned firms, or institutional-controlled firms comparative to publicly controlled firms or firms without controlling shareholders. This is according to [11] due to the lesser conflict between shareholders and managers. Nevertheless, with the presence of minority shareholders in a family-owned firm, a conflict between the two is likely to occur.

Anderson et al. [18] in their study on the debt policy of family-owned firms in the US with a sample of 252 firms from 1993 to 1998 find that the cost of debt in family-owned firms is comparatively low and thus encourages higher level of debt employment in the capital structure, a positive relationship. This findings support the notion that family-owned firms have fewer agency cost issues due to the incentive structure of family-owned firms in the US. The rationale behind this is that perhaps the main concern of the family-owned firms is their long-term relation with the lender; thus, their reputation is their vital care. Since these family-owned firms' investments are generally undiversified investments, they fear of losing the firms as it means the loss for the family as well. Croci et al. [16] also confirm that family-owned firms' main concern is to maintain good rapport with the lenders for the purpose of long-term orientation. However, on the other hand, as argued by [13], family-owned firms are more worried about preserving their control over the firm rather than worrying about bankruptcy risk and insolvency and thus engage more debt in their capital structure. Other example of positive relationship between capital structure and family-owned firms is by [14] where family-owned firms employ high level of debts in their capital structure. They postulate that those family-owned firms use debts as a replacement for independent directors. They also conclude that family-owned firms in their study employ higher debt level to discipline the managers.

Anderson and Reeb [7] investigate the variation of capital structure practice between family-owned firms and non-family owned in the US industrial sector using 2018 firms between the years 1993 and 1999. They categorize family-owned firms are those with 5% of stake, and the founder is part of the director. They find no distinctive difference between family owned and non-family owned, and the founder does not influence debt level of the US industrial firms. Ampenberger et al. [21] discovered that family-owned firms in Germany have a negative impact on the capital structure and this is perhaps due to the involvement of the founder CEO in the management.

Based on what have been reviewed above, literature has been documenting mixed results pertaining to the impact of family owned on firms' debt financing in various countries regardless of the economic landscapes. For instance, [19, 21] find family-owned firms are considerably underleveraged comparative to the non-family-owned firms. In contrast, there are studies that reveal positive relationships, indicating that family-owned firms are more leveraged than the non-family-owned firms [14, 22, 23]. Looking at the financial behavior of the firms, [21] depict family management as the main determinant of lower debt level of family-owned firms. Gottardo and Moisello [22] on the other hand report active family management as the major determinant of high debt level. Other determinants like maintenance of control and influence, growth opportunities, and risk aversion do play a part in the debt financing decisions of family-owned firms [13].

4. Past studies on Indonesia

Indonesia underwent several reformations in its financial system as its financial market activities decades ago were dull and there were a lot of flaws in the firms' financing choices with state-owned banks dominating the debt market and overshadowed the capital market [24]. It was apparent that Indonesian financial systems then needed robust deregulations and reformations. The government control over initial offering prices and the daily movement of stock prices was lifted, providing a fair game between the state and private banks, the choices between debt and equity as well as between internal and external sources of equity. Corporate governance became prevalent in Indonesia since the 1997 Asian financial crisis due to the fact that most firms are exposed to the shock wave of financial crisis. Indonesian government through the capital market regulatory body has started to initiate multiple reforms by starting enacted corporate governance's laws and regulations. Along the way, the government has developed standards and has strengthened enforcement for all listed firms in Indonesian Stock Exchange (IDX) as outlined in the good corporate governance guidelines. All listed firms in IDX should comply with corporate governance regulations [24]. After several financial reformations, trading activities in Indonesia were then started to improve and market capitalization grew alongside the development of Indonesia's financial markets and private sector highlighted by a major bull run in 1990 [25]. At present after several financial reformations and severe experiences during several financial crises, [26] predicts in the long-term perspective of 2016–2020 that Indonesia's average real growth rate is predicted to remain high at 5.5% per year, higher than the average real growth rate of 5.2% of ASEAN (10 countries) compared to China and India of 6.0 and 7.3%, respectively.

Family-owned businesses account for approximately 40% of market capitalization in Indonesia and have substantial impact on several important sectors like property, agriculture, energy, and consumer goods. Data from the Boston Consulting Group show that in the developed market like the US, many of the family businesses are into their fourth or fifth generations. However, only about 30% of Indonesian family businesses survive the first generation and about 9% move into the third generation. This implies that more than half of the family businesses in Indonesia are still in the growth phase with uncertainties in the future, thus making financial decision a crucial element to study [27]. Secondly, corporate governance in Indonesia is distinguished by the fact that the majority of firms are owned and managed by founding family members. Around 67% of listed firms in Indonesia are family controlled [4].

Looking at the journey of Indonesia's financial market for several decades and where it stands now, several studies have documented interesting findings in the literature. For examples, [28] conduct a survey on capital structure and dividend policy on the CEOs of all 180 firms listed on the IDX. The analysis reveals that firms seem to have good access to various sources of funds like debt and equities. Nevertheless, that access is not because of information asymmetry but because of fairly reasonable interest rates, thus no influence of the pecking order theory in this case. Ruslim et al. [29] analyze a sample of 18 Indonesian firms for the period of 2000–2006 and find that profitability has no significant impact on the debt financing of firms in Indonesia, again implying no evidence of pecking order theory influence in the financing decisions in Indonesia which is in line with [28]. Bunkanwanicha et al. [30], on a different strand, incorporate corporate governance arrangement in their study on Indonesia and find that weaker corporate governance seems to have higher debt level especially during financial crisis. They also highlight that country-level determinants could also impact empirical results.

Moosa and Li [24] when studying the financial structure of firms in Indonesia reveal that some firm-level determinants may not have similar impacts on the firms' capital structure like what have been documented in the body of knowledge. They also discover that the financial reformation experienced by the firms has indeed eliminated the inefficient corporate financial policies and financial market during the dominance of state banks.

Saadah and Prijadi [31] examine the capital structure of 53 manufacturing firms in Indonesia over a study period from 2001 to 2008. Using the determinants representing the main capital structure theories, they reveal that the trade-off theory and pecking order theory are quite pronounced, working side by side in the financing decisions of the firms. This implies that no single theory is able to explain the capital structure of firms and thus supports [32] statement that a collaboration of theories is needed to better explain the financing choices of firms. Hardiyanto et al. [33], using a panel data from year 2005 to 2011 on 228 companies, conclude that firms in Indonesia have specific level of debt ratio in their capital structure and try to maintain that debt ratio level for it is believed to maximize firm value. They also argue that certain firm-level determinants do play significant roles in maintaining the debt ratio; thus, managers should take into account the costs that the firm may incur should they adjust their capital structure in striving for value maximization.

Very recently, Haron [25] investigates 365 listed companies using a panel data from year 2000 to 2011 and concludes that POT has significant influence on the capital structure of firms in Indonesia, with several determinants affecting the financing decisions. This is perhaps, according to [25], due to the effects of the financial deregulations taken place where internal financing is also significantly preferred in financing investments and projects, not merely bank loans as previously discussed. An indication of market timing theory at work is also traced where firms seem to time their equity issuance.

Literature on Indonesia has also been compiling evidences where firms with highly concentrated ownership structure suffer with agency problems between the controlling shareholders and minority shareholders [11, 12, 34, 35]. This study therefore reveals the insights on how ownership concentration in Indonesia impacts the financing decisions and can perhaps be inferred to by her neighboring countries for which they are reported to share similar ownership concentration structure and thus fill the gap in the literature.

5. Determinants of capital structure and hypotheses development

5.1. Firm-level determinants

The corporate financing literature has acknowledged the significant impact of ownership concentration on capital structure thus be regarded as important determinants to be examined [34]. Literature has been compiling evidences on several firm-level determinants having significant influence on debt financing decisions and is relevant to either one specific capital structure theory or a mixture of more than one theory at work. The most commonly cited firm-level determinants discussed in the literature are non-debt tax shield (NDTS), firm size, business risk, tangibility, liquidity, profitability, intangibility, growth, age of firms, and share price performance. Frank and Goyal [36] identified and highlighted these determinants as the core factors that are frequently used in empirical capital structure research.

5.2. Ownership concentration

Large shareholders have the incentive and power to monitor and control the action of managers [6]. Debt acts as the controlling mechanism, making it difficult for managers to adjust capital structure according to their own interests. Besides, family-owned firms may prefer debt than equity financing to avoid ownership dilution and thus retain control on the firm. This suggests a positive relationship between family-owned concentrated ownership and capital structure. Li et al. [37] find that ownership structure positively influences debt financing decision of state-owned firms in China. Several studies also find positive relationship between concentrated ownership and leverage like [34, 38, 39].

In contrast, large controlling shareholders in a concentrated ownership can act as a controlling mechanism as a substitute of debt to monitor management activities [1]. Thus, a negative relationship between ownership concentration and debt financing is expected. In addition, large controlling shareholders are also at the position to expropriate their personal interests at the expense of minority shareholders [6]. This increases agency cost for debt, and large controlling shareholders would prefer equity financing to expropriate from minority shareholders; hence, it explains the negative relationship [40]. Ownership concentration is measured based on the shareholdings of 5% and above [11, 35]. The hypothesis for this variable is that: H_1: ownership concentration has a positive influence on debt financing.

5.3. Ownership Identity

Ownership identity can affect capital structure decisions both positively and negatively [17]. Family-owned firms always put long-term commitment as their main priority, making sure it spans at least for two family generations [34]. Having good rapport with the lenders, family ownership is associated with greater availability of credit and much lower cost of debt financing [13]. Thus, family-owned firms become more leveraged comparative to other types of ownership structure or non-family-owned firms. Studies like [14, 22, 23] report a positive relationship between ownership identity (family owned) and leverage.

Nevertheless, ownership identity can also affect debt financing negatively depending on the management's interests and main agenda [34]. Carrying the reputation of being undiversified and risk averse, taking higher level of risk by engaging with more debt will not be in their main financial strategy. Family-owned firms comparative to non-family owned are very much concern over their social reputation, and the fear of a tarnished reputation due to financial distress will keep them away from debt consumption. Thus, these firms will be very much underleveraged as compared to their non-family-owned firms. The alignment of interest between shareholders and managers being a family-owned firm minimizes the agency cost and thus makes issuing debts as manager's disciplinary tool less crucial. Studies like [19, 21] confirm the negative relationship between family owned and leverage. This study therefore hypothesizes that H_2: ownership identity has significant influence on debt financing. This study uses dummy code of '1' for family-owned firms while "0" for non-family-owned firms. The status of the firm, either family owned or non-family owned, is based on the name of the biggest shareholder in the annual report of the firm for the respective years [41].

5.4. Non-debt tax shield (NDTS)

After the MM irrelevance theory, taxes are included in capital structure study and reveal that firms can reap substantial gains from tax shield. But firms are cautioned of the possibility of default in interest payments if debt is employed excessively in the capital structure and thus may lead to financial distress and eventually face bankruptcy risk [36]. To safeguard from such risks of using debt financing, firms may opt to tax loss carry forward, investment tax credits, and depreciation or also known as non-debt tax shield (NDTS). Frank and Goyal [36] argue that NDTS should be negatively correlated with leverage as NDTS is the alternative to tax shields provided by debt financing. Significant negative relationship between NDTS and leverage is reported in [42] on Indonesian firms, supporting [36]. NDTS is represented by annual depreciation expenses to total asset [36]. Thus, following the literature, this study hypothesizes that H_3: NDTS has a negative influence on debt financing.

5.5. Firm size

Size of firm is also documented to have a significant influence on debt financing. Larger firms are seen to have better access to a bigger debt consumption as they are more diversified, thus lesser tendency to fail. This indicates a positive relationship which supports the trade-off theory. Larger firms should be less affected by information asymmetry problems as information regarding the firms is much easier to obtain and more accessible comparatively; thus, debt financing is easily accessible to them. Ameer [42] and De Jong et al. [43] support this trade-off theory explanation on the relationship between firm size and debt financing. However, [25] depicts significant negative relationship between size and debt financing. Perhaps according to [25], the negative relationship is due to the effects of Indonesian financial market deregulation activities where the control over initial offering prices and the daily movement of stock prices were lifted and thus encouraged large firms to issue equity over debt. Firm size is represented by natural logarithm of total asset [25]. The hypothesis is that H_4: firm size has a positive influence on debt financing.

5.6. Business risk

Earnings before interest and taxes (EBIT), also known as operating profit, is a core profit a firm earns from the business it is in and is related to a firm's normal operations and are expected to recur every year unlike the non-recurring items such as gain or loss on sale of assets. Hence, EBIT is a good gauge of how well a firm is being managed and is watched closely by all stakeholders and it measures both sales and cost of a firm. EBIT is also closely linked to firm-level economic factors as changes in economy will affect changes in a firm's earnings (earnings volatility). Earning volatility is commonly translated as business risk of firms as well. Higher earnings volatility may increase the risk of default on debt payments. Therefore, debt financing should be avoided, indicating a negative relationship. Haron [25], Ameer [42], and De Jong et al. [43] find business risk having a significant negative relationship with debt financing among firms in Indonesia. Firms with high degree of risk may prefer equity issuance to debt for business expansion and competencies. As a result, equity holders would seek for higher return as compensation to the higher risk taken on investment. Business risk is represented by yearly change in the firm EBIT [25]. Here, the hypothesis is that H_5: business risk has a negative influence on debt financing.

5.7. Tangibility

Tangible assets help firms obtain more debt from lenders as tangible assets act as collateral, making debt less risky. Lenders are more willing to lend to firms with high tangible assets as these assets are easier to repossess in bankruptcy; thus, a positive relationship is anticipated between tangible assets and debt financing as explained by the trade-off theory. Moosa and Li [24], Bunkanwanicha et al. [30], and De Jong et al. [43] all share similar significant positive relationship between tangibility and debt financing in their studies on Indonesian firms. Tangible asset is represented by net fixed asset over total asset [25, 43]. As for tangibility, the hypothesis is that H_6: asset tangibility has a positive influence on debt financing.

5.8. Liquidity

When a firm is said to be liquid, the internal funds will be quite substantial; thus, the need for debt financing will be lessen. This is explained well by pecking order theory that firms with high liquidity need less debt financing and opt to internal funding given the huge retained earnings of the firm. This reflects a negative relationship between liquidity and debt financing, and this notion is well supported by [24, 25]. Firm liquidity is represented by current asset to current liabilities [24, 25]. The hypothesis is that H_7: firm liquidity has a negative influence on debt financing.

5.9. Profitability

Asymmetric information problem is a concern and can affect the financing choice of a firm. Managers of firms with high profit and cash flows might opt to internal resources first when deciding on investment financing as a mean to mitigate information asymmetry [10] as these are the cheapest funds rather than using external financing, either debt or equity. Hence, profitability is expected to affect debt financing negatively, indicating the support of the pecking order theory. Moosa and Li [24], Haron [25], Ameer [42], and De Jong et al. [43] all share similar result of negative relationship between profitability and debt financing in their studies on Indonesian firms. Firm's profitability is represented by EBIT over total asset [25]. Thus, the hypothesis for this variable is that H_8: firm's profitability has a negative influence on debt financing.

5.10. Intangibility

Intangible assets like copyright, goodwill, patent, trade mark, and research and development costs do have significant impact on debt financing of firms [44]. The trade-off theory and the agency theory suggest a negative association between intangible assets and debt financing, while the pecking order theory implies that firms with more intangible assets confront more asymmetric information problem and thus use more debt financing. Chen and Strange [44] find positive relationship between intangibility and leverage in their study on the Chinese listed firms. Chen and Strange [44] find that intangible assets do help firms in China in confronting information asymmetry problems as intangible assets like goodwill are capable to increase borrower's access to debt in order to mitigate this problem. Intangibility is measured by the ratio of intangible assets to total assets [44]. The hypothesis is that H_9: intangibility has a positive influence on debt financing.

5.11. Growth

Firms with good growth record require huge funds to continue its encouraging growth and investment opportunities for expansion. The agency theory explains that growth firms will choose to issue equities to fund their operations and investments as a signal to the outsiders that they are not facing any underinvestment and asset substitution problems. Therefore, growth is expected to relate negatively with leverage. POT also sees a negative relationship between growth and debt financing as being large firms they are expected to have substantial retained earnings. De Jong et al. [43] support this negative relationship in their cross-country studies that include Indonesian firms. Growth is represented by market value of equity over book value of equity. Following literature, the hypothesis is that H_{10}: firm growth has a negative influence on debt financing.

5.12. Age

With regard to age, the hypothesis is that the older the firm is, the more it is able to accumulate funds and the less it will need to borrow either long term or short term. In other words, a new firm will not have time to retain funds and may be forced to borrow. Consequently, age is likely to be negatively related to debt financing [45]. Older firms have longer track records and therefore a higher reputational value. Age of firm is measured from the year of listing on the stock exchange [44]. The hypothesis is that H_{11}: age has a negative influence on debt financing.

5.13. Share price performance

Equity issuance will be preferred if a firm accumulates a strong share price performance with the present market values comparatively higher than the past market values. On the other hand, firm will repurchase equity if the situation is otherwise. This notion is based on the market timing theory, indicating a negative relationship between share price performance and debt financing. Haron [25] find significant negative relationship between share price performance and debt financing on Indonesian firms. Share price performance is represented by yearly change in year-end share price [24, 25]. The hypothesis for this variable is that H_{12}: share price performance has a negative influence on debt financing.

6. Data and Methodology

6.1. Data

This study analyzes 402 non-financial listed Indonesian firms between 2000 and 2014 (4737 total observations) with data extracted from the Datastream and annual reports of firms. As a normal practice in capital structure research, financial firms (banks, insurance companies, and investments trusts) are excluded from the sample. The 402 sample firms consist of 75% out of 537 listed firms on the IDX (as of December 2016), and this proportion could be regarded as the whole population of firms for generalization purposes. The sample firms cover firms from the various industries of listing that include agriculture, consumer products, industrial, infrastructure and utilities, mining, properties, trade and services, and miscellaneous industry.

Only firms with a minimum of three consecutive observations toward the end of the study period are included in the dataset [25], meaning that the firms should at least be listed on the IDX from the year 2012. Unbalanced panel data are utilized due to the different listing dates of firms within the study period of 2000–2014. **Table 1** presents the structure of the panel data on sample firms for this study.

6.2. Methodology

Debt financing (leverage) in this study, as applied in other capital structure studies, is defined as the ratio of total debt to total asset (at book value) [17, 30, 46]. To examine the determinants of leverage, this study employs the Generalized Method of Moment (GMM). This technique has the advantage of addressing bias due to the presence of lagged dependent variables, or endogeneity of other explanatory variables, associated with the fixed effects in short panels [47], and GMM can be used to control for these issues [48].

To test the hypotheses, the following regression model is employed:

http://dx.doi.org/10.5772/intechopen.70618

$$\begin{aligned} Lev_{it} = \beta_0 Lev_{it(-1)} + \beta_1 OWN_{it} + \beta_2 OWNID_{it} + \beta_3 NDTS_{it} + \beta_4 SIZE_{it} + \beta_5 RISK_{it} \\ + \beta_6 TANG_{it} + \beta_7 LIQ_{it} + \beta_8 PROF_{it} + \beta_9 INTANG_{it} + \beta_{10} GROW_{it} + \beta_{11} AGE_{it} \\ + \beta_{12} SPP_{it} + \varepsilon_{it} \end{aligned} \quad (1)$$

where the dependent variable, Lev_{it}, represents the leverage level of firm i at time t. $Lev_{it(-1)}$ represents the lag leverage and firm-level determinants comprising of ownership concentration (*OWN*), ownership identity (*OWNID*), non-debt tax shield (*NDTS*), firm size (*SIZE*), business risk (*RISK*), asset tangibility (*TANG*), liquidity (*LIQ*), profitability (*PROF*), intangibility (*INTANG*), growth (*GROW*), firm age (*AGE*), and share price performance (*SPP*), and ε_{it} is the error term.

This study takes the first difference of Eq. (1) to eliminate the firm's fixed effects, thereby avoiding any correlation between unobserved firm-specific effects and the explanatory variables.

$$\Delta Lev_{it} = \beta_0 \Delta Lev_{it(-1)} + \sum_{n=1}^{N} \beta_k \Delta X_{kit} + \Delta\epsilon_{it} \quad (2)$$

Eq. (2) denotes the model estimated based on the GMM (first difference). One of the advantages of GMM is that it can handle important modeling concerns, namely the fixed effects and endogeneity of regressors, while avoiding dynamic panel bias. It is important to note that the flexible GMM framework accommodates unbalanced panels, a characteristic of micropanel dataset in this study, as well as endogenous variables [25]. Hence, this study uses GMM for the purpose of estimation.

No. of annual observations for each firm	Number of firms	No. of observations
3	5	15
4	13	52
5	19	95
6	19	114
7	27	189
8	34	272
9	15	135
10	11	110
11	22	242
12	6	72
13	8	104
14	8	112
15	215	3225
Total	402	4737

Table 1. Panel data structure.

To ensure the efficiency of the GMM estimator, this study performs three diagnostic tests which are the Wald test to assess the joint significance of the determinants of leverage (null: all coefficients on the determinants of leverage are jointly equal zero); the AR(2) or second-order autocorrelation test (null: no second-order autocorrelation in the residuals); and the *J*-test, a test for the validity of the instrumental variables representing $Lev_{it(-1)}$ (null: instrumental variables are valid). Estimates derived from the GMM are only consistent if there is no second-order autocorrelation in the residuals and instrumental variables representing $Y_{it(-1)}$ are valid. To check for multicollinearity, this study performs the variance inflation factor (VIF) on each independent variable in the regression model. As a rule of thumb, the VIF for each independent variable should be less than 10 to avoid multicollinearity problem.

7. Analysis and findings

7.1. Descriptive statistics

Table 2 summarizes the descriptive statistics of all variables in this study. Indonesian firms employ mean leverage of 0.3691 in their capital structure. Ownership concentration shows on average 47.64% ownership exceeds 5% shareholding with the maximum and minimum of 100% and 0, respectively. This statistic shows that the ownership structure of public Indonesian firms is highly concentrated. Utama et al. [11] posit that it is quite prevalent for public firms in Indonesia to have only a few shareholders with substantially large holdings (i.e., at least 5%). Profitability shows a mean of 0.0654 ranging from −2.9565 to 2.8310. Business risk on firms as represented by yearly change in firms' EBIT is found to be substantial, shown by

Variable	Mean	Maximum	Minimum	Median	Standard deviation
TD/TA	0.3691	0.9020	0.0998	0.3355	0.1872
Ownership	0.4764	1.0000	0.0000	0.5700	0.3383
Ownership identity	0.5643	1.0000	0.0000	1.0000	0.4959
NDTS	0.0310	0.6045	0.0000	0.0244	0.0384
Firm size	11.5277	16.8969	4.1109	11.5955	1.7817
Risk	−0.0594	28.5000	−29.7739	−0.0275	3.0502
Tangibility	0.3922	0.9852	0.0000	0.3677	0.2504
Liquidity	2.1793	29.8679	0.1027	1.4378	2.6678
Profitability	0.0654	2.8310	−2.9565	0.0672	0.1791
Intangible	0.0164	0.9650	0.0000	0.0000	0.0621
Growth	8.3666	97.8479	0.6000	2.9101	14.2480
Age	15.4104	38.0000	3.0000	15.0000	7.6098
Share price performance	0.0058	2.7810	−4.8121	0.0010	0.2038

Notes: Number of all firms = 402; Number of observations = 4737.

Table 2. Descriptive statistics.

the standard deviation of 3.0502, bigger than the mean of −0.0594. Tangible asset has a much higher mean of 0.3922 compared to intangible asset, 0.0164 as recorded. On firm age, firms in Indonesia have been listed on the stock exchange for 15.4104 years on average, with the longest and shortest listing of 38 years and 3 years, respectively.

7.2. Determinants of leverage

Based on **Table 3**, nine determinants which are ownership, ownership identity, NDTS, size, risk, tangibility, liquidity, profitability, and age of firm are found to significantly influence the debt financing of Indonesian firms throughout the period understudy.

This study depicts a positive relationship between ownership and debt financing. Higher level of concentrated ownership has a positive influence on debt financing ($p = 0.01$), and H_1 is thus supported. This finding supports the findings by [17, 34, 39]. The positive relationship depicted in this study reflects the power and authority of the large controlling shareholders in a highly concentrated ownership environment employing debt as controlling mechanism on

Leverage	TD/TA	VIF
Explanatory variables	(BV)	
Leverage (−1)	0.5348*** [15.0492]	
Ownership	0.1336*** [6.7850]	1.02
Ownership identity	−0.0524* [−1.71113]	1.03
NDTS	−0.7378*** [−3.8734]	1.75
Size	−0.2187*** [−14.7435]	1.12
Risk	−0.0004* [−1.7384]	1.01
Tangibility	0.3063*** [7.1220]	1.25
Liquidity	0.0159** [2.1750]	1.03
Profitability	−0.3759*** [−97.2889]	1.58
Intangible	0.0012 [0.0049]	1.07
Growth	−0.0002 [−0.1438]	1.09
Age	0.0087***[3.4140]	1.06
Share price performance	−0.0794 [−1.5366]	1.03
AR(1) *m*-statistic	−1.1835	
p-Value	0.2366	
AR(2) *m*-statistic	0.2431	
p-Value	0.8080	
J-Statistic	89.3520	
p-Value	0.1997	
Wald test (*F*-statistic)	3932.7750***	
p-Value	0.0000	
Observations	4737	

Notes: ***, **, *denote probability values significant at 1, 5, and 10% levels, respectively. The *t*-statistics in parenthesis are the *t*-values adjusted for White's heteroscedasticity consistent standard errors. The Wald test statistic refers to the null hypothesis that all coefficients on the determinants of debt financing are jointly equal to zero; the *m*-statistic for AR(2) refers to the null of no second-order correlation in the residuals; the *J*-test statistic for the null that the over identifying restrictions are valid. The VIF test of less than 10 confirms that there is no multicollinearity problem.

Table 3. Determinants of debt financing.

the managers. The positive relationship may also be explained by the reluctance of large shareholders to engage with equity financing as to avoid ownership dilution and thus can maintain the control of the firms.

In terms of ownership identity, the result shows that ownership identity has significant influence on debt financing (p = 0.10), thus H_2 is supported. Family-owned firms is found to consume lesser debt financing compared to the non-family-owned firms. This is well explained by the fact that family-owned firms are known with the reputation of being risk averse [19]; thus, debt engagement is very much avoided. The lesser consumption of debt by the family-owned firms depicted could also be the result of the alignment of interest between shareholders and managers, which makes issuing debts as manager's disciplinary tool less crucial for family-owned firms. It is expected that family-owned firms do not suffer from agency cost considering that the owner and the management of firms are the same people, and hence no issue of diverging interests is between the two parties [7].

This study records a negative relationship between NDTS and debt financing (p = 0.01); thus, H_3 is supported. Following the trade-off theory, since engaging to debts means bringing in risks and insolvency to the firms, firms may opt to NDTS. Frank and Goyal [36] argue that NDTS should be negatively correlated with debt financing as NDTS is the alternative to tax shields provided by debt financing. Significant negative relationship between NDTS and debt financing is reported in [42] on Indonesian firms. Looking from the lens of family-owned firms, debt is very much avoided being risk averse and the active monitoring by the family in the firm makes debt less needed as disciplinary tool on the managers and hence explains the negative relationship.

A negative relationship is reported between size and debt financing (p = 0.01), in contrast to H_4 in which a positive relationship is expected. Haron [25] also depicts significant negative relationship between size and debt financing. Perhaps according to [25], the negative relationship is due to the effects of Indonesian financial market deregulation activities where the control over initial offering prices and the daily movement of stock prices were lifted and thus encouraged large firms to issue equity over debt. Nonetheless, looking at the nature of family-owned firms, the fear of power dilution and the concern over business risk and insolvency have hindered the firms to employ higher level of debt in the capital structure. The larger the firms, the more retained earning they have accumulated; thus, debt is the least choice of financing, following the pecking order theory.

Risk is also found to negatively related to debt financing (p = 0.10), and H_5 is then supported. Trade-off theory explains that the higher the debt employment the riskier it gets for the firms in case of default payments; thus, debt financing should be avoided. Haron [25], Ameer [42], and De Jong et al. [43] find business risk having a significant negative relationship with debt financing among firms in Indonesia. One of the distinctive characteristics of family-owned firms is being risk averse for fear of losing the firm in case of bankruptcy risk and insolvency. It is therefore expected of these family firms to avoid debt employment in their capital structure as to avoid the risks that come with it.

This study depicts a positive relationship between tangibility and debt financing (p = 0.01). This finding supports H_6. Tangible assets help firms obtain more debt from lenders as tangible assets act as collateral, making debt less risky. Moosa and Li [24], Bunkanwanicha et al. [30], and De Jong et al. [43] all share similar significant positive relationship between tangibility and debt financing in their studies on Indonesian firms. Degryse et al. [49] argue that the positive effect of tangibility on total debt comes entirely from long-term debt as these tangible assets are used to secure long-term debt. This argument confirms the characteristics of family-owned firms in Indonesia where for the case of family-owned firms, long-term orientation is very crucial in keeping the firm to the family for the next generation as suggested by [16].

Liquidity is reported to relate positively with debt financing (p = 0.05), in contrast to H_7 in which a negative relationship is expected. When firms in Indonesia have high liquidity level, they seem to increase their debt consumption perhaps to reap the tax shield advantage supporting the trade-off theory. Looking at the case of family-owned firms in Indonesia, this finding is in line with the argument by [50] where liquidity is found to positively relate to long-term debt and again being family-owned firms, long-term debt ensures continuity of controlling power for the family which is the main concern for such firms, thus rationalizes the positive relationship depicted in this study.

Profitability is found to relate negatively with debt financing (p = 0.01). H_8 is thus supported. Highly profitable firms in Indonesia choose to use their retained earnings to finance their investments, thus reflecting the influence of pecking order theory in their debt financing decisions. Supporting [24, 30] the negative relationship reported may be the results of the financial reformations taken place in Indonesia which have opened up and encouraged firms to turn to their retained earnings instead of merely bank loans to finance their investments. For the case of family-owned firms, using retained earnings can become the main agenda as to avoid dilution of power and unnecessary intrusion from outsiders via equity financing [13].

Age of firm is positively related to debt financing (p = 0.01), H_{11} is thus supported. Conforming to what has been argued previously in past studies, the older the firm, apparently, will have more impressive track record and thus become less risky comparative to new firms. Being considered as less risky encourages lender to lend more and firms can reap the benefits of debt following the trade-off theory. From the view of family-owned firms, with the impressive track record over the years, these aged family-owned firms enjoy greater availability of credit [16] and a lower cost of debt financing [23].

Nonetheless, results of this study show that three determinants (intangibility, growth, and share price performance) appeared to be insignificant in the debt financing decisions of Indonesian firms despite being reported as important factors in capital structure studies.

8. Conclusion

This study examines the impact of ownership concentration, ownership identity, and other firm-level determinants on debt financing decisions of firms in Indonesia based on the GMM technique. The result from this study is robust to heterogeneity, autocorrelation, endogeneity, and multicollinearity concern. Debt financing in this study is defined as total debt to total asset.

Certain firm-level determinants like ownership concentration, ownership identity, NDTS, size, risk, tangibility, liquidity, profitability, and age of firm do have significant influence on the debt financing of the firms understudy. However, certain hypotheses cannot be supported like size, liquidity and age where the study reveals contrasting results from what have been hypothesized.

The concentrated ownership phenomenon among the emerging market and in this case Indonesia does have a significant impact on debt financing of firms. The positive relationship recorded in this study may be explained by the reluctance of large shareholders to engage with equity financing as to avoid ownership dilution and thus can maintain the control of the firm. In terms of family-owned firms, it is revealed that family-owned firms in Indonesia consume lesser leverage compared to the non-family-owned firms perhaps for several reasons depending on the management of the firm. Literature acknowledges family-owned firms as being risk averse [19]; thus, debt engagement is very much avoided. The lesser consumption depicted could also be the result of the alignment of interest between shareholders and managers, which makes issuing debts as manager's disciplinary tool less crucial for family-owned firms. It is expected that family-owned firms do not suffer from agency cost considering that the owner and the management of firms are the same people, and hence no issue of diverging interests is between the two parties [7].

From the study, it is apparent that large firms with higher profitability in Indonesia seem to employ low level of debt for they fear of bankruptcy risk and insolvency. These large firms seem to use the non-debt tax shield in their capital structure as to avoid the cost of debt. The riskier it gets, the lesser debt engagement it would be for these firms, and they would opt to retained earnings accumulated being a large firm with a high profitability level. The fear of business risk and insolvency reflects the effect of trade-off theory, and at the same time the pecking order theory is also in the picture when internal financing is more preferred. Nevertheless, aged firms with high tangible assets and high level of liquidity seem to engage with a higher level of debt in their capital structure. This must be due to the tax shield advantage that comes with debt employment as explained by the trade-off theory. Another possible explanation is that these aged, very liquid firms with high tangible assets employ debt to mitigate agency conflict that may occur.

The finding from this study has important policy implications. This study reveals that firms in Indonesia do not seem to consider equity issuance as an alternative to debt financing with insignificant impact on the influence of share price performance being detected from the analysis. This may be perhaps, according to Ref. [51], Indonesia has a limited number of non-bank financial institutions and the equity and debt markets are still under developed. This phenomenon also reflects the distinctive characteristic of family-owned firms where controlling power and succession of firms onto the next generation being the main agenda instead of economic advantage. The fear of dilution of power from the intrusion of outsiders through equity issuance has slashed out equity financing in their capital structure agenda. Managers should be sensitive over the interests of the shareholders who are normally the board of directors of the firms to preserve the controlling power among the family forever without any interference from outside. The large shareholders should also be aware of the possibility of expropriation of wealth in the expense of the minority shareholders that may exist.

Therefore, looking what have been revealed from the findings, this study contributes significantly to the existing literature with a deeper insight of the determinants of debt financing of firms in Indonesia. The very recent dataset used and the robust methodology employed have indeed enriched the literature on Indonesia being an emerging market. The nature of family-owned firms does have great influence in the debt financing decisions, and this input is a valuable contribution to the literature of corporate governance particularly regarding ownership concentration in terms of family-owned firms. The policy implications discussed earlier could definitely help in constructing better and more efficient policy in the future.

Being an emerging market, the findings can definitely be extended as a base for future research in the area of corporate financing regardless of the economic landscape, whether developed or emerging market as both markets have been evidenced to share similar significant determinants in deciding the debt financing of the firms. Both developed and emerging markets can also learn from this case study of Indonesia especially on the impact of family-owned firms on debt financing decisions. Other emerging markets particularly can also infer their economic and legal systems standing and learn from Indonesia for being an emerging market they are known to have weak legal systems with less developed financial market comparative to their developed market counterparts. Other emerging markets with high ownership concentration level in their corporate governance can also learn from Indonesia as depicted in this study. Debt can be an effective controlling mechanism to discourage managers to manage cash flows and investments at their own self-interest. Debt can also act as a safeguarding mechanism as to avoid ownership dilution; thus, the large shareholder can maintain their controlling power in the firm.

This study, however, has limitation. Despite relatively utilizing recent data and bigger sample firms compared to the previous limited studies on Indonesia, the results of this study, however, need to be cautiously interpreted. This study does not perform each industry regression individually. All the industries are pooled together as the main focus of this study is to examine the factors affecting debt financing of firms in general without giving particular attention to individual industry. Perhaps for future research, study can be done on individual industry as firms in different industry react differently, responding to certain characteristic of each individual industry.

Author details

Razali Haron

Address all correspondence to: hrazali@iium.edu.my

IIUM Institute of Islamic Banking and Finance, International Islamic University Malaysia, Kuala Lumpur, Malaysia

References

[1] Jensen MC, Meckling W. Theory of the firm: Managerial behavior, agency costs and ownership structure. Journal of Financial Economics. 1976;**3**(4):305-360. DOI: 10.1016/0304-405X(76)90026-X

[2] Jensen MC. Agency costs of free cash flow, corporate finance, and takeovers. American Economic Review. 1986;**76**(2):323-329

[3] Carney RW, Child TB. Changes to the ownership and control of East Asian corporations between 1996 and 2008: The primacy of politics. Journal of Financial Economics. 2013;**107**(2): 494-513. DOI: 10.1016/j.jfineco.2012.08.013

[4] Claessens S, Djankov S, Fan JP, Lang LH. Disentangling the incentive and entrenchment effects of large shareholdings. The Journal of Finance. 2002;**57**(6):2741-2771

[5] Corbetta G, Salvat C. Self-serving or self-actualizing? Models of man and agency costs in different types of family firms: A commentary on comparing the agency costs of family and non-family firms: Conceptual issues and exploratory evidence. Entrepreneurship Theory and Practice. 2004;**28**:355-362. DOI: 10.1111/j.1540-6520.2004.00050.x

[6] Shleifer A, Vishny RWA. survey of corporate governance. The Journal of Finance. 1997;**52** (2):737-783. DOI: 10.1111/j.1540-6261.1997.tb04820.x

[7] Anderson RC, Reeb DM. Founding-family ownership, corporate diversification, and firm leverage. Journal of Law and Economics. 2003;**46**(2):653-684. DOI: 10.1086/377115

[8] La Porta R, Lopez de Silanes F, Shleifer A. Corporate ownership around the world. The Journal of Finance. 1999;**54**(2):471-517. DOI: 10.1111/0022-1082.00115

[9] Modigliani F, Miller M. The cost of capital, corporation finance, and the theory of investment. American Economic Review. 1958;**48**(3):261-297

[10] Myers SC, Majluf NS. Corporate financing and investment decisions when firms have information that investors do not have. Journal of Financial Economics. 1984;**13**(2):187-221. DOI: 10.1016/0304-405X(84)90023-0

[11] Utama CA, Utama S, Amarullah F. Corporate governance and ownership structure: Indonesia evidence. Corporate Governance: The International Journal of Business in Society. 2017;**17**(2):165-191. DOI: 10.1108/CG-12-2015-0171

[12] Carney RW, Hart HN. What do changes in corporate ownership in Indonesia tell us? Bulletin of Indonesian Economic Studies. 2015;**51**(1):123-145. DOI: 10.1080/00074918.2015.1016570

[13] Thiele FK, Wendt M. Family firm identity and capital structure decisions. Journal of Family. Business Management. 2017;**7**(2):221-239. DOI: 10.1108/JFBM-05-2017-0012

[14] Setia-Atmaja L, Tanewski GA, Skully M. The role of dividends, debt and board structure in the governance of family controlled firms. Journal of Business Finance and Accounting. 2009;**36**(7):863-898. DOI: 10.1111/j.1468-5957.2009.02151.x

[15] Mulyani S, Janni AM, Khamimah D. Policy on entry in the use of intellectual property rights (mark) denotes intangible asset as fiduciary security object efforts to support economic development in Indonesia. International Journal of Business, Economics and Law. 2014;**5**(4):51-56

[16] Croci E, Doukas JA, Gonenc H. Family control and financing decisions. European. Financial Management. 2011;**17**(5):860-897. DOI: 10.1111/j.1468-036X.2011.00631.x

[17] Margaritis D, Psillaki M. Capital structure, equity ownership, and firm performance. Journal of Banking and Finance. 2010;**34**:621-632. DOI: 10.1016/j.jbankfin.2009.08.023

[18] Anderson RC, Mansi SA, Reeb DM. Founding family ownership and the agency cost of debt. Journal of Financial Economics. 2003;**68**(2):263-286. DOI: 0.1016/S0304-405X(03) 00067-9

[19] Schmid T. Control considerations, creditor monitoring, and the capital structure of family firms. Journal of Banking and Finance. 2013;**37**(2):257-272. DOI: 10.1016/j.jbankfin.2012. 08.026

[20] Perdana IBP, Kusumastuti R. Analysis of the impacts of family ownership on a company's costs of debt. International Journal of Administrative Science and. Organization. 2011;**18**(2): 143-151

[21] Ampenberger M, Schmid T, Achleitner AK, Kaserer C. Capital structure decisions in family firms: Empirical evidence from a bank-based economy. Review of Managerial Science. 2013;**7**(3):247-275. DOI: 10.1007/s11846-011-0077-2

[22] Gottardo P, Moisello AM. The capital structure choices of family firms: Evidence from Italian medium-large unlisted firms. Managerial Finance. 2014;**40**(3):254-275. DOI: 10.1108/MF-03-2013-0065

[23] Burgstaller J, Wagner E. How do family ownership and founder management affect capital structure decisions and adjustment of SMEs? Evidence from a bank-based economy. The Journal of Risk Finance. 2015;**16**(1):73-101. DOI: 10.1108/JRF-06-2014-0091

[24] Moosa I, Li L. Firm specific factors as determinants of capital structure. Evidence from Indonesia. Review of Pacific Basin Financial Markets and Policies. 2012;**15**(2):1-17. DOI: 10.1142/S021909151150007X

[25] Haron R. Do Indonesian firms practice target capital structure? A dynamic approach. Journal of Asia Business Studies. 2016;**10**(3):318-334. DOI: 10.1108/JABS-07-2015-0100

[26] Economic Outlook for Southeast Asia, China and India 2017. Addressing Energy Challenges [Internet]. Available from: https://www.oecd.org/dev/asia-pacific/SAEO2017_PV.pdf

[27] Why Indonesia. Family Matters – A Guide to Family Owned Businesses in Indonesia [Internet]. 2016. Available from: http://www.gbgindonesia.com/en/main/why_indonesia/2016/family_matters_a_guide_to_family_owned_businesses_in_indonesia_11459.php [Accessed: June 8, 2017]

[28] Ang JS, Fatemi A, Tourani-Rad A. Capital structure and dividend policies of Indonesian firms. Pacific-Basin Finance Journal. 1997;**5**(1):87-103. DOI: 10.1016/S0927-538X(96)00025-X

[29] Ruslim H. Pengujian struktur modal (Teori Pecking Order): Analisis empiris terhad saham di LQ-45. Jurnal Bisnis dan Akuntansi. 2009;**11**(3):209-221

[30] Bunkanwanicha P, Gupta J, Rokhim R. Debt and entrenchment: Evidence from Thailand and Indonesia. European Journal of Operational Research. 2008;**185**(1):1578-1595. DOI: 10.1016/j.ejor.2006.08.025

[31] Saadah S, Prijadi R. Capital structure's dynamic response to exogenous variables: A case of listed manufacturing firms in Indonesia. International Journal of Financial Research. 2012;**3**(2):86-95. DOI: 10.5430/ijfr.v3n2p86

[32] Myers SC. Financing of corporations. Handbook of the Economics of Finance. 2003;**1**(1): 215-253. DOI: 10.1016/S1574-0102(03)01008-2

[33] Hardiyanto AT, Achsani NA, Sembel R, Maulana NA. Testing trade-off theory of capital structure: Empirical evidence from Indonesian listed companies. Economics and Finance Review. 2014;**3**(6):13-20

[34] Driffield N, Mahambare V, Pal S. How does ownership structure affect capital structure and firm value? Recent evidence from East Asia. Economics of Transition. 2007;**15**(3):535-573. DOI: 0.1111/j.1468-0351.2007.00291.x

[35] Siregar SV, Utama S. Type of earnings management and the effect of ownership structure, firm size, and corporate-governance practices: Evidence from Indonesia. The International Journal of Accounting. 2008;**43**(1):1-27. DOI: 10.1016/j.intacc.2008.01.001

[36] Frank MZ, Goyal VK. Capital structure decisions: Which variables are reliably important? Financial Management. 2009;**38**(1):1-37. DOI: 10.1111/j.1755-053X.2009.01026.x

[37] Li K, Yue H, Zhao L. Ownership, institutions, and capital structure: Evidence from China. Journal of Comparative Economics. 2009;**37**(3):471-490. DOI: 10.1016/j.jce.2009.07.001

[38] Cespedes J, Gonzalez M, Molina CA. Ownership and capital structure in Latin America. Journal of Business Research. 2010;**63**(3):248-254. DOI: 10.1016/j.jbusres.2009.03.010

[39] Alimehmeti G, Paletta A. Ownership concentration and effects over firm performance: Evidences from Italy. European Scientific Journal. 2012;**8**(22):39-49

[40] Liu Y, Li Y, Xue J. Ownership, strategic orientation and internationalization in emerging markets. Journal of World Business. 2011;**46**(3):381-393. DOI: 10.1016/j.jwb.2010.07.012

[41] Villalonga B, Amit R. How do family ownership, control and management affect firm value? Journal of Financial Economics. 2006;**80**(2):385-417. DOI: https://doi.org/10.1016/j.jfineco.2004.12.005

[42] Ameer R. Financial liberalization and firms' capital structure adjustments evidence from Southeast Asia and South America. Journal of Economics and Finance. 2010;**37**(1):1-32. DOI: 10.1007/s12197-010-9158-3

[43] De Jong A, Kabir R, Nguyen TT. Capital structure around the world: The roles of firm- and country-specific determinants. Journal of Banking and Finance. 2008;**32**(9):1954-1969. DOI: 10.1016/j.jbankfin.2007.12.034

[44] Chen J, Strange R. The determinants of capital structure: Evidence from Chinese listed companies. Economic Change and Restructuring. 2005;**38**(1):11-35. DOI: 10.1007/s10644-005-4521-7

[45] Hall GC, Hutchinson PJ, Michaelas N. Determinants of the capital structures of European SMEs. Journal of Business Finance and Accounting. 2004;**31**(5–6):711-728. DOI: 10.1111/j.0306-686X.2004.00554.x

[46] Anabila AA, Whang E. Culture, capital structure, and implications for accounting regulation. Journal of Corporate Accounting and Finance. 2017;**28**(2):22-44. DOI: 10.1002/jcaf.22250/full

[47] Batten JA, Vo XV. Foreign ownership in emerging stock markets. Journal of Multinational Financial Management. 2015;**32**:15-24. DOI: 10.1016/j.mulfin.2015.05.001

[48] An Z, Li D, Yu J. Earnings management, capital structure, and the role of institutional environments. Journal of Banking and Finance. 2016;**68**:131-152. DOI: 10.1016/j.jbankfin.2016.02.007

[49] Degryse H, Goeij P, Kappert P. The impact of firm and industry characteristics on small firms capital structure. Small Business Economics. 2012;**38**(4):431-447. DOI: 10.1007/s11187-010-9281-8

[50] Akinlo OO. The effect of working capital on profitability of firms in Nigeria: Evidence from general method of moments (GMM). Asian Journal of Business and Management Sciences. 2011;**1**(2):130-135

[51] Indonesia Crisis Monitoring and Response System (CMRS) [Internet]. 2010. Available from: http://documents.worldbank.org/curated/en/140081468260136422/pdf/706390ESW0P1160CMRS0Detailed0Report.pdf [Accessed: June 12, 2017]

Chapter 2

Review of Tax Shield Valuation and Its Application to Emerging Markets Finance

Tomas Kliestik and Lucia Michalkova

Additional information is available at the end of the chapter

http://dx.doi.org/10.5772/intechopen.70943

Abstract

Due to the existence of tax-deductible expenses, a tax advantage, called tax shield, arises. The aim of the chapter is to identify and define the well-known approaches associated with tax shield, mainly interest tax shield and to analyze the approaches to quantify the present value of interest tax shields. Finally, we identify those that can be used in the conditions of emerging markets.

Keywords: tax shield, valuation, debt, interest, emerging markets

1. Introduction

The issue of tax shields is an increasingly important object of interest for both business managers and academics. Worldwide in recent years, the volume of leveraged buyouts and management buyouts (MBOs) has increased. In this case, debt is an important component of value [1].

Tax expenses generate tax savings (tax shields), which significantly affect business decision-making, especially investment decision-making and capital structure issues. The most important sources of tax savings are interest and depreciation. Therefore, tax shields are divided into two main categories: interest and non-interest tax shields.

More than 50 years of research on tax shield has brought a number of theories to quantify them. The main area of research is the interest tax shield, which has a direct influence on the company's decision about the capital structure, acceptance or non-acceptance of investment projects.

Chapter focuses on the identification and analysis of selected methods for measuring the value of tax shield with an emphasis on the interest tax shield. In Section 2, we define the tax shield and review the main tax shield valuation models. These models are subdivided in accordance with the chosen corporate debt policy. Section 3 is focused on tax shield models when book value of debt is assumed. In Section 4, we summarize the findings from the previous sections and examine which models are applicable in emerging markets. We also analyze which factors affect the value of tax shield and how the identified gaps can be addressed. In Section 5 we sum up the previous information.

2. Main tax shield valuation theories

Within this section, we will focus on defining the tax shield and the breakdown of tax shield theories according to debt policy that divides the theory into two categories: if debt is fixed or if leverage is constant. For investment decision-making, the present value of tax shield is an important category. The criterion for choosing an appropriate method of quantification is the nature of the debt policy which is part of corporate financial management. Debt policy is the source of differences between theories as it determines what discount rate is chosen to quantify the present value of tax shield.

Among economists, there is no consensus about which theory is correct, a source of disagreement is the discount rate used in calculating the present value of tax shield. Copeland et al. [2] argue: *The finance literature does not provide a clear answer about which discount rate for tax benefit of interest is theoretically correct.*

2.1. Definition of tax shield

The tax shield is the result of tax deductibility of business expenses. This is defined as: *A tax shield is a reduction in taxable income for an individual or corporation achieved through claiming allowable deductions such as mortgage interest, medical expenses, charitable donations, amortization and depreciation. These deductions reduce a tax payer's taxable income for a given year or defer income taxes into future years. Tax shields lower the overall amount of taxes owed by an individual taxpayer or a business* [3].

It follows from the previous definition that the source of the tax shield (also called tax benefit or tax advantage or TS) is the different type of business expenses. The most significant sources of expenses include interest and other deductions; therefore tax shields are divided into interest and non-interest. According to Brealey et al. [4], an interest tax shield is defined as: *tax savings resulting from deductibility of interest payments*. According to Damodaran [5], the interest tax shield is expressed in a similar vein: *Interest is tax-deductible, and the resulting tax savings reduce the cost of borrowing to firms.*

The first impulse for the development of different approaches how to quantify tax shield, was the theory of Modigliani and Miller [6]; the authors created the first widely accepted theory of capital structure. The model assumes perfect capital market, risk-free interest rate and zero taxation of corporate income. Capital structure is given by real assets, for examaple, irrelevant to the value of the business. Therefore, it is not important whether the company is levered or not. The main flaw of this theory, however, was the absence of taxes.

This unrealistic assumption has been removed in the modified model of Modigliani and Miller [7], abbreviated *MM* model, resulting in the fact that the value of the company increases with the growth of company's leverage. The newly created value results from tax deductibility of interest and represents the value of tax shield. The value of the levered company is given by Eq. (1) and shown in (**Figure 1**).

$$V_L = V_U + PV(TS) \tag{1}$$

The value of tax shield is simply given as corporate tax rate times the cost of debt times the market value of debt.

$$TS = Tk_D D \tag{2}$$

If the debt is constant and perpetual, the company's tax shield depends only on the corporate tax rate and the value of debt. Then the present value of tax shield equals the discounted value of Eq. (2).

$$PV(TS) = \frac{Tk_D D}{k_D} = TD \tag{3}$$

Eq. (2) is the formula for calculating the interest tax shield based on the Modigliani and Miller theory [7], Eq. (3) is the formula of its present value.[1] It is based on the assumption that the main source of tax shields (hereinafter *TS*) is the interest accruing from the company's leverage.

It should be noted that the tax shield is influenced by three variables: the tax rate, cost of debt and the value of debt. Liu [8], in contrast to the previous formulae, considers tax shield as a variable influenced by four variables: *Tax shield is a function of four variables "net income, interest rate, debt, and tax rate." However, the value of the MM tax shields only includes two variables "debt and tax rate," is independent of interest rate, and cannot be true.*

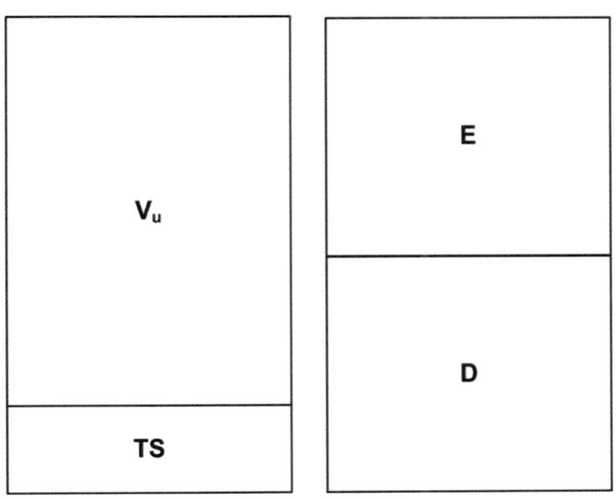

Figure 1. Value of levered company according to Modigliani and Miller [7].

[1]If it is assumed that debt is risky.

Tham and Velez-Pareja define two different methods of calculating the present value of tax shields: *There are two ways to define the present value of tax shield (PVTS). First, the PVTS is simply the tax shield (TS), discounted by the appropriate discount rate for the tax shield* ψ. *Second, the PVTS is the difference in the taxes paid by the unlevered and levered firms* [9].

Fernandez, on the other hand, argues that only one definition is true: *the value of tax shields is the difference between the present values of two different cash flows, each with their own risk: the present value of taxes for the unlevered company and the present value of taxes for the levered company* [10].

These definitions are ambiguous and suggest that the value of tax shield is a function of multiple quantitative and qualitative variables, one of the key variables is debt policy of the company.

2.2. Tax shield valuation theories if debt is constant

2.2.1. Modigliani-Miller model

The first of the analyzed theories is the model of Modigliani and Miller [7] (hereinafter MM), which is outlined in the previous section. According to the assumptions of the model, the company can borrow and lend money on perfect capital markets at risk-free rate and market value of debt is constant. For this reason, the tax savings (tax shield) are risk-free and the appropriate discount rate is risk-free rate. Eq. (4) is similar to Eq. (3).

$$PV(TS) = \frac{Tr_f D}{r_f} = TD \tag{4}$$

The previous model is based on the conditions of an efficient capital market, so its use is limited. Given that the MM model predicts zero cost of financial stress, the enterprise could be funded theoretically only by debt. If the tax rate would not change, then the marginal benefit resulting from the debt is equal to the tax rate, and the value of company changes in proportion to the value of debt.

This model is being criticized for unrealistic and very restrictive assumptions. Nevertheless, the model is known as the basis for the theory of corporate finance, it clearly defines the upper limit of business value.

2.2.2. Other tax shield theories if debt is constant

Similar to the model of Modigliani and Miller, there are other approaches that assume fixed debt. The risk of debt determines the discount rate and its choice varies according to the authors' opinion.

Myers [11] first suggested the adjusted present value (*APV*) method, which is used for the valuation of investment projects. The model is based on several assumptions: the first one is to determine the value of a company as the sum of the unlevered business value and the value of tax shield. Dividend policy impact is neglected. Company generates perpetual cash flow which is known with certainty at time $t = 0$.

The market value of debt is known and debt is perfectly correlated with the value of interest tax savings. Therefore, debt and tax shield are equally risky; both components should be discounted at the same discount factor (cost of debt). The value of tax shield is quantified according to Eq. (5).

$$PV(TS) = \sum_{i=1}^{N} \frac{Tk_d D_{i-1}}{(1+k_d)^i} \tag{5}$$

The Ruback model [12] is based on the assumption that debt is risky because the debt value changes due to the change in the cost of debt. The default option is disregarded. The debt has a constant value (book value) known at $i = 0$. Appropriate discount rate is given by Eq. (6) and cash flow from tax benefits is quantified according to Eq. (7).

$$\rho = r_f + \beta_D r_P \tag{6}$$

$$CF_{TS} = Tk_d B \tag{7}$$

If book value of debt is fixed, the Beta of tax shield is equal to the Beta of debt (β_D). It implies that both the debt and the tax shield share the same systematic risk and therefore the tax shield is discounted at cost of debt. The value of the levered company is measured by *APV* method as the sum of the value of unlevered company and the value of tax shield. Each component of the value is discounted at appropriate discount rate, as follows

$$V_L = \sum_{i=1}^{N} \frac{E(FCF)}{(1+\rho)^i} + \sum_{i=1}^{N} \frac{k_d DT}{(1+k_d)^i} \tag{8}$$

Kaplan and Ruback [13] have logically pursued the previous model. They compared the market value of MBOs (management buyouts) and leveraged recapitalization to the discounted value of their corresponding cash flow forecasts. To estimate the present value of these cash flows, they used the discount rate based on capital asset pricing model (*CAPM*). Cost of capital is measured by weighted average cost of capital before tax according to Eq. (9), which is *CAPM* model for unlevered company.

$$WACC_{BT} = k_u = r_f + \beta_U r_P \tag{9}$$

Business value is measured by discounting capital cash flow using the discount rate for unlevered company. Authors used so-called method "*compressed APV*" (APV_C) which, unlike standard adjusted net present value, assumes that tax shields and cash flow share the same systematic risk. Both are discounted at the same discount rate $k_e = k_u$. The tax shield is more risky than previous models, which indicates the discount rate used.

$$PV(TS) = \sum_{i=1}^{N} \frac{Tk_d D}{(1+k_u)^i} \tag{10}$$

Luehrman [14] focused his work on analyzing the use of *APV* method for business valuation. He criticized using weighted average cost of capital (*WACC*) for evaluating the company because the method is inconsistent in use (the cost of each type of capital is calculated on the basis of the book values instead of the market values and vice versa). Another critical point is leverage, the change of which necessitates a periodic revaluation of *WACC*.

The author suggested using Myers model, two types of cost of capital are used as a discount rate: cost of equity of a comparable company and cost of debt. The condition for this assumption is the existence of debt with the constant value over the entire estimated period.

2.3. Tax shield valuation theories if market leverage ratio is constant

The assumption of fixed debt is simple and unrealistic since the company should know future debt. This financial strategy is relatively binding because it does not reflect sufficiently the economic conditions and the emergence of favorable market conditions (e.g. a fall in interest rates). Therefore, the company should choose a less strict financial strategy.

More realistic debt policy is based on the constant leverage (debt-to-equity and debt-to-value ratio). In the case of constant debt, future interest tax shields have deterministic nature because their future levels are known with certainty at time $i = 0$. The present value of these cash flows may change only in accordance with a change in tax rate or discount rate reflecting both microeconomic and macroeconomic indicators. In the case of constant leverage, future interest tax shields are stochastic and their future values should be estimated only with probability. From the point of view of the discount rate used in this approach, there is a split, as individual authors variously estimate the risk of tax shield.

2.3.1. Miles-Ezzell model

Miles and Ezzell [15, 16], assuming perfect capital market, state that the discount rate for unlevered company, the cost of debt, the tax rate and the market leverage are constant during the existence of the investment project (or the company).

The company value, as well as free cash flow, is stochastic and the company rebalances its capital structure regularly (most frequently every year) to maintain the target leverage. Therefore, the value of debt is known only in the first period; this cash flow is deterministic. In other periods, the value of debt is unknown, so the key component (debt) is stochastic. The tax shield also has deterministic nature in the first period, and in other periods it is stochastic.

An appropriate discount rate for interest tax shield is cost of debt in the first year, it is the unlevered cost of capital in the following years.

$$PV(TS) = \frac{1 + k_u}{1 + k_d} \sum_{i=1}^{N} \frac{Tk_d D_{t-1}}{(1 + k_u)^i} \tag{11}$$

The basic difference among *MM* approach, the theory of Myers and Milles-Ezzell (hereinafter *ME*) model is estimated riskiness of tax shield which determines its present value. *MM* and Myers model are characterized by the discount rate k_d,[2] the risk of tax savings are the same as

[2]Originally the model, MM (1963) involves the use of risk-free interest rate, but Myers model extends this theory to risky debt.

the riskiness of debt. The *ME* approach uses the cost of debt in the first year. Tax savings in the first year are deterministic, as in the *MM* approach (Myers model), which corresponds to the discount factor. In the next years, the cash flow resulting from tax benefits is stochastic and the risk of this flow corresponds to the operational risk of the company.

2.3.2. Harris-Pringle model

Harris and Pringle [17] model (hereinafter *HP* model) is based on the previous model while the constant leverage is assumed. The company continuously rebalances its capital structure to achieve the fixed debt-to-equity ratio. Therefore, debt has a stochastic character because its value is estimated only with some probability and is unknown in all periods, including the first one.

If the value of debt is unknown, tax shield is stochastic, too. An appropriate discount rate is the unlevered cost of capital that takes into account the risk of tax benefit. The present value of the interest tax shield is therefore equal to the formula in Eq. (12).

$$PV(TS) = \sum_{i=1}^{N} \frac{Tk_d D}{(1 + k_u)^i} \tag{12}$$

The authors clarify the benefits of the model as follows: "*the MM position is considered too extreme by some because it implies that interest tax shields are no more risky than the interest payments themselves. The Miller position is too extreme for some because it implies that debt cannot benefit the firm at all. Thus, if the truth about the value of tax shields lies somewhere between the MM and Miller positions, a supporter of either Harris and Pringle or Miles and Ezzell can take comfort in the fact that both produce a result for unlevered returns between those of MM and Miller. A virtue of either Harris and Pringle compared to Miles and Ezzell is its simplicity and straightforward intuitive explanation.*" [17].

2.3.3. Another models assuming constant leverage

The Miles and Ezzell and Harris and Pringle models are the most commonly applied approaches while the constant leverage is assumed. In addition to constant debt, Ruback [12] also developed another model based on fixed leverage. The formula for calculating the present value of interest tax shields is consistent with the Harris and Pringle model.

On the other hand, Lewellyn and Emery [18] suggested three different methods for calculating tax shields. In their view, the Miles and Ezzell method is the most consistent and correct.

Myers, except from model in Section 2.2.2, in Ref. [4], extended its model on the condition of constant leverage (debt to equity ratio): *the risk of interest tax shields is the same as the risk of the project. Therefore, we will discount the tax shields at the opportunity cost of capital (r).* The appropriate discount rate is unlevered weighted average cost of capital.

Other authors combine both approaches (Miles and Ezzell, Harris and Pringle) as well as the Myers model if the company assumes fixed debt. Taggart [19] summarized the valuation models according to impact on personal taxes and suggested using *ME* model if company rebalances debt annually. If the company rebalances debt continuously, then HP model is suitable.

Inselbag and Kaufold [20] recommend using the Myers model if the value of debt is constant; in the case of fixed leverage, the Miles and Ezzell model is suitable.

Damodaran [21] did not mention the formula for the value of tax shield, but Fernandez [22] derived, according to the Damodaran equation (30), the present value of tax shield that is equal to Eq. (13).

$$PV(TS) = \sum_{i=1}^{N} \frac{(k_U DT - (k_D - r_f)D(1-T))}{(1+k_u)^i} \tag{13}$$

Fernandez, in relation to the cost of capital, mentioned *Practioner's method*. It is used by consultants and investment banks. He derived the formula for the present value of tax shield based on the formula for leveraged Beta.

$$PV(TS) = \sum_{i=1}^{N} \frac{(k_u DT - (k_u - r_f)D)}{(1+k_u)^i} \tag{14}$$

Eq. (14) should be always lower than Eq. (13).

Arzac and Glosten [23], based on the approach of Miles and Ezzell, developed a unique method which eliminates the discount rate. They used *"pricing kernel"*, a stochastic discount factor. They derived the formula for the company market value, for the market value of equity and for market value of tax shield using an iterative process.

$$\text{VTS} = \text{TD} - \text{T}\sum_{i=1}^{\infty} E[M_i PP_i] = \text{TD} - \text{TL}\sum_{i=1}^{\infty} E[M_i(S_i - S_{i-1})] \tag{15}$$

The authors then mentioned: *"The value of tax shield depends upon the nature of the equity stochastic process, which, in turn, depends upon the free cash flow process."* [23] If the second part of Eq. (15) is equal to zero, the model is identical to the Modigliani and Miller model.

Grinblatt and Liu [24] developed one of the most general approaches to determine the value of tax shield. Their approach is different from all other models, since the Black-Scholes and Merton option models are applied. The model assumes that the information follows Markov diffusion process; the market is dynamically complete. The model also quantifies any cash flow and tax shield. The approach is mathematically correct, but practically difficult to apply due to many abstract assumptions.

Liu [8] developed the model assuming a dependence of the value of tax shield on four variables: net income, interest rate, debt and tax rate. Tax shield is divided into two parts: *earned tax shield* and *unearned tax shield* depending on whether the interest rate is higher or lower than return on investment (*ROI*). The author himself noted that his theory is inconsistent with other approaches.

2.4. Fernandez model

Fernandez model for calculating the value of tax shield is different than those in previous cases. He argued that his approach is independent of debt policy [10]. The basic idea is that the value of tax shield is not equal to the present value of tax shields, but the value of tax shields (VTS[3]) is the difference between the present value of two cash flows of each with different risk: the present value of taxes paid by unlevered company and the present value of taxes paid by levered company.

$$VTS = G_U - G_L \tag{16}$$

Figure 2 shows the business value according to Ref. [25].

The tax paid by unlevered company is proportional to the free cash flow; they are equally risky. An appropriate discount rate is the unlevered cost of capital in the case of perpetuity. The tax paid by levered company is proportional to the equity cash flow (ECF). The appropriate discount rate for estimating the present value of taxes paid by levered company is the cost of equity, since the risk of both flows is consistent in the case of perpetuity. The value of tax shield is equal to the difference between the present values of these cash flows, as follows

$$VTS = G_U - G_L = \frac{E(T_U)}{k_u} - \frac{E(T_L)}{k_e} = \frac{TV_U}{(1-T)} - \frac{T(E_L)}{(1-T)} = TD \tag{17}$$

Eq. (17) is identical to the *MM* model [7] but Fernandez claimed it could be valid irrespective of debt policy. In the case of constant growth, Eq. (17) is derived to the form of Eq. (18).

$$VTS = G_U - G_L = \frac{T_U}{(k_{T_U} - g)} - \frac{T_L}{(k_{T_L} - g)} = \frac{TDk_U}{(k_u - g)} \tag{18}$$

Despite the revolution of this model, it is criticized. It should be noted that, that equity cash flow is not equal to the taxable income, since any new debt makes equity cash flow increasing without tax increasing. The book value of debt is stochastic and positively correlated with the unlevered equity. Taxes paid by unlevered companies have a lower risk than *ECF* (hence a different discount rate). There is further criticism on the combination of two different approaches (zero growth and non-zero growth) [26].

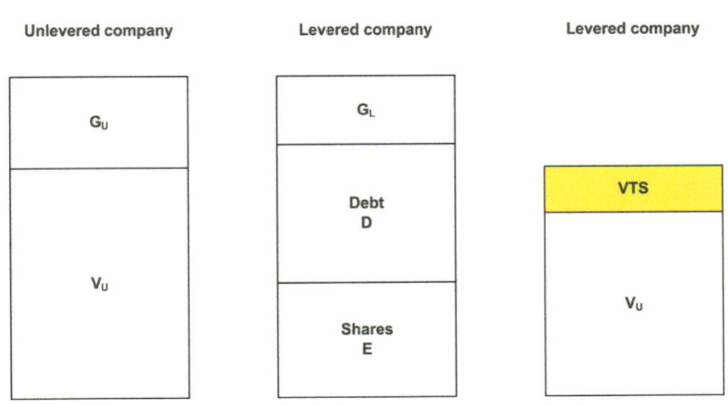

Figure 2. The value of unlevered and levered company according to Fernandez [25].

[3]Fernandez suggested using the term value of tax shield instead of present value of tax shield due to different definitions of the terms.

Cooper and Nyborg argued that Fernandez developed the model based on the combination of two different approaches (*MM* and *ME*) and therefore the value of tax shield is equal to the present value of tax shield. Based on Fernandez approach, the authors found out that the value of tax shield is identical to the Harris and Pringle model in the case of perpetuity [27].

Fernandez [28] subsequently modified the original model. The present value of taxes paid by levered company is, as follows

$$G_L = \frac{T(E_L - PV[\Delta D])}{(1 - T)} \tag{19}$$

Eq. (20) expresses a difference between the present value of taxes paid by unlevered and levered company.

$$VTS = G_U - G_L = TD_0 + TPV[\Delta D] \tag{20}$$

The previous equation indicates that the value of tax shield should depends only on the nature of the stochastic process of the net increase of debt and should not depend on the nature of the stochastic process of the free cash flow. The issue is to estimate the present value of ΔD which requires estimating the discount rate. It depends on the nature of stochastic process of the net increase of debt, it may be:

- fixed debt,
- debt is proportional to the equity value,
- debt increases are as risky as the free cash flow,
- debt of one-year maturity but perpetually rolled over [29].

3. Tax shield valuation theories with book value of debt

There are alternative models based on the book value. Book values are important when deciding on debt policy. Market values better reflect the current value and stock market volatility, nevertheless unreliability of market values highlighted particularly during the financial crisis of 2009.

Another important fact is the use of book values to measure the creditworthiness of businesses. Credit rating agencies (*CRAs*) take into account financial and non-financial factors. Leverage and interest coverage ratio are considered as key determinants of the credit rating and they are quantified by book values.

The last important factor is the weak development of some capital markets, for example, emerging markets. There are relatively few listed companies in Central and Eastern Europe as well as in other emerging markets. The capital market does not provide enough relevant information needed for application of market-based models. Moreover, in these countries, a

http://dx.doi.org/10.5772/intechopen.70943

large number of small and medium enterprises, often family owned, meets the conditions for achieving tax savings, but previous models are not relevant to them.

3.1. Fernandez model for book leverage ratio

Fernandez, in this model, assumed that the company set its debt policy on the basis of target book leverage [30]. Debt is the product of book leverage ratio and book value of equity. The value of unlevered company is equal to, if perpetuity and non-zero growth are assumed, as follows

$$V_U = \frac{FCF(1+g)}{k_u - g} = \frac{EAT(1+g) - gA}{k_u - g} \tag{21}$$

The present value of the debt change ΔD_t is important to know for estimating the value of tax shield.

$$\sum_{i=1}^{\infty} PV[\Delta D_i] = \frac{gD}{k_u - g} \tag{22}$$

If the company estimates the present value of the debt change according to Eq. (22), the value of tax shield with a constant book leverage ratio is equal to Eq. (23).

$$VTS^{BV} = \frac{Tk_u D}{k_u - g} \tag{23}$$

Fernandez highlighted several advantages of using constant leverage instead of market leverage:

- CRAs focus on book value leverage ratios,
- the value of debt does not depend on the movements of the stock markets,
- it is easier to follow for non-quoted companies,
- the empirical evidence provides more support to the fixed book leverage ratio hypothesis [30].

3.2. Velez-Pareja model

Velez-Pareja defined tax shield similar to other authors: "*Tax shields or tax savings TS, are a subsidy that the Government gives to those who incur in deductible expenses. All deductible expenses are a source of tax savings. This is, labour payments, depreciation, inflation adjustments to equity, rent and any expense if they are deductible.*" [31].

If it is assumed that the main source of tax savings is interest, the company achieves the tax advantage if *earnings before interest and taxes* (*EBIT*) plus *other income* are sufficient to offset the interest paid by the company. In this case, the value of tax shield is equal to the tax rate multiplied by *financial expenses* (*FE*). If the value of *EBIT* and *other income* (OI) is less than the amount of *financial expenses*, the company does not pay corporate income tax. Nevertheless it generates the tax shield; its value is equal to corporate tax rate times *EBIT* plus *other income* according to Eq. (24).

$$TS = T \times (EBIT + OI) \text{ if } 0 < EBIT + OI < FE \tag{24}$$

Another possible scenario occurs if the sum of *EBIT* and *OI* is negative. Tax savings do not arise because the company does not pay any tax. In sum, all possible cases are given in Eq. (25).

$$TS = \left\{ \begin{array}{c} T \times FE \text{ if } EBIT + OI \geq FE \\ T \times (EBIT + OI) \text{ if } O \leq EBIT + OI \leq FE \\ 0 \text{ if } EBIT + OI < 0 \end{array} \right\} \tag{25}$$

This is significant for further research; most of the literature dealing with the issue of tax shields is based on Eq. (2). It also means that both new businesses and start-ups can achieve partial tax savings, despite the fact that *EBIT* and *OI* cannot cover the value of financial expenses. Eq. (25) indicates that the value of tax shield should be a function of *EBIT* plus *OI* and not a function of the net income as Liu [8] argued in his theory. Eq. (26) expresses the relation between the dependent and independent variables.

$$TS = Maximum(T \times Minimum(EBIT + OI, FE), 0) \tag{26}$$

Figure 3 shows the course of the function of tax shield with respect to the sum of *earnings before interest and tax* and *other income*.

3.3. Marciniak model

Marciniak [33] suggested *decomposition method* for business valuation. The basis of the method is to divide the value into three different effects:

- cash flow from operating and investing activities,
- tax shield and
- financial effect expressed as a difference between cost of equity and cost of debt.

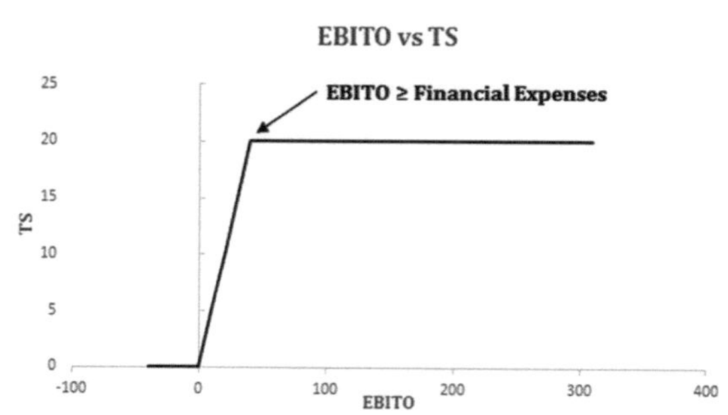

Figure 3. Tax shield as a function of *EBIT* plus other income [32].

The first part, operating and investment cash flow (free cash flow) is discounted at cost of equity (instead of weighted average cost of capital). The tax shield is quantified as the sum of taxes paid on interest (corporate tax rate times interest). Financial effect is the product of debt and a difference between the cost of equity and the cost of debt, it is discounted at the cost of equity. Last component of the business value (financial effect) is positive if the required return on equity is higher than the cost of debt and vice versa.

Eq. (27) expresses the value of levered company as a function of the sum of the present values of these three factors.

$$V_L = \sum_{i=1}^{N} \frac{FCF_i + TI_i + (k_e + k_d)D_{i-1}}{(1 + k_e)^i} \tag{27}$$

Unlike Myers' adjusted present value, decomposition method discounts all cash flows at the same discount rate (the cost of equity). Therefore, this method is similar to the Kaplan and Ruback model. One of the advantages of the model is that it is not necessary to estimate weighted average cost of capital.

Based on the previous method, Marciniak derived the value of tax shield formula expressed in Eq. (28).

$$\mathrm{PV(TS)} = \sum_{i=1}^{N} \frac{k_C BT}{(1 + k_e)^i} \tag{28}$$

This model is similar to Harris and Pringle or Kaplan and Ruback model because the cost of equity is used as a discount factor, assuming book value instead of market value.

4. Emerging markets finance and tax shield valuation

The previous sections show that significant factors of interest tax shield are:

- debt,
- cost of debt (e.g. interest rate),
- corporate tax rate and
- discount factor.

Each of these factors is influenced by other microeconomic and macroeconomic factors. The value of debt determines the capital structure of company and one of the primary objectives is to optimize it. In terms of developed and emerging markets, there are different determinants of capital structure. This issue is a field of research in many studies. Booth et al. [34] investigated capital structure in developing countries. They found that capital structure in developed and developing countries are affected by same firm-specific factors (like debt ratios). Nevertheless, they found out that there are differences such as GDP growth, capital market development and inflation rates.

Bas et al. [35] also investigated capital structure in emerging markets. They examined the capital structure in 25 countries from different regions. It should be noted that according to their study listed companies that prefer equity financing instead of long-term debt financing. They also investigated the effect of company size. Large companies are more diversified and default risk is reduced as a result of higher leverage. Hence, small and large companies have different debt policies. Also, large and traded companies can easily get access to finance that depends more on the economic conditions of the country.

Jong et al. [36] examined the importance of country and firm-specific factors in the leverage choice of companies from 42 countries. They found that the impact of several firm-specific factors (tangibility, company size, growth and profitability) on cross-country capital structure is significant and consistent with conventional theories.

According to the studies mentioned above, the capital structure in emerging markets is determined, in addition to factors similar to those in developed countries, by specific factors. These include the development of the capital market, inflation or the size of businesses [37]. The weak development of the capital market, especially bond market, means that the company cannot take advantage of the possibility of issuing a bond. Therefore, it is not possible to determine the market value of debt, and market value-based theories of the tax shield cannot be applied. Within the models reviewed in the chapter, we can suggest the use of models with a book value of debt because they are suitable for all businesses, regardless of size and tradability of a company on the capital market.

In addition to debt value used (market versus book); it is also questionable to estimate the cost of capital (discount factor). For example, the cost of equity is traditionally estimated by *CAPM* model. However, if the company is non-listed, the model is inappropriate or inaccurate. Also the weighted average cost of capital is difficult to quantify. Damodaran [37] has created the database to help estimate the cost of equity and debt. In addition, a build-up model is often used.

The tax shield is also affected by the tax system and corporate and personal tax rate or loss carried forward, which affects the effective tax rate and tax burden [38–40].

Under the conditions of emerging markets, the tax shield represents a significant source of value and is therefore part of several methods of investment decision analysis. Leasing is a frequent form of financing for small and medium enterprises; net advantage to leasing model includes an analysis of interest and depreciation tax shields; value of tax shield may be a decisive factor for selecting a portfolio of investment projects (using a modified resource-constrained project scheduling problem with discounted cash flows). In addition, other methods of investment decision-making may be adjusted for the existence of a tax shield, like risk analysis [41–44].

5. Conclusion

The chapter deals with the analysis and classification of selected approaches to the quantification of tax shields. Theories are based on the premise of the perfect capital market and a clearly defined corporate debt policy. However, both assumptions cannot be met in the realistic conditions of emerging markets; many businesses in emerging markets are not listed and debt policy is determined based on the book value of debt and not on the basis of a fixed market value of debt or market leverage.

The theories mentioned in this chapter have many gaps that prevent the correct use under conditions of emerging markets. Gradually, new theories are emerging, reflecting real economic conditions, but it makes it difficult to determine which model is correct. In their book, Copeland et al. investigated various models of tax shield, and their opinion on the choice of the appropriate method is: *We leave it to the reader's judgment to decide which approach best fits his or her situation* [2].

Acknowledgements

The chapter is an output of the science project VEGA 1/0428/17 Creation of New Paradigms of Financial Management at the Threshold of the 21st Century in Conditions of the Slovak Republic.

Nomenclature

A	Value of assets
APV	Adjusted present value
APV_C	Compressed adjusted present value
B	Book value of debt
$CAPM$	Capital asset pricing model
CF_{TS}	Cash flow from tax saving
$CRAs$	Credit rating agencies
D	Market value of debt
D_{i-1}	Market value of debt for time $i-1$
ΔD	Net increase of debt
EAT	Earnings after tax
$EBIT$	Earnings before interest and tax
ECF	Equity cash flow
E_L	Equity of levered company
FCF	Free cash flow
FE	Financial expense

g	Growth rate
G_L	Present value of tax paid by levered company
G_U	Present value of tax paid by unlevered company
HP	Harris-Pringle model
I_i	Interest for time i
k_c	Coupon rate
k_d	Cost of debt
k_e	Cost of equity
k_{T_L}	Required return to tax in the levered company
k_{T_u}	Required return to tax in the unlevered company
k_u	Unlevered cost of capital
MBO	Management buyout
ME	Miles-Ezzell model
M_i	Pricing kernel for the time i
MM	Modigliani-Miller model
OI	Other income
PP_i	Principal payment for time i
$PV[\Delta D_i]$	Present value of debt change for time i
$PV(TS)$	Present value of tax shield
r_f	Risk-free rate
ROI	Return on investment
r_P	Risk premium
S_i	Value of the stock for time i
S_{i-1}	Value of the stock for time $i-1$
T	Corporate tax rate
T_L	Tax paid by levered company
TS	Tax shield
T_U	Tax paid by unlevered company
V_L	Value of levered company

VTS	Value of tax shield
VTS^{BV}	Value of tax shield if book leverage ratio is assumed
V_U	Value of unlevered company
$WACC_{BT}$	Weighted average cost of capital before tax
β_U	Unlevered Beta
ρ	Appropriate discount rate

Author details

Tomas Kliestik* and Lucia Michalkova

*Address all correspondence to: tomas.kliestik@fpedas.uniza.sk

Department of Economics, Faculty of Operation and Economics of Transport and Communication, University of Zilina, Zilina, Slovakia

References

[1] Majercak P, Majercakova E. The enterprise valuation and categories of the value. In: M. Culik, editor. Financial Management of Firms and Financial Institutions: 9th International Scientific Conference, Proceedings (Part II.); 9th-10th September 2013; Ostrava, Czech Republic. Ostrava: Technical university of Ostrava; 2013. p. 469-475

[2] Copeland TE, Koller T, Murrin J. Valuation: Measuring and Managing the Value of Companies. 3rd ed. New York: John Wiley & Sons; 2000. 492 p

[3] Investopedia. Tax shield [Internet]. Available from: http://www.investopedia.com/terms/t/taxshield.asp [Accessed: 7 July 2017]

[4] Brealey RA, Myers SC, Allen F. Principles of Corporate Finance. 10th ed. New York: McGraw-Hill/Irwin; 2010. 875 p

[5] Damodaran A. Applied Corporate Finance. 3rd ed. New York: John Wiley & Sons; 2010. 752 p

[6] Modigliani F, Miller MH. The cost of capital, corporation finance and the theory of investment. The American Economic Review. 1958;**48**(3):261-297

[7] Modigliani F, Miller MH. Corporate income taxes and the cost of capital. A correction. The American Economic Review. 1963;**53**(3):433-443

[8] Liu Y. The slicing approach to valuing tax shields. Journal of Banking & Finance. 2009; **33**:1069-1078

[9] Tham J, Velez-Pareja I. Much Ado about Nothing: A Non-technical Comment on the Present Value of The tax Shield (PVTS).Working Paper No. 23. Available at SSRN: https://ssrn.com/abstract=345660 or http://dx.doi.org/10.2139/ssrn.345660 [27 October 2002]

[10] Fernandez P. The value of tax shield is NOT equal to the present value of tax shields. Journal of Financial Economics. 2004;**73**:145-165. DOI: 10.1016/j.jfineco.2002.10.001

[11] Myers SC. Interactions of corporate financing and investment decisions–Implications for capital budgeting. Journal of Finance. 1974;**29**(1):1-25. DOI: 10.1111/j.1540-6261.1974.tb00021.x

[12] Ruback RS. Capital cash flows: A simple approach to valuing risky cash flows. Financial Management. 2002;**31**(2):85-103

[13] Kaplan SN, Ruback RS. The valuation of cash flow forecasts: An empirical analysis. Journal of Finance. 1995;**50**(4):1059-1093

[14] Luehrman TA. Using APV: A better tool for valuing operations. Harvard Business Review. 1997;**75**:145-154

[15] Miles JA, Ezzell JR. The weighted average cost of capital, perfect capital markets, and project life: A clarification. Journal of Financial and Quantitative Analysis. 1980;**15**(3):719-730. DOI: https://doi.org/10.2307/2330405

[16] Miles JA, Ezzell JR. Reformulating tax shield valuation: A note. Journal of Finance. 1985;**40**:1485-1492. DOI: 10.1111/j.1540-6261.1985.tb02396.x

[17] Harris RS, Pringle JJ. Risk-adjusted discount rates – extensions from the average-risk case. The Journal of Financial Research. 1985;**8**(3):237-244. DOI: 10.1111/j.1475-6803.1985.tb00406.x

[18] Lewellen WG, Emery RE. Corporate debt management and the value of the firm. Journal of Financial and Quantitative Analysis. 1986;**21**(4):415-426. DOI: https://doi.org/10.2307/2330689

[19] Taggart RA. Consistent valuation and cost of capital: Expressions with corporate and personal taxes. Financial Management. 1991;**20**:8-20

[20] Inselbag I, Kaufhold H. Two DCF approaches for valuing companies under alternative financing strategies (and how to choose between them). Journal of Applied Corporate Finance. 1997;**10**(1):114-122. DOI: 10.1111/j.1745-6622.1997.tb00132.x

[21] Damodaran A. Damodaran on Valuation: Security Analysis for Investment and Corporate Finance. 2nd ed. New York: Wiley; 2006. 696 p

[22] Fernandez P. Valuing companies by cash flow discounting: Ten methods and nine theories. Managerial Finance. 2007;**33**(11):853-876. DOI: https://doi.org/10.1108/03074350710823827

[23] Arzac RA, Glosten LR. A reconsideration of tax shield valuation. European Financial Management. 2005;**11**(4):453-461. DOI: 10.1111/j.1354-7798.2005.00292.x

[24] Grinblatt M, Liu J. Debt policy, corporate taxes, and discount rates. Journal of Economic Theory. 2008;**141**(1):225-254. DOI: 10.3386/w9353

[25] Fernandez P. Value of tax shields (VTS): 3 theories with "some" sense. SSRN Electronic Journal. 2015: Available at SSRN: https://ssrn.com/abstract=2549005 or http://dx.doi.org/10.2139/ssrn.2549005 [November 19, 2015]

[26] Fieten P, Kruschwitz L, Laitenberger J, Löffler A, Tham J, Velez-Pareja I, et al. Comment on "The value of tax shields is NOT equal to the present value of tax shields". The Quarterly Review of Economics and Finance. 2005;**45**(1):184-187. DOI: https://doi.org/10.1016/j.qref.2004.07.004

[27] Cooper IA, Nyborg KG. The value of tax shields IS equal to the present value of tax shields. Journal of Financial Economics. 2006;**81**(1):215-225. DOI: https://doi.org/10.1016/j.jfineco.2005.07.003

[28] Fernandez P. The value of tax shields is not equal to the present value of tax shields: A correction. IESE: Working Paper No. 581. 2005;**2**

[29] Fernandez P. The value of tax shields and the risk of the net increase of debt. IESE: Working Paper No. 544. 2004;**3**

[30] Fernandez P. A more realistic valuation: Adjusted Present Value and WACC with constant book leverage ratio. Journal of Applied Finance. 2007;**122**. DOI: http://dx.doi.org/10.2139/ssrn.946090

[31] Velez-Pareja I. Return to Basics: Are You Properly Calculating Tax Shields? Análisis Financiero. 2013;**122**:6-17

[32] Velez-Pareja I. Risky Tax Shields: An Exploratory Study . Cuadernos de Administración. 2010;**23**(41):213-235

[33] Marciniak Z. Wykorzystanie Zróżnicowanych Stóp Kosztu Kapitału Do Wyceny Przedsiębiorstw I Oceny Projektów Inwestycyjnych. In: Szyjewskij Z, Grabara JK, Nowak J, editors. Efektywność Zastosowań Systemów Informatycznych 2003 (TOM II); 2003; Warszawa - Szczyrk, Polska. Warszawa: Wydawnictwa Naukowo-Techniczne; 2003. p. 63-92

[34] Booth L, Aizavian V, Demirguc - Kunt A, Maksimovic V. Capital structure in developing countries. The Journal of Finance. 2001;**56**(1):87-130. DOI: 10.1111/0022-1082.00320

[35] Bas T, Muradoglu G, Phylaktis K. Determinants of Capital Structure in Developing Countries. In: European Financial Management Symposium 2010, Asian Finance; 22-24 April 2010; Renmin University of China. Bejing, China: 2010. Available at: http://www.efmaefm.org/0EFMSYMPOSIUM/2010-China/papers/determinants%20of%20capital%20structure%20in%20developing%20countries.pdf [Accessed: 7 July 2017]

[36] Jong de A, Kabir R, Nguyen TT. Capital structure around the world: The roles of firm- and country-specific determinants. Journal of Banking & Finance. 2008;**32**:1954-1969. DOI: 10.1016/j.jbankfin.2007.12.034

[37] Damodaran A. Data [Internet]. Available from: http://pages.stern.nyu.edu/~adamodar/ [Accessed: 7 July 2017]

[38] Jorge Niño T, Salvador Zurita L, Augusto Castillo R. Costo de capital e impuestos en un sistema tributario no integrado y en uno integrado. Generalización del modelo. El Trimestre Economico. 2014;**81**(321):109-132. DOI: http://dx.doi.org/10.20430/ete.v81i321.110

[39] Velez-Pareja I. Tax shield, financial expenses and losses carried forward. Cuadernos de Economica. 2016;**35**(69):663-689. DOI: 10.15446/cuad.econ.v35n69.54352

[40] Simkova N. The Hierarchical Clustering of Tax Burden in the EU27. Journal of Competitiveness. 2015;**7**(3):95-109. DOI: http://doi.org/10.7441/joc.2015.03.07

[41] Wyslocka E, Sczepaniak W. The effectiveness of leasing as a method of financing the development of a company. Polish Journal of Management Studies. 2013;**6**:129-142

[42] Kral P, Janoskova K. Classifying and analysing project resources in project portfolio optimizing process. In: Transport means 2014: proceedings of the 18th international conference; 23-24 October2014; Kaunas, Lithuania. Kaunas: Kaunas University of Technology; 2014. p. 133-136

[43] Grublova E. Attitudes to risk and ability to take risky decisions. Ekonomicko-manazerske spektrum. 2010;**4**(2):58-63

[44] Ruzzier M, Konecnik Ruzzier M. On the relationship between firm size, resources, age at entry and internationalization: the case of Slovenian SMEs . Journal of Business Economics and Management. 2015;16(1):52-73. DOI: http://dx.doi.org/10.3846/16111699.2012.745812

Section 2

Market Efficiency and Market Models

Chapter 3

Testing the Information Efficiency in Emerging Markets

Ceyda Aktan, Eyyup Ensari Sahin and
Ilhan Kucukkaplan

Additional information is available at the end of the chapter

http://dx.doi.org/10.5772/intechopen.70369

Abstract

One of the most common issues for investors regarding markets nowadays is to what extent these markets are efficient as all of them aim to increase their gains and beat the market as much as possible. This competition among them will inevitably result in markets becoming efficient and, therefore, prices quickly adjusting to the new coming information. Eventually, investors will most probably receive only a sum that makes up for the risk they took and the time value of money they invested. This is where market efficiency, its theory and forms come into question. There have been many researches conducted assessing the efficiency of different markets located throughout the world. However, there are still a lot of gaps in research involving emerging economies which needs to be completed for the sake of investment decisions. Therefore, the purpose of this chapter is to is to show how information efficiency relates to the stock markets of emerging economies, how it implicates investors, analyze the stock prices of 24 emerging economies to look for their weak form efficiency, and to put forward a set of commonalities found in results of literature relating to emerging market information efficiency.

Keywords: information efficiency, efficient market hypothesis, emerging economies, weak form of efficiency, anomalies

1. Introduction

One of the most common issues for investors regarding markets nowadays is to what extent these markets are efficient as all of them aim to increase their gains and beat the market as much as possible. But what do we mean by 'efficiency'? The term 'efficiency' is used in many different contexts with different meanings. If we look at the productivity side, efficiency is used to refer to a situation where the quantity produced is at such a level that the more you produce from this point onwards it will lead to a fewer productions of the other. In a similar context, one can also think of Pareto efficiency: distribution or resources to make one better off but at the expense of another [1].

When analysing financial markets, whether these markets are from a developed or from an emerging economy, the term 'efficiency' refers to the informational efficiency of the market, which is about the degree of information reflected in the prices of financial assets [2]. It reflects how the financial asset prices adapt to the incoming information. The quicker it reflects the more informational efficient the market will be, making it hard for these investors to beat the market [3, 4].

In this chapter, we will be explaining the efficient market hypothesis (EMH), which is the main theory behind information efficiency; relevant definitions will be given and the different forms of efficiencies will be identified using previous studies. Possible anomalies will also be talked about. The chapter will end with a discussion on the technical and fundamental analysis in the usage of efficient market hypothesis as the basis of investment policies and an application part, where the stock market prices of the 24 identified emerging economies of the world are analysed using an augmented Dickey-Fuller (ADF) test to observe whether they contain a unit root or not. All of these parts will be explained in relation to information efficiency of emerging economies. There are specific characteristics of these markets that make them attractive for analysis and for investors, such as lower than average income per capita, high volatility, rapid growth, higher than the average return and less-mature capital markets [5]. These characteristics which make emerging economies unique in the study of market efficiency will also be incorporated within the chapter.

2. Efficient market hypothesis

Efficient market hypothesis states that prices of financial assets reflect all information that is available [6]. Although the idea goes all the way back to Bachelier (1900), its development can be pointed mainly to two scientists, Paul A. Samuelson and Eugene F. Fama, who have independently made leading contributions in the 1960s [2]. Samuelson's focus was on temporal pricing models of storable commodities, mechanics of pricing and linear-programming solutions. He stated that if prices contain all the relevant information and participant expectations, then they could not be forecasted [7]. On the other hand, Fama focused more on the measurement of statistical properties of stock prices as well as technical and fundamental analyses, which will be discussed in the last section of the chapter. Fama was the first researcher to use the term 'efficient market' [3] and briefly explained it as 'prices fully reflect all available information' [8–10].

According to EMH, predicting the change in prices and turning them into profit are near impossible and highly unlikely. What drives these changes in price is the new information that is arriving. A particular market, under the theory, can be deemed as efficient if stock prices immediately react to this new-coming information. The information coming in must be unpredictable, by definition, because if future information can be predicted now, then this information would be reflected in today's prices and not in future prices. Adjustment of stock prices to its fair market value in reaction to the new information will cause them to either increase or decrease. It will hence make the stock price movements random and unpredictable [11]. This is also referred to as a **Random Walk Hypothesis**.

The idea of a 'random walk' is closely related to the EMH as it is a financial theory and focuses on investments and claims that present-day stock prices increase or decrease, and this happens randomly and has nothing to do with past stock prices. Thus, the idea is that prices immediately capture the information as was said by the EMH. In this situation, even the most inexperienced investor will obtain a rate of return similar to that of his experienced colleagues [12]. Investors have no chance of achieving gains in these markets without taking on themselves many additional risks. The higher the gains, the higher the risk will be [3, 13].

Therefore, it could easily be said that studying past stock prices (technical analysis) or analysing company's financial information (fundamental analysis) would not benefit the investor. This is important in the case of investors as they look for securities that are undervalued, ones they predict to increase in value in the future. For them the higher the gains, the better it is. However, as we have mentioned, EMH shows that no profits can be made if the market is found efficient because the information about the price changes already would have been captured [12, 14]. But what happens if the market is found to be inefficient? This makes markets in emerging economies more attractive as majority of previously conducted research shows that these stock markets do not follow a random walk and are not efficient [15–20]. The absence of a random walk will mean the inappropriate pricing of stocks away from the fair value and higher risk. This can lead investors to predict future stock prices and gain higher returns [3]. It is expected that stock prices in these markets will increase more than the others because capital allocation in the economy is distorted and the overall economic development of the market is affected [21].

2.1. Principles of EMH

If we want to shortly summarise the points mentioned above, we can say the following as the basic characteristics of an efficient market [22] under the efficient market hypothesis:

- Random walks determine changes in stock prices.
- All new information immediately is reflected within the stock prices. Also, these information cannot be used in order to earn excess profits.
- Not much use can be obtained through a technical analysis.
- Outperforming the market is near impossible, even for the fund managers.
- Economic fundamentals determine and fix the levels of stock prices.

2.2. Forms of efficiency

2.2.1. Weak form of market efficiency

Weak form of market efficiency involves past information and past prices. According to the weak form of efficiency under the EMH, current stock prices fully reflect all of the available past information [11]. All other information such as profit forecasts or announcements of mergers and so on will not have any effect on the current stock prices [13]. This means that no one can analyse past prices of stocks and be able to beat the market.

Under the EMH, there is a reason that this form is named 'weak'. The strength of the efficiency, i.e. degree of weakness, symbolises the type of information available. Historical information plus information on stock prices can be classified as the most easily obtained and costless information. Therefore, it is classified as weak in the efficiency scale by Fama in the EMH [10]. In the weak form of efficiency, investors cannot make a profit from using information that everyone knows [14].

2.2.2. Semi-strong form of market efficiency

In the semi-strong form of efficiency, besides the past information, all the publicly known and available information are also reflected on the price of the financial assets/stocks. This can be the quality information, financial statements, patents as well as information provided by media, investment advisors, annual reports and other information that can be publicly accessible. An important point to note here is that public information does not have to be just financial information [13]. To give an example, consider the cosmetics industry. When analysing cosmetics companies, the relevant information can be the new, published research regarding cosmetics testing.

From the moment these public information that are mentioned above are published, prices of financial assets will immediately adjust itself to become higher or lower according to the nature of the information. Then, it can be deduced that if all investors have access these publicly information, then none of them have an advantage over the other. Therefore, they cannot make excess profit by using a fundamental analysis [11].

Semi-strong and weak forms of market efficiency can be related to each other as the weak form includes past and the semi-strong form includes both past and the public information. It can be deduced that, if one market is found to be efficient in the semi-strong form, then it also must be efficient in the weak form [13].

2.2.3. Strong form of market efficiency

This can be said to be as the strictest version of market efficiency because it not only contains the past and public information but also involves private information. Private information in studies can also be referred to as the inside or insider information. According to the EMH, the strong form of market efficiency can be defined as a market where the prices of financial assets reflect all of the available public and private information. In other words, stock prices in this market reflect all information that exists [23].

If a market is efficient in the strong form, it leaves no room for investors or even insiders from generating profits using information that is not publicly known. For example, let us take the cosmetics company to analyse once more; imagine that its research and development department came up with a breakthrough and they know that this piece of information will cause the company shares to increase by a large amount in the near future. By the time one of the members of this R&D team goes out and buys few of the company's stocks, if strong form of efficiency holds, this information would have already been reflected on the stock price. Hence, that person with insider information would not be able to use this for his/her benefit [11, 13].

It is debateable whether the strong form of market efficiency even exists. The results are contradicting, and research points out that evidence regarding the strong form is inconsistent. Some argue that it is quite impossible for an insider not to benefit from the private information they hold. But, some argue that there is no possibility of keeping secrets. Most countries, today, have certain laws and regulations to prevent insider trading such as the establishment of the Securities and Exchange Commission in the USA. This commission requires owners, directors or corporate officers to report to them in order to limit their harmful activities [23].

2.2.4. *Inefficient markets*

Efficient market hypothesis classifies efficiency into three categories as previously explained. However, when the subject is emerging economies, it would not be correct if we neglect one more important situation: when a market is not found efficient in any of these three forms. We can refer to these markets as **inefficient markets**. Inefficiency, neglecting the random walk, is not a desirable situation. Recent studies point out different techniques to try and solve any mis-assessments. There are studies which show that some markets are inefficient and do not fall under any of the efficiency forms, and the majority of these were observed as to be either developing, emerging or transition economies [15–17]. This will be further mentioned in the following section.

Study conducted by Grossman and Stiglitz argues that it is quite impossible for markets to be perfectly efficient as there will be no reason left for investors to trade in these markets if there were no profits to be made [24]. However, this is a serious situation as, in the long run, it will lead to the collapse of these markets. Also, we all know that trading stocks incur costs, so it is important whether the gains made is sufficient enough to compensate for these costs. This is another question that needs to be kept in mind regarding inefficiencies [7].

2.3. EMH and emerging economies

There are varieties of definitions of emerging economies, but we must be careful in defining it correctly. First of all, a country is classified as emerging when its GDP per capita decreases under a certain level [25]. Then, generally there is low income, frequent economic and political change and rapid growth in these countries. Some other characteristics include high volatility, higher than average return and being less mature capital markets [5]. There is a reason why these countries are named emerging as the basic principle behind them indicates that they try to 'emerge' from their current underdeveloped position and move towards being part of the developed countries, the process which is called **convergence** [25].

Emerging economies can be divided into two groups: developing and transition economies. Transition economies are countries with economies moving towards a market economy from the existing centrally planned economy, such as the Former Soviet Union and China. Developing economies, on the other hand, are countries with economies that are growing and are in the process of becoming industrialised, such as Turkey, Poland, Indonesia, Bangladesh and many more [26].

Especially in the last couple of decades, research on the emerging economies around the world started gaining importance. The reason for this can be attributed to few different factors. Firstly, countries with emerging economies are highly populated and make up a great portion of the world's population as well as land. Secondly, growth in these countries is far more than its developed counterparts. They are beginning to be seen as having diverse environments, whether it is the business, cultural, economic, legal financial or political environments. Researchers want to focus on these diverse environments; analyse, assess and come up with new theories and evidence to understand; and, therefore, improve the welfare of these countries [5]. Application of the EMH is one of them.

It is clear why we keep on stressing the importance of studies conducted on emerging markets in each section. There is an ocean full of information that is yet to be discovered. We can also consider the effects of pull and push factors in the increasing importance. Lack of opportunities and lower returns for investments make up the push factors which are associated with developed stock markets. It pushes investment towards emerging economies. On the other hand, emerging economies tend to have pull factors which attracts these investments. These are reforms (structural and economic), international equity offerings and exchange-rate stabilisation programmes [27].

History is an important concept when assessing market data and the EMH. There needs to be sufficient data in order for us to be able to analyse the efficiency of these stock markets. But the problem with emerging economies is that they are relatively new markets and have very little data. This makes it difficult to obtain healthy results and maybe one of the reasons that majority of these results come up as inefficient. Evidence shows that stock prices take its time when adjusting to information; it may be much better to look over a longer time period in order to obtain results of whether these markets are efficient or not rather than focusing on the short run [28].

2.3.1. Reviewing past research

EMH has made tremendous contribution to the area of finance in the past few decades. Among the three forms of market efficiency, probably the weak form is the most commonly tested form. We can see that research on emerging economies (including developed and transition economies) mainly focuses on the weak form and in some the semi-strong form [29]. Strong form of market efficiency is very difficult to test [23], and there is hardly any evidence of its test on emerging economies. In emerging economies, returns of stocks are said to be highly predictable and the stock markets less efficient than those of emerging economies [30].

For example, Lee et al. investigated the efficiencies of 26 developing countries using panel data stationarity tests between 1999 and 2007, which showed inefficiency of these markets [31]. Kim and Shamsuddin looked at the weak form of efficiency of a group of Asian stock markets using both daily and weekly data from 1990 to 2005. They have found that stock markets in Hong Kong, Japan, Korea, Singapore and Taiwan were efficient in the weak form. But stock markets in Indonesia, Malaysia and the Philippines were found to be inefficient [32]. It is interesting as Korean stock market has been tested for weak form of efficiency by others and found inefficient [15–17]. Istanbul Stock Exchange [currently called Borsa Istanbul (BIST)] was tested for the weak form of efficiency by many and was also found both efficient [30, 33, 34] and inefficient [18–20].

It is important to remember that the data presented in this chapter on the efficiency of emerging economies comprises only an extremely small sample of the entire population of studies. Therefore, we can say that there are many studies, with many different results. The results can show variations among each other, where a study can indicate efficiency, whereas the other shows inefficiency. The reason can be attributed to data being collected from different time periods, whether daily, weekly or monthly data that is being used, or even can be due to the tests that are used. Only recently, studies have pointed out that nonlinearity in stock prices is very important and that they should be taken into account in the tests to prevent the misleading results [35].

2.3.2. *Emerging economies and liberalization*

Liberalization can be defined as a decision made by governments to increase foreign investment and trade. Its aim is for the removal of barriers, lessening of regulations and government controls towards foreigners giving them the right to purchase shares and trade within that country. It is crucial that the impact of liberalization be measured and assessed because it results in both financial and economic changes within the market [36]. To gain the benefits of liberalization, from the second half of the 80s onwards, countries with emerging economies started modifying their laws and allowed foreigners into their markets. The changes of financial liberalization in these emerging economies have been great and led researchers' interest to the area [37].

Some of the research on the liberalization of emerging economies looked at the issue of efficiency of their stock markets. Their point was that if these markets are being opened to foreign investment, are they now more efficient? [38]. According to the EMH, the market's efficiency increases as it becomes more liberalized because liberalization means the market will be made open to the public [37]. Although theoretically true, the effect of liberalization on the efficiency of emerging country's stock market should be further investigated.

2.3.3. *Emerging economies and financial crisis*

One more topic that must be mentioned under emerging economies and EMH is the effect of a financial crisis or a crash of a market to the efficiency of the stock market of that particular country. Financial crisis is counted by researchers as the possible factor of inefficiency. But, yet again, there is not much evidence yet to fully support this theory. A study conducted by Garas and Argyrakis showed a relationship between financial crisis and market efficiency. They have looked at the Athens Stock Exchange stock prices between the years 1987 and 2004 and concluded that during the crisis, the stock market became less efficient, i.e. market showed lower efficiency [39]. However, at the same time, Hoque et al. looked at pre- and postcrisis periods and pointed out that there was no relationship between the crisis and market efficiency [40]. Therefore, it is an area that can be exploited in the near future.

3. Market anomalies

Some stock markets show deviations from the known principles of EMH. These deviations can take place sometimes just once but sometimes can take place repeatedly and are usually referred to as 'anomalies' [14]. Dictionary definition of anomaly is an occurrence that is irregular, is not usual or is strange, and it is usually used to explain scientific issues or technological matters [41]. They reflect inefficient markets. Therefore, this section of the chapter will focus on market anomalies and show if there is a possibility of identifying gaps in the stock market. Gaps, where opportunities for investors are created, allow them to earn above normal profits.

To make it easier to analyse, we can categorise anomalies into three groups (calendar, fundamental and technical). As the name suggests, calendar anomalies focus on a certain time period. Calendar anomalies include anomalies such as day-of-the-week, turn-of-the-year and January effects. Fundamental anomalies include book-to-market ratio, value anomaly, high dividend yield and many more. Lastly, technical anomalies involve a technical analysis to predict future prices. Examples can be moving averages and trading range break anomalies [14]. We will explain few types of market anomalies which are more apparent in emerging economies and more experimented.

3.1. Day-of-the-week effect

Day-of-the-week anomaly, developed originally by French, states that stock returns are not always the same during the week, and different days generate different returns [42]. Majority of the studies show that returns earned on Mondays are usually much lower than the rest of the days, whereas returns generated on Fridays are the highest [43, 44]. Using this knowledge, an investor can buy stocks on a day when the prices are the lowest and sell it when the prices are at the highest point, hence, showing the inefficiency found in the stock market.

Besides the ones that accept the day-of-the-week effect, the remaining are divided into two thoughts: the ones that argue that there is such thing as the day-of-the-week effect, but it is not an anomaly (such as the difference in the trading days and the non-trading problems), and the others (such as econometric methodology, calendar time vs. trading time and the offsetting effect of liquidity hypotheses) who say that it never existed [45].

This anomaly has taken interest of researchers when studying emerging economies because, probably, together with other types of anomalies, it provides an explanation for why these markets are generally inefficient. Let's consider the following studies as examples to the day-of-the-week effect on emerging economies. They provide evidence to both views. Poshakwale studied the Bombay Stock Exchange for the years between 1987 and 1994, to see if the day-of-the-week effect exists within the market. Results of the study showed that the weak form of efficiency did not hold for this market and that the day-of-the-week effect existed [46]. But, to present a different view, Basher and Sadorsky looked at 21 emerging stock markets from around the world. Data was taken from the period between 1992 and 2003. Their results indicated that majority of the emerging markets did not show signs of the day-of-the-week effect except for the Philippines, Pakistan and Taiwan [47].

3.2. January effect

January effect anomaly states that returns generated vary according to the months within the year. In January, the highest returns are expected when compared to the rest of the year. Therefore, January effect is classified under seasonality and, like the day-of-the-week anomaly, has a big impact on the investor's decisions. If seasonality is found, then this means that the EMH will not hold. Investors will then be able to use available information to gain profits over others in the market [27].

However, these are a debate over whether this anomaly still exists or not. According to one view, January effect still exists, whereas another view says that it has lost its momentum and might even have become extinct. But, there is a third view, saying that it might have become extinct in countries like the USA, but it still holds for others, such as in the countries with emerging economies. Study by Patel looked at whether January effect existed in international stock returns, by examining stock returns from 1997 to 2014. Results indicated that this anomaly did not exist in international markets [48]. There were other studies that supported this finding [49, 50]. However, Guler examined data from five emerging economies: Brazil, China, India, Argentina and Turkey. Data was taken from a period between the first trading day of the stock market in each country and the end of 2012. Results, this time, showed the existence of the January effect in China, Argentina and Turkey [51]. Therefore, it could be understood that there are many studies conducted with varying results. This area needs to be deeply investigated as it has a great impact on investment decisions.

3.3. Small-firm effect

The previous two types of anomalies mentioned were part of the calendar anomalies. Small-firm effect, however, is considered to be part of the asset pricing anomalies. It was first put forward by Banz and states that the stock returns are related to the size of the firm [52]. According to the anomaly, the smaller the firm, the higher the expected returns will be. Knowing these will, again, have implications for investors and also relates to the efficiency of the market.

There are few reasons why researchers believe that small firms generate unusually high returns. One of the reasons is that smaller firms have smaller stocks, which contain systematic risks. These risks cannot always be measured correctly. Since they are more prone to risk, small firms will try to compensate it by reflecting it as higher returns. Secondly, when compared to larger firms, they are more focused on increasing their market shares and expanding. Research points out that smaller firms are more likely to reinvest its earnings back into the company and cause the value of its common stock to increase; hence, means increase in returns in the future [53].

Small-firm effect and the January effect are anomalies that actually go hand in hand with one another. Research shows that stock prices of smaller firms were observed to be more affected by the January effect than larger firms [54]. Rogalski and Tinic also stated that returns of smaller firms were much higher in January than any the other months in the year [55]. This can be referred to as an 'anomaly within an anomaly' [56].

It is indicated in research that people who live in countries with emerging economies tend to experience more behavioural biases which makes it more interesting to search for anomalies in the markets of these countries [56]. For example, Chui and Wei examined the size effect in Hong Kong, Korea, Malaysia, Taiwan and Thailand using monthly data from 1977 to 1993. Their results showed that the small-firm effect (size effect) was present in all of the analysed countries except for Taiwan [57]. The effects of these anomalies are important to know, and there is lack of information. Therefore, this particular area in research should be considered and focused more by researchers.

3.4. Other anomalies

As part of the calendar anomalies, we can mention two more: turn-of-the-month effect and turn-of-the-year effect. According to the turn-of-the-month effect, on the last trading day of the month plus the first three days of the next month, an increase in the stock prices is expected. With the same principle, turn-of-the-year effect is about the increase in the stock prices in the last week of December.

Under the fundamental anomalies identified, low price-to-book anomaly states that the lower the price-to-book ratio, the higher the returns will be. Value anomaly takes place when investors over or under estimate the stock returns in the market. Low price-to-earnings (P/E) ratio, which is a common studied anomaly, states that the lower the P/E ratio, the more returns will be [14].

4. Using EMH in investing decisions

For a long time, researchers have tried to understand the behaviour behind stock price movements. Efficient market hypothesis and the random walk theories have surfaced as a result of this search to test these behaviours as Fama mentions in his article [58]. In general, however, there are two common methods for stock price prediction which also helps investor decisions: technical analysis and fundamental analysis. They will be individually explained in the following part.

4.1. Technical analysis

Technical analysis is a theory about past behaviour and deals with the patterns found in stock prices. The theory behind the analysis goes back to Charles Dow, who is the founder of

The Wall Street Journal [59]. His theory, named Dow theory, looks at stock prices and tries to observe the long-term trends in it. Technical analysts, who are also referred to as 'chartists', believe that past information can be used to predict future stock prices as the patterns tend to repeat themselves. This, clearly, shows that technical analysis and random walk theory support opposite views. According to the chartists, information is not as valuable as it was thought in the past. Because, now, the classic demand and supply factors come into the picture. Reaction of stock prices can be so slow that during this time, an investor can have a chance to exploit the situation [11]. Technical analysis can therefore be used by investors to beat the market and exploit the resources in the emerging economies.

4.2. Fundamental analysis

Fundamental analysis is a method used to determine the prices of stocks using both macroeconomic and microeconomic factors, such as the earnings and dividend information of the firm, expected future interest rates and the risk evaluations. Decisions are made according to whether a particular stock is undervalued or overvalued [58].

The problem with fundamental analysis is to choose the correct firm to analyse. For example, in countries with emerging economies, majority of the firms have the potential to generate high returns. However if, as an investor, you want to achieve more, identifying good firms is not enough as everyone else will already have that information. That investor has to be better than its rivals, has to have a better estimate and finds firms that have more potential for higher returns. Therefore, if efficient market hypothesis holds and all the available information is incorporated into the prices, then fundamental analysis becomes even trickier [11].

5. Application: testing the weak form of efficiency of emerging economies

To put the theory in perspective, we have selected 24 countries which have emerging economies, from around the world, based on the MSCI Emerging Markets Index. These markets were classified into three groups within the Index. These are being Americas (Brazil, Chile, Columbia, Mexico and Peru); Europe, Middle East and Africa (the Czech Republic, Egypt, Greece, Hungary, Poland, Qatar, Russia, South Africa, Turkey and the United Arab Emirates); and, lastly, Asia (China, India, Indonesia, South Korea, Malaysia, Pakistan, the Philippines, Taiwan and Thailand).

To test whether the markets within these countries are weak form efficient or not, stock prices need to be analysed. It needs to be checked whether the prices are independent from each other or contain a unit root. Therefore, monthly stock price data was collected from the stock markets of these countries, from their major indices. Data covered the time period between February 2008 and May 2017, which signifies a time from the major 2008 global financial crisis until the current date. These stock prices were placed in the WinRATS programme to test the following hypothesis:

H_0: contains unit root (efficient market) (i.e. H_0: $\gamma = 0$).

H_a: stationary (inefficient market) (i.e. H_a: $\gamma < 0$).

If the null hypothesis holds, then it is said that the data contains a unit root and the market is efficient. However, if the null hypothesis is rejected, meaning that the alternative hypothesis holds, then the data is stationary and the market is not efficient.

There are many tests (linear or nonlinear) that can be used to test for the existence of a unit root. Although nonlinear tests being the most recent ones developed and supported by many researchers, in this application we have used the traditional augmented Dickey-Fuller (ADF) test to look for a unit root within our sample [60].

Dickey-Fuller (DF) test was developed particularly to observe the stationarity of the data and whether it contains a unit root. Augmented Dickey-Fuller test was developed after this classic DF test, and it is said to be more powerful and can even solve more complex models. There are three regression models in the DF test, such as

Model 1: $\Delta y_t = \gamma y_{t-1} + \varepsilon_t$

Model 2: $\Delta y_t = a_0 + \gamma y_{t-1} + \varepsilon_t$

Model 3: $\Delta y_t = a_0 + \gamma y_{t-1} + a_{2t} + \varepsilon_t$

For ADF test, the 'Dickey-Fuller test is augmented by the logs of Δy_t' [61]:

Model 1: $\Delta y_t = \gamma y_{t-1} + \sum_{i=1}^{k} \Delta y_{t-k} + \varepsilon_t$

Model 2: $\Delta y_t = a_0 + \gamma y_{t-1} + \sum_{i=1}^{k} \Delta y_{t-k} + \varepsilon_t$

Model 3: $\Delta y_t = a_0 + \gamma y_{t-1} + a_{2t} + \sum_{i=1}^{k} \Delta y_{t-k} + \varepsilon_t$

In these models, Model 1 has no constant and no trend, whereas Model 2 has a constant but again no trend. Model 3, however, has both constant and a trend. In this test the error terms are assumed to be homoscedastic and are serially independent from each other [61].

Results obtained from the WinRATS programme is presented in **Table 1** below. These results signify the tau values of the model. There will be higher chance to reject the null hypothesis when this obtained tau value is more negative, because it indicates a unit root at the confidence level [62]. Again, using the work of Dickey and Fuller, the resulting values for each country with a sample size of 112 were compared to the critical values provided by them [60]. The identified critical value at the 10% significance level was observed to be 2.73. Any result, after taking its absolute value, found to be above the critical value of 2.73, indicated the rejection of the null hypothesis, and hence the market observed was not efficient.

As mentioned in the previous sections, there are many contradicting results for market efficiency of countries. The reasons can be due to the time period used within the sample, sample size, type of tests used, etc. The general thought behind emerging markets was that these markets are mainly inefficient and therefore offer many opportunities for investors allowing them to generate above average returns. However, our results indicated that out of these 24 economies, only 7 of them were found to be stationary and hence inefficient at the 10% significance level. These economies were from Brazil, the Czech Republic, Egypt, Hungary, Poland, Russia and Taiwan. The rest of the economies were found to contain a unit root and therefore

Country	ADF test results	Country	ADF test results
Chile	−1.4892	Mexico	−1.23757
Brazil	**−2.80201**	Pakistan	−1.51115
China	−1.84112	Peru	−2.33717
Columbia	−0.61411	The Philippines	−0.80674
The Czech Republic	**−3.80316**	Poland	**−3.19045**
Egypt	**−3.15722**	Qatar	−1.67703
Greece	0.68877	Russia	**−2.97182**
Hungary	**−2.80057**	South Africa	−1.20598
India	−1.62649	Taiwan	**−2.78856**
Indonesia	−1.27022	Thailand	−1.22127
South Korea	−2.00885	The United Arab Emirates	−1.55542
Malaysia	−1.06921	Turkey	−0.77993

Table 1. ADF test results of the 24 emerging economies. Note: The bold figures represent significance at 10% level.

can be said to be efficient in the weak form of information efficiency. These results provided an interesting ground for comparison to information efficiency literature, especially focusing on the post-crisis period.

There are many studies in the field and many different results. Looking at previous studies, we can see that when some support our evidence, some does not. For example, Zahid et al. tested the Karachi Stock Exchange (Pakistan) for the weak form of efficiency using various parametric and non-parametric tests, including ADF test, from period 13 March 2000 to 31 October 2011. Their results indicated that the market did not follow a random walk and, therefore, was not efficient [63]. However, our result does not support this and shows efficiency in the weak form. This example shows how using different dates and monthly data can cause the outcome to change.

Phiri, on the other hand, looked at the Johannesburg Stock Exchange to observe whether a unit root exits. Weekly data was collected from five indices, from the period between 31 January 2000 and 16 December 2014. Results of the study showed that, when applying the linear tests such as the ADF test, there was evidence showing the existence of weak form of efficiency, which supports our finding. However, when nonlinear tests were used, such as the Enders and Granger Test, then the results indicated a stationarity and showed inefficiency [29]. This example, now, indicates how the new methods for testing unit roots can be more powerful than the conventional linear tests.

Another interesting result obtained is from China. Our results indicate that the Chinese stock market, although it is perceived as highly speculative and driven by market rumours, is weak form efficient. Studies by Laurence et al., Liu et al. and Lima and Tabak show supporting evidence to our findings, whereas studies conducted by Mookerjee and Yu showed opposing results [64–67].

So, how do these results contribute? First of all, these results clearly break the idea that emerging markets are not efficient, even in the weak form. And, secondly, they specifically indicate a time period as of the financial crisis and are good reference point for researchers if they want to analyse the effects of the crisis on the stock markets.

6. Conclusion

Throughout the chapter we have defined and discussed the possible issues relating to both emerging economies and the information efficiency of their markets. In summary, when analysing financial markets, whether from a developed or from an emerging economy, the term 'efficiency' refers to the informational efficiency of the market, which is about the degree of information reflected in the prices of financial assets. The efficient market hypothesis is one of the most popular theories in this area and states that all existing information is somehow quickly incorporated into the stock prices. In this way everyone will have access to the same information, and no investor can be able to 'beat the market'. This theory has gained more popularity in the recent years with its application to the emerging economies.

But, why studies conducted on emerging economies important? There are specific characteristics of these markets that make them attractive for analysis and for investors, such as lower than average income per capita, high volatility, rapid growth, higher than average return and less mature capital markets. These characteristics actually make emerging economies unique and interesting in the eyes of investors. In emerging economies, returns of stocks are said to be highly predictable and the stock markets less efficient than those of developed economies, giving a chance for investors to exploit the situation and increase their profits.

Studies also point out that not all markets follow the principles of EMH and there exist inefficient markets, i.e. markets that are not efficient in all three forms of efficiency: weak, semi-strong and strong forms, as can be seen from the results of our study in the previous section. These deviations, which are generally referred to as 'anomalies', can take place just once or repeatedly. There are different types of anomalies known. They can be classified under three categories: calendar, technical and fundamental anomalies. All of them point out to the fact that there could be opportunities to exploit by investors.

At the end of the chapter, we have analysed the stock prices given on the major indices of the 24 emerging markets located all around the world in order to see if they are weak form efficient and if there are opportunities that can be exploited. Using the ADF test, data from February 2008 to May 2017 were analysed. The results indicated that out of the 24 markets only 7 of them were inefficient and the rest were weak form efficient, which contradicts the generalised view that emerging economies are inefficient. These results provided an interesting ground for comparison to information efficiency literature, especially focusing on the postcrisis period.

However, knowing that the amount of resources and opportunities are still much higher in emerging economies, it is important to gather as much information about these markets. Whether we use technical analysis to look at past behaviour and sources or we use fundamental analysis to focus on the macro- and microeconomic factors, there is an ocean of information and knowledge waiting to be discovered.

Author details

Ceyda Aktan[1]*, Eyyup Ensari Sahin[2] and Ilhan Kucukkaplan[3]

*Address all correspondence to: caktan@thk.edu.tr

1 University of Turkish Aeronautical Association, Ankara, Turkey

2 Hitit University, Çorum, Turkey

3 Pamukkale University, Denizli, Turkey

References

[1] Williams LV. editor. Information Efficiency in Financial and Betting Markets. Cambridge University Press; Cambridge, UK. 2005

[2] Dimson E, Mussavian M. A brief history of market efficiency. European Financial Management. 1998;**4**(1):91-103. DOI: 10.1111/1468-036X.00056

[3] Clarke J, Jandik T, Mandelker G. The efficient markets hypothesis. Expert Financial Planning: Advice from Industry Leaders. 2001:126-141

[4] Lim KP, Brooks R. Are Chinese stock markets efficient? Further evidence from a battery of nonlinearity tests. Applied Financial Economics. 2009;**19**(2):147-155. DOI: http://dx.doi.org/10.1080/09603100701765182

[5] Kearney C. Emerging markets research: Trends, issues and future directions. Emerging Markets Review. 2012;**13**(2):159-183. DOI: https://doi.org/10.1016/j.ememar.2012.01.003

[6] Busse JA, Green TC. Market efficiency in real time. Journal of Financial Economics. 2002;**65**(3):415-437

[7] Lo AW. The adaptive markets hypothesis. The Journal of Portfolio Management. 2004;**30**(5): 15-29. DOI: 10.3905/jpm.2004.442611@jpm40.2004.30.issue-5

[8] Fama EF. Mandelbrot and the stable Paretian hypothesis. The Journal of business. 1963;**36**(4):420-429. Available from: http://www.jstor.org/stable/2350971

[9] Fama EF. The behavior of stock-market prices. The Journal of Business. 1965;**38**(1): 34-105. Available from: http://www.jstor.org/stable/2350971

[10] Fama EF. Efficient capital markets: A review of theory and empirical work. The Journal of Finance. 1970;**25**(2):383-417. Available from: http://www.jstor.org/stable/2325486

[11] Bodie Z, Kane A, Marcus A. Investments. 5th ed. McGraw Hill; Irvin, United States. 2003

[12] Malkiel BG. The efficient market hypothesis and its critics. The Journal of Economic Perspectives. 2003;**17**(1):59-82. DOI: 10.1257/089533003321164958

[13] Lindner A, Fischer C, Felix A, Scherer V, Warkentin A. Market Efficiency Theory Investment and Valuation of Firms. Universidad de Huelva 03.11.2010. 2010

[14] Latif M, Arshad S, Fatima M, Farooq S. Market efficiency, market anomalies, causes, evidences, and some behavioral aspects of market anomalies. Research Journal of Finance and Accounting. 2011;**2**(9):1-13. ISSN 2222-2847 (Online)

[15] Mun FW, Kee KS. Do Asian stock market prices follow martingales? Evidence from spectral shape tests. Asia Pacific Journal of Management. 1994;**11**(2):345-359. DOI: 10.1007/BF01739207

[16] Ayadi OF, Pyun CS. An application of variance ratio test to the Korean securities market. Journal of Banking & Finance. 1994;**18**(4):643-658. DOI: 10.11114/aef.v2i2.751

[17] Huang BN. Do Asian stock market prices follow random walks? Evidence from the variance ratio test. Applied Financial Economics. 1995;**5**(4):251-256

[18] Balaban E. Informational Efficiency of the Istanbul Securities Exchange and some Rationale for Public Regulation. The Central Bank of The Republic of Turkey Research Department Discussion Paper. 1995;**9502**:39-67

[19] Balaban E, Kunter K. A note on the efficiency of financial markets in a developing country. Applied Economics Letters. 1997;**4**(2):109-112. DOI: http://dx.doi.org/10.1080/758526706

[20] Özer G, Ertokatlı CT. Chaotic Processes of Common Stock Index Returns: An Empirical Examination on Istanbul Stock Exchange (ISE) Market. African Journal of Business Management. 2010;**4**(6):1140-1148

[21] Worthington AC, Higgs H. Random walks and market efficiency in European equity markets. Global Journal of Finance and Economics. 2004;**1**(1):59-78

[22] Beechey M, Gruen DW, Vickery J. The Efficient Market Hypothesis: A Survey. Sydney: Reserve Bank of Australia, Economic Research Department; 2000

[23] Finnerty JE. Insiders and market efficiency. The Journal of Finance. 1976;**31**(4):1141-1148. DOI: 10.2307/2326279

[24] Grossman SJ, Stiglitz JE. On the impossibility of informationally efficient markets. The American Economic Review. 1980;**70**(3):393-408. Available from: http://www.jstor.org/stable/1805228

[25] Bekaert G, Harvey CR. Research in emerging markets finance: Looking to the future. Emerging Markets Review. 2002;**3**(4):429-448

[26] Hoskisson RE, Eden L, Lau CM, Wright M. Strategy in emerging economies. Academy of Management Journal. 2000;**43**(3):249-267

[27] Fountas S, Segredakis KN. Emerging stock markets return seasonalities: The January effect and the tax-loss selling hypothesis. Applied Financial Economics. 2002;**12**(4):291-299

[28] Fama EF. Market efficiency, long-term returns, and behavioral finance. Journal of Financial Economics. 1998;**49**(3):283-306

[29] Phiri A. Efficient market hypothesis in South Africa: Evidence from linear and nonlinear unit root tests. Managing Global Transitions. 2015;**13**(4):369

[30] Ozdemir ZA. Efficient market hypothesis: Evidence from a small open-economy. Applied Economics. 2008;**40**(5):633-641

[31] Lee CC, Lee JD, Lee CC. Stock prices and the efficient market hypothesis: Evidence from a panel stationary test with structural breaks. Japan and the World Economy. 2010;**22**(1): 49-58

[32] Kim JH, Shamsuddin A. Are Asian stock markets efficient? Evidence from new multiple variance ratio tests. Journal of Empirical Finance. 2008;**15**(3):518-532

[33] Buguk C, Brorsen BW. Testing weak-form market efficiency: Evidence from the Istanbul Stock Exchange. International Review of Financial Analysis. 2003;**12**(5):579-590

[34] Karan MB, Kapusuzoglu A. An analysis of the random walk and overreaction hypotheses through optimum portfolios constructed by the nonlinear programming model. Australian Journal of Basic and Applied Sciences. 2010;**4**(6):1215-1220

[35] Gozbasi O, Kucukkaplan I, Nazlioglu S. Re-examining the Turkish stock market efficiency: Evidence from nonlinear unit root tests. Economic Modelling. 2014;**38**:381-384. DOI: https://doi.org/10.1016/j.econmod.2014.01.021

[36] Cajueiro DO, Gogas P, Tabak BM. Does financial market liberalization increase the degree of market efficiency? The case of the Athens stock exchange. International Review of Financial Analysis. 2009;**18**(1):50-57

[37] Kawakatsu H, Morey MR. Financial liberalization and stock market efficiency: An empirical examination of nine emerging market countries. Journal of Multinational Financial Management. 1999;**9**(3):353-371

[38] Lim KP, Brooks RD, Kim JH. Financial crisis and stock market efficiency: Empirical evidence from Asian countries. International Review of Financial Analysis. 2008;**17**(3): 571-591

[39] Garas A, Argyrakis P. Correlation study of the Athens stock exchange. Physica A: Statistical Mechanics and its Applications. 2007;**380**:399-410. DOI: https://doi.org/10.1016/j.physa.2007.02.097

[40] Hoque HA, Kim JH, Pyun CS. A comparison of variance ratio tests of random walk: A case of Asian emerging stock markets. International Review of Economics & Finance. 2007;**16**(4):488-502. DOI: https://doi.org/10.1016/j.iref.2006.01.001

[41] Frankfurter GM, McGoun EG. Anomalies in finance: What are they and what are they good for?. International Review of Financial Analysis. 2002;**10**(4):407-429

[42] French KR. Stock returns and the weekend effect. Journal of Financial Economics. 1980;**8**(1):55-69. DOI: https://doi.org/10.1016/0304-405X(80)90021-5

[43] Raj M, Kumari D. Day-of-the-week and other market anomalies in the Indian stock market. International Journal of Emerging Markets. 2006;**1**(3):235-246. DOI: https://doi.org/10.1108/17468800610674462

[44] Ajayi RA, Mehdian S, Perry MJ. The day-of-the-week effect in stock returns: Further evidence from Eastern European emerging markets. Emerging Markets Finance and Trade. 2004;**40**(4):53-62

[45] Dicle MF, Levendis JD. The day-of-the-week effect revisited: International evidence. Journal of Economics and Finance. 2014;**38**(3):407-437. DOI:10.1007/s12197-011-9223-6

[46] Poshakwale S. Evidence on weak form efficiency and day of the week effect in the Indian stock market. Finance India. 1996;**10**(3):605-616

[47] Basher SA, Sadorsky P. Day-of-the-week effects in emerging stock markets. Applied Economics Letters. 2006;**13**(10):621-628

[48] Patel JB. The January effect anomaly reexamined in stock returns. Journal of Applied Business Research. 2016;**32**(1):317. DOI: http://dx.doi.org/10.19030/jabr.v32i1.9540

[49] Cheung KC, Andrew Coutts J. The January effect and monthly seasonality in the Hang Seng Index: 1985-1997. Applied Economics Letters. 1999;**6**(2):121-123

[50] Coutts JA, Sheikh MA. The January effect and monthly seasonality in the All Gold Index on the Johannesburg Stock Exchange 1987-1997. Applied Economics Letters. 2000;**7**(8):489-492

[51] Guler S. January effect in stock returns, evidence from emerging markets. Interdisciplinary Journal of Contemporary Research in Business. 2013;**5**(4):641-648

[52] Banz RW. The relationship between return and market value of common stocks. Journal of Financial Economics. 1981;**9**(1):3-18

[53] Mghendi F. Testing the small firm effect on stock market returns at the Nairobi securities exchange. Doctoral dissertation, University of Nairobi. 2014

[54] Keim DB. Size-related anomalies and stock return seasonality: Further empirical evidence. Journal of Financial Economics. 1983;**12**(1):13-32

[55] Rogalski RJ, Tinic SM. The January size effect: Anomaly or risk mismeasurement? Financial Analysts Journal. 1986;63-70

[56] Chen TC, Chien CC. Size effect in January and cultural influences in an emerging stock market: The perspective of behavioral finance. Pacific-Basin Finance Journal. 2011;**19**(2): 208-229. Article ID: 62639,9 pages. 10.4236/me.2016.71001

[57] Chui AC, Wei KJ. Book-to-market, firm size, and the turn-of-the-year effect: Evidence from Pacific-Basin emerging markets. Pacific-Basin Finance Journal. 1998;**6**(3):275-293

[58] Fama EF. Random walks in stock market prices. Financial Analysts Journal. 1995;**51**(1): 75-80. DOI: https://doi.org/10.2469/faj.v51.n1.1861

[59] Neely CJ. Technical analysis in the foreign exchange market: A layman's guide. Federal Reserve Bank of St. Louis Review. 1997; Sep:23-38

[60] Omay NC. Testing weak form market efficiency for emerging economies: A nonlinear approach. Doctoral dissertation. 2010

[61] Dickey DA, Fuller WA. Likelihood ratio statistics for autoregressive time series with a unit root. Econometrica: Journal of the Econometric Society. 1981;**49**(4):1057-1072

[62] Konak F, Şeker Y. The efficiency of developed markets: Empirical evidence from FTSE 100. Journal of Advanced Management Science. 2014;**2**(1):29-32

[63] Zahid FM, Ramzan S, Ramzan S. A parametric and non-parametric approach for testing random walk behavior and efficiency of Pakistani stock market. International Journal of Science and Technology. 2012;**2**(5):316-322

[64] Laurence M, Cai F, Qian S. Weak-form efficiency and causality tests in Chinese stock markets. Multinational Finance Journal. 1997;**1**:291-307

[65] Liu X, Song H, Romilly P. Are Chinese stock markets efficient? A cointegration and causality analysis. Applied Economics Letters. 1997;**4**:511-515

[66] Araújo Lima EJ, Tabak BM. Tests of the random walk hypothesis for equity markets: Evidence from China, Hong Kong and Singapore. Applied Economics Letters. 2004;**11**(4):255-258

[67] Mookerjee R, Yu Q. An empirical analysis of the equity markets in China. Review of Financial Economics. 1999;**8**(1):41-60

Chapter 4

Comparison of CAPM, Three-Factor Fama-French Model and Five-Factor Fama-French Model for the Turkish Stock Market

Yaşar Erdinç

Additional information is available at the end of the chapter

http://dx.doi.org/10.5772/intechopen.70867

Abstract

In this study, I try to test the capital asset pricing model (CAPM), three-factor Fama-French (3F-FF) model and five-factor Fama-French (5F-FF) model for the Turkish stock market. The sample is from June 2000 to May 2017. My results show that the five-factor model explains better the common variation in stock returns than the three-factor model and capital asset pricing model. Moreover, the CAPM has no power in explaining monthly excess returns of sorted portfolios. Although three-factor model seems to have significant coefficients, intercepts in this model have significant *t*-values indicating that the model has problems in explaining the portfolio returns. I use equal weight market portfolio for all the models in order to explain the cross-sectional variations in the stock returns.

Keywords: CAPM, three-factor Fama-French model, five-factor Fama-French model, Turkish stock market, size, book to market, profitability, investment

1. Introduction

Borsa Istanbul (BIST) stock exchange was established in 1985 and commenced stock trading on 3 January 1986. Acceptance of BIST as a full member to the World Federation of Exchanges (WFE) was in 1992. As elsewhere, obviously for all investors (institutional or individual), the main goal is to get the highest possible return in a stock market.

This study tests the capital asset pricing model (CAPM hereafter), the three-factor Fama-French model (3F-FF hereafter) and the five-factor Fama-French model (5F-FF hereafter) in the case of the Turkish stock market. This study extends the asset pricing tests in three ways: (a) this study is the first application of the 5F-FF Fama-French model for the Turkish stock market. (b) It expands the test of the 3F-FF model to the Turkish market for a longer period, and this is the first study that covers 17 years of the Turkish data. The main result is that the

5F-FF model explains better the common variation and the cross section of stock returns than the 3F-FF model and the CAPM. (c) I test all the models (CAPM, 3F-FF and 5F-FF) with 48 different market portfolios. 5F-FF model portfolios capture the common variation in stock returns and can explain the cross section in returns.

In Section 2, I give a literature review on asset pricing models and applications. In Section 3, data selection, variable definitions, return periods and filtering data issues are given. Section 4 explains the methodology to apply the CAPM and Fama-French factor models to the Turkish stock market. In this section, explanatory variables and dependent variables are defined. First of all, Fama-French factors are constructed. Then, regression portfolios are constructed by sorting the stocks by their size, book-to-market ratios (B/M), profitability (OP) and investment (INV). In Section 5, I give regression portfolio statistics to see patterns in the behaviour of portfolios. Section 6 defines and estimates factor spanning regressions, which are important to see if an explanatory factor can be explained by a combination of other factors. Having estimated and tested factor spanning regressions, I go on testing of hypothesis of joint significance of portfolio regressions' alphas in Section 7. In this section, I conduct Gibbons-Ross-Shanken (GRS) test for the regression portfolios and give preliminary results of the performance of the CAPM, the 3F-FF and the 5F-FF models for the Turkish case. Section 8 is devoted to the detailed analysis of regressions, and the main messages of these regressions are presented. Section 9 concludes and presents the main findings of the study.

2. Literature review

What kinds of factors determine the price of an asset? Since Markowitz formulated a model of asset pricing [1], the debate on this question continues. The main determinants of asset prices and risk factors that affect the demand for assets and asset prices have been an important issue in finance theory and practice. One can find enormous number of studies on this issue. Earlier studies in this area are by Markowitz, Sharpe, Ross, Fama and French [1–4].

Since the literature on asset pricing model (APM) is very well known and can be reached easily in finance textbooks, I do not go into a detailed explanation of evolution of APM. However, I would like to briefly state that all the asset pricing models developed so far have included risk as the most important determinant. For example, [1] defines the expected return and variance of returns on a portfolio as the basic criteria for portfolio selection.

Markowitz's model requires large data inputs. Because of input drawback, new models have been developed to simplify the inputs to portfolio analysis. William Sharpe's market model [2] is as follows:

$$R_{it} = \alpha_i + \beta_i^* R_{Mt} + e_{it}, \tag{1}$$

where R_{it} is the return of stock i in period t, α_i is the unique expected return of security i, β_i is the sensitivity of stock i to market movements, R_{mt} is the return on the market in period t and e_{it} is the unique risky return of security i in period t and has a mean of zero and finite variance

http://dx.doi.org/10.5772/intechopen.70867

σ^2_{ei}, uncorrelated with the market return, pairwise and serially uncorrelated. This equation explains the return on asset i by the return on a stock market index. β in Eq. (1) is a risk measure arising from the relationship between the return on a stock and the market's return.

Later on, the equilibrium models have been developed. The difference between the market model and the equilibrium model was that asset returns are related to excess market return rather than market return. The first and basic form of the general equilibrium model, which was developed by Sharpe, Lintner and Mossin [2, 4, 5] called capital asset pricing model (CAPM), is given in Eq. (2):

$$R_{it} = R_f + \beta_i{}^* \left(R_{Mt} - R_f\right) + e_{it} \tag{2}$$

where R_{it} is the return of stock i in period t, R_f is risk free rate, β_i is the sensitivity of stock i to excess return on a market portfolio, R_{mt} is the return on the market in period t and e_{it} is the unique risky return of security i in period t and has a mean of zero and variance σ^2_{ei}.

Black et al. [6] derived a new model of the CAPM by relaxing the assumption of risk-free lending and borrowing. Basu [7] considers a different time series model, which is written in terms of returns in excess of the risk-free rate R_f and shows that returns are positively and linearly related to β, as follows:

$$R_{it} - R_{ft} = \alpha_i + \beta_i \left(R_{Mt} - R_{ft}\right) + e_{it} \tag{3}$$

While the CAPM is still the most widely accepted description for security pricing, empirical studies found contradicting evidence (see [7–14]). Therefore, researchers concentrated on finding better models for the behaviour of stock returns and added more explanatory variables into CAPM.

In the early 1990s, one of the most influential researches was by Fama and French [15, 16]. Fama and French [15] reject the market beta associated with the CAPM and instead find that stock size and book-to-market (B/M) ratio better capture the cross-sectional variation in average stock returns. One year later the same researchers proposed that a 3F-FF asset pricing model augmenting the CAPM with size and book-to-market proxies for risk might be a superior description of average returns [16]. After these two influential studies, along with earlier evidence against the CAPM drove the finance community into investigating the reasons behind the anomalies found in [10–14].

Recent studies have found additional factors that seem to exhibit a strong relationship with average returns. Novy-Marx [17] finds that firms with high profitability generate significantly higher returns than unprofitable firms. Aharoni et al. [18] find that a statistically significant relation exists between an investment proxy and average returns. In the wake of these findings, Fama and French [19] expanded the 3F-FF model with *profitability* and *investment*. They reveal that the 5F-FF model performs better than the 3F-FF model in explaining average returns for their sample. The same model was tested using international data [20, 21], and they have found similar results.

This study adds to research conducted on CAPM, three-factor model and the new 5F-FF model by testing all these models on the Turkish stock market.

3. Data selection and issues

3.1. The sample

The data sample used in the analysis consists of monthly price, total return and accounting data downloaded from 'Finnet Data Yayıncılık'. The data set contains nonfinancial 263 firms listed in BIST (Borsa Istanbul or Istanbul stock exchange) for the period between 31.12.1999 and 30.05.2017. The collected accounting data includes total assets, total liabilities, outstanding shares, owner's equity and operating income, where operating income is defined as 'net sales minus operating expenses' and operating expenses is defined as the 'sum of all expenses related to operations'. Data was collected for all available active and dead stocks in Istanbul stock exchange totalling 204 observations. The data was quoted in the Turkish Lira (TRY hereafter).

The downloaded sample included a large amount of stocks, which were already dead at the beginning of the research period, as well as some missing data types and data errors, which ought to be removed.

3.2. Variable definitions

This subsection defines the variables needed in the factor creation process. Market capitalisation or market cap was used as a measure of size for each stock and was calculated by multiplying the price (P) at the 31st of December each year with outstanding shares at the 31st of December for the same year. The price data was obtained from FDY. Book equity was calculated as yearly total assets minus total liabilities from FDY. Book-to-market ratio (B/M) was calculated from the previous two variables by dividing book equity by market cap. Operating profitability (OP) was calculated by dividing operating income by book equity following [22]. Finally, investment (Inv) was calculated as in Eq. (4):

$$\frac{Total\ Assets_{t-1} - Total\ Assets_{t-2}}{Total\ Assets_{t-2}} \tag{4}$$

TRY 3-month Libor rate is used as a proxy of risk-free rate (R_f), while market return (R_m) is approximated by natural log difference of BIST-100 Index of the Istanbul stock exchange. It consists of 100 stocks, which are selected among the stocks of companies listed on the national market (excluding list C companies). Monthly returns for stocks are all calculated as natural log difference of monthly stock data.

3.3. The return period

Fama and French use 6-month gap between the ends of the fiscal year and the portfolio formation date can be considered as convenient and conservative. Since all the accounting data in BIST is available by the end of May of each year, I use 5-month gap. Hence, to ensure that all accounting variables are known by investors, I assume that all accounting information is made public by the end of May, and I use monthly returns from the beginning of June to the end of the following year in May. And, each year at the end of May, I sort the portfolios.

Fama and French [15, 16] used value-weighted returns in their study; however, they also stressed that equal-weighted returns do a better job than value-weighted returns in explaining returns by 3F-FF model. Lakonishok et al. [23] also suggest to use equal-weighted portfolios to investigate the relationship between risk factors and stock returns. Hence, the equal-weighted monthly returns on each portfolio were used in this study.

3.4. Filtering data

At the end of each year, I eliminated firms that have the following specifics: (1) negative book-to-market values were removed, and (2) the companies with yearly increase in their investment, as defined in Eq. (4), which is either less than −50% or higher than 100% in a certain year were eliminated. This would imply that the company in question lost half of its assets, or more than doubled its assets in the given year, which seems very unlikely during normal recurring circumstances.

4. Methodology

4.1. Model definitions

In this study, I test three models, namely, CAPM, 3F-FF model and 5F-FF model for BIST. The model definitions are given below:

$$\mathrm{R}_{it} - \mathrm{R}_{ft} = a_i + \left(R_{Mt} - R_{ft}\right) + e_{it-\mathrm{CAPM}} \tag{5}$$

$$\mathrm{R}_{it} - \mathrm{R}_{ft} = a_i + \left(R_{Mt} - R_{ft}\right) + s_i SMB_t + h_i HML_t + e_{it}(\text{3F-FF model}) \tag{6}$$

$$\mathrm{R}_{it} - \mathrm{R}_{ft} = a_i + \left(R_{Mt} - R_{ft}\right) + s_i SMB_t + h_i HML_t + r_i RMW_t + c_i CMA_t + e_{it}(\text{5F-FF model}) \tag{7}$$

where R_{it} is the return of portfolio i at time t (portfolio creation procedure is given in the following topic); R_{ft} is the risk-free rate approximated by 3-month TRY Libor rate at time t; $R_{it}–R_{ft}$ is the excess return of portfolio i at time t; R_{Mt} is the monthly market return approximated by natural log difference of BIST-100 Index at time t; SMB_t, HML_t, RMW_t and CMA_t are defined in details in the following topic; a_i is the intercept; β_i is the coefficient of $R_{Mt}–R_{ft}$ for portfolio i; s_i is the coefficient of SMB_t for portfolio i; h_i is the coefficient of HML_t for portfolio i; r_i is the coefficient of RMW_t for portfolio i; and c_i is the coefficient of RMW_t for portfolio i.

4.2. Construction of Fama-French factors

The next step in the analysis is to *create sorted portfolios* from which the *Fama and French factor return series* could be calculated. The factors used in the analysis were constructed in a manner similar to the process described in [19], relying solely on 2 × 3 sorts for creating the factors. Other sorting choices might have been used; however, [19] finds no differences in model performance when testing differing sorting methods.

My first data point is at the 31st of December 1999, and the investment variable is calculated as in Eq. (4); the first available year of accounting data used in the sorting process is at the end of fiscal year 2000. The portfolios were sorted at the end of May each year, and therefore the first available return observation in the final analysis is the return of June 2000, sorted according to accounting data at the end of fiscal year 1999. Thus, the time period for the actual analysis is June 2000 to May 2017 or 204 months of return data.

The sorting process is as follows:

(1) First of all, stocks are sorted according to their market cap to define small-sized and big-sized stocks. Fifty percent of the market cap was used as the breakpoint for size. (2) For all other factors, yearly sample 30th and 70th percentiles were used as breakpoints in the sorting method. (3) After the determination of the breakpoints, the stocks in the sample were independently distributed for every year into six size-B/M (where B/M is book-to-market ratio) portfolios, six size-OP (where OP is operational profits divided by book equity showing profitability) portfolios and six size-Inv (where Inv is yearly increase in total assets) portfolios created from the intersections of the yearly breakpoints. (4) All portfolios are value-weighted according to their market cap. (5) Monthly returns were calculated for each of the 18 portfolios. (6) After calculating the sorted portfolio returns, the actual factor returns were calculated.

There are two size groups and three book-to-market (B/M), three operating profitability (OP) and three investment (Inv) groups. The resulting groups are labelled with two letters. The first letter describes the size group, small (S) or big (B). The second letter describes the B/M group, high (H), neutral (N) or low (L); the OP group, robust (R), neutral (N) or weak (W); or the Inv group, conservative (C), neutral (N) or aggressive (A). Stocks in each component are value-weighted to calculate the component's monthly returns (**Figure 1**).

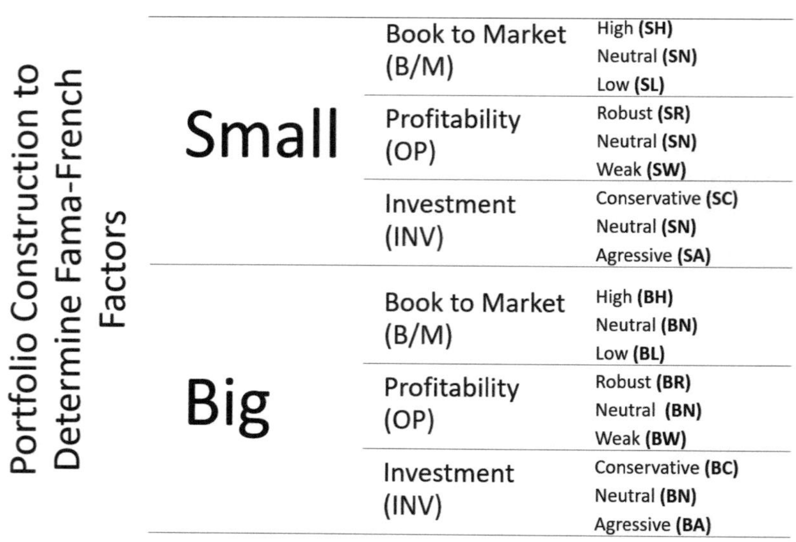

Figure 1. Sorted portfolio groups to construct Fama-French factors.

Eqs. (8)–(14) define calculations of the Fama-French factors:

$$SMB_{B/M} = (SH + SN + SL)/3 - (BH + BN + BL)/3 \tag{8}$$

$$SMB_{OP} = (SR + SN + SW)/3 - (BR + BN + BW)/3 \tag{9}$$

$$SMB_{Inv} = (SC + SN + SA)/3 - (BC + BN + BA)/3 \tag{10}$$

$$SMB = \left(SMB_{B/M} + SMB_{OP} + SMB_{Inv}\right)/3 \tag{11}$$

$$HML = (SH + BH)/2 - (SL + BL)/2 \tag{12}$$

$$RMW = (SR + BR)/2 - (SW + BW)/2 \tag{13}$$

$$CMA = (SC + BC)/2 - (SA + BA)/2 \tag{14}$$

4.3. Regression portfolios and other data used in the regression analysis

Regressions were run on three sets of 16 left-hand-side regression portfolios. Monthly returns for the portfolios were calculated in a manner similar to constructing the factor portfolios;

Book to market (sorted from low to high (BM1 (lowest); BM4 (highest))				
	BM1	**BM2**	**BM3**	**BM4**
S1	S1BM1	S1BM2	S1BM3	S1BM4
S2	S2BM1	S2BM2	S2BM3	S2BM4
S3	S3BM1	S3BM2	S3BM3	S3BM4
S4	S4BM1	S4BM2	S4BM3	S4BM4
Profitability (sorted from robust to weak: PO1 (robust profitability); PO4 (weak profitability))				
	OP1	**OP2**	**OP3**	**OP4**
S1	S1OP1	S1OP2	S1OP3	S1OP4
S2	S2OP1	S2OP2	S2OP3	S2OP4
S3	S3OP1	S3OP2	S3OP3	S3OP4
S4	S4OP1	S4OP2	S4OP3	S4OP4
Investment (sorted from conservative to aggressive: INV1 (conservative); INV4 (aggressive))				
	INV1	**INV2**	**INV3**	**INV4**
S1	S1INV1	S1INV2	S1INV3	S1INV4
S2	S2INV1	S2INV2	S2INV3	S2INV4
S3	S3INV1	S3INV2	S3INV3	S3INV4
S4	S4INV1	S4INV2	S4INV3	S4INV4

For example, S1BM1 shows average of the monthly excess returns of stocks included in the smallest size and lowest book-to-market portfolio.

Table 1. Construction of dependent variables: each notation of a dependent variable in this table shows the monthly excess return of the corresponding sorted portfolio.

Panel A	BM1 (low)	BM2	BM3	BM4 (high)
S1 (small)	7	12	14	19
S2	10	11	14	19
S3	8	8	8	7
S4 (big)	21	15	12	6
Panel B	**OP1 (robust)**	**OP2**	**OP3**	**OP4 (weak)**
S1 (small)	10	9	13	22
S2	11	12	16	15
S3	12	15	12	11
S4 (big)	14	15	11	3
Panel C	**INV1 (conservative)**	**INV2**	**INV3**	**INV4 (aggressive)**
S1 (small)	17	12	12	12
S2	15	15	12	12
S3	14	14	13	12
S4 (big)	8	14	17	14

Table 2. Average number of stocks in regression portfolios.

equal-weighted portfolios were created from independent 4 × 4 sorts with 25th, 50th and 75th yearly sample percentiles as breakpoints for both sorting variables. **Table 1** shows the constructed dependent variables.

Panels A through C in **Table 2** show the average number of stocks in each of the regression portfolios. It is evident from Panel A that high B/M companies are often smaller companies, while low B/M is tilted towards bigger companies. A similar phenomenon can be observed in Panel B, where low operating profitability is a feature of smaller companies and high operating profitability is more often found in stocks with higher market capitalisations.

5. Regression portfolio statistics

In this section, I give descriptive statistics for the regression portfolios and explanatory factors used in the regressions.

The main aim of this research is to see if well-targeted regression models can explain average monthly excess returns on portfolios with large differences in constituent size, B/M, profitability and investment. In **Table 3**, the standard deviations of monthly excess return of portfolios seem to be very high. One of the explanations is that portfolio groups include small numbers of stocks. The second explanation could be the economic crisis experienced in 2001 in Turkey. This crisis created very high volatility in the financial markets, and the daily change in stock market index (viz. BIST-100) reached to 30%. When I exclude data covering the years from 2000 to 2003, standard deviations decrease by 35% on average. On the other hand, it should also be noted that global crisis in 2008 and Greece's haircut in 2010–2011 created very high

http://dx.doi.org/10.5772/intechopen.70867

Excess returns (%)					**Standard deviation (%)**				
Panel A: size/BM portfolios									
	BM1 (low)	**BM2**	**BM3**	**BM4 (high)**		**BM1 (low)**	**BM2**	**BM3**	**BM4 (high)**
S1 (small)	0.40	0.35	0.35	0.66	**S1 (small)**	10.34	11.64	10.57	10.93
S2	−0.03	0.69	0.32	0.67	**S2**	9.69	9.64	10.19	11.42
S3	0.46	0.75	0.28	1.12	**S3**	10.52	10.94	9.71	9.21
S4 (big)	0.43	0.89	0.76	1.09	**S4 (big)**	10.12	11.43	10.55	10.84
Panel B: size/OP portfolios									
	OP1 (robust)	**OP2**	**OP3**	**OP4 (weak)**		**OP1 (robust)**	**OP2**	**OP3**	**OP4 (weak)**
S1 (small)	1.40	0.48	0.89	−0.43	**S1 (small)**	10.66	11.25	10.38	10.45
S2	0.28	0.34	1.24	0.67	**S2**	9.52	9.71	10.53	11.05
S3	1.17	−0.32	0.72	0.49	**S3**	10.50	10.40	9.23	9.52
S4 (big)	1.27	1.10	1.55	−0.01	**S4 (big)**	10.54	11.09	10.42	10.41
Panel C: size/Inv portfolios									
	Inv1 (consv.)	**Inv2**	**Inv3**	**Inv4 (aggr.)**		**Inv1 (consv.)**	**Inv2**	**Inv3**	**Inv4 (aggr.)**
S1 (small)	0.22	0.44	0.42	0.52	**S1 (small)**	10.97	10.67	9.96	10.55
S2	0.63	0.92	0.43	0.46	**S2**	9.33	9.63	10.91	10.70
S3	0.72	0.59	0.80	1.13	**S3**	9.94	10.42	9.34	9.71
S4 (big)	0.73	0.73	0.93	0.93	**S4 (big)**	10.69	10.56	9.98	10.42

Table 3. Average monthly excess returns and standard deviations (for definitions of variables, see Section 4.3).

volatility in many stock markets. In normal circumstances, I would expect the standard deviations to be half of the figures in **Table 3**.

Table 3 shows that big-sized portfolios tend to benefit from high book-to-market ratios. On the other hand, small portfolios tend to benefit from high profitability, while the effect is weak on big portfolios. In Panel A, we see size and book-to-market (B/M hereafter) pairs of portfolios. The highest average monthly excess return portfolios are S3BM4 and S4BM4 with 1.12% and 1.09%, respectively. The Turkish data reveals that big-sized companies (in groups S3 and S4) with high B/M ratios have the highest monthly excess returns. Worst performers are small-sized companies with low B/M ratios.

In Panel B, returns of portfolios sorted and grouped according to their size and profitability are given. The highest returns in the table belong to S1OP1, S4OP1 and S4OP3. In the Turkish stock market, the highest monthly returns coincide with the high profitability. As you will see in the remainder of the study, I think the most important factor determining the returns of stocks is profitability. The main message is that, even if a company is grouped in the smallest size, if its profitability is high, its return is expected to be high. But one peculiar result is that S4OP3, which represents a portfolio with low profitability and the biggest size, has a monthly excess return of 1.55%. One explanation could be that even if the biggest-sized companies have low profitability, if it is an aggressive investing company and the expectation of the market participants is positive, then a monthly average return of 1.55% would be justified. As you may see in Panel C of **Table 3**, big companies with aggressive investing have the highest returns.

6. Factor spanning regressions

Factor spanning regressions are a means to test if an explanatory factor can be explained by a combination of other explanatory factors. Spanning tests are performed by regressing returns of one factor against the returns of all other factors and analysing the intercepts from that regression.

Table 4 shows regressions for the 5F-FF model's explanatory variables, where four factors explain returns on the fifth. In the RM-Rf regressions, the intercept is not statistically significant ($t = -0.55$). Regressions to explain HML, RMW and CMA factors are strongly positive. However, regressions to explain SMB show insignificant intercept, with intercept of −0.27% ($t = -1.34$). These results suggest that removing either the RM-Rf or SMB factor would not hurt the mean-variance-efficient tangency portfolio produced by combining the remaining four factors.

	Intercept	RM-Rf	SMB	HML	RMW	CMA	R^2
RM-Rf							
Coefficient	−0.45		0.34	−0.41	−0.29	−0.21	0.20
t-Stat	−0.55		1.17	−1.81	−1.33	−1.02	
SMB							
Coefficient	−0.27	0.02		0.00	0.07	0.01	0.12
t-Stat	−1.34	1.17		0.07	1.32	0.29	
HML							
Coefficient	−0.55	−0.04	0.01		0.06	0.10	0.19
t-Stat	**−2.19**	−1.81	0.07		0.82	1.50	
RMW							
Coefficient	−1.06	−0.03	0.12	0.06		0.07	0.17
t-Stat	**−4.18**	−1.33	1.32	0.82		1.01	
CMA							
Coefficient	−1.04	−0.02	0.03	0.11	0.07		0.16
t-Stat	**−3.95**	−1.02	0.29	1.50	1.01		

RM-Rf is the equal-weighted return on BIST-100 Index minus the 3-month Tryribor rate. SMB is the size factor, HML is the value factor, RMW is the profitability factor, and CMA is the investment factor. The factors are constructed using individual sorts of stocks into two size groups and three B/M groups, three OP groups or three Inv groups. Bolded and shaded t-statistics indicate the significance at the 5% level.

Table 4. Factor spanning regressions on five factors: spanning regressions using four factors to explain average returns on the fifth (June 2000–May 2017, 204 months).

7. Hypothesis tests of joint significance of the regressions' alphas and regressions

Having presented the methodology and statistical results, in this part, I present an answer to important question if the estimated models can completely capture expected returns. To obtain a more absolute answer to this question GRS f-tests were conducted on results obtained from the first hypothesis' portfolio regressions. The GRS statistic is used to test if the alpha values from regressions are jointly indistinguishable from zero.

If a model completely captures expected returns, the intercept should be indistinguishable from zero. Hence, the first hypotheses are:

H_0: $\hat{\alpha}1 = \hat{\alpha}2 = \ldots = \hat{\alpha}16 = 0$ (*the regression alpha is not significantly different from zero*).

H_1: $\hat{\alpha}1, \hat{\alpha}2, \ldots, \hat{\alpha}16 \neq 0$ (*the regression alpha is significantly different from zero*).

The second hypotheses for all equations are:

H_0: $\hat{\alpha}1 = \hat{\alpha}2 = \ldots = \hat{\alpha}48 = 0$ (*the regression alphas are jointly indistinguishable from zero*).

H_1: $\hat{\alpha}1, \hat{\alpha}2, \ldots, \hat{\alpha}48 \neq 0$ (*the regression alphas are jointly distinguishable from zero*).

Finally, average individual regression alphas and joint GRS regression f-values were used together in order to compare the performance between the tested models.

7.1. The GRS regression equation

The GRS test was developed by Gibbons et al. [24] and serves as a test of mean-variance efficiency between a left-hand-side collection of assets or portfolios and a right-hand-side model or portfolio. The following regression defines the GRS test:

$$fGRS = \frac{T}{N} \times \frac{T-N-L}{T-L-1} \times \frac{\widehat{\alpha}' \times \widehat{\Sigma}^{-1} \times \widehat{\alpha}}{1+\overline{\mu}' \times \widehat{\Omega}^{-1} \times \overline{\mu}} \sim F(N, T-N-L) \quad (15)$$

where $\hat{\alpha}$ is a $N \times 1$ vector of estimated intercepts, $\widehat{\Sigma}$ an unbiased estimate of the residual covariance matrix, $\overline{\mu}$ a $L \times 1$ vector of the factor portfolios' sample means and $\widehat{\Omega}$ an unbiased estimate of the factor portfolios' covariance matrix.

The GRS test is used in this study to determine whether the alpha values from individual model regressions are jointly non-significant and hence to find out if a model completely captures the sample return variation. As intercepts from individual regressions approach zero, the GRS statistic will also approach zero. However, since the GRS statistic derives its results from comparing the optimal LHS and RHS portfolios, the resulting statistic is not strictly comparable between models.

7.2. Model performance

A set of several summary metrics were deployed in order to compare the performance of the asset pricing models. GRS statistics and average alpha values were used as the main two statistics in order to determine how good the different asset pricing models performed in explaining portfolio returns. In addition to these statistics, average absolute alpha spread was added for a more complete picture of the alpha results. Furthermore, different models' explanatory power was measured using R^2 values.

If a capital asset pricing model (CAPM, three-factor model or five-factor model) completely captures expected returns, the intercept (alphas) is indistinguishable from zero in a regression of an asset's excess returns on the model's factor returns.

Table 5 shows the GRS statistics of [24] that tests this hypothesis for combinations of LHS portfolios and factors. The GRS test easily rejects all models considered for all LHS portfolios and RHS factors. The probability, or p-value, of getting a GRS statistic larger than the one observed if the true intercepts are all zero is shown in column 'pGRS'. One can see from **Table 5** that except CAPM in Panel A and Panel C, sets of left-hand-side returns, the p-values round to zero to at least three decimals. Only five-factor model in Panel C has a p-value of 0.30, and it is still significant at the 5% level.

	fGRS	pGRS	Avg $\lvert\alpha\rvert$	Avg $\lvert\alpha - \overline{\alpha}\rvert$	Avg R^2
Panel A: size-B/M portfolios					
CAPM	0.95	2.74	0.57	0.25	0.06
Three-factor (S/BM)	**2.13**	0.00	1.32	0.31	0.34
Five-factor (S/BM)	**2.47**	0.00	0.73	0.72	0.49
Panel B: size-OP portfolios					
CAPM	**4.23**	0.00	0.77	0.49	0.07
Three-factor (S/OP)	**5.63**	0.00	1.41	0.44	0.33
Five-factor (S/OP)	**6.15**	0.00	0.91	0.87	0.50
Panel C: size-Inv portfolios					
CAPM	0.94	2.66	0.66	0.18	0.06
Three-factor (S/Inv)	**2.93**	0.00	1.38	0.19	0.33
Five-factor (S/Inv)	1.33	0.30	0.73	0.74	0.50
Panel D: all portfolios					
CAPM (all)	**3.20**	0.00	0.67	0.30	0.06
Three-factor (all)	**13.37**	0.00	1.15	0.57	0.39
Five-factor (all)	**2.66**	0.00	0.79	0.78	0.49

The table tests the ability of CAPM, 3F-FF and 5F-FF models to explain monthly excess returns on 16 size-B/M portfolios (Panel A), 16 size-OP portfolios (Panel B), 16 size-Inv portfolios (Panel C) and a joint sample of all 48 portfolios (Panel D). For each panel, the table shows the tested model; the GRS statistic testing whether the expected values of all 16 or 48 intercept estimates are zero; the p-value for the GRS statistic; the average absolute value of the intercepts, Avg $\lvert\alpha\rvert$; the average absolute deviation from the average intercept; and the average R^2. Bolded and shaded GRS statistics indicate the significance at the 5% level.

Table 5. Summary of statistics for model comparison tests: summary of statistics for tests of CAPM, 3F-FF and 5F-FF models (June 2000–May 2017, 204 months).

http://dx.doi.org/10.5772/intechopen.70867

Fama and French [19] state that they want to identify the model that is the best (but imperfect) story for average returns on portfolios formed in different ways, and they use absolute value of average alphas ($|\alpha|$) and two more statistics (for a detailed description of these statistics, see ([21], pp. 10). Following [22], in this study I use only average absolute values of alphas ($|\alpha|$) and the average absolute deviation from the average intercept (Avg $|\alpha - \overline{\alpha}|$). Both [19, 22] pay specific importance of the absolute values of alphas. Relatively, small values of Avg$|\alpha|$ or Avg $|\alpha - \overline{\alpha}|$ in equations are regarded as better in identifying the best model. However, as is seen in **Table 5**, Avg$|\alpha|$ of CAPM model in Panel A has the lowest value, but fGRS and pGRS show that we cannot reject the hypothesis that the regression alpha is significantly different from zero. The same case is valid for the CAPM in Panel C in **Table 5**. Therefore, I think concentrating on the magnitude of the alpha values or absolute deviation from the average intercept (Avg $|\alpha - \overline{\alpha}|$) in the equations to decide on the best performing model may not be a healthy approach. Keeping this in mind, my main conclusion from the model comparison tests follows.

The GRS test in Panel D clearly rejects the second hypothesis for all models tested. Furthermore, the GRS test in Panel D suggests that the 5F-FF model is the model closest to a complete description of asset returns. Beware that, as discussed in [19], fGRS values between models cannot be strictly compared. Instead, the fGRS is mainly interpreted as a test to reject or accept a model's explanation of returns on a set of left-hand-side portfolios. The fGRS in [21, 22] is used in comparisons between models only in combination with a comparison of average alpha values. Fama and French [19] instead use the numerator of a GRS regression as a comparison value when choosing which factors to include in a model. In every panel of **Table 5**, explanatory power measured by average R^2 clearly improves with the inclusion of more factors. For this reason, metrics for explanatory power are important in providing additional help to compare these types of asset pricing models.

The main conclusions from the performance comparison tests can be summarised as follows. A GRS test on the joint set of all tested portfolios clearly rejects all tested models as complete descriptions of average returns. The CAPM model elicits the lowest average absolute alpha values of the three tested models throughout all tests but shows a statistically insignificant fGRS value compared to other models. Considering all the evidence in **Table 5**, it is clear that the 5F-FF model shows the strongest performance out of the three models for the sample. In the following section, I provide alpha values from individual left-hand-side portfolio regressions, and I re-examine the alpha values from a different perspective.

8. Regression details

In this part, I give individual regression alphas, the coefficients that were defined in Eqs. (5)–(7), their corresponding t-values and R-squared values in order to provide a more detailed picture of model performance. I concentrate on the significance of alphas. Significant alpha patterns between models are compared and further analysed by looking at regression slopes in **Tables 6–8**.

Dep. variables		Five-factor size-B/M models							Three-factor size-B/M models					CAPM		
		α	Rm-Rf	SMB	HML	RMW	CMA	R^2	α	Rm-Rf	SMB	HML	R^2	α	Rm-Rf	R^2
S1BM1	Coeff.	1.26	−0.07	1.73	0.39	−0.24	0.15	0.45	1.18	−0.06	1.20	0.58	0.44	0.42	−0.06	0.06
	t-Stat	1.69	−1.15	**6.58**	1.88	−1.18	0.79		1.74	−0.88	**6.60**	**2.79**		0.58	−0.84	
S1BM2	Coeff.	1.42	−0.06	2.13	0.78	−0.33	0.06	0.51	1.50	−0.03	1.46	0.99	0.51	0.36	−0.05	0.04
	t-Stat	1.76	−0.85	**7.50**	**3.48**	−1.50	0.28		**2.05**	−0.46	**7.46**	**4.43**		0.45	−0.61	
S1BM3	Coeff.	1.46	−0.05	1.45	0.99	−0.30	0.15	0.47	1.51	−0.04	1.05	1.15	0.48	0.37	−0.07	0.07
	t-Stat	1.94	−0.83	**5.47**	**4.72**	−1.50	0.77		**2.23**	−0.58	**5.81**	**5.54**		0.50	−0.94	
S1BM4	Coeff.	1.76	−0.04	1.55	0.86	−0.31	0.20	0.45	1.75	−0.03	1.13	1.04	0.46	0.68	−0.05	0.05
	t-Stat	**2.23**	−0.61	**5.57**	**3.91**	−1.46	0.97		**2.47**	−0.37	**5.95**	**4.77**		0.88	−0.66	
S2BM1	Coeff.	0.37	−0.07	1.51	0.19	−0.33	0.07	0.41	0.55	−0.05	1.12	0.35	0.43	−0.02	−0.05	0.05
	t-Stat	0.52	−1.20	**6.00**	0.97	−1.74	0.37		0.86	−0.89	**6.55**	1.80		−0.02	−0.73	
S2BM2	Coeff.	1.40	−0.07	1.54	0.48	−0.19	−0.01	0.44	1.51	−0.05	1.18	0.65	0.48	0.71	−0.06	0.06
	t-STAT	**2.00**	−1.14	**6.24**	**2.45**	−0.99	−0.04		**2.43**	−0.88	**7.13**	**3.41**		1.04	−0.88	
S2BM3	Coeff.	0.35	−0.04	1.57	0.73	−0.65	−0.25	0.48	1.02	0.01	0.51	0.75	0.28	0.33	−0.02	0.02
	t-Stat	0.49	−0.64	**6.19**	**3.65**	**−3.38**	−1.32		1.43	0.11	**2.68**	**3.41**		0.46	−0.23	
S2BM4	Coeff.	0.41	−0.03	1.98	1.00	−1.09	−0.33	0.58	1.59	0.04	0.65	1.00	0.33	0.67	0.01	0.00
	t-Stat	0.55	−0.48	**7.51**	**4.81**	**−5.44**	−1.71		**2.02**	0.50	**3.10**	**4.15**		0.83	0.07	
S3BM1	Coeff.	−0.14	0.00	1.43	0.84	−1.19	−0.23	0.54	1.21	0.06	0.54	0.82	0.30	0.44	0.03	0.03
	t-Stat	−0.19	0.00	**5.67**	**4.24**	**−6.18**	−1.26		1.64	0.86	**2.75**	**3.67**		0.60	0.47	
S3BM2	Coeff.	0.24	0.02	1.44	0.84	−1.07	−0.27	0.50	1.48	0.08	0.52	0.82	0.28	0.73	0.05	0.05
	t-Stat	0.32	0.29	**5.37**	**3.97**	**−5.24**	−1.37		1.94	1.06	**2.55**	**3.52**		0.95	0.68	
S3BM3	Coeff.	0.22	0.02	1.32	0.73	−0.51	−0.37	0.45	0.86	0.07	0.29	0.70	0.25	0.26	0.04	0.04
	t-Stat	0.32	0.34	**5.37**	**3.73**	**−2.71**	**−2.02**		1.26	1.01	1.61	**3.35**		0.38	0.60	
S3BM4	Coeff.	1.20	−0.01	1.48	0.88	−0.76	−0.16	0.55	1.95	0.04	0.59	0.91	0.37	1.11	0.01	0.01

Dep. variables		Five-factor size-B/M models							Three-factor size-B/M models					CAPM		
		α	Rm-Rf	SMB	HML	RMW	CMA	R^2	α	Rm-Rf	SMB	HML	R^2	α	Rm-Rf	R^2
	t-Stat	1.93	−0.10	**6.76**	**5.11**	**−4.57**	−0.98		**3.12**	0.68	**3.52**	**4.76**		1.72	0.18	
S4BM1	Coeff.	−0.46	0.05	1.14	0.57	−0.74	−0.65	0.45	0.75	0.11	0.03	0.45	0.17	0.40	0.09	0.09
	t-Stat	−0.64	0.78	**4.46**	**2.79**	**−3.80**	**−3.46**		1.03	1.57	0.15	**2.03**		0.57	1.30	
S4BM2	Coeff.	−0.39	0.08	1.40	0.91	−0.99	−1.00	0.56	1.46	0.16	0.15	0.76	0.24	0.85	0.13	0.11
	t-Stat	−0.51	1.18	**5.20**	**4.28**	**−4.82**	**−5.02**		1.80	**2.05**	0.71	**3.07**		1.06	1.64	
S4BM3	Coeff.	−0.51	0.10	1.06	0.73	−0.66	−1.10	0.53	1.19	0.17	0.18	0.59	0.23	0.70	0.14	0.14
	t-Stat	−0.70	1.63	**4.18**	**3.63**	**−3.38**	**−5.86**		1.59	**2.36**	0.91	**2.58**		0.96	**2.04**	
S4BM4	Coeff.	−0.15	0.03	1.08	0.79	−0.80	−1.01	0.51	1.58	0.10	0.13	0.65	0.20	1.07	0.07	0.07
	t-Stat	−0.20	0.46	**4.04**	**3.78**	**−3.93**	**−5.15**		**2.04**	1.33	0.61	**2.74**		1.40	0.97	

At the end of May each year, stocks are distributed into four size groups using sample quartile breakpoints. Stocks are independently allocated to four B/M groups, using sample quartile breakpoints. The RHS variables are RM-Rf for the CAPM; RM-Rf, SMB and HML for the 3F-FF model; and RM-Rf, SMB, HML, RMW and CMA for the 5F-FF model. The intersections of the two sorts produce 16 size-B/M portfolios. The LHS variables in each set of 16 regressions are the monthly excess returns on the 16 size-B/M portfolios. The factors are constructed using independent 2 × 3 sorts on size and each of the B/M, OP and Inv portfolios. Shaded t-statistics indicate the significance of coefficients at the 5% level of significance. (For the definitions of dependent variables, see **Table 1**).

Table 6. CAPM, 3F-FF and 5F-FF regressions for 16 value-weighted size-B/M portfolios (June 2000–May 2017, 204 months).

Dep. variables		Five-factor size-OP models							Three-factor size-OP models					CAPM		
		α	Rm-Rf	SMB	HML	RMW	CMA	R^2	α	Rm-Rf	SMB	HML	R^2	α	Rm-Rf	R^2
S1OP1	Coeff.	2.85	−0.06	1.83	0.79	0.03	0.09	0.50	2.51	−0.04	1.26	1.00	0.50	1.43	−0.06	0.06
	t-Stat	**3.83**	−0.89	**6.99**	**3.82**	0.13	0.49		**3.72**	−0.69	**6.98**	**4.84**		1.91	−0.89	
S1OP2	Coeff.	1.81	−0.11	1.86	1.04	−0.41	0.27	0.53	1.80	−0.09	1.30	1.24	0.53	0.52	−0.12	0.11
	t-Stat	**2.36**	−1.64	**6.86**	**4.85**	−1.98	1.34		**2.58**	−1.33	**6.98**	**5.81**		0.66	−1.55	
S1OP3	Coeff.	1.81	−0.04	1.21	0.70	−0.39	0.33	0.40	1.76	−0.03	0.81	0.84	0.36	0.91	−0.05	0.05
	t-Stat	**2.36**	−0.66	**4.47**	**3.28**	−1.87	1.64		**2.49**	−0.45	**4.28**	**3.89**		1.25	−0.73	
S1OP4	Coeff.	0.38	−0.03	1.69	0.74	−0.40	0.09	0.47	0.55	−0.01	1.13	0.89	0.45	−0.42	−0.03	0.03
	t-Stat	0.51	−0.53	**6.46**	**3.56**	−1.99	0.45		0.81	−0.14	**6.19**	**4.29**		−0.57	−0.38	
S2OP1	Coeff.	1.13	−0.08	1.42	0.55	−0.09	0.00	0.42	1.12	−0.06	1.08	0.71	0.46	0.30	−0.07	0.08
	t-Stat	1.62	−1.25	**5.80**	**2.82**	−0.49	0.00		1.81	−1.05	**6.53**	**3.74**		0.45	−1.12	
S2OP2	Coeff.	1.33	−0.11	1.42	0.88	−0.20	0.00	0.48	1.44	−0.09	1.07	1.03	0.51	0.38	−0.11	0.12
	t-Stat	1.93	−1.79	**5.88**	**4.60**	−1.07	−0.01		**2.35**	−1.54	**6.54**	**5.51**		0.56	−1.74	
S2OP3	Coeff.	1.09	−0.03	1.59	0.80	−1.09	0.01	0.54	1.96	0.02	0.45	0.80	0.27	1.24	0.00	0.00
	t-Stat	1.52	−0.49	**6.29**	**3.99**	**−5.66**	0.03		**2.65**	0.35	**2.28**	**3.55**		1.67	−0.03	
S2OP4	Coeff.	0.08	−0.02	1.76	0.73	−1.24	−0.23	0.56	1.38	0.04	0.64	0.73	0.28	0.67	0.02	0.02
	t-Stat	0.10	−0.36	**6.76**	**3.57**	**−6.21**	−1.18		1.79	0.58	**3.10**	**3.09**		0.86	0.30	
S3OP1	Coeff.	0.53	−0.03	1.06	0.84	−0.93	−0.43	0.46	1.88	0.02	0.42	0.79	0.27	1.18	−0.01	0.01
	t-Stat	0.71	−0.53	**4.00**	**4.00**	**−4.60**	**−2.17**		**2.55**	0.25	**2.12**	**3.51**		1.59	−0.13	
S3OP2	Coeff.	−0.74	−0.01	1.44	0.93	−0.94	−0.40	0.53	0.43	0.05	0.36	0.89	0.29	−0.33	0.02	0.02
	t-Stat	−1.03	−0.18	**5.74**	**4.70**	**−4.89**	**−2.16**		0.59	0.70	1.85	**3.98**		−0.45	0.23	
S3OP3	Coeff.	0.68	0.03	1.32	0.62	−0.80	0.00	0.48	1.30	0.08	0.46	0.64	0.28	0.70	0.06	0.06
	t-Stat	1.04	0.60	**5.76**	**3.40**	**−4.56**	0.01		**2.01**	1.23	**2.68**	**3.23**		1.08	0.89	
S3OP4	Coeff.	0.07	0.00	1.39	0.82	−1.09	−0.16	0.56	1.26	0.06	0.63	0.83	0.35	0.48	0.03	0.04

Dep. variables		Five-factor size-OP models							Three-factor size-OP models					CAPM		
		α	Rm-Rf	SMB	HML	RMW	CMA	R^2	α	Rm-Rf	SMB	HML	R^2	α	Rm-Rf	R^2
	t-Stat	0.11	0.07	**6.22**	**4.67**	**−6.39**	−0.99		1.94	0.93	**3.59**	**4.17**		0.71	0.50	
S4OP1	Coeff.	−0.07	0.06	1.11	0.68	−0.80	−1.01	0.52	1.60	0.13	−0.04	0.51	0.19	1.23	0.10	0.10
	t-Stat	−0.09	0.88	**4.32**	**3.33**	**−4.09**	**−5.34**		**2.12**	1.76	−0.19	**2.19**		1.67	1.44	
S4OP2	Coeff.	−0.29	0.14	1.30	0.69	−0.72	−1.16	0.56	1.42	0.22	0.02	0.52	0.23	1.03	0.20	0.18
	t-Stat	−0.38	**2.21**	**4.94**	**3.33**	**−3.63**	**−6.02**		1.81	**2.92**	0.10	**2.15**		1.34	**2.63**	
S4OP3	Coeff.	0.40	0.07	0.88	0.54	−0.68	−0.83	0.43	1.85	0.12	0.11	0.42	0.17	1.51	0.11	0.11
	t-Stat	0.52	1.03	**3.29**	**2.57**	**−3.32**	**−4.21**		**2.47**	1.74	0.53	1.83		**2.07**	1.52	
S4OP4	Coeff.	−1.35	0.01	1.03	0.58	−0.86	−0.88	0.48	0.33	0.08	0.11	0.45	0.15	−0.03	0.06	0.06
	t-Stat	−1.83	0.15	**3.98**	**2.86**	**−4.38**	**−4.61**		0.45	1.06	0.56	1.94		−0.04	0.81	

At the end of May each year, stocks are distributed into four size groups using sample quartile breakpoints. Stocks are independently allocated to four OP groups, using sample quartile breakpoints. The RHS variables are RM-Rf for the CAPM; RM-Rf, SMB and HML for the 3F-FF model; and RM-Rf, SMB, HML, RMW and CMA for the 5F-FF model. The intersections of the two sorts produce 16 size-OP portfolios. The LHS variables in each set of 16 regressions are the monthly excess returns on the 16 size-OP portfolios. The factors are constructed using independent 2 × 3 sorts on size and each of B/M, OP and Inv portfolios. Shaded t-statistics indicate the significance of coefficients at the 5% level of significance (for the definitions of dependent variables, see **Table 1**).

Table 7. CAPM, 3F-FF and 5F-FF regressions for 16 value-weighted size-OP portfolios (June 2000–May 2017, 204 months).

Dep. variables		Five-factor size-Inv models							Three-factor size-Inv models					CAPM		
		α	Rm-Rf	SMB	HML	RMW	CMA	R^2	α	Rm-Rf	SMB	HML	R^2	α	Rm-Rf	R^2
S1INV1	Coeff.	1.28	−0.06	1.79	0.62	−0.43	0.36	0.47	1.20	−0.04	1.27	0.83	0.46	0.24	−0.05	0.05
	t-Stat	1.64	−0.83	**6.50**	**2.84**	**−2.07**	1.77		1.69	−0.55	**6.67**	**3.80**		0.31	−0.66	
S1INV2	Coeff.	1.31	−0.05	1.76	0.76	−0.53	0.22	0.49	1.46	−0.02	1.13	0.93	0.45	0.46	−0.04	0.04
	t-Stat	1.75	−0.73	**6.65**	**3.67**	**−2.63**	1.14		**2.10**	−0.31	**6.06**	**4.37**		0.61	−0.55	
S1INV3	Coeff.	1.70	−0.08	1.45	0.78	−0.08	0.18	0.46	1.46	−0.07	1.07	0.97	0.48	0.45	−0.09	0.10
	t-Stat	**2.38**	−1.33	**5.78**	**3.96**	−0.43	0.95		**2.29**	−1.20	**6.27**	**4.94**		0.65	−1.41	
S1INV4	Coeff.	1.42	−0.10	1.47	0.89	−0.19	−0.10	0.45	1.59	−0.08	0.99	1.02	0.44	0.56	−0.10	0.10
	t-Stat	1.88	−1.49	**5.49**	**4.20**	−0.92	−0.49		**2.30**	−1.18	**5.36**	**4.82**		0.76	−1.44	
S2INV1	Coeff.	1.20	−0.08	1.39	0.67	−0.47	0.09	0.46	1.53	−0.05	1.02	0.81	0.46	0.65	−0.07	0.08
	t-Stat	1.80	−1.31	**5.91**	**3.63**	**−2.63**	0.49		**2.54**	−0.92	**6.32**	**4.39**		1.00	−1.09	
S2INV2	Coeff.	1.62	−0.06	1.56	0.57	−0.47	0.21	0.47	1.79	−0.04	1.13	0.73	0.47	0.93	−0.05	0.05
	t-Stat	**2.36**	−1.01	**6.46**	**2.97**	**−2.58**	1.19		**2.87**	−0.65	**6.77**	**3.85**		1.38	−0.75	
S2INV3	Coeff.	0.01	−0.02	1.64	0.75	−0.88	−0.42	0.50	1.17	0.04	0.67	0.75	0.30	0.42	0.02	0.02
	t-Stat	0.01	−0.25	**6.12**	**3.56**	**−4.29**	**−2.11**		1.53	0.57	**3.29**	**3.24**		0.55	0.28	
S2INV4	Coeff.	−0.19	−0.05	1.56	0.80	−1.02	−0.47	0.53	1.22	0.01	0.63	0.78	0.30	0.46	−0.01	0.01
	t-Stat	−0.26	−0.78	**6.04**	**3.95**	**−5.19**	**−2.49**		1.63	0.19	**3.18**	**3.43**		0.61	−0.13	
S3INV1	Coeff.	0.37	−0.02	1.42	0.78	−1.14	−0.04	0.55	1.40	0.04	0.44	0.77	0.28	0.71	0.01	0.01
	t-Stat	0.55	−0.29	**6.02**	**4.16**	**−6.34**	−0.21		**2.02**	0.57	**2.36**	**3.61**		1.02	0.18	
S3INV2	Coeff.	0.14	−0.01	1.26	0.77	−1.05	−0.17	0.48	1.22	0.04	0.31	0.74	0.24	0.59	0.02	0.02
	t-Stat	0.19	−0.16	**4.85**	**3.78**	**−5.29**	−0.88		1.65	0.63	1.55	**3.27**		0.80	0.24	
S3INV3	Coeff.	0.19	0.01	1.31	0.85	−0.94	−0.46	0.56	1.52	0.07	0.49	0.82	0.32	0.78	0.04	0.05
	t-Stat	0.30	0.25	**5.97**	**4.90**	**−5.60**	**−2.85**		**2.36**	1.15	**2.83**	**4.12**		1.19	0.69	
S3INV4	Coeff.	0.67	−0.02	1.50	0.66	−0.77	−0.45	0.51	1.76	0.03	0.58	0.64	0.28	1.13	0.02	0.02

Dep. variables		Five-factor size-Inv models							Three-factor size-Inv models					CAPM		
		α	Rm-Rf	SMB	HML	RMW	CMA	R^2	α	Rm-Rf	SMB	HML	R^2	α	Rm-Rf	R^2
	t-Stat	1.00	−0.35	**6.35**	**3.50**	**−4.29**	**−2.59**		**2.60**	0.53	**3.18**	**3.10**		1.65	0.25	
S4INV1	Coeff.	−0.31	0.08	1.22	0.66	−0.72	−0.87	0.49	1.12	0.15	0.12	0.53	0.20	0.69	0.13	0.12
	t-Stat	−0.41	1.27	**4.59**	**3.14**	**−3.55**	**−4.42**		1.46	**2.03**	0.56	**2.28**		0.92	1.74	
S4INV2	Coeff.	−0.41	0.09	1.12	0.64	−0.73	−0.89	0.49	1.07	0.16	0.06	0.50	0.20	0.68	0.14	0.13
	t-Stat	−0.55	1.44	**4.27**	**3.09**	**−3.65**	**−4.60**		1.42	**2.20**	0.29	**2.18**		0.92	1.91	
S4INV3	Coeff.	−0.49	0.02	1.00	0.67	−0.78	−1.07	0.54	1.32	0.09	0.12	0.52	0.18	0.90	0.07	0.07
	t-Stat	−0.72	0.35	**4.16**	**3.54**	**−4.26**	**−6.08**		1.84	1.29	0.63	**2.35**		1.29	0.99	
S4INV4	Coeff.	−0.38	0.11	0.85	0.59	−0.69	−0.97	0.48	1.20	0.17	−0.03	0.44	0.20	0.88	0.15	0.15
	t-Stat	−0.52	1.65	**3.26**	**2.89**	**−3.45**	**−5.02**		1.61	**2.37**	−0.14	1.92		1.22	**2.10**	

At the end of May each year, stocks are distributed into four size groups using sample quartile breakpoints. Stocks are independently allocated to four Inv groups, using sample quartile breakpoints. The RHS variables are RM-Rf for the CAPM; RM-Rf, SMB and HML for the 3F-FF model; and RM-Rf, SMB, HML, RMW and CMA for the 5F-FF model. The intersections of the two sorts produce 16 size-Inv portfolios. The LHS variables in each set of 16 regressions are the monthly excess returns on the 16 size-Inv portfolios. The factors are constructed using independent 2 × 3 sorts on size and each of the B/M, OP and Inv portfolios. Shaded t-statistics indicate the significance of coefficients at the 5% level of significance (for the definitions of dependent variables, see **Table 1**).

Table 8. CAPM, 3F-FF and 5F-FF regressions for 16 value-weighted size-Inv portfolios (June 2000–May 2017, 204 months).

Looking explicitly at the number of significant alpha values in **Tables 6–8** (at the 5% level of confidence), both the CAPM and the 3F-FF model perform poorly, while 5F-FF model's performance although is not the best but much better. The highest number of significant alpha values belongs to 3F-FF model. This shows that 3F-FF model leaves a high proportion of unexplained part in the behaviour of LHS variables. From the regression tables, it seems that CAPM model has no any significant values for alphas; interestingly enough, none of the coefficients of RM-Rf is significant at the 5% level of confidence, and R^2 terms are too low in CAPMs. In addition to this observation, in none of the models, RM-Rf has no statistically significant coefficient except in a few models (see rows 13, 14 and 15 in **Tables 6–8**).

On the other hand, inspection of alphas in 5F-FF models for size-B/M, size-OP and size-Inv portfolios reveals that very few of alpha values are significant at the 5% level confidence and I think the best performing model (but imperfect) for the Turkish data is the 5F-FF Fama-French model.

There is an interesting pattern in the results of the regression tables (**Tables 6–8**). As the size of the companies in portfolios increases, more factors become statistically significant, and the explanatory power of the 5F-FF model rises. This makes me to think that monthly excess returns of portfolios, covering high-market-cap companies, are more sensitive to SMB, HML, RMA and CMA factors.

Before I present the regression details, readers should be aware that in an OLS regression, R-squared values will always increase with the inclusion of more factors. Another point is that R^2 increases and become much stronger for almost any explanatory power metric when the regressions' explanatory factors are created from return differences in the data itself. In other words, correlation between explanatory variables, which are created from return differences, and dependent variables has to be highly correlated. Hence, R^2s in the equations become stronger and true.

Sundqvist in [22] states that:

> *'The method to construct the factor will hence automatically bring the augmented model's explanatory power in small portfolio regressions closer to the R-squared values found in big portfolio regressions, boosting the average explanatory power more than it would for regressions of randomly picked portfolio sets. This same phenomenon is apparent in all other risk factors, which are included as sorting variables and simultaneously used as explanatory variables created from return differences in the sample data'.*

When the t-values in **Table 6** are analysed, CAPM's results (column labelled with CAPM) are far away from being reliable and informative. None of the t-statistic of RM-Rf (except for S4BM3) is significant at the 5% level of confidence. This might have been due to the fact that BIST-100 Index, which approximates the monthly excess return of the market, is heavily financial stock weighted. However, using different market indices in all models did not improve the results (more information on this issue is given in the discussion of the results in **Table 7**).

In this study, I include only nonfinancial sector stocks registered with the Istanbul stock exchange since the profitability and investment variables' definition is not comparable to the financial stocks. Therefore, I think the coefficient of RM-Rf variable, namely, β_i does not reflect the market risk properly, and CAPM performs poorly.

The 3F-FF regressions find larger *intercept t-values* on most portfolios compared to the 5F-FF regressions, of which three are more than five standard errors from zero. I can find no exceptional characteristics that might shed light into the reasons behind the significant alpha value.

The 5F-FF regressions show high SMB slopes for the portfolio when compared to 3F-FF regressions' slopes. All of the coefficients of SMB variable are statistically significant at the 5% level of confidence in 5F-FF model, while the same metrics have 11 significant coefficients in 3F-FF models. It is somewhat unusual that none of the coefficients of RM-Rf in 5F-FF model regressions are significant at the 5% level of significance. However, as I already discussed above, this may be due to the fact that BIST-100 Index is heavily financially sector stock weighted.

From **Table 6** it is easily seen that (last four rows in the table) excess monthly returns of the biggest-sized company portfolios are best explained by the 5F-FF model. However, as can be seen from the t-statistics, when the company size gets smaller (portfolios starting with the letter S1 and S2), RMW and CMA variables have no effect on excess monthly returns of small-sized portfolios, while SMB and HML variables have significant t-statistics. Assuming that the 5F-FF model is the true definition of the monthly excess returns of portfolios sorted by size and B/M, this result may imply that, when constructing portfolios, the market does not take into account the profitability or investing factors for relatively small-sized companies.

Fama and French [19] note however that one should not expect univariate characteristics and multivariate regression slopes connected to the characteristic to line up. The slopes estimate marginal effects holding constantly all other explanatory variables, and the characteristics are measured with lags relative to returns when pricing should be forward-looking.

The dependent variables are the monthly excess returns of the portfolios sorted by size and profitability (for the definitions of the variables, see **Table 1**). The results in **Table 7** are not much different from the ones that are in **Table 6**. The best performing model is the 5F-FF model. The CAPM has no power to explain the cross-sectional variance of expected returns for the size-B/M, size-OP and size-Inv portfolios I examine. Peculiarly enough, as in the case of **Table 6**, none of the alphas in CAPM are significant at the 5% level of significance. This result could have been due to market return data (RM, represented by BIST-100 Index), which is composed of mainly financial sector companies' price data. To save space not presented in this study, I inform the reader that all of the models (CAPM, three-factor Fama-French model and five-factor Fama-French model) using BIST-TUM Index, which covers all stocks registered with the Turkish stock market, instead of BIST-100 Index, the power of the models in explaining the sorted portfolio monthly excess returns, did not improve. This shows that, at least in the Turkish case, market risk is not a preliminary and strong factor in determining monthly excess returns of portfolios.

When one concentrates on alpha coefficients of the 5F-FF model, it is seen that only 3 of the 16 alphas are statistically significant. But in the case of the 3F-FF model, 9 of the 16 alpha coefficients are significant at the 5% level, showing that three-factor model leaves a high percentage of unexplained part of cross-sectional variance of expected returns.

One of the main messages of the results of the 5F-FF model is that as the size of the companies under investigation increases, the explanatory power of the model rises. It seems from the results of both **Tables 6** and **7** that the best explanatory factor for the monthly excess returns of portfolios is the size factor.

As the size of the companies in portfolios that have been sorted by size and profitability gets smaller, RMW and CMA become ineffective in determining the monthly excess returns of these portfolios (see the coefficients of RMW and CMA in the first six rows of **Table 7**). However, bigger size portfolios have significant RMW and CMA coefficients.

Table 8 gives the results of CAPM, 3F-FF model and 5F-FF model for portfolios that are sorted by size and investment. The CAPM has no power in explaining the returns of portfolios, while the coefficients of the factors in 3F-FF model seem powerful, 8 of the 16 alpha values are significant at the 5% level. This result indicates that the CAPM and 3F-FF model are not the true definition of a model to explain the variations in monthly excess returns of portfolios. However, as in the results of the previous tables (**Tables 6** and **7**), the 5F-FF model in general has statistically significant coefficients for the Fama-French factors, namely, SMB, HML, RMW and CMA. Also, only 2 of the 16 coefficients of intercepts (alphas) are significant at the 5% level of significance.

Variations of the monthly returns of portfolios constructed by big-sized companies are best explained by the 5F-FF model. However, CMA factor turns out to be insignificant when estimating the model for portfolios with relatively small-sized companies.

9. Conclusion

This study adds to the asset pricing literature using the Turkish data. One of the main findings is that CAPM and 3F-FF model cannot explain cross-sectional variations in portfolio returns properly. The best suited model (but not perfect) for the Turkish case is 5F-FF model.

As seen elsewhere [17, 19–23], as the number of explanatory variables increases in the regression portfolios, explanatory power of the equation increases, and the R^2 rises. In the Turkish case, although 3F-FF model has high R^2 compared to the CAPM, more than half of the intercepts of the 3F-FF model are significant at the 5% level, and this shows that SMB and HML factors alone do not explain the cross-sectional variations of portfolio returns.

Besides testing all intercepts individually, we also tested whether all the pricing errors were jointly equal to zero. Gibbons et al. [24] suggested GRS test statistic to test whether all pricing errors are zero. A GRS test on the joint set of all tested portfolios clearly rejects all tested models as complete descriptions of average returns. The CAPM model elicits the lowest average absolute alpha values of the three tested models throughout all tests but shows a statistically insignificant fGRS value compared to other models. The 5F-FF model shows the strongest performance out of the three models for the sample.

http://dx.doi.org/10.5772/intechopen.70867

When I compare the R^2s of all my models (the highest 56%) to the earlier studies done for other countries [15, 16, 19–22] (the R^2s change between 70 and 90%), in general, it is the case that R^2s found in my study are much lower than other R^2s found in other studies. This might be due to the fact that RMW and CMA factors add little in explaining the cross-sectional variations of portfolio returns in Turkey. It is clear that, in the Turkish case, both SMB and HML factors have significant effect on monthly excess returns of portfolios, but further research may be carried on by employing new factors other than RMW and CMA.

Readers should be aware that correlation between explanatory variables, which are created from return differences (as in the case of definition of Fama-French factors), and dependent variables has to be highly correlated. Hence, R^2s in the equations become stronger and true.

Consequently, our empirical results are reasonably consistent with [19–22] findings, and the 5F-FF model was found viable and superior to CAPM and 3F-FF model for the Turkish stock market.

Author details

Yaşar Erdinç

Address all correspondence to: yerdinc65@gmail.com

Bosphorus University, Istanbul, Turkey

References

[1] Markowitz H. Portfolio selection. The Journal of Finance. 1952;**7**(1):77-99

[2] Sharpe WF. Capital asset prices: A theory of market equilibrium under conditions of risk. The Journal of Finance. 1964;**19**(3):425-442

[3] Ross SA. The arbitrage theory of capital asset pricing. Journal of Economic Theory. 1976;**13**(3):341-360

[4] Lintner J. The valuation of risk assets and the selection of risky investments in stock portfolios and capital budgets. Review of Economics and Statistics. 1965;**47**(1):13-37

[5] Mossin J. Equilibrium in a capital asset market. Econometrica. 1966;**34**:68-783

[6] Black F, Jensen MC, Scholes M. The capital asset pricing model: Some empirical tests. In: Black F, Jensen MC, Scholes M, editors. Studies in Theory of Capital Markets. 1st ed. New York, NY: Praeger; 1972. p. 79-121

[7] Basu S. Investment performance of common stocks in relation to their price-earnings ratios: A test of the efficient market hypothesis. The Journal of Finance. 1977;**32**(3):663-682

[8] Bhandari LC. Debt/equity ratio and expected common stock returns: Empirical evidence. The Journal of Finance. 1988;**43**(2):507-528

[9] Jegadeesh N. Evidence of predictable behavior of security returns. The Journal of Finance. 1990;**45**(3):881-898

[10] DeBont WFM, Thaler R. Does the stock market overreact? The Journal of Finance. 1985; **40**(3):793-805

[11] Singleton KJ, Hansen LP. Generalized instrumental variables estimation of nonlinear rational expectations models. Econometrica. 1982;**50**:1269-1286

[12] Singleton KJ, Hansen LP. Stochastic consumption, risk aversion, and the temporal behavior of asset returns. Journal of Political Economy. 1983;**91**:249-265

[13] Parker JA, Julliard C. Consumption risk and the cross-section of expected returns. Journal of Political Economy. 2005;**113**:185-222. DOI: 10.1086/426042

[14] Campbell JY, Cochrane JH. Explaining the poor performance of consumption-based asset pricing models. The Journal of Finance. 2000;**55**:2863-2878. DOI: 10.1111/0022-1082.00310

[15] Fama EF, French KR. The cross-section of expected stock returns. The Journal of Finance. 1992;**47**(2):427-465

[16] Fama EF, French KR. Common risk factors in the returns on stocks and bonds. Journal of Financial Economics. 1993;**33**:3-56

[17] Novy-Marx R. The other side of value: The gross profitability premium. Journal of Financial Economics. 2013;**108**(1):1-28

[18] Aharoni G, Grundy B, Zeng Q. Stock returns and the Miller Modigliani valuation formula: Revisiting the Fama French analysis. Journal of Financial Economics. 2013;**110**(2): 347-357

[19] Fama EF, French KR. A 5F-FF asset pricing model. Journal of Financial Economics. 2015;**116**(1):1-22. DOI: 10.1016/j.jfineco.2014.10.010

[20] Fama EF, French KR. Choosing Factors. Working paper; 2016

[21] Fama EF, French KR. International tests of a 5F-FF asset pricing model. Journal of Financial Economics. 2016;**123**(3):441-463. DOI: 10.1111/j.1540-6261.2008.01368

[22] Sundqvist T. Tests of a Fama-French 5F-FF asset pricing model in the Nordic stock markets [thesis]. Helsinki: Hanken School of Economics; 2017. p. 82 Available from: https://helda.helsinki.fi/dhanken/handle/123456789/167972

[23] Lakonishok J, Schleifer A, Vishny RW. Contrarian investment, extrapolation and risk. The Journal of Finance. 1994;**49**:1541-1578

[24] Gibbons MR, Ross SA, Shanken J. A test of the efficiency of a given portfolio. Econometrica. 1989;**57**:1121-1152

Chapter 5

Comparison of Selected Market Indicators During the Dot-Com Bubble

Wladimir Schubert, Beáta Gavurová,
Viliam Kováč and Martin Užík

Additional information is available at the end of the chapter

http://dx.doi.org/10.5772/intechopen.71381

Abstract

Since the outbreak of the recent financial crisis in 2007, central banks around the world have lowered interest rates while stock markets soared. On the example of North America, Europe, and Asia and in particular the United States, Germany, and China, the situation as of December 2015 is compared on the basis of economic theory and selected key performance indicators to the United States dot-com bubble in the nineties years of the twentieth century. Literature review offers a complex general view on the issue of market bubbles with a historical review of the situation in 2007 and 2008. The only indication of a bubble can be found in the China Securities Index 300, more specifically in the technology sector. The further aim of the paper is related to analyse and compare returns of the explored indices among the regions and the sectors. On a broader level, the study finds that even though there are similarities, the current rise in indices does not qualify for an asset price bubble. Conclusion sums all the observed findings on both the levels – regional and national. Also, it offers suggestions for discussion about the situation on the markets after the financial crisis.

Keywords: market, market bubble, dot-com bubble, financial crisis, market index

1. Introduction and relevance of the topic

The last global financial crisis was set-up by risky mortgage backed security loans and triggered by the default of the Lehman Brothers Holdings in September 2008. This marked the beginning of many policy measures and changes. While central banks around the world began to decrease interest rates in order to boost the economy, stock markets soared. At the same time, the internet is becoming more and more a medium for global interconnection due to technological advancements across all industries. Not only more people connect to the internet every day, also devices actively communicate with one another, coined under the term "the internet of things". Moreover, recent initial public offerings of well-known internet companies such as Groupon, LinkedIn, Facebook, Alibaba Group Holding Limited and funding support programs in the United States, the European Union and China drive the interest of investors for lucrative opportunities.

When looking at the development of certain equity indices in the United States, Germany and China, the rates show record or close to record peaks as seen on **Figure 1**. For the Nasdaq Composite Index such rates were last seen during the dot-com bubble while the Deutscher Aktien Index 30 is almost twice as high as during the dot-com bubble and before the recent financial crisis of 2008. For the China Securities Index 300, the sources from the Bloomberg database even state price-to-earnings ratios as high as 220 times reported profits.

Bringing these circumstances into a global context, an artificial economic boost was created after the crisis that made equity indices soar—just like before the dot-com bubble. Hence, the question arises how the situation as of December 2015 is different if it is at all. Are there signs of an asset price bubble as some research argues [1, 2]?

The dot-com bubble is one of the most disputed bubbles that occurred in the last decades. Each bubble can be modelled according to some rules. Welfare analysis with empirical prediction is subject to examine [3]. Also, the pure statistical tests are suitable to describe bubble [4]. But alternative assessment can be provided by another angle of view on bubbles [5]. Moreover, market bubbles are related to market volatility in general [6].

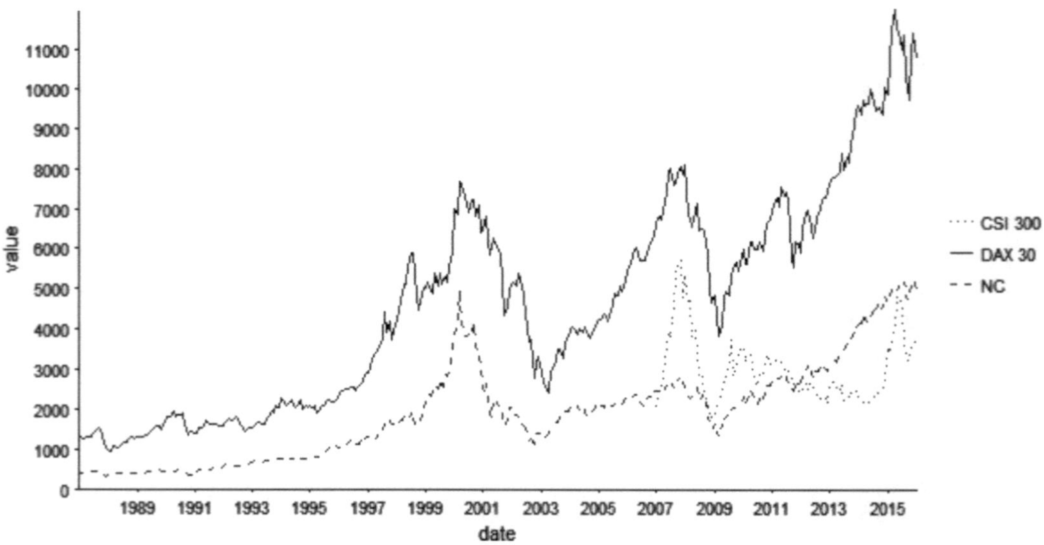

Figure 1. Increase of indices' values across regions. Source: Own elaboration by the authors.

2. Literature review

Since the current situation of peaking indices is too new to expect extensive research on this topic, there are currently only a few similar articles available to the knowledge of the author [7, 8]. Their research, however, is either limited to a single stock, market or pursues another approach. Furthermore, the eventual assessment of a bubble can only happen in retrospect while today's perspective can only try to catch the market sentiment and interpret some key economic indicators.

2.1. Asset price bubble

By the definition of the majority of literature, an asset price bubble is characterised by a substantial deviation from the fundamental value of the asset [9]. On the other hand, according to the efficient market hypothesis, there are three levels of efficiency: weak, semi-strong, strong—which represent the incorporation of information into the price of securities [10]. Hence, under certain assumptions such as that investors perceive information uniformly, securities should trade at their fair value and deviating from the fundamental value should not be possible with respect to the level of efficiency. Despite the critique and controversy of the efficient market hypothesis in recent decades it was confirmed again in 2009 [11]. Nevertheless, severe price deviations did occur and cannot be explained by the efficient market hypothesis. Hence these deviations represent a key flaw in this hypothesis on which much of economy theory relies. In theory, rational investors are expected to base their valuations on fundamentals such as the intrinsic value of an asset which can be approximated by the discounted sum of future cash flows [12]. Since nobody can predict the future, however, projections of future cash flows are likely to be highly subjective. To tackle this issue, the assessment of a bubble can be mainly approached from two dimensions: magnitude and time.

While it is recognised that measuring the fundamental value at the very moment of the occurrence is hardly possible [13]. Therefore, it is suggested that a bubble should be measured by deviations of expected and realised returns over a defined period of time—even decades [14]. Obviously, this can only happen in retrospect since returns cannot be predicted with certainty, especially during times of turmoil in the markets [15].

Beyond the pure stock price, another crucial factor according to equity asset valuation is often taken into account: the price-to-earnings ratio or earnings in general. Commonly speaking, the higher the price-to-earnings ratio increases without substantial news to support a higher valuation, the harder it becomes to justify prices if there is little evidence for future returns other than the pure belief—for instance speculation.

Differentiating a plausible market development and an irrational bubble remains the subject of collective research on expectations and actual future cash flows. In retrospect, only the burst of a bubble, indicated by a substantial depreciation of prices, gives reason to assume that there was one in the first place. That is because a permanent change would require a fundamental reason and not constitute a bubble due to the lack of deviation. Also, there can be an overlap with different types of business cycles. This issue relates to the second dimension by which a bubble has to be assessed – time.

For example, there is an argument that the actual dot-com bubble was quite short and only lasted from 1998 to 2000 [16]. Even though, this might be the time of the actual substantial price deviation, it is important to take into account the circumstance which led to it in the first place. Therefore, a five-stage approach that was described and later refined is favoured in this paper [17]. This is supported by another research, which used a three-stage to five-stage approach, too [18].

Since a single value or theory is unlikely to explain the workings of a complex event of an asset price bubble which is the interplay of irrational humans and algorithm driven economics, it is more likely the combination of these factors.

2.2. Explanations for the occurrence of asset price bubbles

Even though there currently is no guaranteed empirical method to detect an asset price bubble [19], especially in real time, there are still again mainly two methods to approach this issue [20]. The first one is based on rational expectations of the efficient market hypothesis, and the second one on behavioural finance.

Firstly, there are empirical and technical models that are based on the efficient market hypothesis [21, 22]. Even though, such models are able to provide sufficient explanatory power, they are for example limited to historic data [23], certain stocks or companies [24] or more generally, to certain assumptions which were true in the past. Most importantly they lack the major factor of irrational human behaviour that can be observed in certain situations at the stock market, especially during uncertainty due to politics or the introduction of an innovation. Under the category of rational expectations also fall the established economic theories that take into account monetary policies, investment and consumption cycles. For example, there is also an evidence for connecting the emergence of bubbles with the credit creation policies [25].

Secondly, there are qualitative metrics which take into account soft factors such as the current sentiment of the market and irrational human behaviour, including biases as coined under the term behavioural finance. Psychological factors, especially during turbulent times, gain importance while traditional measures lose in relevance [26]. Concepts like herding behaviour and greater-fool theory trump rational economic assumptions such as the efficient market hypothesis and investors willingly forego arbitrage opportunities. Also, soft factors such as human capital, strategic alliances, joint ventures and internet popularity gain in importance [27–29]. Since only forecasts about future cash flows can be made, expectations play an integral role to the development of the market. For example, there is a study showing that during the dot-com bubble financial analysts were more optimistic about internet stocks [30]. Especially in such circumstances fundamental values start to become irrelevant to investors [31]. Also, it must be taken into account that even though there might be an asset price bubble, it can be necessary due to circumstances to ride that bubble instead of acting rationally against the majority of market participants [32]. After all there is nothing so dangerous as the pursuit of a rational investment policy in an irrational world. The financial sector plays also a significant role here [33, 34]. A good example is technical analysis with the Federal Reserve System model which is extensively criticised by theorists for their flaws but used by practitioners nevertheless. The sheer beliefs and usage of such concepts substantially influence the market even without sound academic background [35]. Furthermore, restrictions like short selling, set by a higher body or lock-in periods for stock options, may skew and alter the economic normalisation processes [36]. Moreover, history shows that politicians are reluctant to take countermeasures before an imminent economic threat can be proven because acting on a false alarm would result in a loss in economic output which in consequence would have negative transitioning effects throughout society [37, 38].

So, taking into account the irrational human behaviour is an important factor. Therefore, a holistic combination of both theories efficient market hypothesis and behavioural finance is expected to yield a better result for the explanation and assessment of a bubble formation.

2.3. Other effects

There are argues that there may be many reasons to cause asset price bubbles [39]. There are several research papers which take also nonfinancial but rather information technology oriented factors into account that might influence investors' decisions when buying technology stocks. The reasoning behind such measures is the Anglo-Saxon approach which focuses on growing big and gaining market share at high costs in the beginning while becoming profitable later [40]. Such factors include, for example, page views or visitors and sales in contrast to traditional measures such as earnings before interest, taxes, depreciation and amortisation or net income [41, 42].

3. Data description and methodology

The data set, which is chosen to be analysed, is the appropriate source to examine the desired aims. Also, the selected methods help to reach the outlined result.

3.1. Data description

The source for the most part of the data is the Datastream maintained by Thomson Reuters Corporation. Also, calculations such as price-to-earnings ratio are done by the Datastream and therefore provide a universal basis across the different regions under consideration. Equity indices and ratio calculations for the Deutscher Aktien Index 30 and the China Securities Index 300 were partially extracted from the Bloomberg database since they could not be obtained from the Datastream. December 2015 has been chosen as an end mark of for the underlying data.

3.2. Methodology

The methodology mainly focuses on alternative approaches while still incorporating some impulses from classical economic theory and the efficient market hypothesis. This is in line with many other research papers which are also based on the macroeconomic environment, alternative measures and the expectations of private and institutional investors [43, 44].

Since markets are interconnected as for example confirmed by the study [45], a holistic perspective for comparison is employed. In this regard the industry under consideration must be specified. For this paper, it is the technology sector which is analysed and even though most of the researchers agree that the dot-com bubble occurred in that sector, others have also identified spillover effects into other sectors such as financial, general industrial and non-cyclical services as well [31].

To tackle the research question, first, a combination of macro-economic indicators was used to compare the dot-com bubble with the recent financial crisis. On the one hand, a global perspective is pursued, but on the other hand, data on an aggregate level was not always available. Therefore, the United States, Germany and China are chosen by their economic dominance and highest nominal gross domestic product as representatives in the named regions to base the local economic indicators on. This way a top-down complementary approach from broad regional equity indices to country specific indicators and indices was employed throughout the paper. The term regional in this regard refers to the regions of North America, Europe and Asia, while local refers to the United States, Germany and China.

Additionally, but due to the limited scope of the paper and the main focus being set on the overall economic situation, a rather simple but meaningful test was employed, the Welch-Satterthwaite t-test. This test in the context of this paper is focused on the comparison of means of returns of two samples. With respect to the regular t-test, the Welch-Satterthwaite t-test gives the advantage of yielding accurate results despite unequal variances of the samples. It is, however, important to strictly differentiate the time-period, index and sector under review.

So after an overall evaluation of the economic situation, a distinction is done by the comparison of means of returns between the Nasdaq Composite index and the Datastream technology index in the 1990s of the twentieth century for three phases of the bubble – pre-bubble, inflation and crash. For this purpose, assumptions about the timing of the phases had to be made. The pre-bubble period was chosen to start in December 1990, which marked the lowest point of the Nasdaq Composite index in the nineties years of the twentieth century. The bubble inflation period was set to start in November 1998 since this year is based on the academic research [16], while also marking a relative historic low of the index. The peak obviously occurred in March 2000 and marked the transition to the crash-phase. Here the lowest point before the eventual recovery was chosen – October 2002. For the recent years such a clear distinction was not possible and therefore a time-frame as a whole from April 2009 to December 2015 was chosen, marking a historic low and high, respectively.

Since the movement of the indices alone cannot support nor reject a bubble, a dedicated section takes into account key performance indicators based on which a fundamental value can be estimated.

Due to the limited scope of the paper, the influence of business cycles, exchange rates and non-financial factors such as page-views have been of minor coverage in this paper, and hence provide room for further analysis.

4. Dot-com bubble and financial crisis of 2007

This section builds on the concepts introduced in the literature review and gives specific interpretations on the example of the dot-com bubble and the recent financial crisis which started in 2007.

As already mentioned in introduction, the dot-com bubble can be divided into five stages that were initially described [25] and later refined [17]. First, they argue that there has to be a displacement in the market such as an external shock due to a crisis, a liquidity shortage and so on. Then, normally, the government steps in to calm the situation and the central bank provides liquidity to boost the economy so that credit is created and capital is easily available, for instance capital flood. What is then distinct to a bubble and goes beyond a regular upward movement of a cycle is the euphoria which might be triggered by some disruptive innovation [46]. This might be personal computers, the internet, the internet of things, digital currencies or any other sort of hype. After that, insiders or people close to this industry start to see its limits and begin to sell their stakes—this is when the financial distress occurs. If their sell reaches a critical mass, the bubble crashes and the initial euphoria turns into revulsion so that banks turn cautious to the credits they provide.

4.1. Displacement

In the nineties years of the twentieth century, the breakdown of the Soviet Union and the Japanese Crisis can be identified as two of the major impulses to disrupt the financial world at that time. For the recent financial crisis, it was the bankruptcy of the Lehman Brothers Holdings in September 2008 due to the subprime mortgage crisis. In both cases, the global interconnections of supply chains and markets triggered a spiral of economic decline which is reflected in the respective gross domestic product figures.

4.2. Credit creation

As a monetary initiative, the central banks in the United States, Europe and China reacted in the same way as the Federal Reserve System during the dot-com bubble, namely decrease lending rates in order to provide liquidity and boost the economy. This time, as basically the whole world is affected, even more capital flows into the market—not just from Japan as during the dot-com bubble. In some cases, the governments were even forced to bail out some banks in order to avoid an economic breakdown of financial systems [47]. Economic research and the central banks confirm the relationship of low interest rates, credit creation and rising prices [48–52]. After these measures, the gross domestic product started to increase and corporate profits recovered too – as seen in **Figure 2**.

Also by other measures such as the unemployment rate and the consumer to business confidence, a recovery with some exceptions was observable. Though these measures worked well for the United States, the issues of the recent financial crisis in the European Union did not allow for a swift and substantial recovery as during the nineties years of the twentieth century in the United States as seen in **Figure 3**.

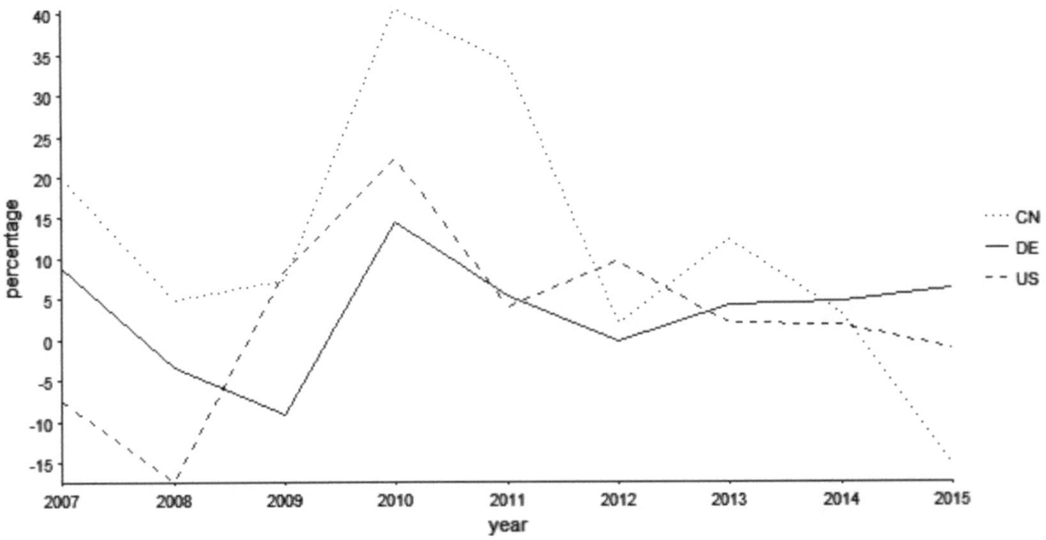

Figure 2. Corporate profit change. Source: own elaboration by the authors.

In the name of the European Central Bank, Mario Draghi promised to further support the economy throughout 2016 and even beyond 2017 if necessary [53]. Putting this promise into perspective and comparing it to the nineties years of the twentieth century, this means that liquidity will flow into the market throughout 2016 and maybe even 2017. Maintaining the interest rate at such low levels, however, increases the risk of a liquidity trap where additional capital in the market does not boost the economy as anticipated due to the neutrality of money in the short-term to long-term [54, 55]. Additionally, current plans to increase the

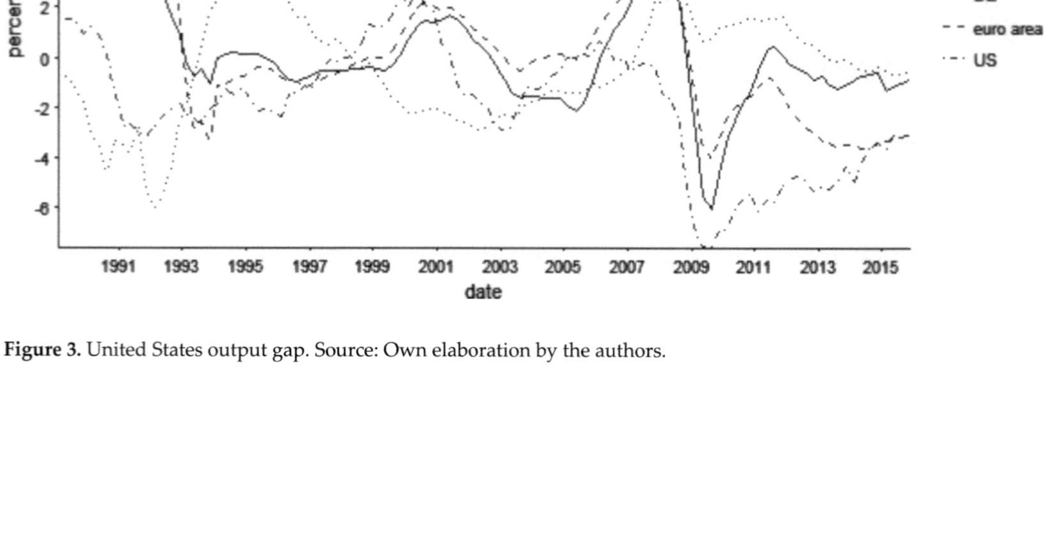

Figure 3. United States output gap. Source: Own elaboration by the authors.

interest rate are damped by the weak support of other indicators. As of 2015, corporate profits stagnate at middle levels and even sharply falling in China in contrast to a steady increase in the middle of the 1990s of the twentieth century in the United States.

4.3. Euphoria

Unique during the dot-com bubble was the creation of euphoria through the personal computer and internet technology hype. Today is different in the way that this technology is innovatively utilised rather than completely new. Nevertheless, there are key concepts which are more strongly emphasised by the media than others, such as artificial intelligence, digital currencies, biotechnologies and so on. However, there is no such strong consensus and focus on one particular technology as during the nineties years of the twentieth century. This marks the difference in motivation for investment between those time frames. During the dot-com bubble, several behavioural concepts such as the law of small numbers, herding, self-attribution bias and others were at play [56, 57]. In the recent years, however, the market sentiment was shaped by political uncertainty while the main driver to invest in stocks is the available liquidity fuelled by the tech-start-up spirit. In the scope of this paper, the following stages are unique to the dot-com bubble since as of December 2015 there was no severe downturn of the indices under analysis, for instance a bubble burst.

4.4. Financial distress and revulsion

All it actually takes to crash a bubble is a critical mass of arbitrageurs who tackle the overvaluation in order for market prices to shift more towards fundamental values. A collapse can happen fundamentally due to the unstable position; the instantaneous cause of the collapse is secondary [58]. The sharp decrease was not triggered by any substantially negative news or announcements. Furthermore, there is an argument that the expiration of a high volume of the lock-up periods expired and provided insiders and arbitrageurs the needed measures to adjust the market and the subsequent fall of the Nasdaq Composite index [36]. More likely it was the interplay and combination of different factors which together created the critical mass that is argued for [59]. Since this critical mass was obviously reached, herding behaviour set in again in the opposite direction—for instance sell—as the news of a downturn spread across media. Eventually, the bubble burst and losses had to be realised which is reflected in most of the indicators shown before, such as the Nasdaq Composite index itself, gross domestic product, corporate profits, the unemployment rate and so on. At this point, banks become more cautious with lending which decreases liquidity in the market and often causes governments and central banks to intervene in order to boost the economy and rebuild trust all over again.

5. Assessment of indices rise in North America, Europe and Asia

The indices' values are assessed throughout their period of rise all over the regions in the world. Mean comparison with key performance indicators are offered.

5.1. Mean comparison

At first, mean comparison is offered to obtain a general view on the explored indices as seen in **Table 1**.

Firstly, the mean comparison showed that on a regional level, for instance in North America, Europe, and Asia, the technology sector showed top returns and one of the highest probabilities for equal means in comparison to the Nasdaq Composite index performance in the nineties years of the twentieth century.

Second, the probabilities increased on a local level for the Nasdaq Composite index, Deutscher Aktien Index 30, the TecDax and the Hang Seng Index. These results, however, have to be interpreted cautiously because the increased probability is most likely due to the prolonged but mild increase before the actual bubble.

Thirdly, the results for the China Securities Index 300 show a considerable similarity to the Nasdaq Composite index in the 1990s of the twentieth century. The probability of equal means for returns is as high as 88.01% for the China Securities Index 300 index and the Nasdaq Composite index in the inflation phase.

5.2. Key performance indicators

The analysis yielded mixed results of the key performance indicators with room for interpretation, including some early warning signals but still the potential to develop either way in the future. On a regional level, the price-to-earnings ratios are as high up as shortly before the actual bubble in the 1990s of the twentieth century as seen on **Figure 4**.

At this point, the irrational exuberance speech by Alan Greenspan from 1996 could be appropriate again. In fact, the Federal Reserve System just increased the federal funds rate to 0.25–0.5% in December 2015. On a local level, the price-to-earnings ratio remains at moderate levels with the exception of the China Securities Index 300, where a peak in the summer of 2015 yet again confirmed the thesis of a bubble from the mean comparison section.

Time span	Nasdaq composite		Datastream technology		Welch-Satterthwaite t-test (%)
	Average monthly return (%)	Standard deviation (%)	Average monthly return (%)	Standard deviation (%)	
December 1990 to October 1998	1.59	4.61	2.03	5.44	54.28
November 1998 to March 2000	6.84	6.90	6.30	9.07	99.57
April 2000 to October 2002	−4.71	10.74	−5.19	13.75	80.43
April 2009 to December 2015	1.70	4.96	1.50	5.28	80.56

Table 1. Nasdaq composite versus Datastream technology phases. Source: own elaboration by the authors.

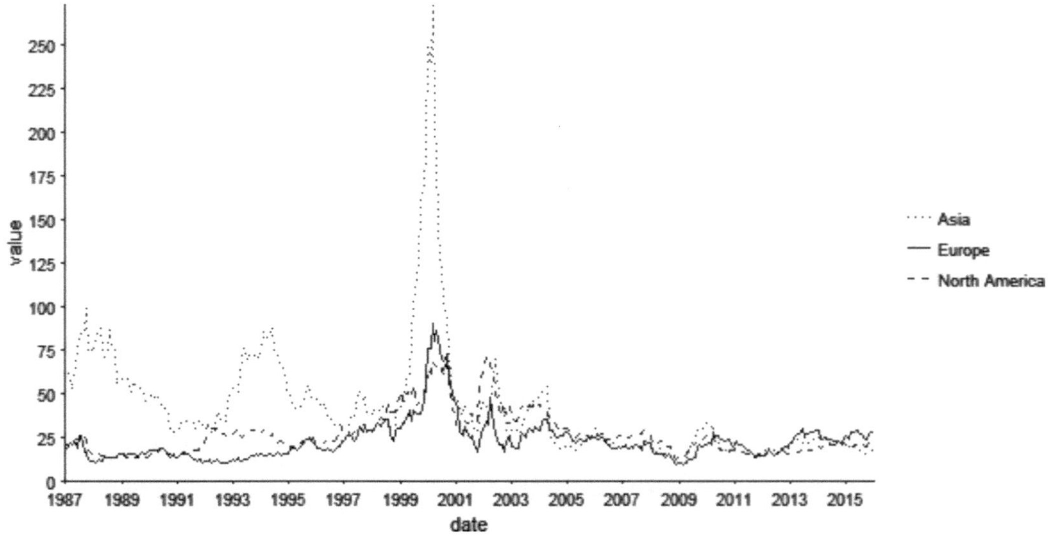

Figure 4. Price-to-earnings ratio by region. Source: Own elaboration by the authors.

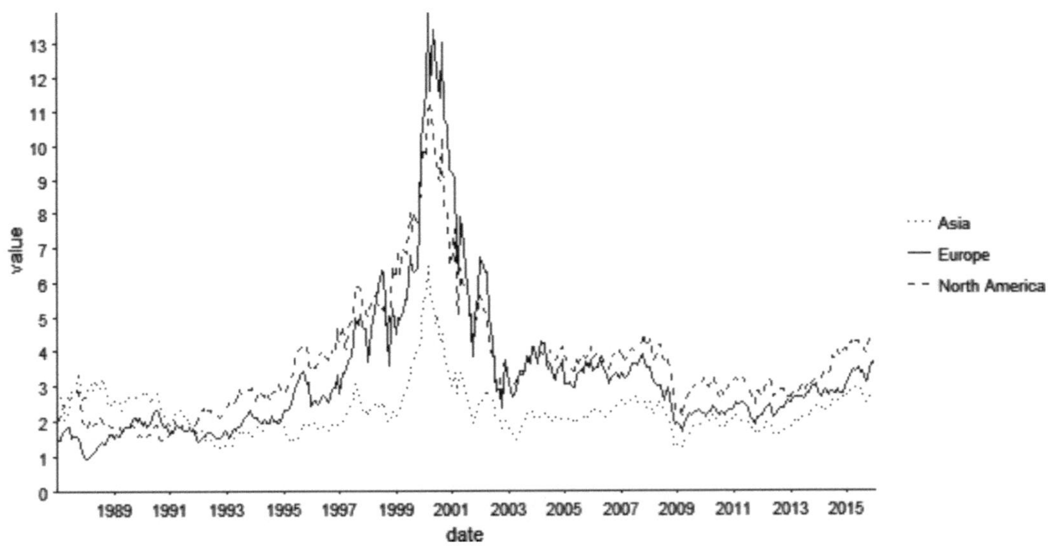

Figure 5. Price-to-book ratio by region. Source: Own elaboration by the authors.

The sales and earnings, for instance earnings before interest, taxes, depreciation and amortisation, figures show mostly support for rising indices with a few exceptions. On a regional level, both sales and earnings are stagnating or even declining, so there is little evidence for optimistic index increases for Europe as a whole. The same is true for all Chinese indices: for instance the Hang Seng Index and the China Securities Index 300. There the sales and earnings are stagnating or declining as well. So at these levels again, the thesis for a possible bubble is strengthened.

Figure 5 shows that on a regional level, the price-to-book ratios are again as high as right before the outbreak of the actual dot-com bubble. Therefore, they should be interpreted as a warning sign for investors. On a local level only the China Securities Index 300 ratio yet again confirms the occurrence of a bubble in middle of 2015 with an extreme peak.

6. Discussion and conclusion

In this section, the results of the comparison between the dot-com bubble and today's crisis are summarised and interpreted. They are grouped into a macro perspective which takes into account the overall economic environment on the one hand. While on the other hand, the indices and ratios of the selected countries and stock exchanges will be interpreted, too. Both perspectives are structured according to the region under consideration.

There are many papers dealing with market bubbles, but only a few of them provide a look in a field of testing the recorded returns in such a way. It is very difficult to compare them. Taking into account the beginning of both situations for instance dot-com bubble and the further financial crisis of 2007, it can be said that they are very similar in many regards. More importantly, the countermeasures in both situations from the central banks were the same: lowering interest rates and providing liquidity. In both cases, the indices responded with a rapid growth and available capital was utilised, finding its way into higher return markets that are also riskier—volatile—by nature. However, there are two differences which must be taken into consideration.

Firstly, during the 1990s of the twentieth century, a new technology—personal computers and the internet—was on the verge of being introduced to average households. The scope of such impact was unforeseeable and the end of the potential for new usages of such technology is not in sight. Today the impact is better, though not perfectly, assessable through the existence of past data and experience from investors' perspectives. As own calculations show, this uncertainty lies inherently in the industry throughout the 1990s of the twentieth century. Despite the governments support for tech start-ups, there is hardly euphoria to the extent as before due to the aforementioned reasons. This result is in line with other current research which finds that even though higher stock valuations in general are possible, they are unlikely and unsustainable [60].

Secondly, the recent crisis is different since it affected the whole world market—not just the high-tech industry—at once in a very severe way, causing global pressure on growth as described before. This is different to the more regional and less of global-scale crises in the 1980s of the twentieth century, for instance Japan, and the 1990s of the twentieth century, for example, the United States, the 1998 Russian financial crisis and the 1997 Asian financial crisis. So the impact of low interest on the economies in the regions under consideration is yet to be seen. Even more, since the start of high volatility in the Chinese economy and the unannounced decrease in interest rates, there is potential for even greater issues in an economy which many countries and regions rely on. This could create a carry-trade similar to the one with Japan and the United States but on a much greater scale.

http://dx.doi.org/10.5772/intechopen.71381

These two points stand in contrast to one another. On the one hand, there is less hype in comparison to the 1990s of the twentieth century in the tech industry, but on the other hand, there is so much capital available due to the previous crisis and current uncertainty that creates more opportunities for speculators.

There is one more level which can be discussed in this paper. It is an index level, where one can have a look at the contemporary trends and also the current development. On this level, the situation looks more diverse, even more so when differentiating between the broad regions and single countries.

Firstly, on a broader regional level, trends indicate an overall increase due to the stimuli across the world by central banks. For the industry under consideration, there are currently no extraordinary trends of a bubble visible. It must be noted, however, that the levels are to some extent as high as before the crisis or before the actual dot-com bubble in the United States. This is especially true for Europe and Asia. Still, as of 2015, earnings were able to grow simultaneously, making up for the increase in prices. Worrying is the recent development of earnings that are most visibly deteriorating in Europe while slightly decreasing in the United States and at least stagnating in Asia. Such trends, however, must be differentiated to normal business cycles.

Secondly, on a national level, the figures show greater amplitudes and interpretations can only be made from a narrow local perspective. In the United States, the Federal Reserve System is confident of being able to increase interest rates due to the regained trust of investors in the stability of the economy even though it is not yet fully recovered. Since it is a rate which acts as an anchor for investors around the world, the signal is necessary though. This action might come early enough to improve the situation while stopping the market from overheating like in the 1990s. In Germany, it is less possible to see the country on its own since it is tied to the euro area monetary union in which the other countries are further away from having recovered from the financial crisis. If the liquidity boost will continue throughout 2016–2017, it gives incentives for speculators and hence rising equity markets. Only the decrease in earnings might lower expectations and hence incentives to speculate. Even more unstable is the situation in China which experienced a major downturn of its economy as shown in the previous sections. This situation is likely to continue throughout 2016 according to business experts [61]. Closest to a bubble-like behaviour and ratios is the trend in summer 2015 for the China Securities Index 300 index. However, the extraordinary deviations cannot be confirmed even though the underlying data is from their database. In either case, this deviation is for the named reasons nowhere near the magnitude of the dot-com bubble. Addressing the research question of whether the current rise in indices across North America, Europe and Asia resembles the dot-com bubble, the answer is negative for the following reasons. While strong short-term deviations as seen in China in the summer of 2015 have occurred, they do not resemble a prolonged deviation of the magnitude in the late 1990s even though they could be called short-term bubbles, in the case of the China Securities Index 300 index in 2015. It can be said that at least the pre-conditions of the overall economies as well as the indices do resemble important trends on a broader level which were visible during the 1990s in the United States. On the other hand, earnings did growth and the increase and the raise in the interest rate by the Federal Reserve System signal the end of the crisis. Depending on the further development of the situation in China and overall economic situation the sentiment can still turn either way. As long as there is cheap liquidity in the market, indices can likely be used for speculation. Moreover, the hype of a new technology might be even found within another sector or a combination of two such as biotechnologies, information technology, virtual reality and healthcare for example. Therefore, the future situation highly depends on the business sentiment and performance of stressed economies such as China and Europe. With these findings, this paper hopes to give a basis for cross regional comparison for the rise of regional and local indices through the combined assessment of different theories and approaches. It remains the opportunity for future research to complement on the limitations and build on this basis.

Author details

Wladimir Schubert[1], Beáta Gavurová[2*], Viliam Kováč[2] and Martin Užík[1]

*Address all correspondence to: beata.gavurova@tuke.sk

1 Berlin School of Economics and Law, Berlin, Germany

2 Department of Banking and Investment, Faculty of Economics, Technical University of Košice, Košice, Slovak Republic

References

[1] Olaberría E. Capital Inflows and Booms in Asset Prices: Going Beyond the Current Account. Centre for Economic Policy Research Policy Portal—voxeu.org. 2013. Available from: http://voxeu.org/article/asset-price-booms-and-composition-capital-inflows [Accessed: 15 July 2017]

[2] Smith N. China Sends Bubbles to North America. Bloomberg View. 2016. Available from: https://www.bloomberg.com/view/articles/2016-06-15/china-sends-bubbles-to-north-america [Accessed: 15 July 2017]

[3] Basco S. Globalization and financial development: A model of the dot-com and the housing bubbles. Journal of International Economics. 2014;**92**(1):78-94. DOI: 10.1016/j.jinteco.2013.10.008. Available from: http://www.sciencedirect.com/science/article/pii/S0022199613001050 [Accessed: 15 July 2017]

[4] Leone V, de Medeiros OR. Signalling the Dotcom bubble: A multiple changes in persistence approach. The Quarterly Review of Economics and Finance. 2015;**55**:77-86. DOI: 10.1016/j.qref.2014.08.006. Available from: http://www.sciencedirect.com/science/article/pii/S1062976914000684 [Accessed: 15 July 2017]

[5] Li C. Log-periodic view on critical dates of the Chinese stock market bubbles. Physica A: Statistical Mechanics and its Applications. 2017;**465**:305-311. DOI: 10.1016/j.physa.2016.08.050. Available from: http://www.sciencedirect.com/science/article/pii/S0378437116305672 [Accessed: 15 July 2017]

[6] Baldi L, Peri M, Vandone D. Stock markets' bubbles burst and volatility spillovers in agricultural commodity markets. Research in International Business and Finance. 2016;**38**(2016):277-285. DOI: 10.1016/j.ribaf.2016.04.020. Available from: http://www.sciencedirect.com/science/article/pii/S027553191630085X [Accessed: 15 July 2017]

[7] Jarrow RA, Kchia Y, Protter P. How to detect an asset bubble. Johnson School Research Paper Series; 2011. Paper No. 28-2010. DOI: 10.2139/ssrn.1621728. Available from: https://papers.ssrn.com/sol3/papers.cfm?abstract_id=1621728 [Accessed: 15 July 2017]

[8] Sornette D, Demos G, Zhang Q, Cauwels P, Filimonov V, Zhang Q. Real-time prediction and post-mortem analysis of the Shanghai 2015 stock market bubble and crash. Swiss Finance Institute Research Paper; 2015. pp. 15-31. DOI: 10.2139/ssrn.2693634. Available from: https://papers.ssrn.com/sol3/papers.cfm?abstract_id=2693634 [Accessed: 15 July 2017]

[9] Shiller RJ. Measuring bubble expectations and investor confidence. National Bureau of Economic Research Working Paper; 1999. Paper No. W10581. DOI: 10.3386/w7008. Available from: http://www.nber.org/papers/w7008.pdf [Accessed: 15 July 2017]

[10] Fama EF. Efficient capital markets: A review of theory and empirical work. The Journal of Finance. 1970;**25**(2):383-417

[11] Fama EF, French KR. Luck versus skill in the cross section of mutual fund returns. Tuck School of Business Working Paper; 2009. Paper No. 2009-56. DOI: 10.2139/ssrn.1356021. Available from: https://papers.ssrn.com/sol3/papers.cfm?abstract_id=1356021 [Accessed: 15 July 2017]

[12] Pinto JE, Henry E, Robinson TR, Stowe JD, Cohen A. Equity Asset Valuation. Hoboken, New York: Wiley; 2010 ISBN: 9780470571439

[13] Rosser JB. From Catastrophe to Chaos: A General Theory of Economic Discontinuities. New York: Springer Publishing; 2000. DOI: 10.1007/978-94-017-1613-0 ISBN: 978940171 6130

[14] Siegel JJ. What is an asset price bubble? An operational definition. European Financial Management. 2003;**9**(1):11-24

[15] Pastor L, Veronesi P. Was there a NASDAQ bubble in the late 1990s?. National Bureau of Economic Research Working Paper; 2004. Paper No. W10581. DOI: 10.3386/w10581. Available from: http://www.nber.org/papers/w10581.pdf [Accessed: 15 July 2017]

[16] DeLong JB, Magin K. A short note on the size of the Dot-Com bubble. National Bureau of Economic Research Working Paper; 2006. Paper No. W12011. DOI: 10.3386/w12011. Available from: http://www.nber.org/papers/w12011.pdf [Accessed: 15 July 2017]

[17] Kindleberger CP, Aliber RZ. Manias, Panics, and Crashes: A History of Financial Crises. New York: Wiley; 2005 ISBN: 9780471467144

[18] Bellotti XA, Taffler RJ, Tian L. Understanding the chinese stockmarket bubble: The role of emotion. Social Science Research Network. 2010. DOI: 10.2139/ssrn.1695932. Available from: https://papers.ssrn.com/sol3/papers.cfm?abstract_id=1695932 [Accessed: 15 July 2017]

[19] Gürkaynak RS. Econometric tests of asset price bubbles: Taking stock. Social Science Research Network. 2005. DOI: 10.2139/ssrn.658244. Available from: https://papers.ssrn.com/sol3/papers.cfm?abstract_id=658244 [Accessed: 15 July 2017]

[20] Windolf PH. Riding the bubble: Financial market crises in 22 OECD-countries. Journal of Economic Issues. 2016;**50**(3):788-813. DOI: 10.1080/00213624.2016.1213588. Available from: https://papers.ssrn.com/sol3/papers.cfm?abstract_id=2527894 [Accessed: 15 July 2017]

[21] Campbell JY, Lo AW, MacKinlay AC. The Econometrics of Financial Markets. Princeton: Princeton University Press; 1997 ISBN: 9781400830213

[22] Bagnoli ME, Kallapur S, Watts SG. Top line and bottom line forecasts: A comparison of internet firms during and after the bubble. Social Science Research Network. 2001. DOI: 10.2139/ssrn.274178. Available from: https://papers.ssrn.com/sol3/papers.cfm?abstract_id=274178 [Accessed: 15 July 2017]

[23] Bharath ST, Viswanathan S. Is the internet bubble consistent with rationality? Social Science Research Network. 2006. DOI: 10.2139/ssrn.943609. Available from: https://papers.ssrn.com/sol3/papers.cfm?abstract_id=943609 [Accessed: 15 July 2017]

[24] Jarrow RA, Kchia Y, Protter P. Is there a bubble in Linkedin's stock price? Johnson School Research Paper Series; 2011. Paper No. 28-2011. DOI: 10.2139/ssrn.1858736. Available from: https://papers.ssrn.com/sol3/papers.cfm?abstract_id=1858736 [Accessed: 15 July 2017]

[25] Minsky HP. Stabilizing an Unstable Economy. New York: McGraw-Hill Education; 2008 ISBN: 9780071592994

[26] Morris JJ, Alam P. Analysis of the dot-com bubble of the 1990s. Social Science Research Network. 2008. DOI: 10.2139/ssrn.1152412. Available from: https://papers.ssrn.com/sol3/papers.cfm?abstract_id=1152412 [Accessed: 15 July 2017]

[27] Majková MS, Solík J, Sipko J. The analysis of chosen business obstacles and problems with the financing of young entrepreneurs in Slovakia. Economics & Sociology. 2014;**7**(3):90-103. DOI: 10.14254/2071-789X.2014/7-3/7. Available from: http://www.economics-sociology.eu/files/11_81_Majkova_Solik_Sipko.pdf [Accessed: 15 July 2017]

[28] Belás J, Bilan Y, Demjan V, Sipko J. Entrepreneurship in SME segment: Case study from the Czech Republic and Slovakia. Amfiteatru Economic. 2015;17(38):308-326. Available from: http://www.amfiteatrueconomic.ro/temp/Article_2387.pdf [Accessed: 15 July 2017]

[29] Belás J, Demjan V, Habánik J, Hudáková M, Sipko J. The business environment of small and medium-sized enterprises in selected regions of the Czech Republic and Slovakia. Ekonomie a Management. 2015;**18**(1):95-110. DOI: 10.15240/tul/001/2015-1-008. Available from: http://www.ekonomie-management.cz/download/1426013199_e667/08_THE+BUSINESS+ENVIRONMENT+OF+SMALL+AND+MEDIUM-SIZED.pdf [Accessed: 15 July 2017]

[30] O'Brien PC, Tian Y. Financial analysts' role in the 1996-2000 internet bubble. Social Science Research Network. 2007. DOI: 10.2139/ssrn.964311. Available from: https://papers.ssrn.com/sol3/papers.cfm?abstract_id=964311 [Accessed: 15 July 2017]

[31] Anderson KP, Brooks C, Katsaris A. Speculative bubbles in the S&P 500: Was the tech bubble confined to the tech sector? Social Science Research Network. 2005. DOI: 10.2139/ssrn.834484. Available from: http://papers.ssrn.com/abstract=834484 [Accessed: 15 July 2017]

[32] Nagel S, Brunnermeier MK. Hedge funds and the technology bubble. European Finance Association 2003 Annual Conference; 2003. Paper No. 446. DOI: 10.2139/ssrn.423940. Available from: https://papers.ssrn.com/sol3/papers.cfm?abstract_id=423940 [Accessed: 15 July 2017]

[33] Belás J, Sipko J, Bilan Y. Regional aspects of business environment creation in the SME segment in Slovakia. Mediterranean Journal of Social Sciences. 2015;**6**(3):637-645. DOI: 10.5901/mjss.2015.v6n3p637. Available from: http://www.mcser.org/journal/index.php/mjss/article/view/6303/6041 [Accessed: 15 July 2017]

[34] Chochoľáková A, Gabčová L, Belás J, Sipko J. Bank customers' satisfaction, customers' loyalty and additional purchases of banking products and services. A case study from the Czech Republic. Economics & Sociology. 2015;**8**(3):82-94. DOI: 10.14254/2071-789X.2015/8-3/6. Available from: http://www.economics-sociology.eu/files/ES_8_3_Chocholakova.pdf [Accessed: 15 July 2017]

[35] Griffioen GAW. Technical analysis in financial markets. Social Science Research Network. 2003. DOI: 10.2139/ssrn.566882. Available from: https://papers.ssrn.com/sol3/papers.cfm?abstract_id=566882 [Accessed: 15 July 2017]

[36] Ofek E, Richardson M. DotCom mania: The rise and fall of internet stock prices. The Journal of Finance. 2003;**58**(3):1113-1138. Available from: http://pages.stern.nyu.edu/~eofek/DotComMania_JF_Final.pdf [Accessed: 15 July 2017]

[37] Gürkaynak RS. Econometric tests of asset price bubbles: Taking stock. Journal of Economic Surveys. 2008;**22**(1):166-186

[38] Hayford MD, Malliaris ATG. Rethinking Monetary Stabilization in the Presence of an Asset Bubble. Social Science Research Network. 2006. DOI: 10.2139/ssrn.1021805. In: Volbert A, Kotz H-H. 2006. Global Divergence in Trade, Money and Policy, pp. 172-191, Cheltenham: Edward Elgar Publishing. Available From: https://papers.ssrn.com/sol3/papers.cfm?abstract_id=1021805. [Accessed: 15 July 2017]

[39] Garber PM. Famous first bubbles: The fundamentals of early manias. Journal of Economic Perspectives. 2001;**4**(2):35-54. Available from: http://web.econ.ku.dk/okocg/Students%20Seminars%C3%98kon-%C3%98velser/%C3%98velse%202007/artikler/Garber-Famous-First-Bubbles-JEP-1990.pdf [Accessed: 15 July 2017]

[40] Heinze A, Fletcher G, Griffiths M. Why Europe is still trailing the US in successful start-ups. The Conversation. 2015. Available from: http://theconversation.com/why-europe-is-still-trailing-the-us-in-successful-start-ups-36915 [Accessed: 15 July 2017]

[41] Trueman B, Wong MHF, Zhang X. The eyeballs have it: Searching for the value in internet stocks. Social Science Research Network. 2000. DOI: 10.2139/ssrn.206648. Available from: https://papers.ssrn.com/sol3/papers.cfm?abstract_id=206648 [Accessed: 15 July 2017]

[42] Sousa M, Pinho M. Is internet industry facing an IPO bubble 2.0?. Social Science Research Network. 2014. DOI: 10.2139/ssrn.2533383. Available from: https://papers.ssrn.com/sol3/papers.cfm?abstract_id=2533383 [Accessed: 15 July 2017]

[43] Johansen A, Sornette D. The Nasdaq crash of April 2000: Yet another example of log-periodicity in a speculative bubble ending in a crash. Social Science Research Network. 2000. DOI: 10.2139/ssrn.224145. Available from: https://papers.ssrn.com/sol3/papers.cfm?abstract_id=224145 [Accessed: 15 July 2017]

[44] Lerner P. Was there a bubble in Nasdaq? Information-based reexamination. Social Science Research Network. 2008. DOI: 10.2139/ssrn.1150510. Available from: https://papers.ssrn.com/sol3/papers.cfm?abstract_id=1150510 [Accessed: 15 July 2017]

[45] Korotayev AV, Tsirel SV. A spectral analysis of world GDP dynamics: Kondratieff waves, Kuznets swings, Juglar and Kitchin cycles in global economic development, and the 2008-2009 economic crisis. Structure and Dynamics: eJournal of Anthropological and Related Sciences. 2010;**4**(1):1-56. Available from: http://escholarship.org/uc/item/9jv108xp [Accessed: 15 July 2017]

[46] Christensen CM, Raynor ME. The Innovator's Solution: Creating and Sustaining Successful Growth. Boston: Harvard Business Review Press; 2013 ISBN: 9781422196571

[47] Collins M. The big bank bailout. Forbes. 2015. Available from: https://www.forbes.com/sites/mikecollins/2015/07/14/the-big-bank-bailout/#5010a6262d83 [Accessed: 15 July 2017]

[48] Wicksell K. The influence of the rate of interest on prices. Economic Journal. 1907;**27**:213-220. Available from: http://www.econlib.org/library/Essays/wcksInt1.html [Accessed: 15 July 2017]

[49] Persons WM. Fisher's the purchasing power of money. Publications of the American Statistical Association. 1911;**12**(96):818-829

[50] Taylor JB. The financial crisis and the policy responses: An empirical analysis of what went wrong. National Bureau of Economic Research Working Paper; 2009. Paper No. W14631. DOI: 10.3386/w14631. Available from: http://www.nber.org/papers/w14631.pdf [Accessed: 15 July 2017]

[51] Ireland PN. The monetary transmission mechanism. In: Boston College Working Papers in Economics. 2005. Paper No. 628. Available from: http://fmwww.bc.edu/EC-P/wp628.pdf Accessed: 15 July 2017

[52] European Central Bank. Transmission mechanism of monetary policy. European Central Bank. 2016. Available from: https://www.ecb.europa.eu/mopo/intro/transmission/html/index.en.html [Accessed: 15 July 2017]

[53] Draghi M. Global and domestic inflation. European Central Bank. 2015. Available from: https://www.ecb.europa.eu/press/key/date/2015/html/sp151204.en.html [Accessed: 15 July 2017]

[54] Levintal O. Financial crisis, equity capital and the liquidity trap. Social Science Research Network. 2009. DOI: 10.2139/ssrn.1304548. Available from: https://papers.ssrn.com/sol3/papers.cfm?abstract_id=1304548 [Accessed: 15 July 2017]

[55] Sutch RC. The liquidity trap, the great depression, and unconventional policy: Reading Keynes at the zero lower bound. Social Science Research Network. 2014. DOI: 10.2139/ssrn.2529025. Available from: https://papers.ssrn.com/sol3/papers.cfm?abstract_id=2529025 [Accessed: 15 July 2017]

[56] Shiller RJ. Irrational Exuberance—Revised and Expanded. 3rd ed. Princeton: Princeton University Press; 2005 ISBN: 9781400865536

[57] Forbes W. Behavioural Finance. New York: Wiley; 2009 ISBN: 9780470028049

[58] Sornette D. Why Stock Markets Crash: Critical Events in Complex Financial Systems. Princeton: Princeton University Press; 2004 ISBN: 9780691118505

[59] Montier J. Behavioural Finance: Insights into Irrational Minds and Markets. New York: Wiley; 2002 ISBN: 9780470844878

[60] Dettmann O. Fed by the Fed: A new bubble grows on Wall St. Social Science Research Network. 2014. DOI: 10.2139/ssrn.2475975. Available from: https://papers.ssrn.com/sol3/papers.cfm?abstract_id=2475975 [Accessed: 15 July 2017]

[61] Moskowitz D. Why the Chinese economy matters so much to the U.S. Investopedia. 2016. Available from: http://www.investopedia.com/articles/investing/012716/why-chinese-economy-matters-so-much-us.asp [Accessed: 15 July 2017]

Chapter 6

Modeling Default Probability via Structural Models of Credit Risk in Context of Emerging Markets

Maria Kovacova and Boris Kollar

Additional information is available at the end of the chapter

http://dx.doi.org/10.5772/intechopen.71021

Abstract

The chapter is focused on the structural models of credit risk introducing basic concepts of risk-neutral world, as well as models and different options for the credit risk quantification. An important part is also the introduction of structural approach for credit risk modeling. Furthermore, the chapter presents basic division of structural models and then presents mathematical derivation of individual apparatuses of models. Among tested models are Merton model, KMV model, Black-Cox model, and Credit Grades model. The practical part is focused on the application of these models under the conditions of local emerging market—Slovakia. Additionally, it pointed out the connection between default probability and credit spreads generated with the use of default mode credit risk models. The main objective is to adjust credit risk model to real market data.

Keywords: credit risk, financial modeling, probability of default, credit spread, structural models

1. Introduction

The chapter is focused on the structural models of credit risk introducing basic concepts of risk-neutral world, as well as models and different options for the credit risk quantification. An important part is also the introduction of structural approach for credit risk modeling. Furthermore, the chapter presents basic division of structural models and then presents mathematical derivation of individual apparatuses of models. Among tested models are Merton model, KMV model, Black-Cox model, and Credit Grades model. The practical part is focused on the application of these models under the conditions of local emerging market—Slovakia. Additionally, it pointed out the connection between default probability and credit spreads generated with the use of default mode credit risk models. The main objective is to adjust credit risk model to real market data.

2. Structural models of credit risk

The main goal of structural models is the objective quantification of credit risk. Objective in the sense is that the process of quantification is not an individual decision of any individual or group of people. On the contrary, the estimation of this risk is the outcome of model, which attempts to describe the causality between the attributes of a particular company applying for a loan (or a company that has already acquired the loan) and the threat that the company will fall into default. We consider market value of its assets to be the main attribute of this company.

The causality mentioned above does not only mean an empirical analysis based on the big set of data and on the choice of proper variables for these data. Correlation does not have to mean causality and prediction. The objective of structural models is to capture the relationship between company fundamentals and the probability of default from time point of view, based on the current market information. The model can then provide a warning of increasing level of credit risk (increasing probability of default) based on changes in company fundamentals. This fact reflects the fundamental and the most important difference between structural and reduced form credit risk models.

Structural models are based on modern financial theory, more precisely on the option pricing theory. The initials of these models are therefore associated with the names of Myron Scholes, Fischer Black, and Robot Merton. These authors contributed significantly to the valuation of options and also laid the foundations for structural models of credit risk. The idea of Black and Scholes [1] to understand corporate liabilities and shares as a derivate written for some corporate assets is considered by Jones et al. [2] to be an even more valuable asset to academic field than the derivation of European option pricing formula itself. It cannot be argued that their approach is the first attempt to quantify credit risk, in particular, the risk of default.

The work of Merton is followed, for example, by Geske [3], who predicts the heterogeneous structure of the company's obligations. This means that he puts both coupon and noncoupon bonds on the side of liabilities. Credit risk is then subsequently valued with the help of barrier option on the company's assets.

Later, the so-called FPT models raised into prominence. Unlike Merton and Geske, they do not assume absolute priority of creditors in the case default, but they work with the idea that part of the value of assets is spent on the costs of bankruptcy or other charge [4]. These assumptions are expressed with the use of coefficients obtained by the empirical observations of defaulted companies and their recovery rates. FPT models assume either a deterministic or stochastic default barrier.

The deterministic barrier is not a constant and it is a function of time, resp. interest rate is a function of time. This type of barrier is used, for example, by Black and Cox [5].

According to Cisko and Klieštik [6], we can divide the structural models into:

- Mark-to-market models are based on the assumption that at the end of the observed risk period, the financial instrument or company will be in one of the n-predefined states.
- Default mode models assume that at the end of the observed risk period, the financial instrument can only be in one of the two states, either default or survival.

3. Default mode models

In this part of this paper, we focus on selected models, which were characterized in the previous sections. In particular, we focus on predicting probability of defaults and credit spreads on empirical data. Because of the fact that the capital market in the Slovak Republic is significantly limited, and it is necessary to know the market price of shares for the purpose of calculation, we have selected company that operates on our market and its shares are traded on the stock exchange, and at the same time, this company is rated by Moody's rating agency.

We use the synthesis of theory and empirical studies of structural models of credit risk. Knowledge from these empirical studies is used, for example, to determine the default barrier height in FPT models. We also limit ourselves only to models with a constant interest rate, as empirical studies show that the stochastic character of the interest rate does not have a significant impact on the credit spread.

4. Calculation of ČEZ, a.s.

The ČEZ Group is the largest energy group operating in Central and Southeastern Europe. Besides the headquarters in Bohemia, it has representation in most of the countries in the region, including Slovakia. To date, ČEZ ranks among the top 10 European energy companies in terms of market capitalization and is the largest company among the new European Union countries. The activities of the ČEZ Group include, in addition to the sale and production of electricity, also telecommunications, informatics, nuclear research, design, construction and maintenance of energy equipment, extraction of raw materials, and processing of various secondary energy intermediates and products. ČEZ is the most profitable and also the least indebted energy company in the region, which reflects its high credit rating. Its stable growth is also achieved due to a balanced portfolio of resources.

The first step is the construction of yield curves for ČEZ, a.s. For the 3, 6, 9, and 12 months horizon, we use the interbank interest rates PRIBOR and for horizons from 2 to 20 years, we use known values of government bonds of Czech Republic. Subsequently, we use the Nelson-Siegel-Svensson method. We construct the yield curves for each year of the prediction, as is shown in **Figure 1**.

Yield curves do not have a traditional shape, except the curve constructed for 2011. The most specific shape is in the case of curve for 2014. In this case, short-term interest rates were higher than government bond rates over 1 year. Changes and natural growth in interest rates occur only in the fifth year. However, the interest rates described by this yield curve follow very low values. Similarly, the low values are also observable in the case of curve constructed for 2015.

In order to determine the market value of assets, we have to stabilize the timeline first, by weighing down the yield on the shares. Consequently, we calculate the market value of assets using the iterative procedures based on Black-Scholes formula [7]. From **Figure 2**, we can see that the shares value of ČEZ, a.s. has a long-lasting character. Shares as the main input of market valuation of assets reflect market reactions to published annual reports and hence

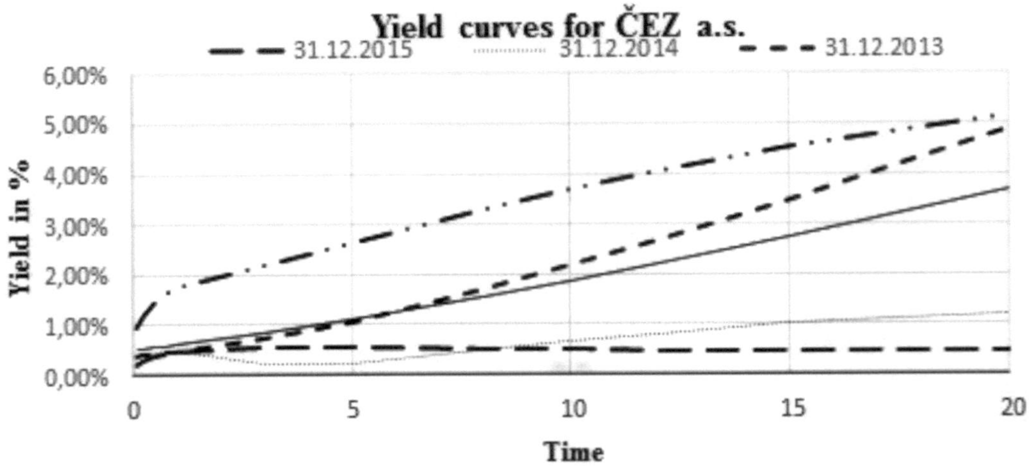

Figure 1. Yield curves for ČEZ a.s.

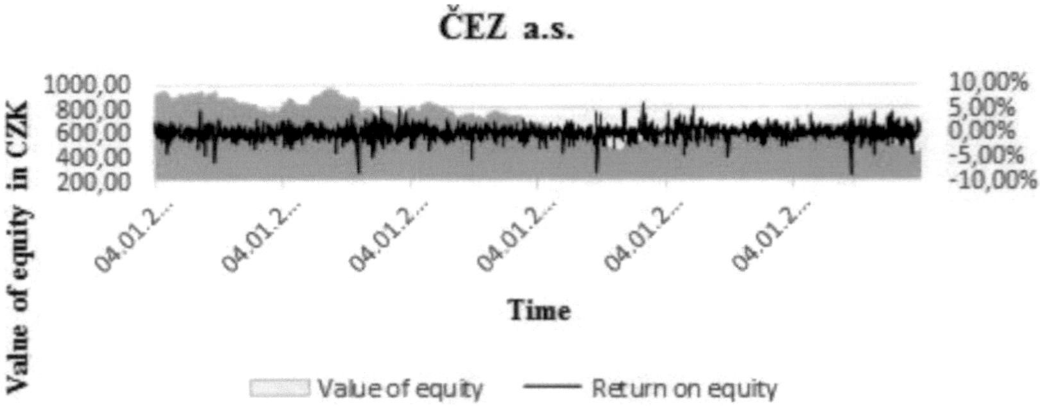

Figure 2. Value of equity for ČEZ, a.s.

reaction to company results. Moody's rating has a worsening tendency just like the value of assets, which has always deteriorated in the past 2 years due to the expected debt growth in the coming years.

Figure 3 shows the development of the equity volatility between 2010 and 2015. We chose the moving average method for the volatility calculation, EWMA, and GARCH (1.1) methods. The highest volatility levels in each of observed periods were the ones generated by GARCH (1.1) model. **Table 1** shows the input data for the calculation of each model. The book value of assets is higher than their market value in the first 3 years of the forecast, which means that the company's assets are underestimated. In the last 2 years, the situation has changed and the market value is higher than the accounting value.

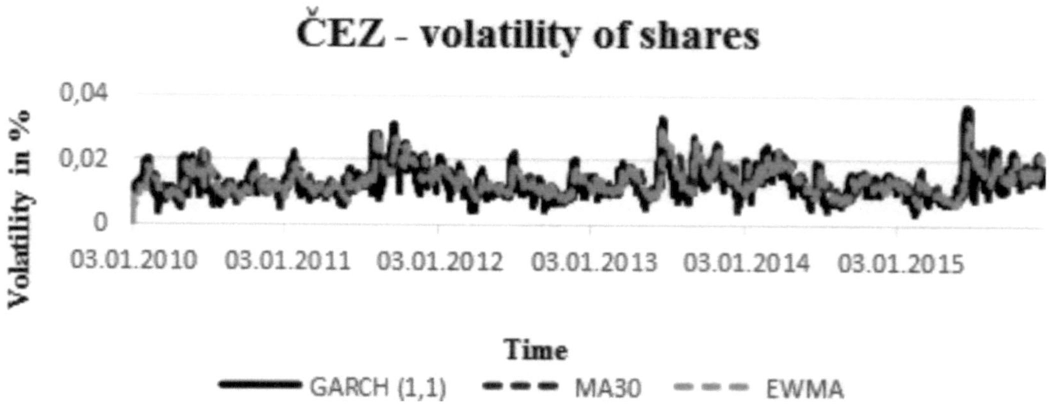

Figure 3. Volatility of shares for ČEZ, a.s.

ČEZ, a.s.		31-12-2015	31-12-2014	31-12-2013	31-12-2012	31-12-2011
Market value of equity		566,369	655,335	632,778	720,103	762,852
Book value of equity		602,686	627,870	641,136	636,070	598,107
Volatility of equity value	MA30	11.57%	12.69%	12.31%	13.86%	14.36%
	EWMA	11.41%	12.52%	12.14%	13.46%	14.35%
	GARCH (1.1)	12.09%	14.07%	17.85%	14.97%	14.95%
Value of debt		330.531	362.019	358.787	360.023	349.083
Market value of shares		237.355	315.662	276.138	363.198	419.756
Volatility of shares value	MA30	22.67%	21.56%	24.24%	19.61%	23.84%
	EWMA	22.53%	21.37%	23.79%	19.29%	23.85%
	GARCH (1.1)	24.11%	22.57%	26.33%	19.71%	25.39%
Default barrier		212,115	235,925	239,252	239,483	237,238

Table 1. Input data for ČEZ, a.s.

We will work with a 20-year time horizon, which is identical to how the individual yield curves were constructed. In the case of the Credit Grades model, we will also need an average rate of return on all debts. Here, we will use the value that the studies and the Credit Grades technical document recommend, and we will work with$\bar{\Lambda}$ = 0.5 [8]. We also choose the volatility of the barrier on the basis of these sources at $\lambda = 0.3$.

Figure 4 shows the probability of default in all models for all calculated volatility types by the end of 2015. The KMV model achieves a significantly lower probabilities of default. In the first half of the predicted time horizon, the probability of default is approaching zero. In short time horizons, the probability of defaults is at minimum values close to zero. This is due to fact

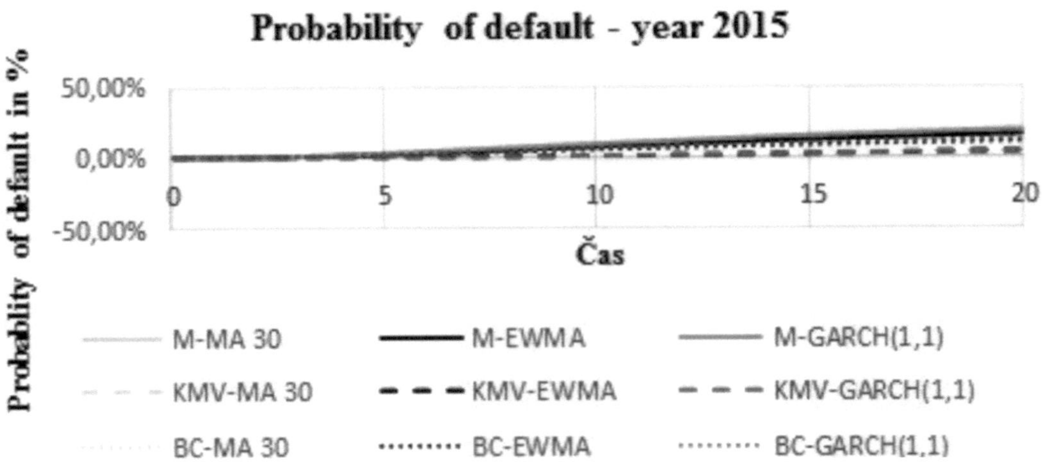

Figure 4. Probability of default in all models for 2015.

that ČEZ a.s. had relatively low volatility of shares during the observed period. The highest Merton probabilities were generated by original Merton model (**Figures 5–12**).

Default curves of ČEZ, a.s. have similar pattern in all models. However, the predicted probability values differ considerably. In a time horizon of up to 1 year, predictions in each of the selected models are close to zero. In the forecast for 2013, there is a sharp increase in the probability of default. This is particularly influenced by the volatility and value of leverage in 2013, which is high in that year in comparison with the other monitored years. In the Black-Cox model, there is an interesting situation when the curves representing the first three seasons are nearing zero. In the long run, they have the highest probability of default in all models for the years 2014 and 2015, which is also influenced by the shape of the yield curves for 2014 and 2015, based on very low interest rates.

The Credit Grades model generates interesting types of curves. Within a short horizon of up to 1 year, the company is virtually safe for all applied models. In the long run, the forecasts vary considerably from 5 to 33%. This is due to both the different design and the ability of models to sensitively react to changes in the input parameters in such a long horizon. Interesting in terms of progress is 2013, which is close to zero in most models, with the exception of the Credit Grades model. The model works with a stochastic barrier, but even then, none of the applied models were able to generate curves with decreasing character. This may be due to the nonrepresentativeness of the sample size.

Credit spreads generated by each model have very similar patterns in all cases. In other applications of these models, we obtained results with negative spreads in the case of KMV model, but not this time. Looking at the reason why this effect does not occur in this case, it is necessary to note the probability of defaults. Over a longer time horizon at higher probability of defaults, the pattern tends to show negative spreads. Therefore, it is better to apply this model to predictions with a shorter time horizon. Another weakness in all three Merton based models is low spreads in short time horizons within 1 year. Highest credit spreads again were however generated by Credit Grades model, because of stochastic barrier.

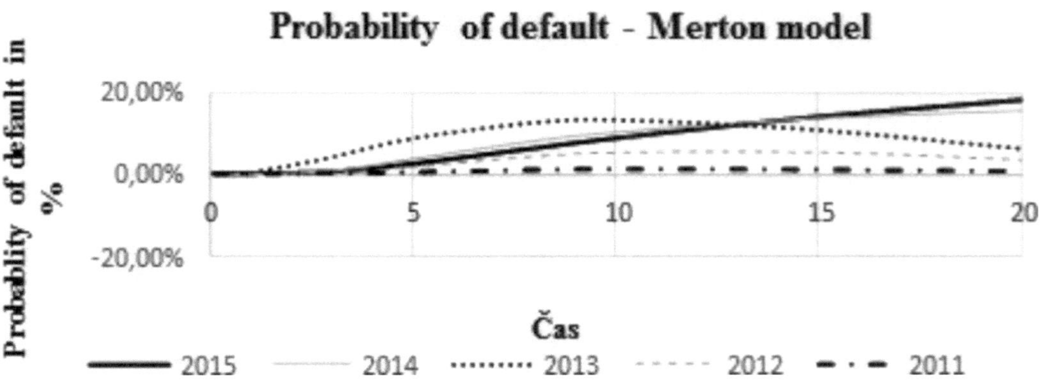

Figure 5. Probability of default for ČEZ, a.s. between years 2011 and 2015—Merton model.

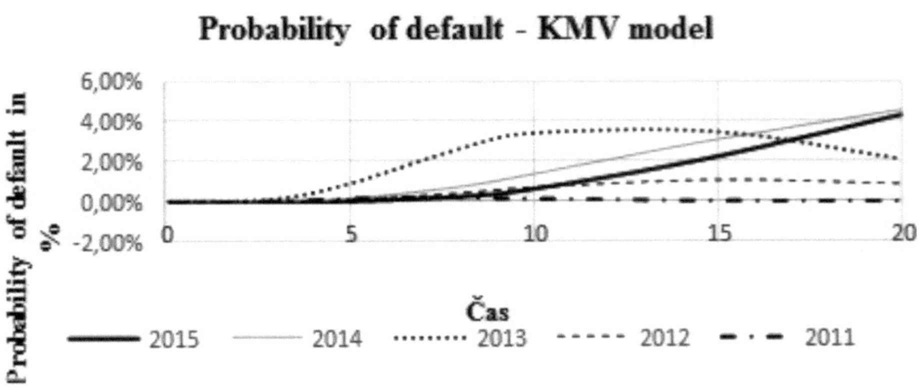

Figure 6. Probability of default for ČEZ, a.s. between years 2011 and 2015—KMV model.

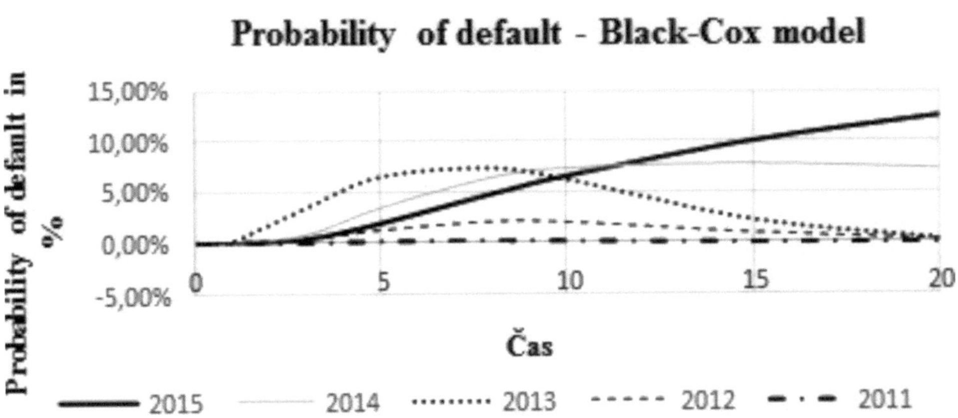

Figure 7. Probability of default for ČEZ, a.s. between years 2011 and 2015—Black-Cox model.

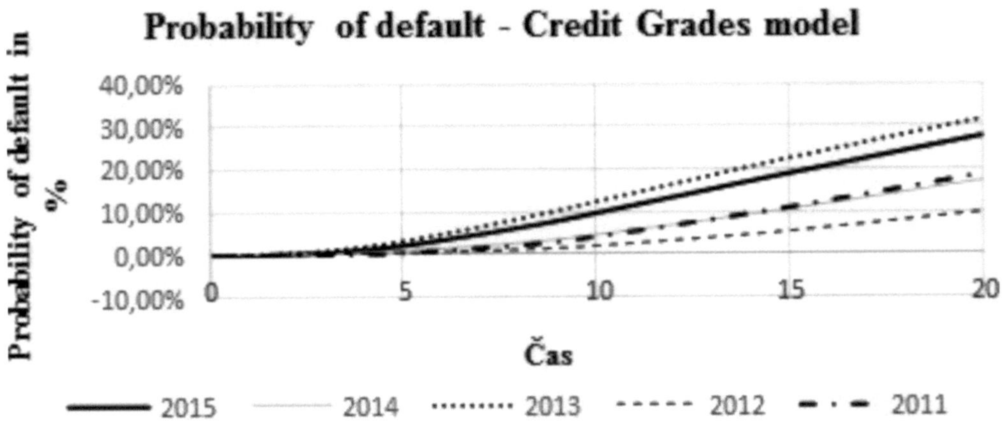

Figure 8. Probability of default for ČEZ, a.s. between years 2011 and 2015—Credit Grades model.

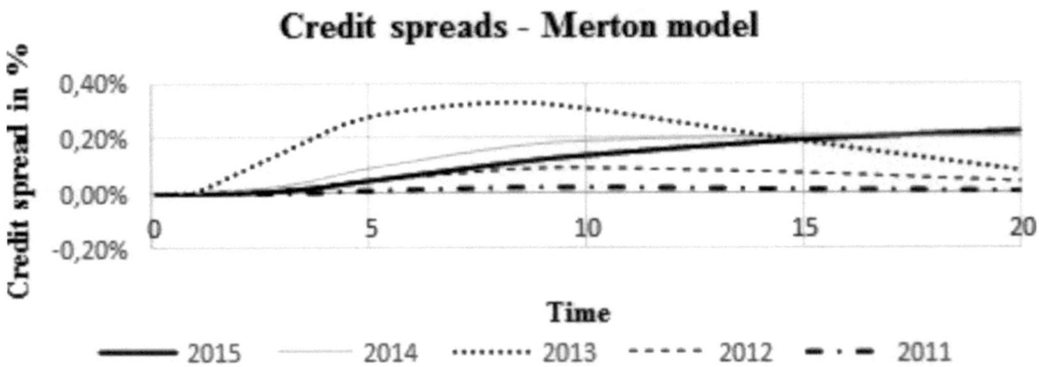

Figure 9. Credit spreads for ČEZ, a.s. between years 2011 and 2015—Merton model.

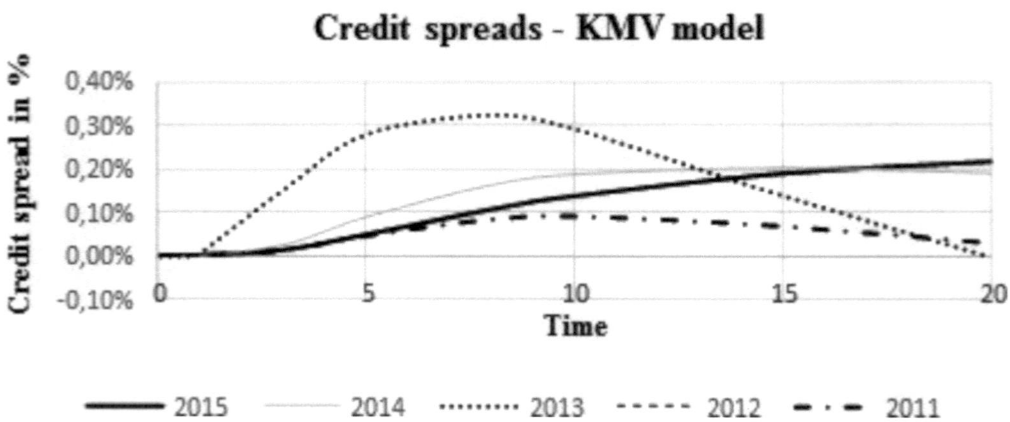

Figure 10. Credit spreads for ČEZ, a.s. between years 2011 and 2015—KMV model.

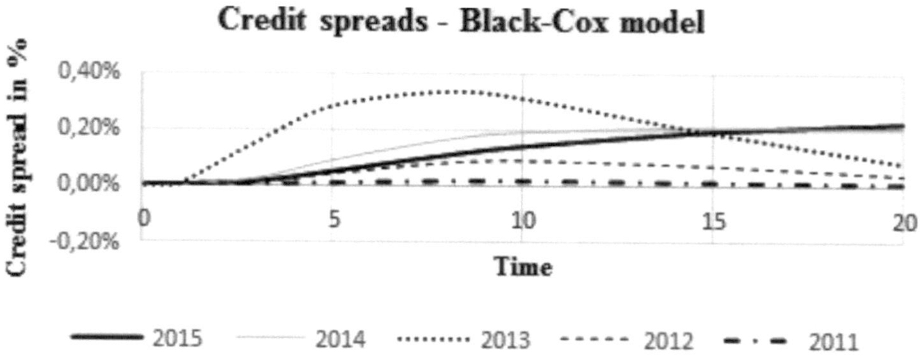

Figure 11. Credit spreads for ČEZ, a.s. between years 2011 and 2015—Black-Cox model.

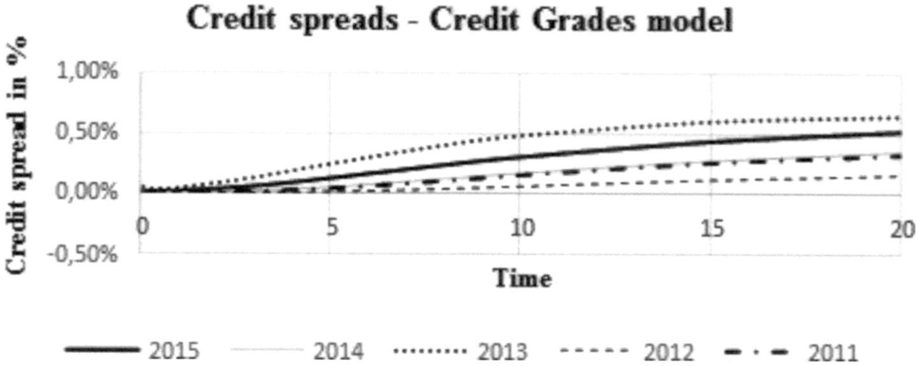

Figure 12. Credit spreads for ČEZ, a.s. between years 2011 and 2015—Credit Grades model.

5. Credit risk quantification with the use of default mode models

Credit spreads generated by selected models have very similar patterns in all cases. Over a longer period at higher probability of defaults, the pattern tends to show negative spreads. Therefore, it is advisable to apply this model to predictions with a shorter time period. Another weakness in all models is low value of spreads in short time horizons within 1 year. Highest credit spreads are generated by Credit Grades model.

While applying the default mode models to companies under the conditions of emerging marker, the problem is to decide whether companies are suitable. We have come across the first barrier of research, as there are only a very small number of companies that have their shares publicly traded on the stock exchange. However, many of these companies are traded on local stock exchanges and their shares are traded only in minimum volumes; and therefore the share price cannot be the basis for calculation of market value. Market value of company and its volatility is one of the basic input parameters of the default mode models.

The next step was the systematization of historical data, in particular the historical values of stocks, buffered indices, as well as interest rates relevant to the stock exchange on which the company is traded. These data were inputs to calculate the market value of assets with the use of iterative procedures. An important source of information is also the analysis and collection of necessary input data from the annual reports of the surveyed companies.

After analyzing the company's historical data, we have identified the input parameters of selected structural credit models and their subsequent quantification. In the process of quantification, not only the calculations but also their synthesis with the studies of credit rating agencies and the works of other authors played an important role. We used the procedure to determine the default barrier height, where we relied on Moody's approach to their commercial KMV model based on Black-Scholes equation. In the case of the Black-Cox model, based on the studies, we chose a default barrier discount rate of 7%. The values recommended by the technical document as well as by other authors have also been used in the Credit Grades model when we worked with the recommended yield rate and barrier volatility.

Finally, we went on to quantify credit risk by using the probability of default and credit spreads within each model. The results of the individual models differ in some cases. Credit Grades modeled in all cases different curves of default probability and credit spreads compared to other models based on the original Merton model. He alone worked with a stochastic barrier, with its volatility having a significant effect on the calculated values.

6. Own approach to determine the probability of default

One of the most criticized assumptions of Merton model, which is the starting model of structural models, is the assumption of a normal distribution of distance from defaults. This critique is also supported by empirical observations. It is for this reason that we have decided to leave the assumption of a normal distribution. The aim was to find a suitable functional relationship between the distance to default and its probability. An extensive statistical sample would be needed to identify such a functional relationship. Since, in pure region, it is not possible to obtain such a sample in view of the underdeveloped capital market, we have attempted to obtain a similar functional relationship that Moody's uses in its commercially successful KMV model. As we mentioned before, KMV is a commercial implementation of Merton's original model.

In 2003, an article was published in the CFO magazine, which contains hundreds of the largest bond issuers on the US capital market. In the article, the probability of default was quantified for companies based on Moody's internal methodology; asset volatility and the leverage of these companies were also presented [9]. Moody's predicts default probability with a 1-year horizon. In addition to this source, Moody's regularly publishes research on defaulted companies on their site in the research section and they have become another source of information for sample augmentation. Due to these studies, we also acquired companies with higher business risk.

From these collected data, we have subsequently calculated distance to default. In the case of risk-free interest rate, which is meant to express the growth of assets in rated company in a risk-neutral world, we have used US dollar yields with a maturity of up to 1 year for 2003 to match the sample of surveyed companies as much as possible. Based on this, it was then possible to assign the Moody's distance to default values. This relationship is shown in **Figure 13**.

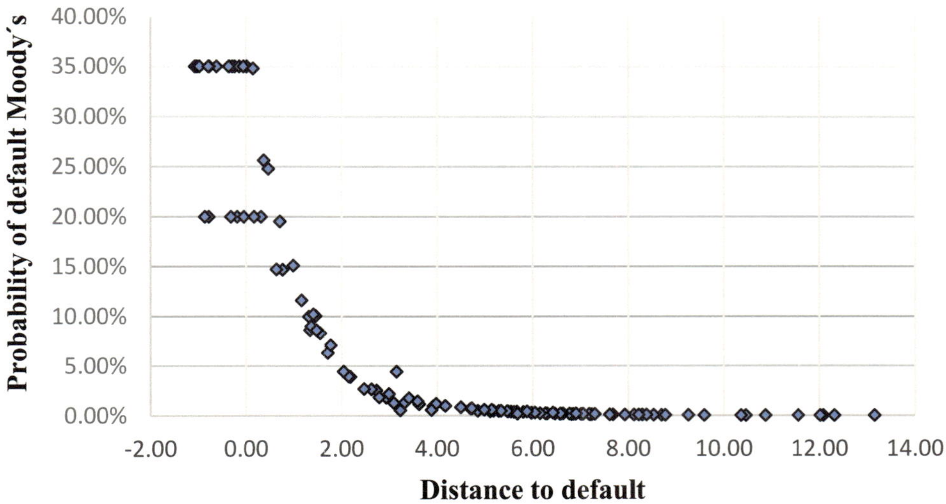

Figure 13. Functionality between distance to default and Moody's probability of default.

Figure 13 shows two areas of anomalies. The first is the area around the probability of defaults at 20%. It is obvious that the negative dependence of distance from defaults and their probability is not ensured. The following conclusions can also be drawn from **Figure 13**:

- The Moody's model assigns probability of default at the level of 35% for defaulted companies and companies with high degree of business risk. Higher values were not even observed in this the model.
- With increasing value of distance to default, its probability decreases exponentially.
- For companies with low degree of business risk and good financial stability, the model assigns a probability of 0.02%. The lower values were not observed for this set of data.

We used these findings to calibrate our own approach to determine the probability of default. In the case of companies that have lower market value of assets than the default point or if their distance to defaults is negative, we can assume default in the near future. Such companies therefore should not be able to meet their obligations and the owners of the capital would thus not apply the purchase option that was written out on the assets of such company. We will associate these companies with the probability of default at 35%. On the contrary, those with a very good financial position, financial stability with a low degree of creditor risk assigned probability at 0.02%. The probability of default for other companies moves between these two extremes of function. Depending on the distance to default based on Moody's (EDF_M) data, the probability of default is described by the following exponential function:

$$EDF_M = 0.1797\, e^{-0.652*DD} \tag{1}$$

The selected functional relationship showed the determination index at 0.9683. The synthesis of the acquired knowledge has determined the resulting function describing the relationship between EDF_M as follows:

$$EDF_M = \begin{cases} 35\% & pre\ DD \leq 0 \\ 0.1797\, e^{-0.652*DD} & pre\ DD > 0 \end{cases} \quad (2)$$

At the same time, $EDF_M \in \langle 0.02\%; 35\% \rangle$. EDF_M expressed in this way, defines the probability of default in a risk-neutral environment. **Figure 14** compares the probability of a default calculated on the base of normal distribution with the probability of default on the base of Eq. (2).

Based on **Figure 14**, we can say that the probability of default—EDF_M calculated with the use of relationship differs from EDF with normal distribution. This is particularly the case for companies with a very low distance to default values. In this extreme, EDF_M values are systematically overestimated. With the increase in distance to default, the opposite situation occurs, and thus the systematic underestimation of probability of default for the normal distribution. For companies with high values of distance to default, these differences are negligible. EDF with normal distribution is asymptotically approaching zero and EDF_M has a minimum of 2%.

Quantification of the probability of default with the use of KMV model takes several forms [10]. Basic and generally known works with a normal distribution of distance to default. However, empirical studies show that this distance varies depending on the probability of default, taking into account several different factors like business sector, its geographical situation as well as other relevant factors. The calibrated relationship between these two variables offered different results in comparison with other models presented in this paper as we can see in **Figure 15**:

To offer better overview, we offer only comparison of default probability for 2 years. From the results, we can see that modeled probabilities of default have an expected progression. During these two curves, there should be two intersections at specific points as we can see in **Figure 15**.

In practice, credit ratings established by renowned agencies are the most commonly used, because they offer sufficient reporting ability in terms of the financial stability of the analyzed companies. However, most of these ratings are in the form of paid service. Moody's officially

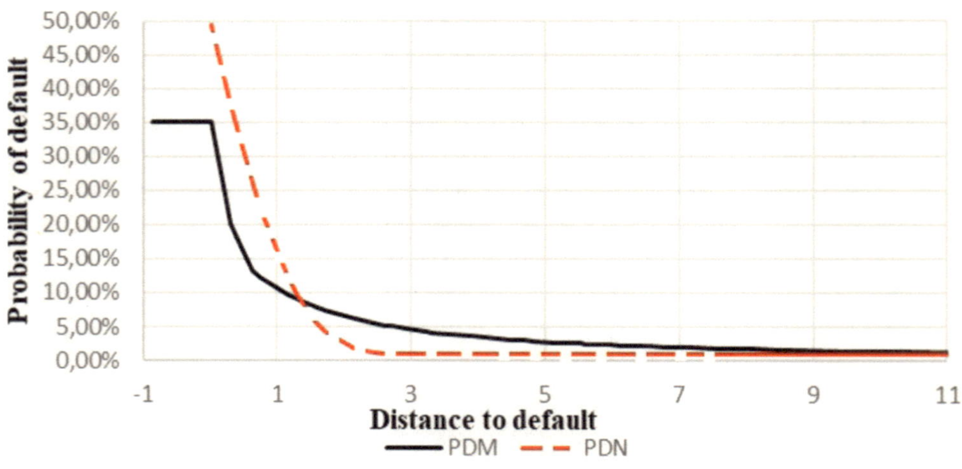

Figure 14. Comparison of functionalities between distance to default and probability of default for normal and calculated distribution.

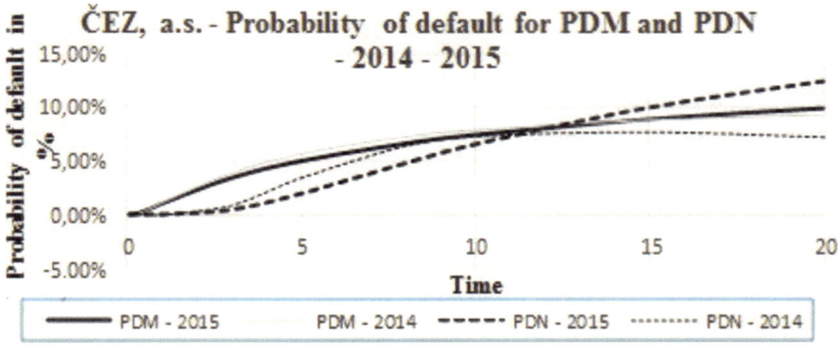

Figure 15. Comparison of probabilities of default with normal and calculated distribution for ČEZ, a.s.

assigns ČEZ, a.s. rating at Baa1 level. The 1-year probability of default level is 1.18%. This value is in the group also assigned by RMA study to this rating as we can see in **Table 2**. Therefore, we can say that our approach to probability of default is relatively close to that one of Moody's agency, also more we would need more data to verify this even further.

EDF_M	**Moody's rating scale**
0.00–0.27%	Aaa
0.28–0.39%	Aa1
0.40–0.49%	Aa2
0.50–0.57%	Aa3
0.58–0.60%	A1
0.61–0.68%	A2
0.69–1.04%	A3
1.05–1.38%	Baa1
1.39–2.08%	Baa2
2.09–4.34%	Baa3
4.35–6.55%	Ba1
6.56–10.20%	Ba2
10.21–14.77%	Ba3
14.78–17.49%	B1
17.50–21.51%	B2
21.52–26.00%	B3
>26.00%/	Caa1

Table 2. Relationship between EDF_M and Moody's rating scale.

7. Conclusion

Despite the fact that numerous models for credit risk quantification have been developed, they differ not only in the way of their construction but also in the amount of input data, in the difficulty of their calculation, and also in the complexity of their usage. In this chapter, we focused on the structural models of credit risk introducing basic concepts of risk-neutral world, as well as models and different options for credit risk quantification. Furthermore, we have tested selected structural models namely Merton model, KMV model, Black-Cox model, and Credit Grades model under the conditions of local emerging market—Slovakia. These calculations were provided on the company data of the ČEZ Group, which is the largest energy group operating in Central and Southeastern Europe. Besides the headquarters in Bohemia, it has its representation in most of the countries in the region, including Slovakia.

The main goal of the chapter was to adjust credit risk model to real market data. Calculation of default curves of ČEZ, a.s. has shown similar pattern in all models. However, the predicted probability values differ considerably. On the other side, the Credit Grades model generated interesting types of curves. Within a short horizon of up to 1 year, the company is virtually safe for all applied models, but in the long run, the forecasts vary considerably from 5 to 33%. This is given by the different design and also by the ability of models to sensitively react to changes in the input parameters in such a long horizon.

Similarly, to default curves also credit spreads generated by each model have similar patterns in all cases. Over a longer period at higher probability of defaults, the pattern tends to show negative spreads. Therefore, it is advisable to apply this model to predictions with a shorter time period. Another weakness in all models is low value of spreads in short time horizons within 1 year. Highest credit spreads are generated by Credit Grades model.

Since one of the most criticized assumptions of Merton model, is the assumption of a normal distribution of distance from defaults, we have decided to leave this assumption and to find a suitable functional relationship between the distance to default and its probability. Based on the collected data, we have calculated distance to default and found out interesting findings. In practice, credit ratings established by renowned agencies are the most commonly used, because they offer sufficient reporting ability in terms of the financial stability of the analyzed companies. Moody's official assigns ČEZ, a.s. rating at Baa1 level. The one-year probability of default level is 1.18%. This value is in the group also assigned by RMA study to this rating.

Therefore, we can summarize that our approach to probability of default is relatively close to that one of Moody's agency, also more we would need more data to verify this even further, but can be successfully applied in the condition of emerging markets.

Acknowledgements

The contribution is an output of the scientific project VEGA 1/0428/17: Creation of New Paradigms of Financial Management at the Threshold of the 21st Century in Conditions of the Slovak Republic.

Author details

Maria Kovacova* and Boris Kollar

*Address all correspondence to: maria.misankova@fpedas.uniza.sk

Department of Economics, Faculty of Operation and Economics of Transport and Communications, University of Zilina, Zilina, Slovak Republic

References

[1] Black F, Scholes M. The pricing of options and corporate liabilities. Journal of Political Economy. 1973;**81**(3):637-654

[2] Jones EP, Mason SP, Rosenfeld E. Contingent claim analysis of corporate capital structures—An empirical investigation. Journal of Finance. červenec 1984, ročník **39**(č.3):s. 611-s. 625. ISSN: 00-22-10-82

[3] Geske R. The valuation of corporate liabilities as compound options. Journal of Financial and Quantitative Analysis. listopad 1977. ročník **12**(č.4):s. 541-s. 552. ISSN: 00-22-10-90

[4] Merton R. On the pricing of corporate debt: The risk structure of interest rates. Journal of Finance. 1974:str. 449-470

[5] Black F, Cox JC. Valuing corporate securities – Some effects of bond indebture provisions. Journal of Finance. 1976;**31**(č. 3):s. 351-s. 367

[6] Cisko Š, Klieštik T. Finančný manažment podniku II. (1st ed., p. 769). Žilina: EDIS Publishers. 2013, ISBN 978-80-554-0684-8

[7] Zmeškal Z, Dluhošová D, Tichý T. Finanční modely – Koncepty, metody, aplikace. Praha: Ekopress. 2013, ISBN 978-80-86929-91-0

[8] Credit Grades – Technical Document: Risk Metrics. 2002. Available on the Internet: http://www.creditrisk.ru/publications/files_attached/cgtechdoc.pdf

[9] Where credit is due: A new study ranks the credit strength of America's top 100 debt issuers. CFO Magazine., November, 2003. Available on the internet: http://www.treas.gov/offices/domestic-finance/debt-management/interest-rate/yield.shtml

[10] Vašíček OA. Credit Valuation. Working Paper, KMV, 1984

Section 3

Mergers and Acquisitions and Corporate Governance

Chapter 7

A Comparative Abnormal Return Analysis of Mergers and Acquisitions in the Emerging Markets

İrem Sevindik and Fazıl Gökgöz

Additional information is available at the end of the chapter

http://dx.doi.org/10.5772/intechopen.71821

Abstract

Financial crisis originated in developed countries in 2008 and has affected M&A activities worldwide. This impact may have irreversible results in emerging market economies. This study aims to examine the spillover effects of 2008 economic crisis, started in developed countries, in emerging markets. In this manner, we have analyzed M&A activities from the acquirer firms' side in BRICS-T countries (namely, Brazil, Russia, India, China, South Africa, and Turkey) for banking industries in pre-and postcrisis periods so that effects of economic crisis can be captured. Significant transactions over $100 million are included in the analysis. Event study methodology, which uses daily market index returns, daily stock returns, and M&A announcement dates to calculate abnormal returns, is employed for the analysis. The cumulative abnormal returns (CARs) are calculated for September 2003–November 2008 (precrisis period) and November 2008–December 2013 (postcrisis) periods. In conclusion there are negative mean CARs in Brazil, India, and Russia, while there are positive mean CARs in China, South Africa, and Turkey in precrisis period. In addition, there are negative mean CARs in South Africa, Brazil, and China, while there are positive mean CARs in Russia, Turkey, and India in *postcrisis* period.

Keywords: mergers and acquisitions, abnormal return analysis, financial crisis, BRICS, Turkey

1. Introduction

Economic activities both inside and outside of a country have direct effects on the firms operating in that country. Furthermore, firm-specific activities such as mergers & acquisitions (M&As), declaring loss, an important exports deal have positive or negative effect on the firms' market value according to the nature of the event.

Aim of the study is to investigate how economic crisis originated in developed countries have affected developing economies. Therefore, we examined the mergers & acquisitions activities of banking sector in BRICS-T countries. Lehman Brothers' crash in September 2008 is assumed to be the trigger of the global financial crisis [1]. With this reasoning, we analyzed cumulative abnormal returns in precrisis (January 2004–September 2008) and postcrisis (November 2008–December 2013) periods to check if there are any differences between these periods. Brazil has negative mean cumulative abnormal returns in pre crisis period as well as the post crisis period. Russia has negative mean cumulative abnormal returns in precrisis period while mean cumulative abnormal returns for Russia are positive in postcrisis period. India has negative mean cumulative abnormal returns in precrisis period, which switches to positive in postcrisis period. China, in the opposite, has positive mean cumulative abnormal returns before crisis but negative mean cumulative abnormal returns after crisis. The mean cumulative abnormal returns in South Africa are positive in the precrisis period and negative in the post crisis period. Turkey has positive mean cumulative abnormal returns in both periods.

Section 2 introduces a literature review about M&As in BRICS-T countries in three different parts. First, literature about M&As during financial crisis is mentioned. Then, literature on abnormal returns in M&As during financial crisis is examined. Finally, financial overview of BRICS-T countries is investigated and shared. In Section 3, data and methodology are mentioned as well as the empirical results. The study is concluded with Section 4.

2. Literature review

Literature reviews has three sub-parts. In first section, M&As during financial crisis, particularly recent financial crisis, are mentioned. In second section, abnormal returns in cross-border M&As during financial crisis are investigated. In final section, there is a summary of financial overview of BRICS-T countries.

2.1. Mergers and acquisitions during financial crisis

It has been argued that M&As[1] are closely related to the stock markets' welfare. [2] suggests that M&A activities are not closely related to the business cycle but the state of the economy. In other words, if economy is in a good condition, stock markets have desired conditions for the firms to raise capital and grow their profitability [3]. On the other hand, in the opposite situation, that is, if economy is in a narrow condition, firms tend to be more conservative about M&A.

M&As are assumed to be a way of foreign direct investment[2] (FDI) and they follow a wave path due to economic state [4]. M&A wave between 2003 and 2007 (precrisis period) indicated that cross-border M&As had increased compared to the recession periods. Especially in 2005, there had been a number of FDI flows to the developed countries, and the quantity and the

[1]M&A is a way of economic growth strategies by combining or consolidating of companies.

[2]FDI is a company's investment to another company operating in a different country.

value of M&As were the highest since 2000 [4]. In 2006, M&A activities started to rise in emerging countries. Until the second half of 2007, M&As continued increasing but after that they started to fall and got even worse in the first half of 2008 compared to 2007 [4].

Collapse of Lehman Brothers is assumed to be the trigger of financial crisis in September 2008 [1]. Hence, economic crisis caused a drastic fall in M&As.

On the other hand, according to [5], financial crisis originated in developed countries in 2008 did not have the same large impact on emerging economies. The crisis emerged in United States, spread immediately to Europe but it only affected the specific regions and countries so harsh.

While some banks utilized M&A as an expansion strategy, some banks used it into their advantage during crisis. Banks in emerging economies such as China, Brazil and Russia acquired undervalued banks in developed countries as their prices in the stock markets fell [3]. Banks that are in healthy conditions in terms of capital and liquidity took the advantage of increasing their market share through M&As [6].

2.2. Abnormal returns of cross-border M&As during financial crisis

There is a broad literature about generating abnormal returns[3] through M&As. However, there are not many studies in investigating the abnormal returns during 2007–2008 crisis. In addition, the results of the studies are mixed.

The research that does not include 2008 crisis is as follows. [7] examined 507 cross-border M&As between 1985 and 1998. They found negative and significant abnormal returns. In another study, [8] investigated cross-border M&A activities of 15 international banks between 1982 and 1987. They concluded that there had been negative and significant abnormal returns. In a single country study, [9] investigated M&As in U.S. between 1989 and 1999. He found that U.S. targets earn significantly positive abnormal returns while U.S. bidders' wealth gains are insignificant. In another research conducted in the U.S., [10] used the data for bank-holding companies in United States between 1980 and 1990 in order to determine abnormal returns. Results revealed significantly negative abnormal returns. On the other hand, [11] found that there had been significant positive returns using 216 large publicly traded U.S. bank M&As between 1987 and 1999. In a cross-border study, [12] employed 73 cross-border banks M&As (from advanced economies to emerging economies) between 1998 and 2005. They found significant and positive abnormal returns. In Europe, [13] achieved the existence of positive abnormal returns for the shareholders of target banks cross-border M&As between 1989 and 1996. In another study in Europe, [14] found positive abnormal returns using the data from European banks between 1988 and 1997. [15] gathered the data for 98 large M&As in Europe between 1985 and 2000. They found that domestic M&As created positive returns. [16] suggested that value created would be larger if the target firm was in advanced economy using 425 cross-border M&As in India between 2000 and 2007.

[3] Abnormal return is the return on a security that is different from the expected return.

In order to investigate the effects of Asian crisis, [17] used a data of nine emerging countries namely Argentina, Brazil, Chile, Indonesia, Philippines, South Korea, and Thailand between 1988 and 2002. They concluded that acquirer firms show no significant difference in abnormal returns pre and postcrisis periods. On the other hand, [18] studied the M&As in eight East Asian countries between 1997 and 2003 in order to determine market reaction to M&As during Asian crisis. Their results showed that market reaction was negative in Indonesia, Malaysia, the Philippines, South Korea, and Thailand where the bank structure was less well settled.

The results of the studies that investigate the effects of 2008 crisis are mixed. [19] utilized the M&A data in Europe between 2007 and 2010 to evaluate whether M&A differed in crisis period. They concluded that there were insignificant abnormal returns on the event date. On the other hand, abnormal returns were generated positively at the completions. However, [20] used 80 M&As in UK, USA, Canada, Germany, Japan, and France between 1999 and 2009 to determine stock returns of bidder firms. Abnormal returns precrisis and postcrisis period was not significantly different from zero. In another research, [3] examined 883 cross-border M&A deals in banking sector between 2004 and 2012. They concluded that only in M&As from emerging countries targeting developed countries, returns of the shareholders were significantly positive after the crisis. Finally, [21] gathered the M&A data for 20 emerging countries namely BRICS-T countries and Chile, Colombia, Czech Republic, Egypt, Hungary, Indonesia, Malaysia, Mexico, Morocco, Peru, Philippines, Poland, Taiwan and Thailand between 1997 and 2013. They concluded that M&As created positive abnormal returns. In addition, they found out that abnormal returns had increased after crisis for target firm's stock.

In conclusion, results of the studies are mixed and they change according to the period.

2.3. Financial overview of BRICS-T countries in precrisis and postcrisis periods

In previous sections, it has been mentioned that there exists M&A waves. According to [22], there had been six M&A waves before the 2008 crisis, which are 1887–1907, 1919–1933, 1955–1975, 1980–1989, 1992–2002, and finally 2003–2007.

Table 1 shows the quantity and transaction value of cross-border M&As in BRICS-T countries between 2002 and 2016 [23]. In Brazil, cross-border M&As have value of $17 billion in 2003. It increased by 65% in 2004 and reached to $26 billion. In 2005, there is a decrease by 58% and the value is $15 billion. Then in 2006, there is a jump in the value and it has reached to $74 billion. In 2007, there is a fall by 72% in value. M&As have the peak value in 2008 during the precrisis period. There is a drastic fall in value in 2009 due to crisis. In 2010, M&As have the peak value in postcrisis period. It started declining afterwards. In Russia, the value of cross-border M&As is $35 billion in 2003, and in 2004, the value has declined by 72%. In 2005, the value has jumped to $63 billion and during the precrisis period, M&As have the peak value in 2007. In 2008, the value has decreased by 52% and in 2009 the decrease is 43%. Then, the value has been tripled in 2010. Cross-border M&As have their peak value in 2012 in postcrisis period. In India and China, cross-border M&As have the peak value in 2007 in precrisis period and in 2010 in postcrisis period. In India, there is a jump in cross-border M&A value in 2005 (4.5 times higher than 2004), and in China, there is a high increase in 2005 as well (6.25 times higher than 2004).

http://dx.doi.org/10.5772/intechopen.71821

	Brazil		Russia		India		China		South Africa		Turkey	
	Quantity	Value	Quantity	Value	Quantity	Value	Quantity	Value	Quantity	Value	Quantity	Value
1992–2002	2627	213	1942	35	n/a	n/a	410	9	3541	140	587	11
1999–2002					2578	29						
2003	209	17	488	35	706	6	53	2	260	11	82	1
2004	269	26	398	25	762	8	101	4	241	27	64	3
2005	269	15	468	63	1251	36	96	25	244	16	120	31
2006	373	74	654	52	1446	34	117	14	338	28	167	21
2007	857	53	966	159	1504	56	210	40	289	34	238	23
2008	932	105	1718	82	1400	49	204	21	436	26	267	19
2009	497	71	3285	36	1293	41	245	48	369	33	183	7
2010	689	160	3684	109	1328	60	288	53	370	27	245	23
2011	816	93	3211	88	1042	35	266	46	356	21	269	13
2012	801	69	2532	115	1070	37	261	38	382	16	321	24
2013	612	69	2021	67	955	32	264	48	333	11	364	19
2014	559	56	1915	18	1084	31	302	44	402	20	363	16
2015	669	50	1819	32	1241	51	475	68	448	45	345	18
2016	613	45	1819	40	1271	49	671	132	418	22	226	7

Table 1. Quantity and Transaction Value of Cross-border M&As in BRICS-T Countries between 1992 and 2016 (value in billion dollars).

In South Africa, values of M&As follow an increasing pattern until 2007. M&As have their peak value in 2007 in precrisis period and in 2009 in postcrisis period. Finally, in Turkey, M&As have their peak value in 2005 in precrisis period and 2012 in postcrisis period.

3. Empirical study

In this part, first, data, methodology, and the hypothesis are explained. Then empirical results are represented.

3.1. Data, methodology, and hypothesis

Our study uses daily market index returns, daily stock returns, and M&A announcement dates (event date) between January 2003–September 2008 and November 2008 and December 2013. We utilize the data from Bloomberg database for cross-border bank M&A activities in Brazil, Russia, India, China, South Africa, and Turkey. Our data consists of cross-border M&As with a transaction value over $100 million.

Event study is employed for the analysis. Event studies aim to determine whether there are abnormal returns around the date an event is announced to the market. Abnormal returns are the returns that are less or more than normal returns when the related event is announced. These returns are usually related with the performance of the market index returns [24, 25]. The event is the M&A announcement date. There could be different event windows, which include the announcement date. In this study, we investigate abnormal returns for different event window lengths:

- Two days before and two days after the event date (−2, +2)
- A day before and a day after the event date (−1, +1)
- The event day and a day after the event date (0, +1)

We choose market model in order to estimate market α[4] and β[5] over a prediction period, which is 128 days prior to and 9 days prior to event date, that is, (−128, −9). The market model is as follows:

$$R_{it} = \alpha_i + \beta_i R_{mt} + e_{it} \tag{1}$$

R_{it} stands for the return of the ith security at time t and R_{mt} denotes the return of the market at time t.

Then, abnormal return (AR) is calculated using predicted $\alpha_i and\ \beta_i$:

$$AR_{it} = R_{it} - \widehat{\alpha_i} - \widehat{\beta_i} R_{mt} \tag{2}$$

AR_{it} represents abnormal return for the ith bank at time t and R_{it} is the actual return on bank i.

Later, average aggregate abnormal return (AAR) is calculated:

$$AAR_t = \frac{1}{N}\sum_{i=1}^{N} AR_{it} \tag{3}$$

After that, by adding daily abnormal returns up, cumulative abnormal returns are obtained:

$$CAR_{i(T_1-T_2)} = \sum_{t=T_1}^{T_2} AR_{it} \tag{4}$$

Here, CAR_i is the cumulative abnormal return for bank i over the event window T_1 and T_2.

Finally, average aggregate cumulative abnormal return is calculated (AACAR):

$$ACAR(T_1, T_2) = \frac{1}{N}\sum_{i=1}^{N} CAR_i(T_1, T_2) \tag{5}$$

and (T_1, T_2) are (0, +1), (−1, +1), and (−2, +2).

---

[4]Return on security when the expected return on market is zero.

[5]Responsiveness of a security to the market return.

3.2. Empirical results

This section introduces the empirical results. First, abnormal returns for the entire period are shown without separating the before/after crisis periods in Section 3.2.1. Then, abnormal returns for pre / post crisis periods are given in Sections 3.2.2 and 3.2.3, respectively.

3.2.1. Aggregate daily abnormal returns

This part introduces the aggregate results, which means that abnormal returns of the M&A activities are included to the analysis without considering pre- and post-crisis periods. A total of 36 banks with M&A transaction values over $100 million are taken into consideration.

Table 2 shows average aggregate daily abnormal returns two days before after the event date. The AARs before and on the announcement date are negative and significant at 5% while AARs are positive and significant at 5% significance level. The AARs increase through the event window. In other words, the AAR two days before the event day is −0.043, it is −0.040 on the day before the event day, and it is larger but still negative on the event day. One day after the event day, the AAR reaches to the largest value. There are excess returns on the M&As. On the second day, AAR decreases again.

Table 3 shows aggregate CARs for the related event window. In 5-day event window (−2, +2), CAR is −0.042, and it is statistically significant at 5%. Then, in 3-day event window (−1, +1), CAR increases to −0.018, and this value is statistically significant at 5%. Finally, in 2-day event window, CAR increases to −0.007, and it is statistically significant at 5%.

Event day[1]	Average abnormal returns (%) (AAR)
−2	−0.043
−1	−0.040
0	−0.029
1	0.022
2	0.001

[1]M&A announcement day.

Table 2. AARs for the Related Event Associated with M&A Activities.

Event window[1]	Average CAR (%)
−2, +2	−0.042
−1, +1	−0.018
0, +1	−0.007

[1]Time period that includes several days prior and after the event.

Table 3. CARs for the Related Event Windows Associated with M&A Activities.

Table 4 shows the distribution of 5-day CARs. The results show that there are negative abnormal returns in Brazil and Russia, while there are positive cumulative abnormal returns in China, India, South Africa, and Turkey. The results are significant at 5% significance level. In terms of 5-day CARs, Brazil has the lowest CAR among other countries, and it is followed by Russia. Although, there is positive CAR in India, South Africa, Turkey, and China have more CAR than India. CARs in South Africa and Turkey are very close. China has the largest CAR among these countries in 5-day event window.

Table 5 shows the distribution of 3-day CARs. Brazil, Russia, and India have negative CARs while China, South Africa, and Turkey have positive CARs. The results are significant at 5% significance level. In 3-day event window, Brazil has the least CAR among other countries and it is followed by India and Russia. While India has slightly positive CAR in 5-day event window, it has negative CAR in 3-day event window. South Africa and Turkey have positive CAR in 3-day event window as well as the 5-day event window. Turkey has the largest CAR among other countries in 3-day event window.

Table 6 shows the distribution of 2-day CARs. Brazil, Russia, and India have negative CARs while China, South Africa, and Turkey have positive CARs. The results are significant at 5% significance level. In 2-day event window, Brazil has the least CAR and it is followed by Russia and India. Turkey has the largest CAR among other countries in 2-day event window as well as 2-day event window.

Table 7 shows the distribution of mean CARs. On an average, Brazil, India, and Russia have negative cumulative abnormal returns and China, South Africa, and Turkey have positive

Name of the country	CAR (−2, +2) (%)
Brazil	−0.287
China	0.017
India	0.001
Russia	−0.006
South Africa	0.013
Turkey	0.014

Table 4. Distribution of 5-day CARs (−2, +2) in BRICS-T countries.

Name of the country	CAR (−1, +1) (%)
Brazil	−0.129
China	0.007
India	−0.012
Russia	−0.011
South Africa	0.012
Turkey	0.026

Table 5. Distribution of 3-day CARs (−1, +1) in BRICS-T countries.

http://dx.doi.org/10.5772/intechopen.71821

cumulative abnormal returns between 2003 and 2013 for banking industry. The results are significant at 5% significance level.

3.2.2. *Daily abnormal returns in precrisis period*

This section introduces the abnormal return analysis results of M&As in banking sector during the pre-crisis period, that is, between September 2003 and November 2008. In this manner, 22 banks M&As with a M&A transaction value more than $100 million have been investigated.

Table 8 shows AARs for pre-crisis period. There are negative AARs before and on the event date. However, there are positive abnormal returns after the announcement date. The results

Name of the country	CAR (0, +1) (%)
Brazil	−0.071
China	0.011
India	−0.009
Russia	−0.015
South Africa	0.014
Turkey	0.026

Table 6. Distribution of 2-day CARs (0, +1) in BRICS-T countries.

Name of the country	Mean CAR (%)
Brazil	−0.162
China	0.012
India	−0.007
Russia	−0.011
South Africa	0.013
Turkey	0.022

Table 7. Distribution of mean CARs in BRICS-T countries.

Event day	Average abnormal returns (%)
−2	−0.057
−1	−0.051
0	−0.037
1	0.032
2	0.004

Table 8. AARs for the Related Event Windows Related to M&A Activities Before Crisis (2003-2008/9).

are significant at 5% significance level. Two days before the announcement day AAR is −0.057 and 1 day before the event day it increases to −0.051. On the announcement day, AAR increases to −0.037 and 1 day after the event day, it turns to positive and has its peak value. In other words, the AARs follow an increasing path until 1 day after the announcement day. Two days after the announcement date, it decreases but it is still positive. This figure is very similar to the aggregate case in Section 3.2.1.

Table 9 shows CARs for 5-day, 3-day, and 2-day event windows. There are negative cumulative abnormal returns in precrisis period. The values tend to increase as the event window gets narrower to the event date. The results are significant at 5% significance level.

Table 10 shows 5-day CARs in BRICS-T countries. In Brazil, India, and Russia, CARs are negative and significant at 5% level. In China, South Africa, and Turkey, CARs are positive and significant at 5% level. Brazil has the least CAR and it is followed by India and Russia in 5-day event window. China has the largest CAR in 5-day event window in precrisis period and it is followed by South Africa and Turkey. Note that Turkey had the largest CAR in the aggregate case.

Table 11 shows the distribution of 3-day cumulative abnormal returns in BRICS-T countries in precrisis period. In Brazil, India, and Russia, CARs are negative and significant at 5% level. In China, South Africa, and Turkey, cumulative abnormal returns are positive and significant at 5% level. Brazil has the least CAR in 3-day event window during the precrisis period. However, the CAR value has increased with respect to 5-day event window. Russia and India follow Brazil and their CAR values have decreased compared to 5-day event window. China still has the largest CAR but the values have decreased in 3-day event window. CARs in South Africa and Turkey have increased in 3-day event window

Event window	Average CAR (%)
−2, +2	−0.053
−1, +1	−0.019
0, +1	−0.006

Table 9. CARs for the Related Event Windows in Response to M&A Activities Before Crisis (2003-2008/9).

Name of the country	CAR (−2, +2) (%)
Brazil	−0.368
China	0.064
India	−0.025
Russia	−0.039
South Africa	0.041
Turkey	0,009

Table 10. Distribution of 5-day CARs (−2, +2) in BRICS-T countries before crises (2003–2008/2009).

Table 12 shows the distribution of CARs in two-day event window. Brazil, India, and Russia have negative abnormal returns while China, South Africa, and Turkey have positive abnormal returns. The results are significant at 5% significance level. Brazil has the least CAR in 2-day event window. This value of CAR in 2-day event window is larger than the value of CAR in 3-day event window. CAR for Russia in 2-day event window is less than CAR in 3-day event window and CAR for India in 3-day event window is larger than CAR in 2-day event window. China still has the largest CAR in 2-day event window and the value has increased compared to the 3-day event window. CAR in South Africa has increased while CAR in Turkey has decreased in 2-day event window with respect to 3-day event window.

Table 13 shows the distribution of mean CARs in BRICS-T countries for precrisis period. Accordingly, Brazil, India, and Russia generates negative and statistically significant abnormal

Name of the country	CAR (−1, +1) (%)
Brazil	−0.157
China	0.057
India	−0.035
Russia	−0.044
South Africa	0.047
Turkey	0.018

Table 11. Distribution of 3-day CARs (−1, +1) in BRICS-T countries before crises (2003–2008/2009).

Name of the country	CAR (0, +1) (%)
Brazil	−0.077
China	0.067
India	−0.026
Russia	−0.061
South Africa	0.051
Turkey	0.013

Table 12. Distribution of 2-day CARs (0, +1) in BRICS-T countries before crises (2003–2008/2009).

Name of the country	Mean CAR (%)
Brazil	−0.201
China	0.062
India	−0.029
Russia	−0.048
South Africa	0.046
Turkey	0.014

Table 13. Distribution of mean CARs in BRICS-T countries before crises (2003–2008/2009).

returns while China, South Africa, and Turkey obtains positive cumulative abnormal returns between September 2003 and September 2008 for banking industry for M&A transactions with a value more than $100 million. Brazil has the least mean CAR and it is followed by Russia and India while China has the largest mean CAR and South Africa and Turkey follow it.

3.2.3. *Daily abnormal returns in postcrisis period*

This section introduces abnormal returns in M&As in the banking industry during the postcrisis period, that is, between November 2008 and December 2013. In this manner, 14 bank M&As with a M&A transaction value more than $100 million have been investigated.

Table 14 shows the AARs for the related event window in postcrisis period. Two days before the announcement date, AAR is positive; 1 day before the announcement date AARs is negative; and on the event date, AAR is positive. One-day and 2-day after the event date, AARs are slightly negative. The results are significant at 5% significance level.

Table 15 shows CARs for the related event windows in postcrisis period. In 5-day event window, CAR is positive and in 3-day and 2-day event windows cumulative abnormal returns are negative. Average CAR has the largest value in 5-day event window, the least value in 3-day event window. The results are significant at 5% significance level.

Table 16 shows distribution of the 5-day CARs in BRICS-T countries in postcrisis period. Brazil has the least CAR among other countries. South Africa and China follow Brazil. Note that South Africa had positive CAR in precrisis period. Russia has the largest CAR and it is followed by

Event day	Average abnormal returns (%)
−2	0.002
−1	−0.002
0	0.001
1	−0.001
2	−0.001

Table 14. AAR for the Related Event Windows in Response to M&A Activities After Crisis (2008/11-2013).

Event window	Average CAR (%)
−2, +2	0.002
−1, +1	−0.004
0, +1	−0.001

Table 15. CARs for the Related Event Windows in Response to M&A Activities After Crisis (2008/11-2013).

http://dx.doi.org/10.5772/intechopen.71821

India and Turkey. Another remarkable points are that India had negative CAR in precrisis period and China had the largest positive CAR in precrisis period

Table 17 shows the distribution of 3-day CARs in BRICS-T countries in postcrisis period. South Africa now has the least CAR among other countries in 3-day event window. CAR value in Brazil does not change compared to the 5-day CAR but the CAR value in South Africa has decreased. CAR values in China and India have also decreased while CAR in Turkey has increased. Russia has the largest CAR among other countries and the value has increased.

Table 18 shows the 2-day CARs in BRICS-T countries during postcrisis period. The figure is similar to the 3-day CAR case. South Africa has the least CAR and its value has not changed.

Name of the country	CAR (−2, +2) (%)
Brazil	−0.045
China	−0.007
India	0.026
Russia	0.050
South Africa	−0.044
Turkey	0.019

Table 16. Distribution of 5-day CARs (−2, +2) in BRICS-T countries after crises (2008/2011–2013).

Name of the country	CAR (−1, +1) (%)
Brazil	−0.045
China	−0.018
India	0.010
Russia	0.055
South Africa	−0.059
Turkey	0.036

Table 17. Distribution of three-day CARs (−1, +1) in BRICS-T countries after crises (2008/2011–2013).

Name of the country	CAR (0, +1) (%)
Brazil	−0.052
China	−0.017
India	0.008
Russia	0.076
South Africa	−0.059
Turkey	0.042

Table 18. Distribution of 2-day CARs (0, +1) in BRICS-T countries after crises (2008/2011–2013).

Name of the country	Mean CAR (%)
Brazil	−0.047
China	−0.014
India	0.015
Russia	0.063
South Africa	−0.054
Turkey	0.032

Table 19. Distribution of mean CARs in BRICS-T countries after crises (2008/2011–2013).

The CAR value in China has increased slightly. CARs in India have decreased while the CARs in Russia and Turkey have increased.

Table 19 shows the distribution of mean CARs in BRICS-T countries in postcrisis period for M&A transactions with a value more than $100 million. Brazil, China, and South Africa have negative and statistically significant mean CARs while India, Russia, and Turkey have positive and statistically significant mean CARs. South Africa has the least mean CAR and Brazil and China follow it. Russia has the largest CAR and Turkey and India follow Russia.

4. Conclusion

Economic activities have direct impact on firms operating in a country and M&A activities have a close relationship with the economic welfare. If stock markets have desired conditions, there are more M&A activities. When there is an economic recession, firms are more conservative about M&A activities.

Although many researchers have worked on the abnormal returns during M&As, there are only a few studies on capturing abnormal returns of M&As during financial crisis. In this manner, we investigate M&A activities with a transaction value more than $100 million in banking industry in BRICS-T countries before and after the financial crisis in 2008. Studies have shown that positive abnormal returns are generated after 2008 crisis in the emerging markets [3, 21].

According to our results, in precrisis period, Brazil has the least mean CAR with a value −0.201 among BRICS-T countries. Russia and India follow Brazil with CAR values −0.048 and −0.029, respectively. China has the largest mean CAR value, that is, 0.062. South Africa and Turkey follow Russia with mean CARs 0.046 and 0.014, respectively. In postcrisis period, now, South Africa has the least mean CAR among BRICS-T countries. Note that mean CAR in South Africa is positive before crisis and it is negative after crisis. Brazil still has negative mean CAR in postcrisis period with an increased value compared to precrisis period. China has negative mean CAR value, which is −0.014 in post crisis period. Mean CAR in China is positive in precrisis period and it is negative in postcrisis period and this figure is similar to South Africa case. Russia has the largest and positive mean CAR in postcrisis period. The value of mean CAR in Russia is negative in precrisis period and it is positive in postcrisis period with a value 0.063. India has positive mean CAR in postcrisis period with a value 0.015, while it is negative in precrisis period. Mean CAR in Turkey remains positive mean in postcrisis period and the value is increased to 0.032. In conclusion, Russia has negative mean CAR in precrisis period while mean CAR for Russia is positive in postcrisis period. This result is compatible with [3, 21]. India has negative mean CAR in precrisis period, which switches to positive in postcrisis period, which is compatible with previous research [21]. China, in the opposite, has positive mean CAR in precrisis period but negative mean CAR in postcrisis period. The mean CAR in South Africa is positive in the precrisis period and negative in the post crisis period. These results are in line with the previous research. This is due to the sample and the period differences. Turkey has positive mean cumulative abnormal returns in both pre- and postcrisis periods. Mean CARs are higher in the postcrisis period. This result supports the previous research [21].

In further, we might conclude that 2008 crisis had a significant effect on M&As (over $100 million) in BRICS-T countries. Consequently, abnormal return analysis would give precious results for investigating M&As in the emerging financial markets.

Author details

İrem Sevindik[1]* and Fazıl Gökgöz[2]

*Address all correspondence to: isevindik@baskent.edu.tr

1 Faculty of Economics and Administrative Sciences, Baskent University, Ankara, Turkey

2 Faculty of Political Sciences, Ankara University, Ankara, Turkey

References

[1] Mishkin FS. Over the cliff: From the subprime to the global financial crisis. NBER Working Paper Series, 16609; 2010

[2] Nelson RL. Merger Movements in American Industry, 1895–1956, NBER Books. Princeton: NBER; 1959

[3] Rao-Nicholson R, Salaber J. Impact of the financial crisis on banking acquisitions: A look at shareholder wealth. International Journal of the Economics of Business. 2015;**22**(1):87-117

[4] Burksaitiene D. Cross-border mergers and acquisitions: An analysis of activity. The 6th International Scientific Conference "Business and Management 2010". Selected papers 2010. DOI: 10.3846/bm.2010.005

[5] Rao-Nicholson R, Salaber J. Impact of the financial crisis on cross-border mergers and acquisitions and concentration in the global banking industry. Thunderbird International Business Review. 2015a;**58**(2):161-173. DOI: 10.1002/tie.21731

[6] Berger A, Bouwman C. Bank liquidity creation. The Review of Financial Studies. 2009; **22**:3779-3837

[7] Amihud Y, Lev B, Travlos NG. Corporate control and the choice of investment financing: The case of corporate acquisitions. The Journal of Finance. 1990;**45**:603-616

[8] Cornett MM, Örs E, Tehranian G. Bank performance around the introduction of a section 20 subsidiary. The Journal of Finance. 2002;**57**:501-521

[9] Kiymaz H. Cross-border acquisitions of US Financial Institutions: Impact of macroeconomic factors. Journal of Banking & Finance. 2004;**28**(6):1413-1439

[10] Knapp M, Gart A, Becher D. Post-merger performance of bank-holding companies 1987–1998. Financial Review. 2005;**40**:549-574

[11] DeLong GL, DeYoung R. Learning by observing: Information spillovers in the execution and valuation of commercial bank M&As. The Journal of Finance. 2007;**62**:181-216

[12] Williams J, Liao A. The search for value: Cross-border bank M&A in emerging markets. Comparative Economic Studies. 2008;**50**(2):274-296

[13] Rad AT, Van Beek L. Market valuation of European bank mergers. European Management Journal. 1999;**17**(5):532-540

[14] Cybo-Ottone A, Murgia M. Mergers and shareholder wealth in European banking. Journal of Banking & Finance. 2000;**24**(6):831-859

[15] Beitel P, Schiereck D, Wahrenburg M. Explaining M&a success in European banks. European Financial Management. 2004;**10**(1):109-139

[16] Gubbi SR, Aulakh PS, Ray S, Sarkar MB, Chittoor R. Do International acquisitions by emerging-economy firms create shareholder value: The case of Indian firms. Journal of International Business Studies. 2010;**41**(3):397-418

[17] Chari A, Ouimet P, Tesar L. Acquiring Control in Emerging Markets: Evidence from the Stock Market. Cambridge, MA: National Bureau of Economic Research; 2004

[18] Celine C, Lepetit L, Bautista C. How did the Asian stock markets react to bank mergers after the 1997 financial crisis? Pacific Economic Review. 2008;**13**(2):171-182

[19] Beltratti A, Paladino G. Is M&a different during a crisis? Evidence from the European banking sector. Journal of Banking & Finance. 2013;**37**(12):5394-5405

[20] Amewu G. Implication of mergers and acquisitions on stock returns before and during the 2007–2009 credit crunch: An event study. African Review of Economics and Finance. 2014;**6**(1):102-119

[21] Arık E, Kutan AM. Do mergers and acquisitions create wealth effects? Evidence from twenty emerging markets. Eastern European Economics. 2015;**53**(6):529-550

[22] Kummer C, Steger U. Why merger and acquisition (M&a) waves reoccur: The vicious circle from pressure to failure, strategic. Management Review. 2008;**2**(1):44-63

[23] M&A Statistics by Countries. (n.d.). Available from: https://imaa-institute.org/m-and-a-statistics-countries/ [Accessed: June 15, 2017]

[24] Rao RKS. Financial Management: Concept and Application. 3rd ed. Cincinnati: South-western College Publishing; 1995

[25] Cowan AR. Nonparametric event study tests. Review of Quantitative Finance and Accounting. 1992;**2**(4):343-358

Chapter 8

Corporate Governance and Financial Performance in the Emerging Markets: Do ADRs Perform any Better than Non-Cross-Listed Firms?

Naz Sayari and Bill Marcum

Additional information is available at the end of the chapter

http://dx.doi.org/10.5772/intechopen.72297

Abstract

We investigate the impact governance standards have on financial performance of firms operating across various political and socioeconomic regimes. Specifically, we examine the performance of non-cross-listed emerging market firms that implement corporate governance standards similar to those mandated of firms listed on US exchanges. Using cross-sectional time-series analysis, we find that a more rigorous corporate governance structure is associated with better performance (as measured by return on assets (ROA)) among non-cross-listed firms. Cross-listed firms, whose common stock trades as American Depository Receipts (ADRs) and who are subject to the same listing requirements as domestic US firms, exhibit no evidence of improved performance. We also find that the positive performance effect of improving corporate governance is mitigated among firms with higher market risk (i.e., beta).

Keywords: corporate governance, financial performance, market risk, emerging markets, American depository receipts (ADRs)

1. Introduction

Since the passage of the Sarbanes-Oxley Act (SOX) in 2002 and stiffened restrictions imposed by the US Securities and Exchange Commission in 2003, corporate governance in the US has been significantly strengthened. A substantial amount of research into the impact of these governmental initiatives indicates that American firms have exhibited enhanced board oversight with more effective control systems, reduced their risk taking and experienced an increase in value [1–7]. A number of researchers have also investigated the relationship between these more stringent governance rules and the financial performance of publicly held corporations trading in US markets, as well as the performance of firms operating under a more rigorous governance environment in other developed countries [8–11]. However, the relationship between corporate governance and the performance of firms operating in the emerging markets has drawn little attention [12–15], while the comparison of cross-listed emerging market (EM) firms issuing American Depository Receipts (ADRs), that are required to abide by SEC restrictions, and non-cross-listed EM firms have received even less [16–19]. In this study, we address the governance – performance relationship for cross-listed (ADR) firms trading on US markets and non-cross-listed EM firms. To do this we use the corporate governance score of companies that is provided by the *Bloomberg Professional* database and corporate governance rules mandated by the *New York Stock Exchange* (NYSE) or the *National Association of Securities Dealers Automated Quotations* (NASDAQ) for firms trading on their exchanges; the rules are identified in Section 303A of the NYSE's Listed Company Manual.

Investors have shown an increasing interest in emerging market countries in recent years. Despite the many evident problems associated with political instability, lacking infrastructure and uncertain property rights protections, the latent potential for substantial growth in these untapped markets is clearly present. Both corporate leaders and politicians have begun to signal their recognition that the influx of capital is the key to sustained economic development and growth. To attract this requisite capital in a competitive global economy, more robust corporate governance standards are beginning to evolve; either by government mandate or through self-imposed corporate standards. To examine the impact of enhanced governance standards on corporate performance, we focus on firms operating in countries identified by Bloomberg's 2014 Emerging Market rankings for which there are available data. In this study we apply a two-step Generalized Least Squares (GLS), random effects model and company specific data on a large sample of firms over the 2008–2014 period.

Given that emerging market countries are endeavoring to compete for a slice of the global economic pie, this study provides both theoretical insight and practical relevance related to international corporate governance practices and the impact it has on creating and maintaining investor confidence. We find that stronger governance is associated with higher financial performance among the non-cross-listed EM firms, but we were unable find any significant evidence for the cross-listed ADRs. Furthermore, CEO duality has a negative impact on financial performance only for ADR firms, while none of the other governance standards have a significant effect on firm performance. Finally, among cross-listed firms, it appears to be important to separate the chief executive's position and authority from that of the chairman of the board, so that the authority of the board of directors (BOD) is not usurped or mitigated. This is important because it strengthens the mechanisms used to monitor management, which leads to enhanced financial performance. A CEO lacking appropriate oversight by the BOD may have the incentive and certainly the ability to accept investments that self-benefitting, but prove harmful to the firm in the long run [20, 21]. Finally, the findings also reveal that market risk negatively moderates the governance-performance relationship in the emerging markets. As a firm's market risk increases, the positive effect on financial performance associated with strengthening corporate governance significantly declines. The results indicate that strong corporate governance is an important element toward improving financial performance among EM firms; however, reducing the risk of an equity investment and controlling for stock price volatility is of primary importance for investors.

2. Conceptual framework and hypotheses development

2.1. Corporate governance and financial performance

SOX (2002) was established in an effort to mitigate, if not completely eliminate, major corporate scandals. The SEC implemented the new law in 2006 in the form of enhanced corporate governance standards, which are codified in Section 303A of the NYSE's Listed Company Manual and the NASDAQ's Rule 4000 and apply to cross-listed ADRs (in particular to level 2 and 3 ADRs) as well as US domiciled firms. Bonding Theory provides an explanation for the voluntary adoption of these rather rigorous, "best practice" governance rules among EM firms. EM firms have an incentive to "bond" to a regulatory regime with higher standards than their own markets in an attempt to signal a commitment to these standards [22]. From this perspective, US governance directives serve as a global model of "best practices," providing a codified benchmark of corporate transparency, which restrains the self-serving behavior of all stakeholders as well as management [23].

Global investors typically are skeptical when EM firms exhibit good performance, because they are concerned about the accuracy and consistency of their financial reports. In order to provide confidence and attract investors, some emerging markets companies have made impressive strides in their governance over the last decade by "bonding" their companies to globally accepted best practice rules [24]. However, the impact of this improved corporate governance on firm performance remains ambiguous in the extant literature. For example, Brown and Caylor [9] create a corporate governance measure for US firms based on 51 firm-specific provisions over the 2003–2005 period and show that the governance score is significantly and positively related to a firm's value. Chhaochharia and Grinsten [3] run an event study over the post-SOX (2002) announcement period across US firms and, in contrast to Brown and Caylor [9], observe that firms that are less compliant with the new corporate governance rules earn positive abnormal returns compared to firms that are less compliant. Similarly, Aebi et al. [8] examine corporate governance mechanisms and firm performance for the US banking industry during the crises 2007–2008 and show that corporate governance factors (i.e., board independence and board size) are not statistically significant and/or are negatively related to performance. Among cross-listed ADRs, Litvak [18] also finds similar findings to that of Aebi et al. [8]. By comparing the stock price reaction of SOX-exposed ADRs to SOX-unexposed foreign firms, Litvak [18] observes that the impact of SOX on ADRs is negative and that firms that rigorously apply the governance standards experience the greatest declines in their stock prices.

The results reported regarding the governance-performance relationship for US firms as well as ADRs reveal that countries with more developed financial markets do not react significantly to a change in the governance regime. This is partly related to the fact that the costs of complying with these rules outweigh the benefits in markets that are already heavily regulated [3, 18, 19]. In comparison to developed markets, financial markets in emerging countries are relatively inefficient and incomplete. However, in order to compensate for the negative perception of their riskier market conditions, the emerging markets have provided incentives in an effort to strengthen corporate governance so that the interests of all stakeholders are protected (i.e., investors and creditors) [25]. It follows then that we expect that stronger governance to have a positive effect on financial performance among EM firms. Also, based on the evidence in the extant literature, we do not expect to find a significant relationship between governance and performance among cross-listed ADRs. Therefore, we hypothesize the following:

H1: Stronger corporate governance will increase financial performance in the emerging markets over time.

2.2. The individual corporate governance standards and their impact on financial performance

In addition to examining firms' overall corporate governance score with respect to financial performance, in this study we further investigate the impact of four individual governance standards. Three of these standards (i.e., board independence, establishing a formal ethics policy and three committees) are compulsory for all public US firms as well as cross-listed ADRs trading on the NYSE or NASDAQ. While US governance standards are not mandatory for the EM firms, in an effort to minimize the potential for conflicts of interest between major and minority shareholders and to build trust among potential foreign investors, voluntary adoption of these standards has increased during the last decade [26, 27].

While SOX (2002) mandates that listed firms have a majority of independent directors, US governance rules do not require the CEO and the chairman of the board to be held separately. Nonetheless, over the last 10 years, it appears as though American companies began providing a clearer distinction between the responsibilities of management and the board [28, 29]. The academic literature seems to support the distinction: CEOs simultaneously holding the position of chairman of the board are more likely to select board members who fail to qualify as independent [30–32]. Furthermore, separating the CEO role from that of the chairman also separates the interests of the CEO from that of the shareholders [33].

The emerging markets literature is mixed with regard to the impact of Independent Directors and CEO Duality on firm performance. Black et al. [34] examines the relationship between board independence and performance, as measured by Tobin's Q, and finds a positive association between the two variables in Korea, a negative association in Brazil and no association in India. Similarly, Mahadeo [35] uses survey data to test the impact of board diversity on the short-term performance of firms trading on the exchange of Mauritius and finds that a higher proportion of independent directors negatively impacts performance. Nonetheless, the results also provide evidence that companies in Mauritius have been employing "best practices" corporate governance since a mandated code change in 2005. In this case, "best practices" include increasing the number of independent directors and appointing independent board chairpersons to avoid CEO duality. Moreover, Ramdani and Witteloostuijn [36] examine the effect of board independence in addition to CEO duality on the performance of firms in Indonesia, Malaysia, South Korea and Thailand. They find that both having a greater percentage of independent directors on the board and CEO duality positively affects performance. The authors also observe that board size has a negative moderating impact on the positive relationship between CEO duality and performance.

An application of Bonding Theory leads us to expect that EM firms will likely converge toward a corporate governance structure consistent with that of the US, thereby voluntarily subjecting themselves to a rigorous set of "best practices" rules. Moreover, in this study, we scrutinize the governance – performance relationship over a longer term. Although the short-term effect of these standards on performance might diverge, we expect that, given enough time, EM firms will converge toward a US governance structure, regardless of any compulsory standard. Given that CEO duality is negatively associated with strong corporate governance structure, while board independence is positively associated with strong governance among US firms, we expect to find a positive relationship between strong governance and performance in the emerging countries, and hypothesize the following:

H2: A higher proportion of independent directors on the board will increase the financial performance of EM firms over time.

H3: CEO duality will result in decreased financial performance for EM firms over time.

In accordance with SOX (2002), listed companies in NYSE and NASDAQ must have nomination, compensation and audit committees to identify potential courses of action for the board of directors [37]. The nomination committee directs the process governing board appointments and provides recommendations regarding candidates for directory positions [38]. The compensation committee exists to oversee the process by which bonuses and salaries are awarded to senior executives or other employees to prevent gratuitous compensation. The board of directors relies on audit committees to manage internal controls, risk management and financial reporting. In general, committees are assigned specific roles and responsibilities with the intention of improving a firm's governance and enhanced governance should increase investor returns through higher stock prices. Research suggests that there is a positive association between the committee structure of boards and firm performance among US firms [39]. Still, studies also reveal that as the percentage of outsiders on these boards increases, financial performance decreases [40]. On the whole, there remains a considerable gap in the governance literature and therefore little guidance for policymakers regarding the importance of board committees for effectively enhancing firm performance [41].

According to SOX (2002), listed firms also are required to establish a well-defined ethics policy and code of conduct for directors, officers and employees that clearly identifies the applicable rules of behavior as well as the various responsibilities of every employee in the organization. Donker et al. [42] examines the relationship between the corporate ethics behavior of firms and the performance of Canadian firms listed on the Toronto Stock Exchange. They find that by establishing a code of ethics, a company increases profitability. If a firm applies a code of ethics effectively, individual and organizational dilemmas can be resolved promptly. This, in turn, increases the efficiency of the decision-making process. Furthermore, corporations that effectively apply an ethics policy improve their image and reputation, which likely produces a positive effect on financial performance. Overall, we expect that EM firms will adopt a bonding strategy and subject themselves to a more robust governance structure, resulting in the establishment of a greater number of committees that support the board of directors.

Additionally, firms will forge formal ethics policies to enhance the decision-making process as well as their market image. In line with the findings in the extant literature, and following Bonding Theory, we hypothesize the following:

H4: EM Firms with a greater number of committees will exhibit better financial performance over time.

H5: EM firms with formal ethics policies will exhibit better financial performance over time.

2.3. The moderating effect of risk on governance-performance relationship

Prior literature documents a negative relationship between contemporaneous risk and governance; perhaps because establishing an effective corporate governance regime protects shareholders and creditors and serves to reduce the expropriation of power by managers and controlling shareholders [43–45]. Earlier studies also document risk as an important determinant of a firm's financial performance [46, 47]. For firms in the emerging markets, however, identifying an appropriate measure of risk can present problems when estimating the cost of capital because of the time-varying nature of the integration of these markets into the global economy. Nonetheless, the exposure of a firm to the risks inherent in its local market remains an important element of the overall risk assessment [48–50]. Although, research has demonstrated that both market risk and governance have a significant impact on the financial performance of firms, it remains necessary to develop a more complex and dynamic theoretical model than has been previously considered; a model that reflects how market risk moderates the governance-performance relationship in the emerging markets. We therefore posit the following hypotheses for each of the aforementioned governance indicators:

H6: Greater market risk negatively moderates the relationship between an EM firm's governance score and its financial performance over time.

H7a: Greater market risk negatively moderates the relationship between an EM firm's independent directors and its financial performance over time.

H7b: Greater market risk positively moderates the relationship between CEO Duality and financial performance among EM firms over time.

H7c: Greater market risk negatively moderates the relationship between number of committees and financial performance among EM firms over time.

H7d: Greater market risk negatively moderates the relationship between the presence of an ethics policy and financial performance among EM firms over time.

3. Empirical study

3.1. Data and variable measurement

In this study we analyze the impact of corporate governance on the financial performance of a sample of EM firms and ADRs based in 22 emerging countries over a period extending from 2008–2014. Our analysis is restricted to this seven-year period because of the scarcity of reliable governance data before 2008. The countries are drawn from the 22 best performing emerging markets for the year 2014, as ranked by the *Bloomberg Visual Data*. The ranking is based on each country's GDP growth, inflation, the level of government debt, the annual change in government debt, currency purchasing power, and total investment as percentage of GDP. The 22 emerging countries in ranked order are: China, South Korea, Malaysia, Chile, Thailand, Panama, Peru, Latvia, Poland, Czech Republic, Columbia, Turkey, Hungary, Russia, Brazil, Philippines, Mexico, Indonesia, South Africa, Morocco, India and Egypt. Unfortunately, Morocco, Latvia, Egypt and the Czech Republic have been dropped from the sample because of missing firm-year observations. Moreover, our sample of ADRs excludes Malaysia, Chile, Thailand, Panama, Peru, Poland, Colombia, Philippines and India, either because these ADRs do not exist or because the data are missing for these countries. In total, the sample comprises 10,045 non-cross listed EM firm-year observations of companies that are publicly traded on the stock market of 18 EM countries and 610 cross-listed ADR firm-year observations of companies trading on the NASDAQ and NYSE in the US.

The financial and corporate governance data on the EM firms and ADRs were accessed through the *Bloomberg Database*. Financial performance is measured by the return on assets ratio (ROA), estimated by dividing a company's annual net income by its total assets. In the literature, ROA is frequently used as a measure for profitability and financial performance, especially in studies investigating corporate governance structure [51–53]. A firm's Governance Score was attained from the Bloomberg Professional database and is based on the extent of a company's governance disclosure, where the score ranges from 0.1 for companies that disclose a minimum amount of governance data to a maximum of 100. The *Independent Directors* variable is measured as the number of independent directors on the board divided by the board size; *Committees* is measured as the total number of committees (including audit, nomination and compensation committees) established by the company and ranges between a value of 0 and 3; *CEO Duality* is employed as a dummy variable that takes a value of 1 if the CEO of the company also serves as the chairman of the board and 0 otherwise; *Ethics policy* also is a dummy variable that takes a value of 1 if the company has a formal ethics policy and 0 otherwise. Finally, we include a market-based measure of risk, the CAPM-beta, as a moderator between governance and performance, because of its frequent use in the literature [30, 43, 44, 54]. For each firm, beta (β_t) is estimated for each year t based on daily stock prices: a beta greater than 1 indicates that a stock is more volatile than the market.

To control for potentially confounding, exogenous factors, we include a number of company, industry and country-level variables. At the firm level, we control for leverage because of its significant impact on performance through the cost of capital and capital budgeting decisions [55, 56]. Leverage is measured as the ratio of total debt to total assets. We also include Tobin's Q to control for investment and growth opportunities, because it diverges considerably across countries and captures important elements of firm performance [57, 58]. Tobin's Q is measured as the sum of a firm's market capitalization, total liabilities, preferred equity and minority interest divided by total assets. We also control for firm size, which is computed as the log of a firm's total assets. Industry effects are captured using nine indicator variables; one for each Industry Classification Benchmark (ICB) code. The nine relevant industries include oil and gas, basic materials, industrials, consumer goods, health care, consumer services, telecommunications, utilities, financials and technology. Finally, we employ an indicator variable for each country to control for possible fixed effects related to the national origin of a firm.

3.2. Descriptive statistics and correlations

Descriptive statistics for the cross-listed ADRs and non-cross listed EMs are presented in **Table 1**. The results show that ADR firms generate a higher governance disclosure score than the EM firms. Also, cross-listed ADRs tend to have a larger proportion of independent board members, are almost twice as likely to have a formal ethics policy as EM firms and tend to have more committees. Conversely, EM firms are much more likely to have to have a CEO that also serves as chairman of the board (i.e., CEO duality). In comparing the estimated betas of the two groups of firms, it becomes apparent that ADRs are riskier than EM firms, but this may stem from the residual elements of local market segmentation [48–50]. Finally, the profitability of EM firms appears greater over this period than that of the ADR firms, suggesting that there is a notable difference, not only in the governance structure of these firms, but also in the performance between cross-listed ADRs and non-cross-listed EM firms.

Variables	Mean	Median	Std. Dev.	%25	%75
EM firms					
ROA	6.161	5.006	9.139	1.922	9.818
Governance score	46.844	44.643	7.742	42.857	51.786
Committees	2.074	2	.966	1	3
Independent directors	44.178	42.860	13.739	33.333	54.550
CEO duality	0.237	0	0.425	0	0
Ethics policy	0.433	0	0.496	0	1
Leverage	0.237	0.200	0.179	0.093	0.346
Firm size	7.203	7.156	2.082	5.850	8.487
Tobin's Q	0.424	0.300	0.607	0.020	0.751
Beta	0.954	0.972	0.738	0.781	1.141
ADRs					
ROA	5.633	4.895	9.370	1.285	9.151
Governance score	50.248	50	9.560	42.857	57.143
Committees	2.219	3	0.953	1	3
Independent directors	48.063	44.444	19.784	33.333	62.500
CEO duality	0.160	0	0.368	0	0
Ethics policy	0.827	1	0.379	1	1

Variables	Mean	Median	Std. Dev.	%25	%75
Leverage	0.217	0.182	0.167	0.084	0.313
Firm size	9.510	9.266	1.648	8.463	10.276
Tobin's Q	0.328	0.166	0.543	0.005	0.588
Beta	1.080	1.060	0.330	0.888	1.244

This table provides descriptive statistics for the cross-listed ADRs and non-cross listed EM firms in the sample. A firm is defined cross-listed if it was continuously cross-listed in the US market for the period 2008–2014. All cross-listed and non-cross listed firms are publicly traded EM firms that are from *Bloomberg's* Best Emerging Markets 2014 list.

Table 1. Descriptive statistics cross-listed ADRs and non-cross-listed EM firms.

The Pearson correlation coefficients and corresponding significance levels are reported in **Table 2**. Prior to estimating the determinants of financial performance presented in the theory and hypotheses above, we perform a preliminary screening for collinearity. **Table 2** reveals no evidence of collinearity among the independent variables; no Pearson correlation exceeds $|0.418|$ and the variance inflation factors in later multivariate estimations remain small. Moreover, in line with the theory, the correlation estimates indicate that the Governance Score, Independent Directors, the Number of Committees and CEO Duality are significantly and positively correlated with financial performance ($p < 0.01$), while the coefficient estimate on CEO Duality is negative but insignificant. An examination of the correlation estimates between risk, performance and governance, reveals that the estimated betas are positively and significantly correlated with CEO Duality ($p < 0.10$) and the Number of Committees ($p < 0.05$), while they are negatively correlated with Ethics Policy. Although we expect a negative correlation between risk and the Number of Committees, the positive correlation might be related to the relatively large size of the firms establishing a greater number of committees. That is, given the positive and significant correlation between firm size and risk ($p < 0.01$), a positive correlation between risk and the Number of Committees is not surprising.

3.3. Empirical model

In this study a two-step Generalized Least Squares (GLS) random effects model is employed to capture both cross-sectional and time-series variation in the data. We implement a double transformation of the data to correct for autocorrelation as well as potential heteroskedasticity problems, in which the data are corrected for unobservable, firm-specific and time-invariant effects [59, 60]. The Two-step GLS random effects regression analyses are specified from a general model that represents return on assets (ROA), our proxy for financial performance, as a function of various corporate governance indicators and control variables. In the first model, financial performance is defined as a function of an overall governance disclosure score as shown in Eq. (1):

$$ROA_{it} = \beta_0 + \beta_1 \text{Governance\_Score}_{it} + \text{Controls}_{it} + \varepsilon_{it.} \quad (1)$$

	ROA	Governance score	Committees	Board independence	CEO duality	Ethics policy	Leverage	Firm size	Tobin's Q	Beta
ROA	1.000									
Governance Score	0.097	1.000								
	0.000[a]									
Committees	0.034	0.327								
	0.009[a]	0.000[a]	1.000							
Independent Directors	0.039	0.226	0.263							
	0.002[a]	0.000[a]	0.000[a]	1.000						
CEO Duality	−0.001	−0.062	0.021	0.107						
	0.943	0.000[a]	0.103[c]	0.000[a]	1.000					
Ethics Policy	0.047	0.418	0.146	0.172	−0.021					
	0.000[a]	0.000[a]	0.000[a]	0.000[a]	0.110	1.000				
Leverage	−0.161	−0.119	−0.012	−0.031	0.065	−0.094				
	0.000[a]	0.000[a]	0.342	0.018[b]	0.000[a]	0.000[a]	1.000			
Firm Size	−0.019	0.402	0.210	−0.054	−0.143	0.215	−0.133			
	0.144	0.000[a]	0.000[a]	0.000[a]	0.000[a]	0.000[a]	0.000[a]	1.000		
Tobin's Q	0.303	−0.025	−0.117	−0.161	−0.056	−0.007	0.042	−0.138		
	0.000[a]	0.054[b]	0.000[a]	0.000[a]	0.000[a]	0.599	0.001[a]	0.000[a]	1.000	
Beta	−0.053	−0.001	0.028	−0.017	−0.021	−0.026	−0.008	0.122	−0.025	
	0.000[a]	0.951	0.029[b]	0.198	0.103[c]	0.046[b]	0.526	0.000[a]	0.053[b]	1.000

This table provides Pearson Correlation coefficients and corresponding *p*-values for the cross-listed ADRs and non-cross listed EM firms in the sample.
[a]Significance at the 0.01 level.
[b]Significance at the 0.05 level.
[c]Significance at the 0.10 level.

Table 2. Pearson correlation for the full sample.

In the second model, each of four governance variables are incorporated into the governance – performance regression for each of the samples as in Eq. (2):

$$\begin{aligned} ROA_{it} = {} & \beta_0 + \beta_1\, CEO\_Duality_{it} + \beta_2\, Independent\_Directors_{it} \\ & + \beta_3\, Committees_{it} + \beta_4\, Ethics\_Policy_{it} + Controls_{it} + \varepsilon_{it.} \end{aligned} \tag{2}$$

The third model introduces beta as a moderator variable for risk into the governance-performance regression and includes an interaction variable for the governance disclosure score with Beta as exhibited in Eq. (3):

$$\begin{aligned} ROA_{it} = {} & \beta_0 + \beta_1\, Governance\_Score_{it} + \beta_2\, Beta_{it} \\ & + \beta_3\, Beta_{it}{}^{*}\, Governance\_Score_{it} + Controls_{it} + \varepsilon_{it.} \end{aligned} \tag{3}$$

Finally in the fourth model, we employ a moderator variable, the CAPM Beta. This governance-performance regression includes an interaction term for each of the four governance indicators with Beta as displayed in Eq. (4):

$$\begin{aligned} ROA_{it} = {} & \beta_0 + \beta_1\, CEO\_Duality_{it} + \beta_2\, Independent\_Directors_{it} \\ & + \beta_3\, Committees_{it} + \beta_4\, Ethics\_Policy_{it} + \beta_5\, Beta_{it} \\ & + \beta_6\, Beta_{it}{}^{*}\, CEO\_Duality_{it} + \beta_7\, Beta_{it}{}^{*}\, Independent\_Directors_{it} \\ & + \beta_8\, Beta_{it}{}^{*}\, Committees_{it} + \beta_9\, Beta_{it}{}^{*}\, Ethics\_Policy_{it} + Controls_{it} + \varepsilon_{it} \end{aligned} \tag{4}$$

As discussed in the Data and Variable Measurement section, the sample employed to estimate Eqs. (1) and (3) comprise 10,045 non-cross listed EM firm-year observations and 610 cross-listed ADR firm-year observations. However, in Eqs. (2) and (4), the sample is reduced to 5709 non cross-listed EM firms and 324 ADRs, as a result of missing observations for the four corporate governance indicators.

4. Results

4.1. The direct effect of governance factors on financial performance

To test hypotheses 1 through 5, we examine the influence of governance on firm performance using Eqs. (1) and (2). The results of estimating of Models (1) and (3) are presented in **Table 3** and reveal the impact of the governance score on the financial performance (i.e., ROA) of EM firms and ADRs, respectively. The estimate of Model (1) provides evidence supporting hypothesis 1 in that an increase in the governance score ($p < 0.05$) is likely to increase the financial performance of an EM firm, while the estimate of Model (3) shows a positive but insignificant coefficient on the governance score variable for the ADRs. The estimates of Models (2) and (4) provide the results of the four corporate governance indicators on financial performance for EM and ADR firms, respectively. Model (2) reveals no evidence of a relationship between the individual corporate government variables and performance for EM firms. Model (4), however, shows that CEO Duality negatively affects the financial performance of cross-listed ADR firms ($p < 0.10$).

	EM firms		ADRs	
	(1)	(2)	(3)	(4)
Governance score	0.010**		0.009	
	(0.005)		(0.014)	
Committees		0.002		0.000
		(0.006)		(0.028)
Independent directors		−0.004		−0.006
		(0.012)		(0.035)
CEO duality		0.013		−0.122*
		(0.017)		(0.065)
Ethics policy		−0.011		−0.078
		(0.016)		(0.077)
Leverage	−0.088***	−0.086***	−0.094***	−0.146***
	(0.005)	(0.008)	(0.029)	(0.034)
Firm size	0.060***	0.081***	−0.042	−0.023
	(0.009)	(0.012)	(0.041)	(0.042)
Tobin's Q	0.112***	0.131***	0.291***	0.357***
	(0.005)	(0.007)	(0.028)	(0.035)
Industry fixed effects	Yes	Yes	Yes	Yes
Country fixed effects	Yes	Yes	Yes	Yes
Constant	0.210***	0.118**	0.565***	0.589***
	(0.037)	(0.056)	(0.145)	(0.177)
Observations	14,045	5709	610	324
R^2	0.111	0.088	0.559	0.721
Chi^2	1018.5	559.5	225.6	259.5

This table shows the outcomes of cross-sectional time-series two-step GLS regressions of Return on Assets (ROA) on the governance score, four individual governance standards and control variables. It reports the standardized coefficients on the independent variables as well as standard errors in parentheses.

*Significance at the 0.1 level.

**Significance at the 0.05 level.

***Significance at the 0.01 level.

Table 3. Two-step GLS regressions of governance factors on return on assets.

Overall, we find that stronger governance (as measured by the overall Governance Score) is associated with better financial performance among non-cross-listed EM firms, but we find no evidence of an impact on the performance of cross-listed ADRs. Also, there is no evidence of a positive effect by any of the individual governance rules on the performance of EM firms. CEO Duality, however, appears to be associated with weaker performance among the ADR firms over time.

4.2. The moderating effect of risk on governance-performance relationship

We examine the results of hypotheses 6 and 7 using the interaction terms as specified in Eqs. (3) and (4). **Table 4** provides the estimates of the regressions that include interactions between Governance Score and the four governance indicators with a moderating variable, Beta. Model (1) indicates that, when the moderating variable is introduced, the direct effect of the Governance Score on firm performance remains significant and positive ($p < 0.05$), while the interaction term has a significant but negative association with performance in EM firms ($p < 0.05$), providing evidence for hypothesis 6. Similarly, in Model (2) we observe that, although the direct effects of all four governance indicators are not significant, the moderating effect of beta on Ethics Policy, Number of Committees and performance are significant and negative, providing evidence in support of hypotheses 7c and 7d. The results further reveal that the independent variables Ethics Policy and Number of Committees are significant, conditional on the inclusion of the interaction variable, Beta into the model. Nevertheless, we find no evidence in support of the moderating effect of risk on the governance-performance relationship in Models (3) and (4) among the ADR firms.

	EM firms		**ADRs**	
	(1)	**(2)**	**(3)**	**(4)**
Governance score	0.010**		0.009	
	(0.005)		(0.014)	
Committees		0.005		0.006
		(0.006)		(0.028)
Independent directors		−0.002		0.028
		(0.012)		(0.037)
CEO duality		0.011		−0.108
		(0.017)		(0.080)
Ethics policy		−0.001		0.037
		(0.017)		(0.083)
Beta	0.061	−0.880	2.303	5.902
	(0.052)	(1.129)	(1.728)	(8.043)
Beta*governance score	−0.396**		−0.902	
	(0.162)		(0.935)	
Beta*independent directors		−0.350		−2.227
		(0.457)		(3.350)
Beta*CEO duality		0.618		−3.308
		(0.888)		(5.837)
Beta*ethics policy		−2.063***		−4.196
		(0.785)		(7.735)

	EM firms		ADRs	
	(1)	(2)	(3)	(4)
Beta*committees		−0.874***		−0.006
		(0.241)		(2.570)
Leverage	−0.090***	−0.091***	−0.120***	−0.184***
	(0.006)	(0.008)	(0.029)	(0.032)
Firm Size	0.061***	0.081***	0.013	0.030
	(0.009)	(0.012)	(0.039)	(0.038)
Tobin's Q	0.112***	0.131***	0.290***	0.339***
	(0.005)	(0.007)	(0.027)	(0.032)
Industry fixed effects	Yes	Yes	Yes	Yes
Country fixed effects	Yes	Yes	Yes	Yes
Constant	0.204***	0.121**	0.627***	0.701***
	(0.037)	(0.055)	(0.134)	(0.161)
Observations	14,045	5709	610	324
R^2	0.116	0.096	0.554	0.745
Chi^2	1044.3	595.5	245.0	326.6

This table shows the outcomes of cross-sectional time-series two-step GLS regression model for the moderating effect of risk (measured by beta) on the relationship between return on assets (ROA) and the governance score, as well as four individual governance standards. It reports the standardized coefficients on the independent variables as well as standard errors in parentheses.

*Significance at the 0.1 level.

**Significance at the 0.05 level.

***Significance at the 0.01 level.

Table 4. The moderating effect of risk on governance-performance relationship.

Overall, the results indicate that the existence of a formal ethics policy in the emerging markets may signal a sincere commitment to a strengthened governance structure, which improves the profitability of EM firms. However, in the presence of relatively high market risk (i.e., Beta), the performance enhancing attributes of an ethics policy are mitigated. Given that Governance Score is a continuous variable while the Number of Committees is a categorical variable, we provide graphical analyses to depict the interaction between risk (Beta) and the Governance Score as well as the interaction between risk and the Number of Committees in **Figures 1** and **2**, respectively. **Figure 1** shows that lower risk EM firms enjoy greater benefits in the form of performance from more rigorous governance standards than the higher risk firms. Similarly, **Figure 2** reveals that lower risk EM firms see greater performance gains from adding committees.

4.3. Supplementary analyses

Given the frequent use of market capitalization of equity as an alternative performance measure in the accounting and finance literature, we assess the robustness of the governance-performance

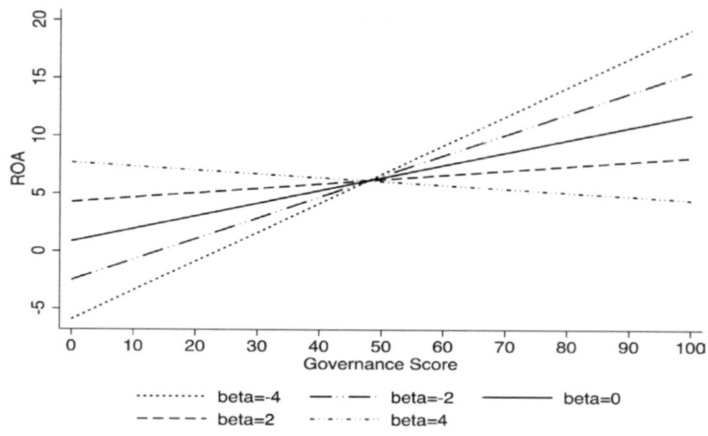

Figure 1. The moderating effect of risk on Governance Score-Performance relationship in the EMs.

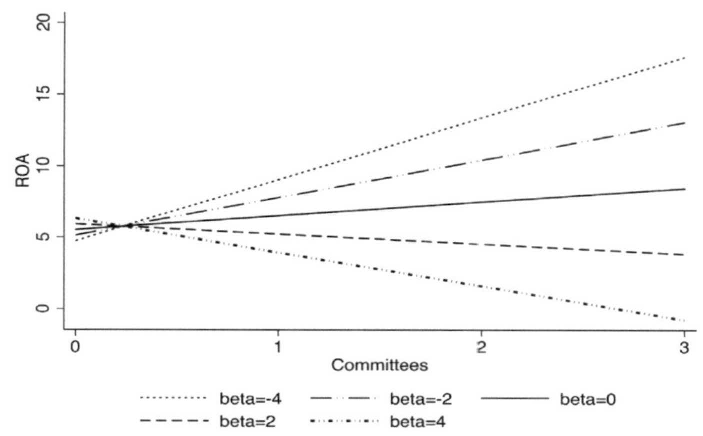

Figure 2. The moderating effect of risk on Committees-Performance relationship in the EMs.

models with regard to our measure of financial performance by substituting the market-to-book value of equity ratio (M/B) for ROA [61–63]. Specifically, M/B is calculated as the ratio of the total market value of a firm's equity to its book value of equity; it is interpreted as the multiple by which the market values a firm's net assets. **Table 5** provides the results of estimating the models using M/B as the relevant performance metric. Results reveal that the positive effect of the Governance Score on performance remains significant ($p < 0.10$) for EM firms [Model (1)] and insignificant for the cross-listed ADRs [Model (3)]. An examination of the impact of the individual governance variables on M/B indicates that the parameter estimate on CEO Duality becomes negative and significant ($p < 0.05$) for EM firms [Model (2)], suggesting that CEO Duality weakens corporate governance mechanisms and reduces the long-term potential wealth creation of the firm. In line with the extant literature, the results also show that an increase in Independent Directors ($p < 0.05$) increases firm value [36]. In contrast, but consistent with Aebi et al. [8], we find a negative relationship between firm performance and the specific corporate governance variables, Number of Committees ($p < 0.10$) and Ethics Policy ($p < 0.01$) for cross-listed ADRs [Model (4)].

The equity of cross-listed firms are offered on the market as Level 1, 2 or 3 ADRs. Level 1 ADRs are traded over-the-counter and require the least amount of compliance and regulatory oversight by the SEC. Level 2 and 3 ADRs are required to adhere to all of the financial reporting standards mandated by SOX (2002). If compliant, level 2 and 3 ADRs trade on the major US stock exchanges (i.e., NASDAQ and NYSE). Given the regulatory differences between level 1

	EM firms		**ADRs**	
	(1)	**(2)**	**(3)**	**(4)**
Governance score	0.011*		0.003	
	(0.006)		(0.017)	
Committees		−0.005		−0.060*
		(0.007)		(0.033)
Independent directors		−0.011		0.082**
		(0.015)		(0.040)
CEO duality		−0.044**		−0.018
		(0.021)		(0.079)
Ethics policy		−0.010		−0.259***
		(0.020)		(0.089)
Leverage	0.021***	−0.005	0.003	0.047
	(0.007)	(0.010)	(0.040)	(0.043)
Firm size	0.008	0.045***	0.031	0.061
	(0.009)	(0.012)	(0.053)	(0.047)
Tobin's Q	0.745***	0.826***	0.913***	0.999***
	(0.007)	(0.009)	(0.036)	(0.040)
Industry fixed effects	Yes	Yes	Yes	Yes
Country fixed effects	Yes	Yes	Yes	Yes
Constant	0.004	−0.062	−0.449**	−0.686***
	(0.035)	(0.052)	(0.184)	(0.194)
Observations	14,045	5709	610	324
R^2	0.793	0.802	0.869	0.932
Chi^2	15934.0	10435.4	1004.5	1186.0

This table shows the outcomes of cross-sectional time-series two-step GLS regressions of market value (measured by market-to-book ratio) on the governance score, four individual governance standards and control variables. It reports the standardized coefficients on the independent variables as well as standard errors in parentheses.

*Significance at the 0.1 level.

**Significance at the 0.05 level.

***Significance at the 0.01 level.

Table 5. Two-step GLS regressions of governance factors on market value.

and level 2 and 3 ADRs, we test the sensitivity of our results on the ADR sample. Eqs. (1) and (2) are re-estimated using a restricted sample that includes only level 2 and 3 ADRs. **Table 6** presents the results of Models (1) and (2) using ROA as the performance measure (dependent variable) and Models (3) and (4) using M/B. A comparison of the results of Models (3) and (4) using the full sample (in **Table 4**) with Models (1) and (2) using the restricted sample (in **Table 6**), reveals that both the sign and the statistical significance of the parameter estimates remain similar with regard to the governance-performance relationship when level 1 ADRs are excluded from the sample. Therefore, using ROA as the performance measure, level 2 and 3 ADRs exhibit no evidence of improved performance given an enhanced governance structure.

When M/B is employed as a performance measure, a comparison of Model (4) in **Table 6**, using the restricted sample, with Model (4) in **Table 5**, using the full sample, reveals that the statistical significance of some of the parameter estimates decrease or disappear. When level 1 ADRs are excluded from the sample, the variables Independent Directors and Ethics Policy become statistically insignificant, while Number of Committees continues to have a negative and statistically significant impact on market value for level 2 and 3 ADRs. In addition, similar to the findings of Model (3) in **Table 5** that uses the full model, governance score still remains insignificant in Model (3) (**Table 6**) when level 1 ADRs are excluded from the sample.

	ROA		**Market value**	
	(1)	**(2)**	**(3)**	**(4)**
Governance score	0.020		0.010	
	(0.015)		(0.020)	
Committees		−0.055		−0.099**
		(0.037)		(0.047)
Independent directors		0.008		0.078
		(0.040)		(0.051)
CEO duality		−0.095		0.101
		(0.073)		(0.093)
Ethics policy		−0.079		−0.204
		(0.095)		(0.125)
Leverage	−0.097***	−0.049	0.069	0.089
	(0.033)	(0.040)	(0.046)	(0.054)
Firm size	−0.088*	−0.038	−0.163**	−0.126
	(0.049)	(0.063)	(0.068)	(0.082)
Tobin's Q	0.264***	0.313***	0.847***	0.941***
	(0.036)	(0.047)	(0.049)	(0.062)
Industry fixed effects	Yes	Yes	Yes	Yes
Country fixed effects	Yes	Yes	Yes	Yes
Constant	0.359**	0.220	−0.292	−0.274
	(0.181)	(0.206)	(0.248)	(0.266)

	ROA		Market value	
	(1)	(2)	(3)	(4)
Observations	358	212	358	212
R^2	0.679	0.698	0.883	0.909
Chi^2	179.5	157.1	593.1	563.0

This table shows the outcomes of cross-sectional time-series two-step GLS regressions of return on assets (ROA) and market value (measured by market-to-book ratio) on the governance score, four individual governance standards and control variables for the level 2 and 3 ADRs. It reports the standardized coefficients on the independent variables as well as standard errors in parentheses.

*Significance at the 0.1 level.

**Significance at the 0.05 level.

***Significance at the 0.01 level.

Table 6. Two-step GLS regressions of governance factors on ROA and market value for level 2&3 ADRs.

5. Conclusion

This study examines the association between corporate governance and financial performance among cross-listed ADRs and non-cross listed EM firms. It appears unlikely that cross-listed ADRs, which are required to submit to regulatory oversight and must remain in compliance with the US governance rules, experience an improvement in performance as a result of the enhanced governance structure. In fact, ADR firms do not appear to perform any better than non-cross listed EM firms, which do not abide by these rules. The study further investigates whether market risk (i.e., Beta) has a moderating effect on the governance-performance relationship and finds that risk reduces the positive association between governance and performance in the emerging markets.

In this study, a two-step Generalized Least Squares (GLS) random effects model is employed to capture both cross-sectional and time-series variation in the data. The results of estimating various models reveal that enhanced governance leads to improved financial performance among non-cross-listed EM firms, when the strength of a firm's corporate governance is measured as a cumulative score (in this article the variable Governance Score). However, there is no evidence that any of the individual governance measures (i.e., CEO Duality, Independent Directors, Ethics Policy and Committees) affect EM firm performance, when performance is measured as ROA. Also, consistent with findings presented in the extant literature [10], we find that a cumulative corporate governance score provides no evidence of an impact on the ROA of cross-listed ADR firms. Still, among the individual governance indicator variables, CEO Duality produces a mitigating effect on ROA (performance).

When the market-to-book equity ratio (M/B) is employed as the measure of performance, ADRs with a formal ethics policy and greater established committees exhibit a reduction in their performance. In contrast, an enhanced governance structure improves the M/B of non-cross-listed EM firms, and also restricting the dual role of the CEO appears to have a positive effect. Finally results of the study also show that market risk is a factor that negatively affects the governance-performance relationship among EM firms. That is, higher market-risk firms fail to experience an improvement in their financial performance even while applying US best practice governance rules.

In general, the results indicate that non cross-listed EM firms voluntarily "bond" themselves to US best practice governance rules in an effort to become integrated into the global financial market; presumably to attract capital and customers. Non-cross-listed EM firms appear to experience a benefit from building a stronger governance structure and it is reflected in better performance over time. Nevertheless, enhancing the governance structure of a firm ultimately does not appear to compensate for the presence of risk – higher risk firms experience substantially less reward for stalwart governance. In this regard, reducing the incidence of CEO duality looks like an effective solution to protect investors and creditors from risk-taking activities of overly powerful managers and to increasing the impact on long-term performance.

Author details

Naz Sayari[1]* and Bill Marcum[2]

*Address all correspondence to: nazsayari@yahoo.com

1 Middle East Technical University, Department of Business Administration, Ankara, Turkey

2 Wake Forest University, School of Business, Winston-Salem, NC, USA

References

[1] Beasley MS, Carcello JV, Hermanson DR, Neal TL. The audit committee oversight process. Contemporary Accounting Research. 2009;**26**(1):65-122

[2] Chang JC, Sun HL. Crossed-listed foreign firms' earnings informativeness, earnings management and disclosures of corporate governance information under SOX. The International Journal of Accounting. 2009;**44**(1):1-32

[3] Chhaochharia V, Grinstein Y. Corporate governance and firm value: The impact of the 2002 governance rules. The Journal of Finance. 2007;**62**(4):1789-1825

[4] Cohen DA, Dey A, Lys TZ. Real and accrual-based earnings management in the pre-and post-Sarbanes-Oxley periods. The Accounting Review. 2008;**83**(3):757-787

[5] Cohen J, Krishnamoorthy G, Wright A. Corporate governance in the post Sarbanes-Oxley era: Auditors' experiences. Contemporary Accounting Research. 2010;**27**(3):751-786

[6] Jain PK, Kim JC, Rezaee Z. The Sarbanes-Oxley act of 2002 and market liquidity. Financial Review. 2008;**43**(3):361-382

[7] Wang X. Increased disclosure requirements and corporate governance decisions: Evidence from chief financial officers in the pre and post–Sarbanes-Oxley periods. Journal of Accounting Research. 2010;**48**(4):885-920

[8] Aebi V, Sabato G, Schmid M. Risk management, corporate governance, and bank performance in the financial crisis. Journal of Banking & Finance. 2012;**36**(12):3213-3226

[9] Brown LD, Caylor ML. Corporate governance and firm valuation. Journal of Accounting and Public Policy. 2006;**25**(4):409-434

[10] Dalton DR, Dalton CM. Integration of micro and macro studies in governance research: CEO duality, board composition, and financial performance. Journal of Management. 2011;**37**(2):404-411

[11] Epps RW, Cereola SJ. Do institutional shareholder services (ISS) corporate governance ratings reflect a company's operating performance? Critical Perspectives on Accounting. 2008;**19**(8):1135-1148

[12] Bai CE, Liu Q, Lu J, Song FM, Zhang J. Corporate governance and market valuation in China. Journal of Comparative Economics. 2004;**32**(4):599-616

[13] Braga-Alves MV, Shastri K. Corporate governance, valuation, and performance: Evidence from a voluntary market reform in Brazil. Financial Management. 2011;**40**(1):139-157

[14] Gibson MS. Is corporate governance ineffective in emerging markets? Journal of Financial and Quantitative Analysis. 2003;**38**(1):231-250

[15] Klapper LF, Love I. Corporate governance, investor protection and performance in emerging markets (No. 2818). The World Bank. 2002

[16] Jayaraman N, Shastri K, Tandon K. The impact of international cross listings on risk and return: The evidence from American depository receipts. Journal of Banking & Finance. 1993;**17**(1):91-103

[17] Litvak K. The effect of the Sarbanes-Oxley act on non-US companies cross-listed in the US. Journal of Corporate Finance. 2007;**13**(2):195-228

[18] Litvak K. Sarbanes-Oxley and the cross-listing premium. Michigan Law Review. 2007;**105**: 1857-1898

[19] Litvak K. The long-term effect of the Sarbanes-Oxley act on cross-listing Premia. European Financial Management. 2008;**14**(5):875-920

[20] Hayward ML, Shepherd DA, Griffin D. A hubris theory of entrepreneurship. Management Science. 2006;**52**(2):160-172

[21] Malmendier U, Tate G. Who makes acquisitions? CEO overconfidence and the market's reaction. Journal of Financial Economics. 2008:**89**(1):20-43

[22] Coffee JC Jr. The Future as History. The prospects for global convergence in corporate governance and its implications. Northwestern University Law Review. 1999;**93**(1): 641-708

[23] Coffee JC. Law and the market: The impact of enforcement. University of Pennsylvania Law Review. 2007;**156**(2):229-311

[24] Aguilera RV, de Castro LRK, Lee JH, You J. Corporate governance in emerging markets. Capitalisms and Capitalism in the Twenty-First Century. 2012:319

[25] Allen F. Corporate governance in emerging economies. Oxford Review of Economic Policy. 2005;**21**(2):164-177

[26] Claessens S, Yurtoglu BB. Corporate governance in emerging markets: A survey. Emerging Markets Review. 2013;**15**:1-33

[27] Francis B, Hasan I, Song L, Waisman M. Corporate governance and investment-cash flow sensitivity: Evidence from emerging markets. Emerging Markets Review. 2013;**15**:57-71

[28] Garrett AD. Comparison of United Kingdom and United States approaches to board structure. Corporate Governance Law Review. 2007;**3**(2):93-114

[29] Tuggle CS, Sirmon DG, Reutzel CR, Bierman L. Commanding board of director attention: Investigating how organizational performance and CEO duality affect board members' attention to monitoring. Strategic Management Journal. 2010;**31**(9):946-968

[30] Ashbaugh-Skaife H, Collins DW, LaFond R. The effects of corporate governance on firms' credit ratings. Journal of Accounting and Economics. 2006;**42**(1):203-243

[31] Conyon MJ, Peck SI. Board control, remuneration committees, and top management compensation. Academy of Management Journal. 1998;**41**(2):146-157

[32] Imhoff EA. Accounting quality, auditing, and corporate governance. Accounting Horizons. 2003;**17**(2003):117-128

[33] Jensen MC. The modern industrial revolution, exit, and the failure of internal control systems. The Journal of Finance. 1993;**48**(3):831-880

[34] Black BS, De Carvalho AG, Gorga É. What matters and for which firms for corporate governance in emerging markets? Evidence from Brazil (and other BRIK countries). Journal of Corporate Finance. 2012;**18**(4):934-952

[35] Mahadeo JD, Soobaroyen T, Hanuman VO. Board composition and financial performance: Uncovering the effects of diversity in an emerging economy. Journal of Business Ethics. 2012;**105**(3):375-388

[36] Ramdani D, Witteloostuijn AV. The impact of board independence and CEO duality on firm performance: A quantile regression analysis for Indonesia, Malaysia, South Korea and Thailand. British Journal of Management. 2010;**21**(3):607-627

[37] Bates EW, Leclerc RJ. Boards of directors and risk committees. The Corporate Governance Advisor. 2009;**17**(6):16-18

[38] Dumitrascu M, Gajevszky A. Corporate governance committees in European Union emerging economies. Annals of Faculty of Economics. 2013;**1**(1):618-630

[39] Klein A. Firm performance and board committee structure. The Journal of Law and Economics. 1998;**41**(1):275-304

[40] Klein A. Economic determinants of audit committee independence. The Accounting Review. 2002;**77**(2):435-452

[41] Finegold D, Benson GS, Hecht D. Corporate boards and company performance: Review of research in light of recent reforms. Corporate Governance: An International Review. 2007;**15**(5):865-878

[42] Donker H, Poff D, Zahir S. Corporate values, codes of ethics, and firm performance: A look at the Canadian context. Journal of Business Ethics. 2008;**82**(3):527-537

[43] Bargeron LL, Lehn KM, Zutter CJ. Sarbanes-Oxley and corporate risk-taking. Journal of Accounting and Economics. 2010;**49**(1):34-52

[44] Bhojraj S, Sengupta P. Effect of corporate governance on bond ratings and yields: The role of institutional investors and outside directors. The Journal of Business. 2003;**76**(3):455-475

[45] Orlitzky M, Benjamin JD. Corporate social performance and firm risk: A meta-analytic review. Business and Society. 2001;**40**(4):369-396

[46] Bromiley P. Testing a causal model of corporate risk taking and performance. Academy of Management Journal. 1991;**34**(1):37-59

[47] Purdy BM, Langemeier MR, Featherstone AM. Financial performance, risk, and specialization. Journal of Agricultural and Applied Economics. 1997;**29**(1):149-161

[48] Bekaert G, Harvey CR. Emerging equity market volatility. Journal of Financial Economics. 1994;**43**(1):29-77

[49] Harvey CR. The risk exposure of emerging equity markets. The World Bank Economic Review. 1995;**9**(1):19-50

[50] Bruner RF, Lie W, Kritzman M, Myrgren S, Page S. Market integration in developed and emerging markets: Evidence from the CAPM. Emerging Markets Review. 2008;**9**(2):89-103

[51] Bhagat S, Bolton B. Corporate governance and firm performance. Journal of Corporate Finance. 2008;**14**(3):257-273

[52] Core JE, Holthausen RW, Larcker DF. Corporate governance, chief executive officer compensation, and firm performance. Journal of Financial Economics. 1999;**51**(3):371-406

[53] Shleifer A, Vishny RW. A survey of corporate governance. The Journal of Finance. 1997;**52**(2):737-783

[54] McGuire JB, Sundgren A, Schneeweis T. Corporate social responsibility and firm financial performance. Academy of Management Journal. 1988;**31**(4):854-872

[55] Jermias J. The relative influence of competitive intensity and business strategy on the relationship between financial leverage and performance. The British Accounting Review. 2008;**40**(1):71-86

[56] Opler TC, Titman S. Financial distress and corporate performance. The Journal of Finance. 1994;**49**(3):1015-1040

[57] Gozzi JC, Levine R, Schmukler SL. Internationalization and evolution of corporate valuation. Journal of Financial Economics. 2008;**88**(3):607-632

[58] Lang LH, Stulz RM. Tobin's Q, corporate diversification, and firm performance. Journal of Political Economy. 1994;**102**(6):1248-1280

[59] Halaby CN. Panel models in sociological research: Theory into practice. Annual Review of Sociology. 2004:507-544

[60] Mátyás L, Sevestre P, editors. The Econometrics of Panel Data: Fundamentals and Recent Developments in Theory and Practice. Vol. 46. Springer Science & Business Media; 2008

[61] Chakravarthy BS. Measuring strategic performance. Strategic Management Journal. 1986;**7**(5):437-458

[62] Daniel K, Grinblatt M, Titman S, Wermers R. Measuring mutual fund performance with characteristic-based benchmarks. The Journal of Finance. 1997;**52**(3):1035-1058

[63] Jain BA, Kini O. The post-issue operating performance of IPO firms. The Journal of Finance. 1994;**49**(5):1699-1726

Section 4

Working Capital Management

Chapter 9

Financing of Working Capital Requirement and Profitability: Evidence from Borsa Istanbul Chemical, Petroleum, Rubber, and Plastic Sector

Burcu Dinçergök

Additional information is available at the end of the chapter

http://dx.doi.org/10.5772/intechopen.72760

Abstract

This study investigates the relationship between the maturity of debt used to finance working capital requirement and profitability. The firms in Borsa Istanbul chemical, petroleum, rubber, and plastic sector are analyzed using two-step generalized method of moments (GMM) method over the 2005–2015 period. The results show a concave-shaped relation between the short-term financial debt that is used to finance the working capital requirement and profitability. The ratio of short-term financial debt increases profitability up to a point, and over this point, the effect of short-term debt on profitability is found to be negative. Furthermore, for financially flexible firms, the breakpoint of the short-term financial debt and profitability relation occurs at the higher levels of the short-term financial debt-to-working capital requirement ratio.

Keywords: working capital requirement, profitability, short-term financial debt, chemical, petroleum, rubber and plastic sector, GMM method

1. Introduction

Working capital management is one of the most important issues in corporate finance due to its effects on the profitability, liquidity, and risk of firms. When the literature on working capital management is reviewed, it can be seen that many of the studies are generally focused on the investment in working capital requirement (WCR) and firm performance [1–7].[1] While studies

[1]In this study working capital requirement (WCR) is defined as the difference between current assets and accounts payable.

show that investment in WCR has an important effect on the profitability of firms, another issue, at least as important as investment in WCR, is the linkage between profitability and WCR financing. Since the types and maturities of financing sources have a direct impact on the costs and the risks of firms, it is expected that how WCR is financed will also have an effect on profitability. The literature on the relationship between WCR financing and profitability is very limited (i.e., there is only one study by Banos-Caberollo, Garcia-Teruel, and Martinez-Solano [8]). To the best of our knowledge, there is no study in Turkey related with this subject.[2]

Financial managers consider the general economic conditions, industrial factors, legal regulations, firm-specific factors, and the reaction of the lenders when deciding on the maturity and the type of the financing instruments they choose. At the same time, appropriateness, risk, cost, the financial leverage effect, flexibility in usage, timing, and the possible claims on management are also taken into account in the selection processes [10].

There are many advantages of using short-term debt in financing WCR. The most important advantage of short-term debt is its cost advantage. Normally, short-term debt is less costly than long-term debt. In addition, compared with long-term debt, short-term debt is easier to obtain and provides more flexibility over spending. But, short-term funds are riskier than long-term funds. This risk is due to the immediate payment of the short-term obligations, the refinancing requirement, and the uncertainty in interest rates when refinancing requirement arises. It is known that firms may face bankruptcy when they have difficulties in payment of short-term funds and when these funds are not renewed [11]. Due to these risks, the cost advantage of short-term debt is not limitless.

As stated by Banos-Caberollo, Garcia-Teruel, and Martinez-Solano, usage of short-term funds provides a cost advantage to the firms when a low percentage of WCR is financed by short-term debt. However, if a high percentage of WCR is financed by short-term debt, an additional increase in short-term debt will increase the risk of repayment as well as the risk of renewing the funds and will cause the lenders to demand higher interest rates from the firms. Therefore, at lower levels of short-term debt-to-WCR ratios, the expected relationship between the proportion of short-term funds used to finance WCR and profitability is positive, but at higher levels of the short-term debt-to-WCR ratios, the expected relationship is negative [8].

The first aim of this study is to reveal the relationship between the proportion of short-term funds used in WCR financing and profitability in the Borsa Istanbul chemical, petroleum, rubber, and plastic sector. If the relationship turns out to be as expected, then the level at which the short-term debt-to-WCR ratio turns from positive to negative will also be investigated. To do this, the firms operating in the chemical, petroleum, rubber, and plastic sector in Borsa İstanbul over the 2005–2015 period are analyzed using two-step GMM method. This study finds a concave-shaped relation between the proportion of short-term financial debt that is used to finance WCR and profitability. The ratio of short-term financial debt increases profitability up to the breakpoint, but the effect of short-term debt on profitability turns to negative above this point.

[2]In Turkey, Poyraz analyzed the effects of working capital financing strategies on a single bank using multiple regression analysis [9]. Their methodology and scope are very different from our study.

http://dx.doi.org/10.5772/intechopen.72760

Another important point regarding this issue is whether the WCR financing and profitability relationship of financially flexible firms show differences in comparison to other firms. Compared with the other firms, financially flexible firms can obtain credit more easily and in better terms, and their refinancing risk is lower as well. Therefore, it is expected that for these types of firms, the breakpoint of WCR financing and profitability relation occurs at higher levels of short-term debt-to-WCR ratios. The second aim of this study is to determine whether the breakpoint of financially flexible firms and other firms differs or not.

The remainder of the study is organized as follows. The first part gives a review of the literature; WCR financing and profitability relationship is explained in the second part. Data and methodology are described in the third part, and the findings are explained and evaluated in the fourth part. The conclusion is presented in the last part of the paper.

2. Literature review

The literature on working capital management is generally focused on the relationship between investment in WCR and profitability.

Deelof investigated the effect of working capital management on Belgian firms' corporate profitability over the 1992–1996 period. They used fixed effects and ordinary least squares methods and found that the reduction in the number of days accounts receivable, the number of days inventories and the number of days accounts payable all have a positive effect on profitability [1].

For the small and medium enterprises in Portugal, Pais and Gama analyzed the effect of working capital management on profitability over 2002–2005 period. The results of the panel data analysis show a negative relationship with profitability for the number of days accounts receivable, the number of days inventory, and the number of days accounts payable. But when controlled for endogeneity, the relationship between the number of days accounts receivable and profitability is reversed [7].

Controlling for unobservable heterogeneity and possible endogeneity, Banos-Caberollo, Garcia-Teruel, and Martinez-Solano show a non-monotic relationship between the level of working capital and profitability. It is also stated in the study that firms have an optimal working capital level and that deviation from that level harms profitability [12].

Using multiple regression analysis, Vahid, Elham, Mohsen, and Mohammedreza conducted an analysis on a number of companies in the medicine and cement industries in Iran over the 2006–2009 period. The results showed that an increase in the average collection period, inventory turnover in days, average payment period, or net trading cycle decreases profitability. As for the effect of cash conversion cycle on profitability, the results are found to be insignificant [2].

For Indian manufacturing companies, Singhania, Sharma, and Rohit analyzed the effect of working capital management on profitability by taking into account the impact of macroeconomic variables on this relationship. Utilizing correlation and fixed-effects estimation methods, it is revealed that the cash conversion cycle has a negative effect on profitability. Decreasing the number of days accounts receivable and increasing the number of days accounts payable increase the profitability ratios of Indian manufacturing companies. Also, it is stated that global macroeconomic factors should be taken into consideration in formulating working capital strategies [13].

A different study in the field of working capital management belongs to Aktas, Croci, and Petmezas in which the authors analyzed the effects of working capital management on the stock and operating performance of a large sample of firms in US between 1982 and 2011. The results of the study show that firms have an optimal working capital level and divergence from this level harms to the stock and operating performance of the firms. The authors also documented that working capital management increases corporate performance through corporate investment channel [14].

In Turkey, Öz, and Güngör, Akbulut, Coşkun, and Kök, Kendirli, and Konak and Şamiloğlu, and Demirgüneş analyzed the effect of working capital management on profitability [3–6, 15]. Öz and Güngör analyzed the effect of working capital management indicators on the profitability of a number of Turkish manufacturing firms on Borsa Istanbul over the 1992–2005 period. Using panel data analysis, it is documented that receivable turnover, payable turnover, inventory turnover, and net trade period negatively affect profitability [3].

Şamiloğlu and Demirgüneş used multiple regression analysis to determine the effect of working capital management on profitability of Turkish manufacturing firms that are listed on Borsa Istanbul over 1998–2007 period. The results show that accounts receivable, inventory period, and leverage ratios negatively affect profitability, whereas firm growth has a positive effect on it. From the other variables, cash conversion cycle, size, and fixed financial assets are found to be insignificant [15].

Using regression and ANOVA, Akbulut analyzed the effect of cash conversion cycle on profitability on Turkish manufacturing firms that are quoted on Borsa Istanbul over 2000–2008 period. As a result of the study, it is found that there is a negative relationship between cash conversion cycle and profitability [4].

Using dynamic panel data analysis, Coşkun and Kök analyzed the effects of cash conversion cycle, inventory period, accounts receivable period, and accounts payable period on profitability of a number of Turkish manufacturing firms over the period of 1991–2005. The results show a negative relationship between cash conversion cycle, inventory period, and accounts receivable period on profitability. But the relationship between accounts payable period and profitability is found to be positive [5].

Using multiple regression analysis, Kendirli and Konak analyzed the working capital management and profitability relationship for the firms that are quoted on Borsa Istanbul Tourism Index. The study covers the 2010–2014 period. The study finds that although cash conversion cycle has a positive effect on profitability, the coefficients of the components of cash conversion cycle such as the accounts receivable period and accounts payable period are found to be insignificant. Looking at the control variables, we observe that the sign of the relationship between leverage and profitability is negative, whereas the effect is positive for the total assets ratio [6].

The only study that investigates the relationship between WCR financing and profitability belongs to Banos-Caberollo, Garcia-Teruel, and Martinez-Solano. Banos-Caberollo, Garcia-Teruel, and Martinez-Solano analyzed the WCR financing-profitability relationship using a two-step GMM method for small and medium enterprises over the 1997–2012 period in Spain. The results show that there is a concave relationship between short-term WCR financing and profitability [8].

In Turkey, Poyraz analyzed the effects of working capital financing strategies on a single bank using multiple regression analysis. In the study, current ratio, long-term debt ratios, short-term debt ratio, and permanent capital ratios were used as independent variables. As a result it is found that there is a significant relationship between current ratio and profitability. As for the other variables, the relationship was found to be insignificant [9].

As can be seen from the literature review, although there is a large number of studies on the relationship between WCR investment and profitability, the studies on the effects of WCR financing on profitability is very limited. Therefore, the aim of this study is to extend the literature on this subject by conducting an analysis for an emerging country, namely, Turkey. The results of this study will help managers increase the profitability of their firms by shedding light on the degree of short-term financing they use to increase the profits of the firms.

3. The relationship between short-term debt usage in WCR financing and profitability

Working capital financing strategies depends on the extent of utilization of short-term or long-term financing sources in funding working capital. Under an aggressive financing strategy, the firm funds its temporary working capital and a part of its permanent working capital with short-term debt, whereas under a conservative financing strategy, the firm funds its permanent working capital and a part of temporary working capital with long-term debt. The hedging approach, on the other hand, lies in the middle of these two approaches in which the firm funds its permanent working capital with long-term debt and temporary working capital with short-term debt. The effects of these approaches on profitability and risk are different. While aggressive approaches provide the highest profitability with the highest risk, the conservative approaches provide the lowest profit with the lowest risk. As for the profitability and risk, hedging approach lies in the middle [16].

When the working capital requirement is heavily financed through short-term debt, it provides various cost advantages to firms. The first advantage comes from the fact that the nominal interest rates on short-term debt are generally lower than the interest rates on long-term debt. The difference is called as the term premium. The term premium, which is the total of inflation and default premiums, increases as debt maturity lengthens. Since the inflation uncertainty rises with maturity, the inflation premium of short-term debt is lower than the inflation premium of long-term debt. The default premium of short-term debt is also lower than the default premium of long-term debt, because it is charged for one period. The shareholder-creditor conflict is limited in this short period of time. These types of agency conflicts can be immediately compensated by charging higher interest rates at the end of short maturities. For all of these reasons, the default premium on short-term debt is less than the default premium on long-term debt [17].[3]

Another cost advantage of short-term debt is that firms that use short-term funds only borrow the amount that they need. So, the interest that is paid on short-term funds is the interest cost of the money that is actually used. This is especially important for the firms that have seasonal fluctuations in their current assets. However, in terms of long-term debt, firms may borrow more than their needs.

The third cost advantage of short-term debt is related to agency costs. Short-term debt requires making periodical payments and declaring periodical information about the main operations of the firms. Myers stated that short-term debt usage decreases underinvestment and asset substitution problems [18]. Also, Stulz noted that short-term debt is a strong device in the monitoring of management [19]. In a theoretical model developed by Rajan and Winton, it is shown that management can be monitored with minimum effort using short-term funds [20]. As a result, it can be said that short-term debt usage decreases agency costs.

In addition to all of the cost advantages stated above, there are refinancing and interest rate risks of using short-term funds. At the end of short-term debt maturity, the firms that use short-term funds may need new funds and can obtain new funds from the current interest rates that exist on the market. Refinancing may be more difficult for the firms that currently have high short-term debt-to-WCR ratios. Since the default risk is higher for these firms, the lenders may charge higher interest rates for bearing that risk. Short-term borrowing can negatively affect profitability in such cases.

To sum up, the cost advantage of using short-term funds depends on the current proportion of WCR that is financed with short-term debt. If a firm currently has a low short-term debt-to-WCR ratio, additional short-term borrowing will decrease costs and increase profitability. However, if the stated ratio is high, additional borrowing will increase the costs of the firm—due to the increased financial risk—and therefore hamper profitability. Based on these reasons, we expect a concave-shaped relation (reversed U-shaped relation) between the proportion of short-term funds in WCR financing and profitability. The first aim of this study is to reveal whether the expected relationship exists in chemical, petroleum, rubber, and plastic sector of Istanbul Stock Exchange in the period analyzed. The results obtained from the analysis show the peak point up to which short-term debt-to-WCR ratios increase profitability.

Financial flexibility is defined as the ability to react to the unexpected changes of cash flows and investment opportunities by obtaining and using the minimum cost funds [21]. When compared to other firms, financially flexible firms can utilize the minimum cost funds whenever they need. Due to the difference of such firms in obtaining short-term funds, it is expected that the cost advantage of short-term debt prevails up to higher short-term debt-to-WCR ratios. In another saying, it is expected that the breakpoint occurs at higher levels of short-term debt-to-WCR ratios for that type of firms [8].

[3]The default premium on long-term debt is higher especially for the financially weak firms. Since the shareholder-creditor conflict is higher in these types of firms, this increases the default premium [17].

http://dx.doi.org/10.5772/intechopen.72760

3.1. Data and methodology

In this study, 25 manufacturing firms that were quoted to Borsa Istanbul over the 2005–2016 period are analyzed. The balance sheets and income statements are obtained from the "Data Stream" database. The observations with negative WCF are excluded from the analysis.

The study is conducted using panel data analysis. As explained by Kennedy, there are four main advantages of using this method. One advantage is that panel data analysis controls for heterogeneity among firms. Uncontrolled heterogeneity may lead to omitted variable problems. Secondly, the time series dimension of panel data reduces the problems associated with multicollinearity. Thirdly, panel data analysis permits the testing of hypotheses that cannot be solely tested by time series or cross-sectional analysis alone. Finally, since panel data analysis takes into account dynamic adaptation processes, it has advantages over both time series and cross-sectional analyses [22].

Due to the endogeneity problem, the two-step generalized method of moments (GMM) method based on the study of Arellano-Bond is utilized in this study [23]. The endogeneity problem arises when the correlation between the independent variables and the error term is different than zero. The best way to solve this problem is to use instrumental variables [24]. Since the least squares method leads to biased results when instrumental variables are used, two-step least squares or GMM methods are generally preferred. The models that are used in this study are estimated using the Arellano-Bond estimator.[4]

Following the study of Banos-Caberollo, Garcia-Teruel, and Martinez-Solano, the following model is constructed (Model 1) [8]:

$$ROE_{i,t} = \beta_0 + \beta_1 WCF_{i,t-1} + \beta_2 WCF^2_{i,t-1} + \beta_3 SIZE_{i,t-1} + B_4 GROWTH_{i,t-1} + \beta_5 LEV_{i,t-1} + \varepsilon_{i,t} \quad (1)$$

The dependent variable $ROE_{i,t}$ is the return on equity and is calculated by dividing net profit by total equity. $WCF_{i,t-1}$ is a variable that shows the proportion of WCR that is financed with short-term financial debt. Working capital requirement is calculated by subtracting accounts payable from current assets. Since the expected theoretical relationship between $ROE_{i,t}$ and $WCF_{i,t-1}$ is nonlinear, the square of $WCF_{i,t-1}$ is added to the model. The positive and negative effects of short-term financing can be determined by using $WCF_{i,t-1}$ and the square of $WCF_{i,t-1}$. The $SIZE_{i,t-1}$ variable measures the natural logarithm of total assets, and it is added to the model in order to control the firm size. $GROWTH_{i,t-1}$ shows the growth in sales and is calculated by dividing the difference between sales in year t and in year t−1 to the sales in year t-1. $GROWTH_{i,t-1}$ is added to the model to control for the growth rates of the firms. The last control variable is $LEV_{i,t-1}$, and it is calculated by dividing total debt by total assets. $\varepsilon_{i,t}$ is the error term. All of the independent variables are used in their 1-year lagged forms (**Table 1**).

The negative $WCF_{i,t-1}$ values are excluded from the analysis. The breakpoint is mathematically calculated by $\frac{-\beta_1}{2\beta_2}$ equation. If there exist a concave relation between the proportion of WCR

[4]See Greene for details about the Arellano-Bond estimator [25].

Variable	Definition	Calculation
$ROE_{i,t-1}$	Return on equity	$\text{Net Profit}_{i,t-1}/\text{Total Equity}_{i,t-1}$
$WCF_{i,t-1}$	Working capital financing	$\text{Short Term Financial Debt}_{i,t-1}/\text{Working Capital requirement}_{i,t-1}$
$WCF^2_{i,t-1}$	The square of working capital financing	$\text{Short Term Financial Debt}_{i,t-1}/\text{Working Capital Requirement}_{i,t-1})^2$
$SIZE_{i,t-1}$	Size	$\text{Ln(Total Assets}_{i,t-1})$
$GROWTH_{i,t-1}$	Growth	$(\text{Sales}_{t-}\ \text{Sales}_{t-1})/\text{Sales}_{t-1}$
$LEV_{i,t-1}$	Leverage	$\text{Total Debt}_{t-1}/\text{Total Asset}_{t-1}$

Datasource: Datastream.

Table 1. Variable definitions.

that is financed with short-term debt and profitability, β_1 is expected to be positive, whereas β_2 is expected to be negative.

After the calculation of breakpoint using Model 1, dummy variables $WCFL_{i,t-1}$ and $WCFL_{i,t-1}$ are added to the Model 1 for the firms that have low and high $WCF_{i,t-1}$ values. If the value of $WCF_{i,t-1}$ is between zero and the breakpoint, the dummy variable $WCFL_{i,t-1}$ takes the value of $WCF_{i,t-1}$; otherwise, $WCFL_{i,t-1}$ takes the value of the breakpoint. The other dummy variable $WCFH_{i,t-1}$, takes the value of the difference between $WCF_{i,t-1}$ and breakpoint if $WCF_{i,t-1}$ is greater than the breakpoint; otherwise, $WCFH_{i,t-1}$ takes the value of zero.

Following Ghosh and Moon, Banos-Caballero, Garcia-Teruel, and Martinez-Solano, the robustness of the findings in Model 1 is checked by utilizing the following model [8, 26]:

$$ROE_{i,t} = \beta_0 + \beta_1 WCFL_{i,t-1} + \beta_2 WCFH_{i,t-1} + \beta_3 SIZE_{i,t-1} + B_4 GROWTH_{i,t-1} + \beta_5 LEV_{i,t-1} + \varepsilon_{i,t} \quad (2)$$

Many studies pointed out the importance of low leverage ratios in providing financial flexibility (see [27–29]), while many others stated the importance of holding medium or high levels of cash [30–32]. Some studies showed that both leverage and cash ratios have a role in providing financial flexibility ([21, 33, 34]). In this study firstly firms are grouped according to their cash ratios. The firms that have cash ratio above the median value are accepted as "financially flexible." Secondly, the firms are grouped based on their leverage ratios. The firms that have leverage ratios below the median value are accepted as "financially flexible." In the third categorization, we combined the cash and leverage ratios. The firms that have leverage ratios in the bottom 75% of all firms and cash ratios in the top 75% of all firms are accepted as financially flexible. The dummy variables take the value of 1 if a firm is financially flexible; otherwise, they take the value of zero:

$$ROE_{i,t} = \beta_0 + (\beta_1 + \delta_1 DUM_{i,t-1})WCF_{i,t} + (\beta_2 + \delta_2 DUM_{i,t-1})WCF^2_{i,t-1} + \beta_3 SIZE_{i,t} + B_4 GROWTH_{i,t-1} + \beta_5 LEV_{i,t-1} + \varepsilon_{i,t} \quad (3)$$

The breakpoint is determined by using the equation $-(\beta_1 + \delta_2)/2(\beta_2 + \delta_2)$.

4. Findings

Table 2 presents the descriptive statistics on profitability, the proportion of short-term financial debt in WCF financing, size, growth, and leverage ratios.

As seen in **Table 2**, the average return on equity (ROE) of the chemical, petroleum, rubber, and plastic sector firms over the period of analysis is 6.6%. The mean value of WCF is 0.29, which means that 29% of the working capital requirement is financed by short-term financial debt. The average size of the firms is 13.15, and the average sales growth is 22%. Leverage, which shows the proportion of total debt in total assets, is 19% on average. The standard deviations of ROE, WCF, GROWTH, and LEV ratios are 0.21, 0.23, 1.14, and 0.14, respectively.

The first column of **Table 3** shows the estimation results of Model 1. The coefficient of $WCF_{i,t-1}$ variable is positive and statistically significant at the 1% significance level. The coefficient of $WCF_{i,t-1}^2$ is negative and is also statistically significant but at the 5% significance level. Utilizing equation $\frac{-\beta_1}{2\beta_2}$, the breakpoint is found to be 0.52. With the control variables, only the result of the growth variable is found to be statistically significant, but the coefficient of this variable is negative.

The breakpoint of 0.52, which is found by utilizing Model 1, is used for classifying the firms as WCRL and WCRH. In Model 2, if $WCR_{i,t-1}$ is between 0 and 0.52, $WCRL_{i,t-1}$ takes the value of $WCR_{i,t-1}$; otherwise, if $WCR_{i,t-1}$ is greater than 0.52, it takes the value of 0.52. $WCRH_{i,t-1}$ variable takes the value of the difference between $WCF_{i,t-1}$ and 0.52 when $WCF_{i,t-1}$ is greater than 0.52; otherwise, it takes the value of zero. The estimation results of Model 2 show that the coefficients of $WCFL_{i,t-1}$ and $WCFH_{i,t-1}$ are positive and negative, respectively. Both are statistically significant. The concave-shaped relationship between WCF and profitability is also supported by the findings of Model 2.

Table 3 presents the results of Model 1 and Model 2.

In **Table 4**, firms are categorized according to their leverage ratios in column 1, cash ratios in column 2, and leverage and cash ratios in column 3. In the first column, the firms which have cash ratios (cash/total assets) are above the median value and are accepted as "financially flexible." In the second column, the firms that have leverage ratios (total debt/total assets) under

	Number of observation	Mean	Standard deviation	10. centile	Median	90. centile
ROE	222	0.066	0.211	−0.145	0.099	0.237
WCF	222	0.291	0.226	0.005	0.260	0.604
SIZE	222	13.155	1.502	10.838	13.219	14.879
GROWTH	205	0.215	1.138	−0.091	0.119	0.417
LEV	222	0.193	0.136	0.033	0.185	0.399

Table 2. Descriptive statistics.

Variables	ROE	
	(1)	(2)
$ROE_{i,t}$	−0.205*** (0.00777)	−0.208*** (0.0103)
$WCF_{i,t-1}$	0.376*** (0.138)	
$WCF_{i,t-1}^2$	−0.363** (0.149)	
$WCFL_{i,t-1}$		0.232*** (0.0725)
$WCFH_{i,t-1}$		−0.344*** (0.0819)
$SIZE_{i,t-1}$	0.00835 (0.0104)	0.00164 (0.0146)
$GROWTH_{i,t-1}$	−0.00260*** (0.000615)	−0.00281*** (0.000566)
$LEV_{i,t-1}$	−0.150 (0.0946)	−0.125 (0.101)
$OROE_{i,t}$	−0.364*** (0.0143)	−0.369*** (0.0130)
Constant	−0.00410 (0.129)	0.0883 (0.185)
Observation	161	161
Number of firms	25	25

The results of Model 1 estimation are presented in the first column. The results of Model 2 estimation are presented in the second column. Standard errors are presented in parentheses. ***p < 0.01, **p < 0.05.

Table 3. WCF and profitability relation.

Variables	LEV (1)	CASH (2)	LEV + CASH (3)
$ROE_{i,t}$	−0.182*** (0.0254)	−0.222*** (0.0184)	−0.185*** (0.0205)
$WCF_{i,t-1}$	0.604*** (0.132)	0.623*** (0.121)	0.528*** (0.127)
$WCF_{i,t-1}$*D	−0.306*** (0.0824)	−0.190** (0.0938)	−0.260** (0.116)
$WCF_{i,t-1}^2$	−0.739*** (0.125)	−0.604*** (0.107)	−0.520*** (0.145)
$WCF_{i,t-1}^2$ *D	0.536*** (0.113)	0.226 (0.152)	0.314* (0.175)
$SIZE_{i,t-1}$	−0.0285 (0.0244)	0.0285* (0.0150)	−0.000461 (0.00971)
$GROWTH_{i,t-1}$	−0.00342*** (0.000774)	−0.00336*** (0.000590)	−0.00153** (0.000654)
$LEV_{i,t-1}$	−0.159 (0.123)	−0.264** (0.118)	−0.143* (0.0760)
$OROE_{i,t}$	−0.333***	−0.381***	−0.392***
Constant	0.463	−0.270	0.119
	0.308	0.185	0.12

***p<0.01, **p<0.05, *p<0.1.

Table 4. Financial flexibility, WCF and profitability.

the median are accepted as "financially flexible." In the third column, the firms that have cash ratios in the top of 75% of all firms and have leverage ratios in the bottom 75% of all firms are accepted as financially flexible. Dummy variables are used to discriminate the financially flexible firms. The dummy variable takes the value of 1 if the firm is financially flexible; otherwise,

http://dx.doi.org/10.5772/intechopen.72760

it takes the value of zero. For the firms that are financially flexible, the breakpoint is found by the equation of $-(\beta_1+\delta_2)/2(\beta_2+\delta_2)$, whereas the breakpoint is calculated by utilizing $\frac{-\beta_1}{2\beta_2}$ equation for the other firms. When the firms are categorized according to their leverage ratios, the breakpoint of financially flexible firms is found to be 0.74, and it is 0.41 for the others. When the categorization is based on cash ratios, the breakpoint for financially flexible firms is found to be 0.57, while it is 0.52 for the other firms. As for the last classification, which is based on cash and leverage ratios, the results show that the breakpoint for financially flexible firms is 0.65, while it is 0.51 for the other firms. These results show that financially flexible firms can finance a greater portion of WCR to increase their profitability, WCF.

The results of financial flexibility, WCF, and profitability are presented in **Table 4**.

5. Conclusion

In this study, the relationship between the proportion of short-term financial debt used to finance WCR and profitability is investigated. To do this the firms that are quoted on Borsa Istanbul chemical, petroleum, rubber, and plastic sector over 2005–2015 period are analyzed using a two-step GMM method. The results showed that WCR financed with short-term financial debt has a positive effect on profitability up to a breakpoint. Above this point the effect on profitability is found to be negative. In other words, the relationship between short-term financial debt used to finance WCR and profitability is a concave-shaped relationship. The firms with low short-term financial debt-to-WCR ratios can increase their profitability by increasing the proportion of WCR that is financed with short-term financial debt, whereas the firms with high short-term financial debt-to-WCR ratios will harm their profitability by increasing the proportion of short-term financial debt in WCR financing. Further analysis also revealed that the breakpoint for financially flexible firms occurs at higher levels of short-term financial debt-to-working capital requirement ratios.

In the working capital literature, studies are generally focused on the relationship between investment in WCR and profitability. But the results of this study revealed that the financing of WCR is at least as important as the investment in WCR in terms of profitability. This study also sheds light about the benefits and limits of using short-term financial debt in WCR financing for managers.

Since there may be sectoral differences among different sectors that may affect the results, further research may be conducted on other sectors to reveal these differences.

Author details

Burcu Dinçergök

Address all correspondence to: burcu.dincergok@atilim.edu.tr

Atılım University Management Department, Ankara, Turkey

References

[1] Deelof M. Does working capital management affect profitability of Belgian firms. Journal of Business Finance & Accounting. 2003;**30**(3&4):573-587

[2] Vahid TK, Elham G, Mohsen AK, Mohammedreza E. Working capital management and corporate performance: Evidence from Iranian companies. Procedia: Social and Behavioral Sciences. 2012;**65**:1313-1318

[3] Öz Y, Güngör B. Çalışma sermayesi yönetiminin firma karlılığı üzerine etkisi: Imalat sektörüne yönelik panel veri analizi. Atatürk İktisadi ve İdari Bilimler Dergisi. 2007;**10**(2):1-14. http://e-dergi.atauni.edu.tr/ataunisosbil/article/viewFile/1020000442/1020000436

[4] Akbulut R. IMKB'de imalat sektöründeki işletmelerde işletme sermayesi yönetiminin karlılık üzerine etkisini ölçmeye yönelik bir araştırma. İstanbul Üniversitesi İşletme Fakültesi Dergisi. 2011;**40**(2):195-206

[5] Coşkun E, Kök D. Çalışma sermayesi politikalarının karlılık üzerine etkisi: Dinamik panel uygulaması. Ege Akademik Bakış. 2011;**11**:75-85

[6] Kendirli S, Konak F. İşletme Sermayesi Yönetiminin Firma Performansı Üzerindeki Etkisi: BIST Gıda, İçecek Endeksi Uygulaması. Akademik Bakış Dergisi. 2014;**41**:1-17

[7] Pais MA, Paulo MG. Working capital management and SME'S performance: Portuguese evidence. International Journal of Managerial Finance. 2005;**11**(3):341-358

[8] Banos-Caballero S, Garcia-Teruel PJ, Martinez-Solano P. Financing of working capital requirement, flexibility and SME performance. Journal of Business Economics and Management. 2016;**17**(6):1189-1204

[9] Poyraz E. İşletme sermayesi finanslama stratejilerinin karlılık oranları üzerindeki etkisi: Akbank T.A.Ş uygulaması. Dokuz Eylül Üniversitesi İİBF Dergisi. 2012;**27**(1):47-56

[10] Aksoy A, Yalçıner K. İşletme Sermayesi Yönetimi. Detay Yayıncılık; 2013. 488 p

[11] Brigham EF, Houston JF. Fundamentals of financial management. 10th edition. Thomson/South Western; 2004. 831 p

[12] Banos-Caballero S, Garcia-Teruel PJ, Martinez-Solano P. How does working capital affect the profitability of Spanish SMEs. Small Business Economics. 2012;**39**:517-529

[13] Singhania M, Sharma N, Rohit JY. Working capital management and profitability: Evidence from Indian manufacturing companies. Decision. 2014;**41**:327-337

[14] Aktas N, Croci E, Petmezas D. Is working capital management value-enhancing? Evidence from firm performance and investments. Journal of Corporate Finance. 2015;**30**:98-113

[15] Şamiloğlu F, Demirgüneş K. Effect of working capital management on firm profitability: Evidence from Turkey. The International Journal of Applied Economics and Finance. 2008;**2**(1):44-50

[16] Van Horne JC, Wachowicz JM. Fundamentals of financial management. 13th edition. London: Pearson; 2008. 719 p

[17] Jun SG, Jen FC. Trade-off model on debt maturity structure. Review of Quantitative Finance and Accounting. 2003;**20**(1):5-34

[18] Myers S. Determinants of corporate borrowing. Journal of Financial Economics. 1977;**5**: 147-175

[19] Stulz R. Does financial structure matter for economic growth? A corporate finance perspective. Working paper. Ohio: Ohio State University. 2000

[20] Rajan R, Winton A. Covenants and collateral as incentives to monitor. Journal of Finance. 1995;**50**:1113-1146

[21] Byoun S. Financial flexibility and capital structure decision. SSRN Electronic Journal. 2011:1-48. Available at https://papers.ssrn.com/sol3/papers.cfm?abstract_id=1108850

[22] Kennedy P. A Guide to Econometrics. 6th ed. Blackwell Publishing. 2008

[23] Arellano M, Bond SM. Some test of specification for panel data: Monte Carlo evidence and an application to employment equations. Review of Economics Studies. 1991;**58**(2):227-297

[24] Baum CF. An Introduction to Modern Econometrics Using Stata. Stata Press; 2006

[25] Greene WH. Econometric Analysis. 5th ed. Prentice Hall; 2003. 1026 p

[26] Ghosh A, Moon D. Corporate debt financing and earnings quality. Journal of Business Finance and Accounting. 2010;**37**(5-6):538-559

[27] Billet MT, King TD, Mauer DC. Growth opportunities and the choice of leverage, debt maturity, and covenants. Journal of Finance. 2007;**62**:697-730

[28] Lins KV, Servaes H, Tufano P. What drives corporate liquidity? An international survey of cash holdings and lines of credit. Journal of Financial Economics. 2010;**98**:160-196

[29] Campello M, Graham JR, Harvey CR. The real effects of financial constraints: Evidence from a financial crisis. Journal of Financial Economics. 2010;**97**:470-487

[30] Faulkender M, Wang R. Corporate financial policy and the value of cash. Journal of Finance. 2006;**61**(4):1957-1990

[31] Kalcheva I, Lins KV. International evidence on cash holdings and expected managerial agency problems. Review of Financial Studies. 2007;**20**:1087-1112

[32] Harford J, Mansi S, Maxwell W. Corporate governance and firm cash holdings in the US. Journal of Financial Economics. 2008;**87**:535-555

[33] DeAngelo H, DeAngelo L. Capital structure, payout policy, and financial flexibility. Working Paper. 2007. Available at http://ssrn.com/abstract=916093

[34] Gamba A, Triantis A. The value of financial flexibility. Journal of Finance. 2008;**63**(5): 2263-2296. http://dx.doi.org/10.1111/j.1540-6261.2008.01397.x

Chapter 10

The Effects of Working Capital Management on Mining Firm's Profitability: Empirical Evidence from an Emerging Market

Mutlu Başaran Öztürk and Gizem Vergili

Additional information is available at the end of the chapter

http://dx.doi.org/10.5772/intechopen.71800

Abstract

Working capital management decisions are the most important among the financial decisions in terms of companies. Working capital expresses financing and management of the short-term investment; in other words, profitability and liquidity are among the main factors affecting the objectives of the companies. The management of working capital components in emerging markets such as Turkey, where financial markets have inadequate depth and financial product diversity, with insufficient saving volume and capital accumulation, is an important topic. In this chapter, we examine the relationship between the components of working capital and profitability; a sample consisting of Istanbul Stock Exchange (ISE) listed mining firms for the period of 2009Q4–2015Q3 that has been analyzed under a panel data analysis. The main reason for choosing the mining sector is because it is the most strategic sector in developing countries. As a result, empirical findings of the study show that growth (firm growth in sales) and INVP (inventory period) affect ROA (return on assets), which represent firm profitability positively, while size (firm size) affects firm profitability negatively. On the other hand, the other independent variables included in the regression model LEV (leverage), CCC (cash conversion cycle), and ACRP (accounts receivables period) have no statistically significant effects on firm profitability for mining sector in Turkey.

Keywords: working capital, working capital management, emerging markets, profitability, mining firms

1. Introduction

Working capital, which represents the current assets of firms, is one of the main factors affecting business objectives such as profitability and liquidity. The fulfillment of payment obligations, increasing operating volume, and providing superiority to the competitor firms are closely related to working capital management. In fact, working capital management is not only limited to managing short-term assets but also involves short-term liabilities.

Working capital consists of cash and cash equivalents, receivables, and inventories. There are also many factors that influence working capital and its components; therefore, businesses need to be cautious in such decisions and should make detailed analyses. Working capital components' contribution to the purpose of the companies depends on the optimum management of it. In emerging markets where there are insufficient saving volume and capital accumulations, and inadequate financial market depth and financial product diversity are the main problems, working capital management is becoming more important.

This study has been done on mining sector firms in Turkey, which is one of the developing countries, in order to show the relationship between the components of working capital and profitability. In theoretical part of the study, literature review, importance of working capital management in emerging markets, and also general properties of mining companies are handled. In empirical part, panel data analysis is carried out 2009Q4–2015Q3 in mining sector, which is a strategic sector especially for the developing countries. The conclusion section includes a general evaluation and results.

2. The importance of working capital management in emerging markets

Emerging markets concept was used in economic literature for the first time by the International Finance Corporation (IFC) in 1981. IFC is one of the five[1] organizations affiliated to the World Bank. Emerging markets is a concept that is used to represent the markets of countries with high economic potential. These countries are expected to be ranked in the "developed country" class in the future and offer high-return opportunities to their investors [1]. These countries that grow very fast compared to developed countries also have higher risks associated with the sudden stop in economic growth, the sudden fluctuations in asset prices, and the economic and political instability.

According to the "Global Economic Prospects and the Developing Countries" published by the World Bank, developing countries constitute 80% of the world population and also represents 20% of the global economy. The number of multinational corporations operating in emerging markets is now over 20,000. According to *The Economist*, multinational corporations anticipate that 70% of their future growth will be from the emerging markets [2].

The concept of emerging markets has expanded to include almost all developing countries in the period from its existence to nowadays. The rapid development of trade in emerging markets, the efforts of financial liberalization, the growth in financial market, and the need to diversify international portfolio managers have caused investors and companies to focus on the

[1]The World Bank Group consists of five complimentary organizations. These are International Bank for Reconstruction and Development (IBRD), International Development Association (IDA), International Finance Corporation (IFC), Multilateral Investment Guarantee Agency (MIGA), and International Center for Settlement of Investment Disputes (ICSID).

http://dx.doi.org/10.5772/intechopen.71800

emerging markets of developing countries. According to the IFC, portfolio investments have continued to grow in emerging markets since the 1980s, with the exception of the financial crisis period. The geographical location of some of the developing countries is presented in **Table 1**.

Working capital management is even more important in emerging markets due to insufficient development of financial markets and inadequate capital accumulation. Global crises, which are more and more frequent today with increasing national and international competition, have made working capital management more important especially for developing country firms. The KPMG 2010 report about working capital management states that firms around the world place more emphasis on management of working capital after the crisis [4].

Working capital consists of funds linked to production factors for the period starting from the beginning of production to income generation [5]. Working capital refers to the firm's investment in short-term assets that can be converted into cash in less than a year. Cash and cash equivalents, inventories, and receivables that are current asset items in a balance sheet make up the components of working capital. However, management of working capital is not just about current assets; it also involves short-term liabilities. Especially in Western literature, working capital is stated as a "net working capital" which can be reached by the formula "current assets-current liabilities."

A manufacturing company fulfills three main functions such as production, sales, and collection. The components of working capital are internally related. If these three main functions are performed simultaneously in a company, there will not be a need for working capital. In this study, working capital concept is expressed as a total amount of current assets.

Middle and Eastern Europe	East Asia and Pacific	Latin America and Caribbean	South Asia	South Europe and Middle Asia	Sub-Sahara and Africa	Middle East and North Africa
Russia Federation	China	Argentina	Bangladesh	Azerbaijan	Angola	Afghanistan
The Czech Republic	Indonesia	Bolivia	India	Bulgaria	Burkina Faso	Algeria
Hungary	Malaysia	Brazil	Maldives	Croatia	Cameroon	Egypt
Lithuania	The Philippines	Chile	Nepal	Kazakhstan	Çahad	Iraq
Poland	South Korea	Colombia	Pakistan	Romania	Gambia	Iran
Slovenia	Taiwan	Mexico	Sri Lanka	*Turkey*	Kenya	Jordan
Estonia	Thailand	Paraguay		Turkmenistan	Nigeria	Kuwait
Georgia	Vietnam	Peru		Albania	South Africa	Morocco
Ukraine	Fiji	Uruguay		Bosnia and Herzegovina	Sudan	Saudi Arabia
Armenia	Cambodia	Venezuela		Moldova	Somalia	Tunisia
	Papua New Guinea	Nicaragua		Tajikistan		United Arab Emirates

Resource: [3].

Table 1. Developing countries according to geographical locations.

Effective management of working capital, which directly affects the company's liquidity and profitability, is important in terms of business finance. The management of working capital components also contributes business goal. This contribution is intended to maximize the net present value of the companies. Financial manager needs to consider and evaluate the cash-generating power of the company in the crisis period as well as interest in maximizing the net present value of the company during normal [6].

The main components of working capital, as previously mentioned, comprise current assets and short-term liabilities. The main objective of working capital management is to keep an optimal balance among each of the working capital components [7]. Working capital, which represents the current assets of companies, is one of the main factors affecting the profitability and liquidity of the company. The type of working capital management has an important effect on profitability and liquidity of the companies [8]. There needs to be a significant balance that working capital has to establish between these two factors. In other words, focusing on only optimal liquidity or profitability can have a negative effect on financial performance [9]. The optimal level of working capital for the companies can be achieved by balancing profitability and liquidity. The idle part of the working capital leads to decline in profitability, while the deficit in working capital causes the default risk.

The fact that working capital components are influenced by many factors necessitates financial managers to be careful in their decisions and financial analysis. Companies try to keep an optimal level of working capital that maximizes their value. Accomplishment of this aim depends on efficient working capital management.

3. Literature review

In finance literature, importance of working capital management has been a common thought among researchers. There have been various studies to analyze the relationship of working capital components and the profitability of firms. A lot of different indicators are used to represent working capital components like cash conversion cycle, inventory period, payment period, leverage, growth, etc. For the profitability of a firm, in different kinds of studies, we can see these indicators as return on asset ratio, return on equity and gross operating profit, net profit margin, etc. Some of them reveal that there is a positive relationship between working capital components and profitability, while others suggest that there is a negative relationship or no statistically significant relationship.

Some researchers are seen to use just return on asset indicator as a profitability measurement, as we have done in our study. For Turkey, Şamiloğlu and Demirgüneş [10] analyzed the effect of working capital management on firm profitability for the period of 1998–2007 manufacturing firms listed in Istanbul Stock Exchange (ISE). They have chosen return on assets as the measure of profitability. Empirical findings of the study showed that accounts receivables period, inventory period, and leverage affect firm profitability negatively, while growth (in sales) has a positive effect [10]. For Cyprus, Charitou et al. [11] investigated the effects of working capital management on firm's financial performance in an emerging market. Their data set consisted of 43 firms listed in the Cyprus Stock Exchange for the period of

1998–2007. Empirical results indicated that the cash conversion cycle and all its major components, namely, days in inventory, days in sales outstanding, and creditors payment period, were associated with firms' profitability. Days in inventory is inversely related to profitability. The sales growth has a positive coefficient with return on assets, meaning that growth leads to increase profitability [11]. In both studies, while inventory period has a negative effect, growth in sales has a positive effect on return on assets as a profitability measurement.

Making use of return on equity as a measure of profitability, Sharaf and Haddad [12] examined the relationship between working capital management and profitability using panel data analysis for a sample that consists of 43 industrial companies listed in the Amman Stock Exchange in Jordan, during the period of 2000–2012. The results show a significant negative relationship between cash conversion cycle and profitability, whereas a positive relationship between payables deferral period and return on equity as a measurement of profitability [12].

For Kenya, Mathuva [13] looked at the influence of working capital management components on corporate profitability for companies listed on the Nairobi Stock Exchange (NSE) for the period of 1993–2008. Net operating profit was chosen as the dependent variable. The key findings from the study were, firstly, a highly significant negative relationship was found between the time it takes for firms to collect cash from their customers (accounts collection period) and profitability. This means that the more profitable a firm is the shorter the cash collection time will be from their customers. Secondly, a highly significant positive relationship was found between the period taken to convert inventories into sales (the inventory conversion period) and profitability. In our study also, we obtained the same result that the inventory period positively affects firm profitability. This means that firms which maintain sufficiently high inventory levels reduce costs of possible interruptions in the production process and loss of business due to scarcity of products. This reduces the firm supply costs and protects them against price fluctuations. Thirdly, a highly significant positive relationship was found between the time it takes the firm to pay creditors (average payment period) and profitability. This implies that the longer a firm takes to pay its creditors, the more profitable it is [13].

Some of the researchers used gross operating profit as a profitability indicator in their studies. Rahman et al. [14] examined the relationship between working capital management and profitability of 10 sample companies listed in Chittagong Stock Exchange (CSE) of Bangladesh with primary and secondary data. The study clearly asserts that sample companies listed in CSE have enough scope to enhance their profitability by the use of working capital in more efficient ways [14]. On the other hand, Husain and Alnefaee [15] selected to analyze the impact of working capital management and the profitability of 18 listed agriculture and food companies of Saudi Arabia for the period of 2009–2014. Gross operating profit as dependent variable and average collection period, average payment period, inventory turnover in days, and cash conversion cycle as independent variables were used. The regression analysis revealed that there is no significant impact of working capital management on profitability for this sample [15].

Many researchers have focused on the relationship between different types of profitability measures and working capital management. Most of these studies support the conclusion that there is a negative relation between profitability and working capital management measures, like the average collection period, inventory turnover in days, and cash conversion cycle. Ahmadi et al. (2012) investigated the relationship between working capital and profitability at companies of food industry group member Tehran Stock Exchange. They used operational profit as profitability. The results showed that average accounts collection period, average inventory turnover period in days, average payment period, and cash conversion cycle have a negative relation with profitability [16]. On the other hand, Arbidane and Ignatjeva (2013) examined the effect of working capital on profitability of Latvian manufacturing firms on the sample of 182 firms for the period of 2004 to 2010. For profitability, return on assets and gross operating profitability indicators were determined. The results of the research that has been performed in relation to Latvian manufacturing enterprises confirm the existence of a correlation between components of working capital and profitability [17]. Aregbeyen (2013) analyzed the effect of working capital management on the profitability of a sample of 48 large manufacturing firms quoted on the Nigerian Stock Exchange (NSE) for the period of 1993–2005. Profitability was alternatively measured by gross operating profit, net operating income, and return on assets. The results indicated that the firms have been inefficient in their working capital management, and this caused significant reductions in profitability. Manufacturing firm in Nigeria should shorten average collection period, average pay period, inventory turnover days, and reduce their cash conversion cycle to be successful [18]. Moreover, Alavinasab and Davoudi [19] who focused on return on assets and return on equity ratios for profitability measurement selected 147 listed companies on Tehran Stock Exchange for the period of 2005–2009. The results show a negative significant relationship between cash conversion cycle and both return on assets and return on equity [19]. Singhania et al. [20] used cash conversion cycle as a measure of working capital management, whereas gross operating profit was a proxy for the firms' profitability. The sample consisted of Indian manufacturing companies of BSE-500 index of the Bombay Stock Exchange for the period from 2005 until 2012. The results revealed that cash conversion cycle of a company has a negative correlation with its profitability [20]. Furthermore, Şamiloğlu and Akgün [21] examined the relationship between working capital management and performance, using variables such as profitability between accounts receivables period, account payable period, and cash conversion cycle on Istanbul Stock Exchange (ISE). One hundred and twenty manufacturing firms were selected for a period of 10 years from 2003 to 2012. The results showed that a significant and negative relationship exists between accounts receivables period and return on asset, return on equity, operating profit margin, and net margin in manufacturing industry [21].

All the researchers above have investigated the effects of working capital components on the profitability of firms. To carry out a somewhat similar research but in a different country and sector, namely, the Turkish mining sector, research data and method section describes the variables that will be used for the investigation and also the data sample.

4. General properties of mining firms

Mining is one of the most important sources of income and foreign exchange for countries. For this reason, the mining sector has become a strategic sector among countries. About 30 million people work in mines around the world. Considering the amount of employment each miner has created employment for other workers in different sectors and also the family members they are obliged to look at, mining is a giant sector closely related to 300 million people in the world [22].

There are some differences that distinguish the mining industry from other sectors. These features are:

- When the mines are produced, they cannot be replaced because of depletion.
- The investment repayment period is quite long.
- No chance of choosing a location.
- Operation has to be at the place of production.
- A labor-intensive sector that contributes to employment.
- The high cost of regeneration when activities are interrupted.

The mining sector, which has great importance in development and economic progress of countries, creates significant added value. Share of mining in GNP is 5% in the USA, 4% in Germany, 3.7% in Canada, 6.5% in Australia, 22% in Russia Federation, 8.5% in Chile, 6.5% in South Africa, 3% in Brazil, and 1.2% in Turkey. While the share of mining in GNP was 44% in the 1940s in Turkey, it started to decrease gradually in the 1950s. After the transition to the planned economy period, this deceleration accelerated to 1% in the 2000s [23].

Turkey's mineral resources are almost as diverse as mineral sources of a continent. There are more than 40 different minerals in Turkey. Despite of all inadequacies related to searching for boron, marble, thorium, trona, zeolite, pumice, and celestite mines, Turkey has the largest reserves for these elements. However, the mining sector in Turkey plays a very small role in the Turkish economy. While Turkey ranks 29th among the 152 countries in terms of the variety of mineral resources produced, Turkey is in the tenth place when it is based on production made in the form of mining. According to producer countries, Turkey is ranked 52nd with the share of 0.16%. The amount of value added created by this production reaches 2–2.5 billion dollars, and its share in GNP is around 1–1.5%, depending on the years. When the mining sector and other sectors based on mining sector are considered together, the share of added value in GNP is around 12%, which means that 22 billion dollars has been created [24].

5. Research data and method

5.1. The objectives and importance of the study

The aim of this study is to reveal the relationship between working capital components (firm size, leverage, firm growth in sales, cash conversion cycle, accounts receivables period, inventory period) and profitability (return on assets) in the mining sector firms which trade in the Istanbul Stock Exchange (ISE). The data are taken from balance sheets and income statements of companies, quarterly from 2009Q4 till 2015Q3, and analyzed using the panel data analysis. Other goals include showing the impact of working capital on profitability in emerging markets and making managers understand the effect of working capital decisions on profitability.

5.2. Study sample and variables

The study sample includes mining sector firms listed on the Istanbul Stock Exchange (ISE) during the period of 2009Q4–2015Q3. All financial statements have been obtained from https://www.kap.org.tr/tr/. The study covers six companies operating in mining sector. The names of the companies included in analysis are shown in **Table 2**.

	ISE	Business fields	Net working capital[a]
1	İhlas Real Estate Project Development and Trade, Inc.[b]	Metallic ore production	17,648,656
2	İpek Natural Energy Resources Research and Production, Inc.	Crude oil and natural gas production	1,830,100
3	Koza Gold Enterprises, Inc.	Coal mining	1,829,124
4	Koza Anatolia Metallic Mining Operations, Inc.	Metallic ore production	1,481,806
5	Metal Real Estate, Inc.	Coal mining	−8,296,551
6	Park Electricity Production Mining Industry and Trade, Inc.	Coal mining	178,655,858

Resource: [25].

[a]Net working capital is calculated by "current assets-current liabilities." These amounts are from the third quarter of 2015.

[b]İhlas Real Estate Project Development and Trade, Inc., which has been working as a İhlas Mining until April 14, 2017 has finished the mining part field of the company due to major work accidents, long-term bureaucratic procedures, difficulties in applying the mining law and regulations, fluctuating price movements, etc.

Table 2. Mining companies operating in Istanbul stock exchange (ISE).

This study investigates the effects of firm size, leverage, firm growth in sales, cash conversion cycle, accounts receivables period, and inventory period on firm profitability. The dependent variable of the regression model is the return on assets. Formulas of variables are given in **Table 3**.

Variables	Formula	Literature
Dependent variable		
ROA	Net income/total assets	Şamiloğlu and Demirgüneş [10] Alavinasab and Davoudi [19] Singhania et al. [20] Madhou et al. [27] Muralıdhara and Shollapur [28] Sharaf and Haddad [12] Şamiloğlu and Akgün [21]
Independent variables		
Size (firm size)	$In_{\text{Total Assets}}$ (natural logarithm of total assets)	Şamiloğlu and Demirgüneş [10] Singhania et al. [20] Madhou et al. [27] Sharaf and Haddad [12] Şamiloğlu and Akgün [21] Muralıdhara and Shollapur [28]

Variables	Formula	Literature
Lev (leverage)	Total debt/total assets	Şamiloğlu and Demirgüneş [10] Singhania et al. [20] Madhou et al. [27] Muralıdhara and Shollapur [28] Şamiloğlu and Akgün [21]
Growth (firm growth in sales)	$(Sales_t - Sates_{t-1}) / Sales_{t-1}$	Şamiloğlu and Demirgüneş [10] Singhania et al. [20] Sharaf and Haddad [12]
CCC (cash conversion cycle)	(ACRP + INVP)-(accounts payables × 365)/cost of sales	Şamiloğlu and Demirgüneş [10] Alavinasab and Davoudi [19] Singhania et al. [20] Madhou et al. [27] Sharaf and Haddad [12] Husain and Alnefaee [15]
ACRP (accounts receivables period)	(accounts receivables × 365)/sales	Şamiloğlu and Demirgüneş [10] Singhania et al. [20] Sharaf and Haddad [12] Husain and Alnefaee [15] Şamiloğlu and Akgün [21] Muralıdhara and Shollapur [28]
INVP (inventory period)	(inventories × 365)/cost of sales	Şamiloğlu and Demirgüneş [10] Singhania et al. [20] Sharaf and Haddad [12] Şamiloğlu and Akgün [21] Muralıdhara and Shollapur [28] Husain and Alnefaee [15]

Table 3. Dependent variable and independent variables.

Definition of dependent variable: profitability

ROA: return on assets is used for profitability measurement. The reason of choosing is that ROA represents the ratio of how much a firm has earned on its assets [26].

Definitions of independent variables: working capital components

Size: firm size is measured by the natural logarithm of total assets. The size of the firm can change according to small or large companies' situation. While large companies can obtain more favorable, extended credit terms from suppliers, smaller ones may be required to pay immediately. Another size of a firm that can make a difference is that bigger companies can purchase larger quantities of products [29].

Lev: leverage shows the rate of the company's debt relative to its assets and its potential risks. In other words, how much the assets of the firm is financed by external debt.

Growth: firm growth in sales is a percentage that represents an increase, decreases in sales volume from period to period, and has an impact on working capital behavior [12].

CCC: cash conversion cycle is a main comprehensive and powerful measure of managing working capital and assessing liquidity in companies [30]. CCC shows the time between spending cash for resources and cash receipts from product sales [31].

ACRP: accounts receivables period reflects in how many days receivables are collected and gives some indication of how fast companies can collect payments from sales.

INVP: inventory period is also called as inventory collection period. It indicates the frequency with which firms convert their cumulative of raw material into finished goods and then sell those products.

5.3. Research methodology

Regression models created using the panel data are called panel regression models. Other names for panel data are pooled data, micro panel data, pooled time series and cross-sectional data, longitudinal data, etc. Pooled panel regression model that is frequently used in the literature will be used in this study. Pooled data are elements of both time series and cross-sectional data [32].

Panel regression model used in the study is as follows:

$$ROA = a_i + \beta_{i1}(SIZE) + \beta_{i2}(LEV) + \beta_{i3}(GROWTH) + \beta_{i4}(CCC) + \beta_{i5}(ACRP) + \beta_{i6}(INVP) + \varepsilon_i \quad (1)$$

According to the Hausman test results that will be mentioned later, in this study the fixed effect model that was found appropriate to was used.

5.4. Constraints of the study

In this study, mining sector listed in Istanbul Stock Exchange (ISE) is chosen as a sample. Although there are many operating mining companies in Turkey, few companies are open to the public. Only quoted companies are included in the study because financial information of unquoted companies is not readily available. This constitutes the greatest constraint of the research. Also, the dates of publicly traded companies are different from each other; therefore, data set is limited between 2009Q4 and 2015Q3.

5.5. Empirical results

5.5.1. Descriptive statistics

Descriptive statistics for dependent and independent variables are calculated in the panel data form. The results are given in **Table 4**.

When we look at the values given in **Table 5**, we can say that size, growth, CCC, and INVP have negative values so the distribution is left tailed. Other variables are positive so the distribution is right tailed.

5.5.2. Stationarity tests

The stationarity of series is tested with Augmented Dickey-Fuller test; Im, Pesaran, and Shin W-stat test; Phillips-Perron test; and Levin, Lin, and Chu test. These tests were developed to observe the stationarity of the data and whether it contains a unit root. In this sample the series contain unit root so the first differences of the series have been used in analysis to avoid

http://dx.doi.org/10.5772/intechopen.71800

	ROA	Size	Lev	Growth	CCC	ACPR	INVP
Mean	4.944843	2.866556	2.411620	0.736065	4.376339	3.351357	4.570842
Median	3.260348	2.977405	2.220768	0.958676	4.863107	3.500431	5.099591
Maximum	12.47728	3.068666	5.768931	2.043083	8.224957	8.139257	6.474505
Minimum	0.826349	2.630181	0.457901	0.009356	0.104758	0.024990	1.000000
Std. Dev.	3.842894	0.163158	0.922734	0.410556	1.690290	1.628396	1.705792
Skewness	0.658287	−0.221510	1.642497	−0.012713	−1.031479	0.071150	−1.346429
Kurtosis	1.797728	1.160462	5.600206	2.790192	3.378884	2.999412	3.419309

Table 4. Summary statistics for the main study variables.

	ROA	Size	Lev	Growth	CCC	ACPR	INVP
ROA	**1.000000**						
Size	−0.657983	**1.000000**					
Lev	−0.028854	−0.413378	**1.000000**				
Growth	0.038117	−0.099312	0.284882	**1.000000**			
CCC	0.197224	0.273313	−0.578595	−0.117231	**1.000000**		
ACPR	0.106368	0.241622	−0.348518	−0.080037	0.721644	**1.000000**	
INVP	0.165374	0.386480	−0.702069	−0.154342	0.908750	0.579284	**1.000000**

Table 5. Correlation matrix.

spurious regressions. Stationarity test results are shown in **Table 6**. The lag length of variables subjected to test is determined by Schwarz information criteria.

As seen in **Table 6**, no variables has reached the probability value greater than 0.05. In other words, the data is stationary. As a result, stationarity of the data has made possible to establish this model.

5.5.3. Regression analysis

There are two different types of panel data analysis. One of them is fixed effects, and the other one is random effect model. In this study, panel data fixed effect model is used. The Hausman test is used to select this model, and the result shows that it gives better results than the random effect panel data analysis (**Table 7**). The hypotheses are as follows:

H_0: Random effect model is appropriate.
H_1: Random effect model is inappropriate (fixed effect model is appropriate).

The Hausman test results explicitly show that the null hypothesis (H_0), which states "random effect model is appropriate," is rejected, since p value (0.0000) is less than 0.05. Based on the Hausman test results, fixed effect model panel data analysis is appropriate for this model (**Table 8**).

Variables	Augmented Dickey-Fuller		Im, Pesaran, and Shin W-stat		Phillips-Perron		Levin, Lin, and Chu	
	t-Statistic	p-Value	t-Statistic	p-Value	t-Statistic	p-Value	t-Statistic	p-Value
ROA	−6.748	0.0000	−6.943	0.0000	9.442	0.0000	−6.754	0.0000
Size	−4.839	0.0000	−3.898	0.0000	7.3447	0.0000	−4.839	0.0000
Lev	5.980	0.0000	−6.280	0.0000	5.6167	0.0000	−2.418	0.0000
Growth	11.980	0.0000	−11.700	0.0000	7.538	0.0000	−7.408	0.0000
CCC	5.5775	0.0000	−9.794	0.0000	5.469	0.0000	−7. 951	0.0000
ACPR	9.616	0.0000	−9.214	0.0000	11.569	0.0000	−9.987	0.0000
NPV	3.935	0.0000	−9.400	0.0000	5.872	0.0000	−8.707	0.0000

Table 6. Stationarity tests of variables.

	Correlated random effects (Hausman test)		
Test summary	Chi square statistic	Chi square f.	Prob.
Cross-sectional random	30.041109	6	0.0000

Table 7. Hausman test results.

Dependent variable	ROA			
Method	Panel fixed effect model			
Sample period	2009Q4–2015Q3			
Sample number	136			
Variable	**Coefficient**	**Std. error**	**t-Statistic**	**Prob.**
C	48.21348	4.341295	11.10578	0.0000
Size	−16.72289	1.451334	−11.52243	0.0000
Lev	−0.031608	0.338043	−0.093504	0.9257
Growth	0.339326	0.745787	0.454990	0.0050
CCC	−0.363589	0.357237	−1.017780	0.3109
ACPR	−0.047350	0.188328	−0.251424	0.8019
INPV	1.366229	0.338755	4.033088	0.0001
Adj.	0.712325			
F-statistic	13.20995			
Prob. (F-statistic)	0.000000			
Durbin-Watson	1.725998			

Table 8. Panel data analysis results.

The purpose of the panel data analysis is to find out the significant impact of working capital components on profitability of mining companies, which are listed in Istanbul Stock Exchange (ISE). **Table 8** shows the results of regression analysis pertaining to ROA (return on assets) and components of working capital including size (firm size), Lev (leverage), growth (firm growth in sales), CCC (cash conversion cycle), ACRP (accounts receivables period), INVP (inventory period). The adjusted R^2 of the model is 0.712 which indicates that 71.2% of the variation in the dependent variable is explained by the model. The Durbin-Watson test statistic tests the null hypothesis that the residuals from a regression are not autocorrelated against the alternative. The Durbin-Watson statistic ranges in value from 0 to 4. A value near 2 indicates non-autocorrelation; a value toward 0 indicates a positive autocorrelation; and a value toward 4 indicates a negative autocorrelation. In this study the result of Durbin-Watson test is 1.7259, which means that there is no autocorrelation. In addition, prob. value of F-statistic (0.0000) is less than 0.05 so the model is statistically significant.

6. Conclusion

The significance of working capital management has increased even more in developing countries with insufficient capital accumulation after the global financial crisis. The researches reveal that companies that are operating in developing countries and succeed in working capital management are affected less in financial crisis. This study empirically investigated the relationship between working capital components and profitability of a sample of six mining sector firms quoted on Istanbul Stock Exchange (ISE) for the period from 2009Q4 to 2015Q3. The independent variables are size (firm size), Lev (leverage), growth (firm growth in sales), CCC (cash conversion cycle), ACRP (accounts receivables period), and INVP (inventory period). The dependent variable of this study is ROA (return on assets) that represents firm profitability.

The results of regression analysis show that growth (firm growth in sales) and INVP (inventory period) affects ROA (return on assets) positively, while size (firm size) affects firm profitability negatively. The other independent variables included in the regression model Lev (leverage), CCC (cash conversion cycle), and ACRP (accounts receivables period) have no statistically significant effects on firm profitability for mining sector in Turkey.

The whole results of study can be disclosed step by step. The positive relationship between INVP (inventory period) and ROA (return on assets) can be explained by the companies' tendency of holding more stocks from 2009 to 2015 that indicates the post crisis period. In this period, it is considered that mining firms invested in stocks to protect against the increases in stock price or aimed to earn by possible increases in stock price.

Other positive relations are found between growth (firm growth in sales) and ROA (return on assets). Firms especially in developing countries tend to credit sale in the post crises period in order to increase sales amounts. As a result, because of this reason, sales amounts are growing compared to the previous period. Growth in sales leads to more efficient use of firms' assets, and in this case, it can affect its profitability in a positive way.

There is a negative relationship between size (firm size) and ROA (return on assets) in this study. As the firm size increases, assets are growing, and more resources are allocated to the assets. It is considered that cost of financing resulting from the increase of investment amount to current and fixed assets has a negative effect on return on assets.

The study was conducted only taking into account internal factors related to the firms. In the future studies, external factors (general economic situation, inflation, etc.) can be taken into account. If the data of firms operating in mining sectors, which are nonpublic companies, are found reliably, analyses can be applied on a wider sample.

Author details

Mutlu Başaran Öztürk[1]* and Gizem Vergili[2]

*Address all correspondence to: mbozturk@ohu.edu.tr

1 Niğde Ömer Halisdemir University, Niğde, Turkey

2 Afyon Kocatepe University, Afyonkarahisar, Turkey

References

[1] Atik H. Finansal krizlerin gölgesinde yükselen piyasa ekonomileri [thesis]. Türkiye Kalkınma Bankası A.Ş. Araştırma Müdürlüğü: Ankara; 2005

[2] Capital [Internet]. 2015. Available from: https://www.capital.com.tr/yonetim/liderlik/gelismekte-olan-piyasalardaki-is-modelleri. [Accessed: 2017-06-20]

[3] World Bank, Global Economic Prospects and Developing Countries [Internet]. 2009. Available from: http://documents.worldbank.org/curated/en/586421468176682557/Global-economic-prospects-2009-commodities-at-the-crossroads [Accessed: 25-06-2017]

[4] KPMG. [Internet]. 2010. Available from: http://www.kpmg.com/cn/en/issuesandinsights/articlespublications/pages/cash-matters- 201003.aspx [Accessed: 2017-06-26]

[5] Aksoy A, Yalçıner K. İşletme Sermayesi Yönetimi. Gazi Kitabevi: Ankara; 2008

[6] Waide JH, Maier SF. Managing Corporate Liquidity an Introduction to Working Capital Management. Canada: John Wiley & Sons Inc; 1995

[7] Korankye T. Empirical analysis of working capital management and its impact on the profitability of listed manufacturing firms in Ghana. Research Journal of Finance and Accounting. 2013;**4**(1):124-131 Stable URL: http://www.iiste.org/Journals/index.php/RJFA/article/viewFile/4050/4178

[8] Deloof M. Does working capital management affects profitability of Belgian firms? Journal of Business Finance and Accounting. 2003;**30**(3-4):573-587

[9] Shin HH, Soenen HL. Efficiency of working capital and corporate profitability. Financial Practice and Education. 1998;**8**:37-45

[10] Şamiloğlu F, DemirgüneŞ K. The effect of working capital management on firm profitability: Evidence from Turkey. The International Journal of Applied Economics and Finance. 2008;**2**(1):44-50

[11] Charitou MS, Elfani M, Lois P. The effect of working capital management on firm's profitability: Empirical evidence from an emerging market. Journal of Business & Economics Research. 2010;**8**(12):63-68

[12] Sharaf RF, Haddad FS. The relationship between working capital management and profitability for industrial companies listed in Amman stock exchange. Jordan Journal of Business Administration. 2015;**11**(2):509-524

[13] Mathuva DM. The influence of working capital management components on corporate profitability: A survey on Kenyan listed firms. Research Journal of Business Management. 2010;**4**(1):1-11

[14] Rahman MM, Uddin MN, Ibrahim S. Measuring the relationship between working capital management and profitability: Empirical evidence from Bangladesh. Journal of Accounting and Finance. 2015;**15**(8):120-132

[15] Husain S, Alnafaee S. The effects of working capital management on profitability of firms: Evidence from agriculture and food industry of kingdom of Saudi Arabia. Journal of Emerging Issues in Economics, Finance and Banking (JEIEFB) An Online International Research Journal. 2016;**5**(1):1684-1698

[16] Ahmadi M, Arasi IS, Garajafary M. Studying the relationship between working capital management and profitability at Tehran stock exchange: A case study of food industry. Research Journal of Applied Sciences, Engineering and Technology. 2012;**4**(13):1868-1874

[17] Arbidane I, Ignatjeva S. The relationship between working capital management and profitability: A Latvian case. Global Review of Accounting and Finance. 2013;**4**(1):148-158

[18] Aregbeyen O. The effects of working capital management on the profitability of Nigerian manufacturing firms. Journal of Business Economics and Management. 2013;**14**(3):520-534. DOI: 10.3846/16111699.2011.651626

[19] Alavinasab SM, Davoudi E. Studying the relationship between working capital management and profitability of listed companies in Tehran stock exchange. Business Management Dynamics. 2013;**2**(7):01-08

[20] Singhania M, Sharma N, Rohit JY. Working capital management and profitability: Evidence from Indian manufacturing companies. Decision. 2014;**41**(3):313-326. DOI: 10.1007/s40622-014-0043-3

[21] Şamiloğlu F, Akgün Aİ. The relationship between working capital management and profitability: Evidence from Turkey. Business and Economics Research Journal. 2016;**7**(2):1-14. DOI: 10.20409/berj.2016217492

[22] Mining Sector. [Internet]. 2015. Available from: http://www.isguvenligi.net/iskollari-ve-is-guvenligi/madencilik-sektorunde-is-sagligi-ve-guvenligi/. [Accessed 27-06-2017]

[23] Mining Sector. [Internet]. 2015. Available from: http://www.maden.org.tr/genel/bizden_detay.php?kod=6620&tipi=5&sube=0. [Accessed 28-06-2017]

[24] Mining Sector. [Internet]. 2015. Available from: http://www.maden.org.tr/genel/bizden_detay.php?kod=6620&tipi=5&sube=0. [Accessed 28-06-2017]

[25] KAP. [Internet]. 2015. Available from: https://www.kap.org.tr/tr/. [Accessed: 2017-06-29]

[26] Melicher RW, Leach JC. Entrepreneurial Finance. 3rd ed. Mason, Ohio: South-Western Cengage Learning; 2009

[27] Madhou A, Moosa I, Ramiah V. Working capital as a determinant of corporate profitability. Review of Pacific Basin Financial Markets and Policies. 2015;**18**(4):1-17. DOI: 10.1142/S0219091515500241

[28] Muralıdhara, Shollapur, MR. Effect of working capital management on firm's profitability: Evidence from selected Indian retail firms. Finance India. Indian Institute of Finance. 2016:**XXX**(4):1251-1263

[29] Soekhoe SG. The Effects of Working Capital Management on the Profitability of Dutch Listed Firms. [Thesis]. Netherland: University of Twente; 2012

[30] Richards V, Laughlin E. A cash conversion cycle approach to liquidity analysis. Financial Management. 1980;**9**(1):32-38

[31] Jose ML, Lancaster C, Stevens JL. Corporate returns and cash conversion cycles. Journal of Economics and Finance. 1996;**20**(1):33-46

[32] Gujurati. Basic, Econometrics. 4th ed. New York; McGraw-Hill Companies; 2004

Chapter 11

The Effect of Working Capital Management on Profitability in Emerging Countries: Evidence from Turkey

Samet Evci and Nazan Şak

Additional information is available at the end of the chapter

http://dx.doi.org/10.5772/intechopen.70871

Abstract

This study aims to reveal the tradeoff between working capital components and firm's profitability by using the data of the firms listed on Borsa Istanbul Industry Index in Turkey. Annual data of 41 firms are used for the period 2005–2016 in the study. The working capital components and firm's profitability tradeoff was examined via the fixed effects panel regression model. Dependent variable is defined as return on assets; independent variables are cash conversion cycle, inventory conversion period, and payables deferral period; and control variables are sales growth, the ratio of short-term financial debts to short-term debts, and the ratio of fixed assets to total assets. Findings show the existence of tradeoff working capital management profitability. A negative relationship exists between return on assets and payables deferral period, cash conversion cycle, the ratio of short-term financial debts to short-term debts, and the ratio of fixed assets to total assets while return on assets is positively related to inventory conversion period and sales growth.

Keywords: working capital management, profitability, panel data analysis, emerging countries, Turkey

1. Introduction

Global economic integration for developing countries through economic liberalization and democratization is accepted as the best way to overcome destitution and discrimination [1]. At this point, the industry sector plays a significant role. According to the World Bank data, the share of the industry sector in the gross domestic product (GDP) of emerging countries such as China, India, and Brazil in 2016 is 40, 29, and 21%, respectively [2]. For Turkey, which is among the emerging countries, the industry sector is important for the country economy in terms of value added export and employment [3]. According to the World Bank data, the industry sector's share in GDP is 32% [2]. The share of the industry sector in exports is around 92% [4]. In this case, the industry sector will remain important for the Turkish economy in the future.

The industry sector, which plays a key role in the Turkish economy, is faced with many problems such as lack of qualified workforce, inadequacy of infrastructure and technology, weak competition power, and difficulties in marketing and financing. The financing problem is one of the most important problems faced by these firms. These firms need to be able to use their existing resources effectively and be self-sufficient because of the scarcity of funding resources and the insufficient accumulation of capital. Working capital, which is seen as the lifeblood of a business, has an important role in the return of the owner's reckoning, and has a decisive influence on liquidity [5], is important at this point.

Firms need working capital to begin its business operations, carry on its activities efficiently, and meet its short run obligations [6]. Working capital management is concerned with the day-to-day activities rather than long-term investment decisions [7]. Working capital is a part of firm's current assets, which are converted into cash within a year or less [8]. In this sense, working capital components (WCC) are cash, cash equivalents, inventories, accounts receivables, and accounts payables.

Investment in the working capital components is important for all industrial enterprises to be powerful financially. A firm can collect its receivables in a short time and restrict credit sales to reduce account receivables and increase cash inflows. However, rigid sales policies and low credit sales would lead to loss of sales, thus causing profits to fall [6]. On the other hand, high inventory levels and flexible credit sales policy can contribute to increased sales. Because sales on credit allow the customer to examine the product before paying, it may increase sales [9]. There are some advantages to work with high inventory levels such as preventing customer losses caused by not having enough stock level and protecting against price volatilities [10]. However, the high inventory and loose trade credit policies lead to the locking of the money to the working capital [9]. In this context, firms that invest heavily in inventory and accounts receivables may be exposed to low profits [11]. Another component that has an impact on the working capital requirement is accounts payables. Deferment of payments to suppliers can enable the firm to evaluate the product bought and may be a cheap and flexible funding source. But, postponing payments can be expensive, if the firm has got a discount for early payment [9]. In this case, the level of accounts payables of the firm may affect the firm's profitability.

The style of WCM may have a considerable influence on the profitability, risk, and liquidity of the firm [12]. The firm that invests more in current assets is more liquid than a firm that does not invest. This will reduce the firm's liquidity risk, while decreasing overall rate of return, because the return of current assets is less than the return of other assets [13]. While lower investment in the working capital expressed as aggressive working capital policy is associated with higher returns and higher risk, more investment in the working capital expressed as conservative working capital policy is associated with lower return and lower risk [14]. The firm has to choose between aggressive and conservative working capital policies depending on its purpose [15].

Effective WCM is a significant factor affecting the survival of the firm, the continuity of its activities, and the maintenance of liquidity and profitability [16]. Excessive working capital

http://dx.doi.org/10.5772/intechopen.70871

like inadequate working capital has led many businesses to fail and prevent their growth [17]. WCM is important due to the effect on profitability of firm, firm's risk, and the firm value [18]. In this context, this study aims to reveal the tradeoff between WCC and firm's profitability by using the data of the firms listed on Borsa Istanbul (BIST) Industry Index in Turkey.

This study, which investigates the impact of the WCM on the profitability of Turkish industrial firms, is considered to contribute on the determination of working capital investment levels of these firms, determination of the distribution among the working capital components, effective use of scarce resources, and resource supply and sustainability of future investments by applying a working capital that will increase the profitability. There are a number of studies covering the developed countries in the literature, while there are limited studies covering the emerging countries. It is anticipated that the study will contribute to the literature in terms of comparing the relationship between the WCM and profitability of industrial firms of emerging countries like Turkey. It is thought that the study with these aspects will be beneficial to both managers and researchers.

2. Literature review

There are studies in the literature that examine WCC-firm's profitability tradeoff in terms of different countries and different sectors. The findings obtained from these studies vary depending on the method and data set used. Some of these studies are summarized in **Table 1**.

Authors	Sampling	Variables	Method	Results
In [9]	Hindalco Industries Limited in India	Dependent variables: Profit before tax to total assets ratio Independent variables: Current ratio, liquid ratio, working capital ratio, inventory turnover ratio, receivables turnover ratio and working capital to total assets	Correlation analysis and a multivariate regression model	Findings show that the working capital components are related to profitability of Hindalco Industries Limited
In [21]	Firms in the manufacturing sector listed on BIST in Turkey	Dependent variables: Gross profit ratio Independent variables: The number of days accounts receivable, the number of days of inventory, the number of days accounts payable and net trade cycle Control variables: Financial fixed assets, sales growth, financial liabilities	Panel regression analysis	The relationship between the profitability and inventory turnover ratio, receivables turnover ratio, payable deferral period and net trade cycle is negative
In [25]	Brazilian used companies	Dependent variables: Return on assets, return on sales and return on equity Independent variables: Cash conversion efficiency, debt ratio, days of working capital, days receivable and days inventory	Multiple linear regression	The study shows a negative relationship for return on assets and return on sales with days inventory. Also return on assets has a negative relationship with debt ratio.
In [28]	Manufacturing firms listed in Centre for	Dependent variables: The profit before depreciation tax accounts return on assets	Correlation analysis, panel	The study shows a positive relationship for inventory days

Authors	Sampling	Variables	Method	Results
	Monitoring Indian Economy	Independent variables: Debtors days, inventory days, creditors days, cash velocity, working capital policy, net working capital leverage, size, current ratio	regression analysis	and debtors days with the profitability.
In [22]	Manufacturing corporations listed on Dhaka Stock Exchange in Bangladesh	Dependent variables: Return on asset and net profit margin Independent variables: Receivables Collection Period, inventory turnover period, payable deferral period, cash conversion cycle, current ratio and quick ratio	Single regression analysis	The meaningful relationship exists between the firms' profitability and the working capital components
In [20]	Production and trade firms listed on BIST in Turkey	Dependent variables: Gross profit ratio Independent variables: Inventory turnover ratio, receivables turnover ratio, payable deferral period, net trade cycle Control variables: Ratio of financial fixed assets, firm size, financial leverage ratio	Panel regression analysis	The relationship between gross profit ratio and independent variables is negative
In [27]	Firms in textile industry listed on Karachi Stock Exchange in Pakistan	Dependent variables: Profitability Independent variables: Cash management, account receivables, inventory and account payables	Regression analysis	Cash, account receivables and inventory except accounts payables have a positive relationship with profitability.
In [29]	Manufacturing firms listed on BIST in Turkey	Dependent variables: Return on assets, tobin-q Independent variables: Cash conversion cycle, inventory conversion period, account receivable period, accounts payable period and current ratio	Panel regression analysis	Return on assets has a negative relationship with account receivable period and cash conversion cycle while having a positive relationship with current ratio.
In [36]	Manufacturing firms in Egypt, Kenya, Nigeria and South Africa	Dependent variables: Net operating profit Independent variables: Number of days accounts payable, number of days inventories, the number of days accounts receivables and cash conversion cycle Control variables: firm size board size.	Panel regression analysis	Cash conversion cycles have a negative relationship with net operating profit
In [19]	Firms in the retail sector listed on BIST in Turkey	Dependent variables: Gross profit ratio Independent variables: Inventory turnover ratio, receivables turnover ratio, payable deferral period, net trade cycle	Panel regression analysis	The existence of firms' profitability- working capital components tradeoff is invalid.
In [8]	Cement companies in Kenya	Dependent variables: Firm's profitability Independent variables: Cash conversion cycle Control variables: Sales growth, depth ratio and current ratio	Multivariate regression model	Cash conversion cycle is negatively related to firm's profitability

Authors	Sampling	Variables	Method	Results
In [6]	Indian construction companies	Dependent variables: Return on assets Independent variables: Quick ratio, current ratio, debtors turnover, creditors turnover	Correlation and regression analysis	Working capital ratio is negatively related to firm's profitability
In [24]	Cement firms listed on Karachi Stock Exchange in Pakistan	Dependent variables: Return on assets Independent variables: Current Ratio, quick ratio, net current assets to total assets, working capital turnover ratio, inventory turnover ratio	Panel regression analysis	Findings show that the working capital components is related to the profitability of cement firms
In [23]	Manufacturing and conglomerates firms listed in Nigeria	Dependent variables: Return on assets and return on equity Independent variables: Average payment period, average collection period and inventory turnover period Control variables: Firms' size and leverage	Panel regression analysis	Working capital components except inventory turnover are significant determinants of firm's profitability. Also the negative relationship is observed between average collection period and profitability
In [26]	Firms in Cement Industries listed on Bombay Stock Exchange in India	Dependent variables: Return on Investment Independent variables: Working capital turnover ratio, fixed asset turnover ratio, debtors turnover ratio, inventory turnover ratio, quick ratio, current ratio, firm's size, leverage ratio	Multiple regression analysis	There is not a significant effect of working capital ratio, debtor's turnover ratio, fixed assets turnovers ratio, inventory turnover ratio except current ratio, quick ratio on return on investment
In [34]	Firms in food sector listed on BIST in Turkey	Dependent variables: Return on assets Independent variables: The number of days accounts receivables, the number of days of inventories, the number of days accounts payable, cash conversion cycle Control variables: Current ratio, firm's size, leverage ratio	Panel regression analysis	The number of days accounts receivables and current ratio have a negative and meaningful effect on firms' profitability. But the negative insignificant effect is observed between cash conversion cycle and firms' profitability

Table 1. Overview of the studies about WCC-firm's profitability tradeoff.

3. Methodology

In the study, the impact of WCM on profitability is analyzed via panel data regression model. The panel data models, which allow more consistent estimation results by including both time and cross-sectional properties, are modeled in different ways according to effect of the cross section and time properties [30]. In this context, the models in which both constant and slope parameters are constant with respect to cross section and time unit are called as pooled panel data models and are defined as follows:

$$Y_{it} = \alpha_0 + \sum_{k=1}^{K} \alpha_k X_{kit} + e_{it}; \quad \mathrm{i} = 1, 2, \ldots \mathrm{N}; \quad \mathrm{t} = 1, 2 \ldots, \mathrm{T} \tag{1}$$

The subscript i in the model is a cross-sectional unit such as an individual or a firm; t represents the time dimension. Y_{it} is the dependent variable, and X_{kit} denotes k independent variables with cross sectional unit i and time t. In the model, α_k is the vector of the (kx1) size parameter that does not vary according to the i cross-section unit and time dimension, and α_0 is also the constant term. e_{it} is the error term that is independent and identically distributed with 0 mean and σ^2 variance for all i cross-section units and t time periods (IID) [31].

If both the time and the cross-section are affecting the model, the panel data model takes the name of the two-way panel data model. The model is called as a one-way panel data model if the effect is only a cross-sectional unit or a time effect.

In the case where unit and/or time effect cause changes in some or all of the parameters of the model, the panel data models are named fixed effects panel data model. If the fixed effects model is one way, model is shown as following:

$$Y_{it} = \alpha_i + \sum_{k=1}^{K} \alpha_k X_{kit} + e_{it} \tag{2}$$

Similar to previous model, Y_{it} is the dependent variable and X_{kit} denotes k independent variables with cross sectional unit i and time t. α_i is the individual specific coefficients for the cross-sectional unit, while the t time dimension is constant. Similarly, α_k is the vector of the (kx1) size parameter that does not vary according to the i cross-section unit and t time dimension. The model is also named as covariance model or dummy variables model. Unobserved individual effects are achieved by using specific dummy variables:

$$Y_{it} = \mu_i D_N + X'_{it}\beta + e_{it} \tag{3}$$

D_N is the vector of dummy variables [30]. If the model contains both cross section and time effects, the two-way fixed effect model is determined as the following model:

$$Y_{it} = \mu_i + \lambda_t + X'_{it}\beta + e_{it} \tag{4}$$

X_{it} is the vector of independent variables. In the two-way fixed effects models, μ_i is the individual specific coefficients, λ_t is the time effects, and β is also the vector of coefficients [30].

The model in which the cross section and/or time effect is included as a component of the model error term is defined as the random effects model. If the random effects model is one way, model is generally expressed as:

$$Y_{it} = \alpha_i + \beta X_{it} + e_{it} \tag{5}$$

$$\alpha_i = \alpha_0 + \mu_i \tag{6}$$

$$u_{it} = \mu_i + e_{it} \tag{7}$$

As explained in the fixed effects model, Y_{it} is dependent variable, and X_{it} is the vector of independent variables. Individual effects consist of a combination of α_0, which does not have unit and time effects, and μ_i, which contains the specific cross section effects. The cross section effects and e_{it} error term are added to the model as a component of u_{it} error term, and the

http://dx.doi.org/10.5772/intechopen.70871

model is predicted with act of knowledge [31]. If both the specific unit effects μ_i and the specific time effects λ_t are expressed as a component of the error term e_{it}, the two-way random effects model is mentioned. The two-way random effects model is determined as,

$$Y_{it} = \alpha_0 + \beta X_{it} + e_{it} \tag{8}$$

$$e_{it} = \mu_i + \lambda_t + u_{it} \tag{9}$$

The Hausman (1978) test determines whether the fixed effects model or the random effects model is appropriate for panel data analysis [31]. Hausman suggests that the null hypothesis for the test is an appropriate model of the random effects model, which implies that there is no relationship between cross section and explanatory variables [32]. The alternative hypothesis indicates that the appropriate model is the fixed effect model. Hausman test statistic (H) is estimated by the following formula using the variance covariance matrix:

$$H = \left(\widehat{\beta}_{FE} - \widehat{\beta}_{RE}\right)' \left(V\left(\widehat{\beta}_{FE} - \widehat{\beta}_{RE}\right)\right)^{-1} \left(\widehat{\beta}_{FE} - \widehat{\beta}_{RE}\right) \tag{10}$$

Hausman test statistics fits the asymptotic χ^2 distribution with parameter k. V is the variance covariance matrix of the difference between the estimators. $\widehat{\beta}_{FE}$ and $\widehat{\beta}_{RE}$ are the fixed effects and random effects estimators, respectively. As a result of the analysis, it is determined whether the predicted model is a fixed effects model or a random effects model [30].

4. Data and variables

In this study, the tradeoff between WCC and firm's profitability is examined via the annual data for the period 2005–2016 of 41 firms listed on BIST Industrial Index in Turkey. In order to examine WCC firm's profitability tradeoff, dependent variable is defined as return on assets (ROA); independent variables are cash conversion cycle (CCC), inventory conversion period (ICP), payables deferral period (PDP), and control variables are sales growth (SG), the ratio of short-term financial debts to short-term debts (FDSD), and the ratio of fixed assets to total assets (FATA).

ROA widely used and accepted as measure of profitability [23] indicates the rate of return provided by firm's assets [13]. CCC measures the effectiveness of the working capital [9, 22]. CCC expresses the time spent between the expenses for purchasing raw materials and the collection of sales [9, 11, 12]. Longer CCC means the more investment in the working capital [9, 11], in other words, the more current asset financing needs [8]. CCC consists of three components: receivables collection period, ICP, and PDP. ICP refers to the time required for the conversion of raw materials to finished goods and then the sale of these products. PDP is the average time firm's suppliers give it to pay for its purchases [33]. The other component of CCC, receivables collection period, was not included in the study, since this variable was not statistically significant in the models formed. SG, FDSD, and FATA as control variables were also used to increase the reliability level of the models established in the study [34]. All variables and its formulations in the study are shown in **Table 2**.

	Variables	Formulas
Dependent variables	Return on assets (ROA)	Net profit/total asset
Independent variables	Cash conversion cycle (CCC)	(receivables collection period + inventory conversion period) − payables deferral period
	Inventory conversion period (ICP)	(Inventories/cost of goods sold)×365
	Payables deferral period (PDP)	Accounts payable/cost of goods sold)×365
Control variables	Sales growth (SG)	Change in sales (%)
	The ratio of short-term financial debts to short-term debts (FDSD)	Short-term financial debts/short-term debts
	The ratio of fixed assets to total assets (FATA)	Fixed assets/total assets

Table 2. Descriptions of the variables.

5. Empirical results

Panel regression analysis was used to investigate the tradeoff between WCC and the profitability of the 41 firms listed on BIST Industrial Index in Turkey. In the panel data analysis, variables include both time and cross section size. According to time and cross-section effects, it is determined that the model should be predicted to be one way or two ways. For this purpose, the LR test has performed with the maximum likelihood method, and the findings are given in **Table 3**. The calculated test statistics are interpreted according to the 1% significance level.

For the two-way effects test, the null hypothesis is formed no cross section and time effects in the model. Because the value of the test statistic for the two-way effect is 279.1188 at 1% significance level, the null hypothesis is rejected. This result shows that it is a two-way effect. Then, the presence of the cross section and time effects was tested separately with the movement from the findings that it was a two-way effect. The null hypothesis for cross section effect analysis is that the standard error of cross section is equal to zero. According to the analysis results, the null hypothesis is rejected at 1% significance level, since the value of the test statistic is 262.4951. In this case, there is a cross section effect in the panel data model. The existence of time effect was also examined, and the test statistic was calculated as 3.981432 at 5% significance level. According to this result, the null hypothesis cannot be rejected at the 1% significance level with no time effects.

Score test, Breusch-Pagan Lagrange Multiplier test, and Hausman tests were applied to identify the suitable model in the study. It was determined whether the analysis should be done

Tests	Two-way effects	Cross-section effects	Time effects
χ^2 *testi*	279.1188	262.4951	3.981432
Prob.	0.000	0.000	0.023

Table 3. Test results of cross section and time effects.

with the pooled model, the random effects model, or the fixed effects model. Both the score test and the Breusch-Pagan Lagrange Multiplier test analyze the pooled model against the random effects model. The null hypothesis suggests that the pooled model is appropriate, and that there is no random effect that reflects the existence of heterogeneity. Score test statistic was calculated as 8586.81 at 1% significance level, and the Breusch-Pagan Lagrange Multiplier test statistic was also estimated as 479.82 at 1% significance level. The null hypothesis is rejected relative to the 1% significance level. According to both tests, it is determined that the pooled model is not a suitable model. After it is defined that the pooled model is not suitable, it will be determined whether the model is a fixed effect model or a random effects model with the Hausman test. The test results are given in **Table 4**.

Because the Hausman test statistic was calculated as 25.46, the null hypothesis is rejected at 1% significance level. Hausman test shows that the model is a fixed effect model. The fixed effects panel data model results are given in **Table 5**.

The findings in **Table 5** show that all predicted parameters and model are significant at 1% significance level. Modified Wald test was applied to examine heteroskedasticity in the model. The null hypothesis for the modified Wald test is constructed as:

$$H_0 = \sigma_i^2 = \sigma^2 \quad \textit{for all } i \tag{11}$$

$$H_1 = \sigma_i^2 \neq \sigma^2 \tag{12}$$

The null hypothesis is rejected according to the test result at 1% significance level. There is a heteroskedasticity problem in the model. Autocorrelation was investigated with modified Bhargava et al., Durbin-Watson, and Baltagi-Wu LBI tests. The test result is assessed by

	Coefficients			
	(b)	**(B)**	**(b-B)**	**Sqrt(diag(V_b-V_B))**
	fe	**re**	**Difference**	**S.E.**
PDP	−0.0004057	−0.0003602	−0.0000455	0.000034
ICP	0.000696	0.0005636	0.0001324	0.0000612
CCC	−0.0004332	−0.0003739	−0.0000593	0.000036
SG	0.0847359	0.0862303	−0.0014943	
FDSD	−0.0595096	−0.0650816	0.005572	0.0042299
FATA	−0.2220324	−0.1595819	−0.0624505	0.0142161

b = consistent under Ho and Ha, B = inconsistent under Ha, efficient under Ho, Ho: difference in coefficients not systematic.
chi2(6) = (b-B)′[(V_b-V_B)^(−1)](b-B) = 25.46.
Prob > chi2 = 0.0003.

Table 4. Hausman test results.

	Coef.	Std. error	t stat.	Prob.	[95% conf. interval]
PDP	−0.0004057	0.0001086	−3.73*	0.000	(−0.0006193, −0.0001922)
ICP	0.000696	0.0002185	3.19*	0.002	(0.0002665, 0.0011255)
CCC	−0.0004332	0.0001124	−3.85*	0.000	(−0.0006542, −0.0002121)
SG	0.0847359	0.0126799	6.68*	0.000	(0.0598066, 0.1096653)
FDSD	−0.0595096	0.0168587	−3.53*	0.000	(−0.0926546, −0.0263646)
FATA	−0.2220324	0.0346947	−6.40*	0.000	(−0.2902438, −0.1538209)
Constant	0.2240622	0.0218885	10.24*	0.000	(0.1810283, 0.2670962)

F test stat. = 16.92 (prob. = 0.000).
Modified Wald test for groupwise heteroskedasticity: 918.72 (prob. = 0.000).
Modified Bhargava et al. Durbin-Watson = 1.3899562.
Baltagi-Wu LBI = 1.7238703.
Pesaran test of cross sectional independence = 6.814 (prob. = 0.000).
*indicates significance at the level 1%.

Table 5. The fixed effects panel data model results.

comparing it with two values which indicate no autocorrelation. Since test statistics are smaller than 2, it can be said that it is autocorrelation. Pesaran test was performed to examine the cross-sectional dependence in the model. The null hypothesis of no cross-sectional dependent is rejected at 1% significance level. For this reason, resistance fixed effect panel data model results were obtained by using in [37] estimator, which provided consistent estimates in the case of heteroskedasticity, autocorrelation, and cross-sectional dependent [35].

When the resistive fixed effects model presented in **Table 6** is examined, it is seen that the coefficients do not change, but t statistics and confidence intervals calculated by using Driscoll and Kraay standard errors change. These estimates give consistent results in the case of heteroskedasticity, autocorrelation, and cross-sectional dependent.

	Coef.	Driscoll and Kraay Std. Error	t stat.	Prob.	[95% conf. interval]
PDP	−0.0004057	0.0000774	−5.24*	0.000	(−0.0005761, −0.0002354)
ICP	0.000696	0.0002746	2.53**	0.028	(0.0000916, 0.0013003)
CCC	−0.0004332	0.000068	−6.37*	0.000	(−0.0005828, −0.0002835)
SG	0.0847359	0.0173669	4.88*	0.000	(0.0465118, 0.1229601)
FDSD	−0.0595096	0.0172452	−3.45*	0.005	(−0.0974661, −0.0215532)
FATA	−0.2220324	0.0302661	−7.34*	0.000	(−0.2886475, −0.155417)
Constant	0.2240622	0.0127534	17.57*	0.000	(0.1959921, 0.2521324)

F test stat. = 329.63 (prob. = 0.000).
*Significance at the level 1%.
**Significance at the level 5%.

Table 6. Resistance fixed effect panel data model.

According to the estimation results presented in **Table 6**, it was found that PDP, CCC, FDSD, and FATA have a negative effect on ROA. An increase of one-unit in PDP, CCC, FDSD, and FATA would induce a decrease of 0.0004057, 0.0004332, 0.0595096, and 0.2220324 on ROA, respectively. On the other hand, ICP and SG have a positive effect on the ROA. An increase of one-unit in ICP and SG would induce an increase of 0.000696 and 0.0847359 on ROA, respectively.

Although the studies in the literature are different in the way of both the country and the sector, similar results were obtained with other studies in the literature that a negative relationship exists between CCC which measures the efficiency of WCM, PDP, and ROA [6, 8, 22, 23, 29, 34]. Besides, the finding of this study is similar to in Ref. [27, 28] who report a positive relationship between ICP and ROA.

6. Conclusion

In emerging countries like Turkey, the development of the industrial sector plays a key role in the development of the country's economy. Firms in this sector need to solve the financing problem, which is one of the most important problems to survive in markets based on competition. Industrial firms need to become greater in their profitability by effectively managing their working capital in order to reduce the need for external financing due to scarce resources. In this context, this study aims to reveal the tradeoff between WCC and firm's profitability by using the data of the firms listed on BIST Industry Index in Turkey.

In the study, panel regression analysis was used to investigate the tradeoff between WCC and the profitability of the 41 firms listed on BIST Industrial Index. Dependent variable is defined as ROA; independent variables are CCC, ICP, and PDP; and control variables are SG, FDSD, and FATA. For the model estimation in the study, it was determined that the model had a cross section effect by performing the LR test. The Hausman test defined that the fixed effects panel data model should be applied for analysis. In the fixed effect model, the coefficients and the model were determined to be statistically significant at the 1% significance level.

The results of the study show the existence of a meaningful relationship between firms' profitability and WCC. In the industrial firms in the study, the decrease in CCC contributed to the increase of ROA. While the other variables remain constant, the increase in ICP raises the firm's profitability. This situation may be expressed as the fact that the benefit provided by meeting the customers' demands on time by keeping stocks is more than the cost of holding stocks. Another consequence of the study is that industrial firms can become greater ROA by reducing the duration of PDP. It can be said that the discounts provided by the suppliers for timely payments may contribute to the firm's profitability. According to the results of the study, a negative relationship exists between FDSD and FATA variables and ROA, while a positive relationship exists between SG and ROA. While an increase in sales volume of the firms may positively affect ROA, the increase in short-term financial liabilities may raise the financial risk of the firms and decrease the firm's profitability.

Both the findings obtained in the study and the studies in the literature reveal that there is an impact of WCM on the industrial firm's profitability in emerging countries such as Turkey. In this context, decreasing the cash return period of the firms will reduce the funds used for the financing of the current assets and contribute to increase their asset profitability. In addition to this, the firms should benefit from discounting by reducing the payables deferral period, which will help increase the firm's profitability. Besides, industrial firms can contribute to raise the firm's profitability by increasing Inventory conversion period and sales.

Author details

Samet Evci* and Nazan Şak

*Address all correspondence to: sametevci@osmaniye.edu.tr

Osmaniye Korkut Ata University, Faculty of Economics and Administrative Sciences, Osmaniye, Turkey

References

[1] Raynard P, Forstater M. Implications for Small and Medium Enterprises in Developing Countries. United Nations Industrial Development Organization; 2002. p. 1-90

[2] The World Bank. World Development Indicators: Structure of Output [Internet]. Available from: http://wdi.worldbank.org/table/4.2# [Accessed: 2017–07-01]

[3] Türkiye sanayisine sektörel bakış. Tusiad Basın Bülteni. 2008;**08**(47):1-8

[4] Sanayi Üretim Endeksi ve İmalat Sanayi Değerlendirme Raporu. Bilim, Sanayi ve Teknoloji Bakanlığı. 2017:1-4

[5] Pandey S, Jaiswal VK. Effectiveness on profitability: Working capital management. SCMS Journal of Indian Management. 2011;January–March:73-80

[6] Kandpal V. An analysis of working capital management in select construction companies. Journal of Commerce & Management Thought. 2015;**6**(1):7-31. DOI: 10.5958/0976-478x.2015.00001.4

[7] Masocha R, Dzomonda O.The mediating role of effective working capital management on the growth prospects of small and medium enterprises in Polokwane municipality. In: SAAPAM Limpopo Chapter 5th Annual Conference; 2016. p. 157-165

[8] Afande FO. Relationship between working capital management and profitability of cement companies in Kenya. Research Journal of Finance and Accounting. 2015;**6**(7):154-182

[9] Deloof M. Does working capital management affect profitability of Belgian firms. Journal of Business Finance and Accounting. 2003;**30**(3):573-587

[10] Blinder AS, Mancini LJ. The resurgence of inventory research: What have we. The Journal of Economic Survey. 1991;**5**:291-328

[11] Singh JP, Pandey S. Impact of working capital management in the profitability of Hindalco Industries Limited. The Icfai University. Journal of Financial Economics. 2008;**6**(4): 62-73

[12] Shin H, Soenen L. Efficiency of working captial management and corporate profitability. Financial Practice and Education. 1998;Fall/Winter:37-45

[13] Keown AJ, Martin JD, Petty JW. Foundations of Finance: The Logic and Practice of Financial Management. 9th ed. Pearson Education Limited: England; 2017

[14] Banos-Caballero S, Garcia-Teruel PJ. How does working capital management affect the profitability of Spanish SMEs. Small Business Economics. 2012;**39**:17-529. DOI: 10.1007/s11187-011-9317-8

[15] Nazir MS, Afza T. A panel data analysis of working capital management policies. IBA Business Review. 2009;**4**(1):143-157

[16] Thapa PDP. How does profitability get affected by working capital management in food and beverages industry. Journal of Advanced Research in Management. 2013;**2**(8):2-4. DOI: http://dx.doi.org/10.14505/jarm.v4.2(8).01

[17] Grass M. Control of Working Capital. Essex: Grower Press Limited; 1972

[18] Smith K. Profitability versus liquidity trade off in working capital management. In: Smith KK, Paul S, editors. Reading on the Management of Working Capital. West Publishing Company; 1980. p. 549-562

[19] Toroman C, Sönmez AR. Çalışma sermayesi ve karlılık arasındaki ilişki: Perakende ticaret sektörü üzerine bir uygulama. Erzincan Üniversitesi Sosyal Bilimler Enstitüsü Dergisi. 2015;**8**(1):15-24

[20] Dursun A, Ayrıçay Y. Çalışma sermayesi-karlılık ilişkisinin IMKB örneğinde 1996-2005 dönemi analizi. Atatürk Üniversitesi İktisadi ve İdari Bilimler Dergisi. 2012;**26**(3):199-214

[21] Öz Y, Güngör B. Çalışma sermayesi yönetiminin firma kârlılığı üzerine etkisi: Imalat sektörüne yönelik panel veri analizi. Sosyal Bilimler Enstitüsü Dergisi. 2007;**10**(2)

[22] Quayyum ST. Relationship between working capital management and profitability. International Journal of Business and Management. 2012;**7**(1):58-69. DOI: 10.5539/ijbm.v7n1p58

[23] Azeez OT, Abubakar MA, Olamide FT. Analysis of the effects of working capital management on profitability of listed Nigerian conglomerate companies. FWU Journal of School Sciences. 2016;**10**(1)

[24] Shahzad F, Fareed Z, Zulfiqar B. Impact of working capital management on firm's profitability:A case study of cement industry of Pakistan. European Researcher. 2015;**91**(2): 86-93. DOI: 10.13187/er.2015.91.86

[25] Ching HY, Novazzi A, Gerab F. Relationship between working capital management and profitability in Brazilian listed companies. Journal of Global Business and Economics. 2011;**3**(1):1-14

[26] Pandey NS, Sabamaithily S. Working capital management on profitability: Cement industry in India. SCMS Journal of Indian Management. 2016;April–June:81-95

[27] Muhammad M, Jan WU, Ullah K. Working capital management and profitability: An analysis of firms of textile industry of Pakistan. Journal of Managerial Sciences. 2012;**6**(2):155-165

[28] Arunkumar ON, Radharamanan T. Analysis of effects of working capital management on corporate profitability of Indian manufacturing firms. International Journal of Business Insights & Transformation. 2011;**5**(1):71-77

[29] Aksoy EE. İşletme sermayesi yönetimi ile firma performansı ilişkisi: 2008 krizi örneği. Finans Politik & Ekonomik Yorumlar. 2013;**50**(586):9-21

[30] Greene WH. Econometrics Analysis. 5th ed. New Jersey: Prentice Hall International; 2002

[31] Baltagi B. Econometric Analysis of Panel Data. 3rd ed. USA: John Wiley & Sons Ltd; 2005

[32] Hausman JA. Specification tests in econometrics. Econometrica. 1978;**46**:1251-1271

[33] Brigham EF, Ehrhardt MC. Financial Management: Theory and Practice. 14th ed. USA: South-Western; 2014

[34] Keskin R, Gökalp F. Çalışma sermaye yönetiminin firma karlılığı üzerine etkisi: panel veri analizi. Doğuş Üniversitesi Dergisi. 2016;**17**(1):5-25

[35] Tatoğlu FY. Panel Veri Ekonometrisi. 2nd ed. İstanbul: Beta Yayınları; 2013

[36] Ukaegbu B. The significance of working capital management in determining firm profitability: Evidence from developing economies in Africa. Research in International Business and Finance. 2014;**31**:1-16

[37] Driscoll JC, Kraay AC. Consistent covariance matrix estimation with spatially dependent panel. Review of Economics and Statistics. 1998;**80**:549-560

Section 5

Financial Economics and Digital Currency

The Impact of Exchange Rate Uncertainty on Domestic Investment: Panel Evidence from Emerging Markets and Developing Economies

Bilge Canbaloglu and Gozde Gurgun

Additional information is available at the end of the chapter

http://dx.doi.org/10.5772/intechopen.71195

Abstract

This study attempts to suggest empirical evidence about the impact of exchange rate uncertainty on the domestic investment for 25 emerging markets and developing economies (EMDEs) for the time line covering the years between 2004 and 2014. Exchange rate uncertainty is modeled by selecting one of the volatility models of GARCH(1, 1), EGARCH(1, 1), or GJR-GARCH(1, 1) for individual countries. The study aims to offer a broad point of view about the impact of exchange rate uncertainty on domestic investment through a feasible generalized least square panel data model by deeming the economic growth, real interest rate, and 2008/2009 global financial crisis (GFC). The empirical results show that the impact of exchange rate uncertainty on domestic investment for EMDEs is found to be positive and significant, which may indicate the existence of risk neutral or insensitive domestic investors to exchange rate uncertainty in these countries. On the other hand, the study also proves that the effect of economic growth is positive and significant on domestic investment, whereas the impact of GFC on domestic investment is negative and significant. However, the impact of real exchange rate on domestic investment is found to be negative but insignificant.

Keywords: exchange rate, uncertainty, domestic investment, emerging markets and developing economies, panel data model

1. Introduction

Although the effects of exchange rate uncertainty on the economic variables such as economic growth, trade, export, and foreign direct investment have been investigated broadly in the existing literature, the researches examining the impact of exchange rate uncertainty on the domestic investment have been limited. The existing studies suggest mixed and inconclusive evidence on the relationship between uncertainty and investment. Hartman [1] and Able [2] argue that heightened uncertainty about the price of output gives rise to higher investment and, in turn, enhances economic activity under the assumptions of risk-neutral competitive firms and constant returns to scale production function. Their assumptions ensure convexity of the marginal profitability of capital in output price and input costs. On the other hand, a larger body of literature provides explanation for the response of investment to uncertainty by focusing on the real option feature of investment. Making an analogy between an investment opportunity and a stock option in a financial market, Dixit and Pindyck [3] argue that if investment is irreversible, uncertainty raises the value of accumulating cash and waits for new developments that would dispel uncertainty. Heightened uncertainty is likely to increase the value of this "wait and see" option and thus reduce investment spending temporarily. Building on the model of Dixit and Pindyck [3], Darby et al. [4] examine impacts of exchange rate uncertainty on domestic investment. They argue theoretically that rising exchange rate volatility may increase or decrease investment, depending on particular industry involved. Furthermore, Campa and Goldberg [5] show that exchange rate variability has relatively weak and insignificant effects on investment in US manufacturing sectors, depending on the size and sign of sectoral exposure to exchange rates.

In order to observe the impact of flexible exchange rate regime on the real economic activity, Lafrance and Tessier [6] aim to reveal the reaction of investments such as manufacturing industry, machinery and equipment sectors, and foreign direct investment to the levels of Canadian dollar and the volatility of Canadian dollar by implementing VAR structures. They conclude that the exchange rate and their volatility do not really impact the investment activities in Canada. Harchaoui et al. [7] offer another study that focuses on the general impact of exchange rates on the investment in Canada for the time line between 1981 and 1997 by examining industry level data of 22 Canadian manufacturing industries. First, their findings suggest that the response of investment to exchange rate fluctuations rely on whether there exist high or low exchange rate uncertainties. Second, the findings conclude that the impact of exchange rate depreciation on the total investment is positive, when exchange rate uncertainty is at low levels. Furthermore, Caglayan and Torres [8] investigate the association between exchange rate and exchange rate volatility and capital investment of Mexican manufacturing firms. They conduct a panel data analysis on the firms for the period of 1994–2003. Their findings indicate that exchange rate depreciation affects the investment positively (negatively) through export (import) channel. In addition, they find that the investments of export-oriented firms and the firms producing nondurable goods are more sensitive to the exchange rate volatility.

There are also researches investigating the direct impact of exchange rate uncertainty on the domestic investment at macro level. Serven [9] conducts a study investigating the real exchange rate uncertainty and private investment for 61 developing countries in a panel data set for the time span between 1970 and 1995. The real exchange rate volatility is retrieved by employing GARCH(1, 1) model. He finds that the impact of real exchange rate uncertainty on the private investment is negative and significant. In additionally, this impact gets larger at higher levels of uncertainty underlying "threshold effects." He also concludes that the real exchange rate impact on the investment depends on the level of trade openness and financial sector development. The significant and negative linkage between the exchange rate uncertainty and investment gets stronger as the environment of higher trade openness and weaker financial system. Soleymani and Akbari [10] investigate this relationship by constructing a fixed effect panel data model covering only 15 Sub-Saharan countries for the time span between 1975 and 2006. They employ GARCH(1, 1) model when measuring the exchange rate volatility. They conclude that these low-income countries allocate considerable amount of their spending for imported goods. Safdari and Soleymani [11] also study the exchange rate uncertainty and domestic investment relationship for six Middle East and North African countries, namely Algeria, Egypt, Iran, Morocco, Syrian Arab Republic, and Tunisia for the time period between 1975 and 2006. As for methodology, they build fixed effect approach of panel model, and they measure the exchange rate volatility GARCH(1, 1) model for each country. Their findings suggest that domestic investments in these countries suffer from the exchange rate uncertainty, since investments depend on the imported capital goods in these countries. Furthermore, Bahmani-Oskooee and Hajilee [12] investigate 36 countries (involving both developed and developing economies) individually for the time line between 1975 and 2008 by employing ARDL approach. Their findings reveal that effect of exchange rate volatility on domestic investment is negative and significant in Chile, France, Malawi, South Africa, and UK, while this impact is found positive and significant in Colombia, Italy, Singapore, Sweden, and United States. More recently, Chowdhury and Wheeler [13] examine the exchange rate and output uncertainty on the fixed private investments for Canada, Germany, the United Kingdom, and the United States by implementing VAR models. They conclude that neither shocks of output uncertainty nor exchange rate uncertainty has a significant impact on the fixed private investments for these selected countries.

All in all, the impact of exchange rate uncertainty on investment is not clear cut both in the theoretical and empirical literature. This study aims to contribute to the existing literature by exploring the impact of exchange rate uncertainty on the domestic investment for EMDEs in several aspects. First, 25 countries, within the group of emerging and developing countries and employing floating exchange rate regimes, are considered in order to construct panel data model for the time span of 2004–2014. Since the study is not confined to a specific region in the world and pools the countries under panel data model, it attempts to offer a general view about the impact of exchange rate uncertainty on the domestic investment for EMDEs. The time span of the study also offers more recent results. Second, exchange rate volatility of each country is modeled with GARCH(1, 1), EGARCH(1, 1), and GJR-GARCH(1, 1) models. The most appropriate model for volatility measure is selected for each country. Third, this study also employs feasible generalized least square (GLS) panel model approach, which may suggest more robust results when compared to fixed effect panel data models.

2. Data and exchange rate uncertainty measure

The countries studied in this study are EMDEs that implement floating exchange rate regimes, namely Brazil, Chile, Colombia, Georgia, Hungary, India, Indonesia, Kenya, Madagascar, Mexico, Moldova, Mongolia, Papua New Guinea, Paraguay, Peru, Philippines, Poland, Serbia,

Seychelles, South Africa, Tanzania, Thailand, Turkey, Uganda, and Uruguay.[1] The countries are determined due to the availability of the data. The time span covers the period of 2004–2014. The econometric model is defined in Eq. (1)

$$INV_{it} = \delta_i + \beta_1 GPD\_G_{it} + \beta_2 RIR_{it} + \beta_3 VOL_{it} + v_{it} \tag{1}$$

$$INV_{it} = \delta_i + \beta_1 GPD\_G_{it} + \beta_2 RIR_{it} + \beta_3 VOL_{it} + \beta_4 CRI + u_{it} \tag{2}$$

The domestic investment, INV, is the gross capital formation as a percentage of GDP. As a controlling variable, the growth of gross domestic product (GDP_G) and real interest rate (RIR) in percentages is included in the model. The data related to these variables are obtained from World Development Indicator and IMF statistical databases[2]. In addition, a dummy variable (CRI) is added to the model as in Eq. (2) in order to control the effects of the GFC. As the impacts of the crisis deepened in the aftermath of collapse of Lehman Brothers in September 2008, the most severe impacts are observed in 2009. Hence, the dummy variable for the crisis is put for the year 2009.

VOL represents the volatility (i.e., uncertainty) of nominal domestic exchange rate against US Dollar, EXC. The daily returns of each country's nominal exchange rate, employed for the volatility models, are obtained as in Eq. (3):

$$R_t = \ln\left(\frac{EXC_t}{EXC_{t-1}}\right) \times 100 \tag{3}$$

In the literature of volatility models, generalized autoregressive heteroskedasticity (GARCH), exponential GARCH, and GJR-GARCH models are the most prominent ones. Therefore, GARCH(1, 1), EGARCH(1, 1), and GJR-GARCH(1, 1) models are implemented on each country's exchange rate returns.

The GARCH model, proposed by Bollerslev [14], is based on that the conditional variance of returns depends on the lagged values of conditional variance and error terms. The GARCH(1, 1) model is expressed as in Eq. (4):

$$\sigma_t^2 = \omega + \alpha\varepsilon_{t-1}^2 + \beta\sigma_{t-1}^2 \tag{4}$$

The GARCH(1, 1) model is defined, where $\omega > 0, \alpha \geq 0, \beta \geq 0$, and $\alpha + \beta < 1$.

In order to detect asymmetries of returns on the volatility, Nelson [15] developed EGARCH model. The EGARCH(1, 1) model is defined as in Eq. (5):

[1] Country classification is based on International Monetary Fund (IMF) country classifications. Exchange rate classifications follow the de facto classification of the IMF's Annual Report on Exchange Arrangements and Exchange Restrictions (AREAER) 2016.

[2] Only the real exchange rate data for Turkey and Poland are retrieved from the Borsa Istanbul and National Bank of Poland.

$$\ln\left(\sigma_t^2\right) = \omega + \alpha\left|\frac{\varepsilon_{t-1}}{\sigma_{t-1}}\right| + \gamma\left[\frac{\varepsilon_{t-1}}{\sigma_{t-1}}\right] + \beta\ln\left(\sigma_{t-1}^2\right) \quad (5)$$

The γ coefficient indicated the asymmetry in the EGARCH model. $\gamma>0$ implies that positive shocks on the returns of exchange rate induce the volatility more when compared to the negative shocks, whereas $\gamma<0$ indicates that negative shocks have more effect on volatility than positive shocks [16].

The GJR-GARCH, developed by Glosten, Jagannathan and Runkle [17], is another model that attempts to reveal asymmetry in the volatility modeling. The GJR–GARCH(1, 1) is modeled as in Eq. (6):

$$\sigma_t^2 = \omega + \alpha\varepsilon_{t-1}^2 + \gamma I_{t-1}^{-}\varepsilon_{t-1}^2 + \beta\sigma_{t-1}^2 \quad (6)$$

I_{t-1}^{-}, which is a dummy variable, equals to 1 where $\varepsilon_{t-1}<0$ and zero otherwise. The asymmetry effect is measured by γ coefficient. If $\gamma>0$ indicates that negative shocks on the exchange rate returns have more impact on the volatility than positive shocks, while $\gamma<0$ is the sign that positive news has more impact on the volatility than negative news [16].

Since each country's exchange rate data show different patterns, each country's exchange rate volatility is modeled with GARCH(1, 1), EGARCH(1, 1) and GJR-GARCH(1, 1) models. The exchange rate uncertainties of Chile, Georgia, Kenya, Philippines, Thailand, Uganda and Uruguay are modeled with GARCH(1, 1), since exchange rate volatilities of these countries' provide the assumptions of GARCH(1, 1) models more when compared to the other volatility models. Each GARCH(1, 1) model provides that $\alpha+\beta<1$, and the α and β terms in each GARCH(1, 1) model are found to be statistically significant as in **Table A1**. The Ljung-Box-Q statistics (Q^2) of squared standardized residuals are not found to be statistically significant for lags of 1 and 10, which may indicate no autocorrelation between residuals for all GARCH(1, 1) models. In addition, the ARCH-LM (Lagrange Multiplier) test statistic for each country is found to be statistically insignificant, which points out that there is no ARCH effect in the residuals up to order two for all GARCH(1, 1) models.

Brazil, Hungary, Madagascar, Moldova, Papua New Guinea, Paraguay, Peru, South Africa, and Tanzania give the most reliable results for EGARCH(1, 1) model as in **Table A2** and **Table A3**. The coefficients of ω, α, and β are found to be statistically significant in each model. The asymmetry coefficients (γ) of Brazil, Hungary, Madagascar, Papua New Guinea, Paraguay, South Africa, and Tanzania are found to be negative and statistically significant, which indicates leverage effect and implies that the negative news on the exchange rate returns has more impact on the volatility than positive news. On the other hand, the asymmetry coefficients (γ) of Moldova and Peru are found positive and significant, which indicates that positive shocks on the returns affect volatility more when compared to the negative shocks. As for autocorrelation between residuals, the estimated Ljung-Box-Q statistics (Q^2) of squared standardized residuals are found to be statistically insignificant for each country under EGARCH(1, 1) model. Furthermore, there exists no ARCH effect in residuals up to order two for all estimated EGARCH(1, 1) models according to ARCH-LM test.

On the other hand, the exchange rate volatilities of Colombia, India, Indonesia, Mexico, Mongolia, Poland, Serbia, Seychelles, and Turkey are most properly modeled with GJR-GARCH(1, 1) model as offered in **Table A4** and **Table A5**. The ω, α, and β coefficients are found to be statistically significant. The asymmetry coefficient (γ) is found positive and statistically significant for Colombia, India, Indonesia, Mexico, Mongolia, Poland, Serbia, and Turkey, which points out leverage effect and is a sign that negative shocks on the exchange rate returns have more impact on the volatility when compared to the positive shock. On the other hand, for only Seychelles, the asymmetry coefficient (γ) is found negative and statistically significant, which suggests that positive news has more impact on volatility than the negative shocks. The acquired Ljung-Box-Q statistics (Q^2) of squared standardized residuals imply that no autocorrelation between the residuals for these GJR-GARCH(1, 1) models. Additionally, no ARCH effect exists in the residuals of GJR-GARCH(1, 1) model of each country.

As a summary, the exchange rate uncertainties of the countries, which are estimated by selecting the most appropriate volatility models, are offered in **Table 1**[3]:

Country	Exchange rate uncertainty model	Country	Exchange rate uncertainty model
Brazil	EGARCH(1, 1)	Paraguay	EGARCH(1, 1)
Chile	GARCH(1, 1)	Peru	EGARCH(1, 1)
Colombia	GJR-GARCH(1, 1)	Philippines	GARCH(1, 1)
Georgia	GARCH(1, 1)	Poland	GJR-GARCH(1, 1)
Hungary	EGARCH(1, 1)	Serbia	GJR-GARCH(1, 1)
India	GJR-GARCH(1, 1)	Seychelles	GJR-GARCH(1, 1)
Indonesia	GJR-GARCH(1, 1)	South Africa	EGARCH(1, 1)
Kenya	GARCH(1, 1)	Tanzania	EGARCH(1, 1)
Madagascar	EGARCH(1, 1)	Thailand	GARCH(1, 1)
Mexico	GJR-GARCH(1, 1)	Turkey	GJR-GARCH(1, 1)
Moldova	EGARCH(1, 1)	Uganda	GARCH(1, 1)
Mongolia	GJR-GARCH(1, 1)	Uruguay	GARCH(1, 1)
Papua New Guinea	EGARCH(1, 1)		

Table 1. Countries and their exchange rate uncertainty models.

3. Methodology and empirical results

When investigating the exchange rate uncertainty on the domestic investment under the panel data model expressed as in Eq. (1), the panel data analysis is carried out by following the steps in Aktas et al. [19]. The panel data consist of countries which may involve individual effects of

[3] The annual volatility for each country is derived by multiplying σ_{daily} and $\sqrt{T}$ since the volatility escalates with the square root of time [18].

http://dx.doi.org/10.5772/intechopen.71195

countries (denoted as δ_i). Therefore, F-test is implemented so as to determine whether the model is fixed effect model or pooled least square model [20]. The null hypothesis and test result of F-test having degrees of freedom as F (n-1, nT-n-k)[4] are given in **Table 2**. F-test statistic is statistically significant at 1% significance level, which indicates the model can be fixed effect model.

The model can also include random effect. In order to test whether the model involves random individual effects, Breusch and Pagan (1980) Lagrange Multiplier (LM) test having Chi-square distribution with a degree of freedom of 1 is employed [20]. The null hypothesis and test statistics of the Breusch Pagan LM are given in **Table 3**. The test result, statistically significant at 1% significance level, points out that the model can include random individual effects.

Since the model could involve either fixed effect or random effect, a well-known test Hausman (1978) is conducted. The Hausman test, having a null hypothesis of no correlation between unobservable individual effects and regressors (i.e., Random effect model), has a chi-square distribution with degrees of freedom of k [21]. The null and alternative hypotheses and test statistics of Hausman specification test are suggested in **Table 4**. The Hausman test indicates that the model is a fixed effect model, since the test statistic is significant at 5% significance level.

The fixed effect model is found to be appropriate to estimate the parameters in the main model. After constructing fixed effect model, the Wald test for groupwise heteroskedasticity is implemented in order to detect heteroskedasticity of the residual of fixed effect model [22]. The test has a chi-square distribution with a degree of freedom of n. The chi-square test statistics (25) is found to be 1833.61 with a prob. value of 0.000, which indicates the existence of groupwise heteroskedasticity in the residuals of the fixed effect model. It is also necessary to check the serial correlation in the panel data model, since serial correlation may offer biased

The null hypothesis	F statistics	Prob. value
Ho: $\delta_i = 0$ (no individual effect)	F(24, 247) = 24.01	0.000

Table 2. Null hypothesis and test result of F-test.

The null hypothesis	F statistics	Prob. value
Ho: $\sigma^2_{\delta i} = 0$ (no random effect)	Chi (1) = 544.93	0.000

Table 3. Null hypothesis and test result of Breusch Pagan LM test.

Null and alternative hypotheses	F statistics	Prob. value
Ho: Random effect model Ha: Fixed effect model	Chi (3) = 8.11	0.0439

Table 4. Null and alternative hypotheses and test result of Hausman test.

[4] n, T and k are number of groups (countries), number of years and number of regressors in the model, respectively.

standard errors, hence indicating less efficient parameter estimations. Thus, the serial correlation test developed by Wooldridge (2002) is utilized under the null hypothesis of no serial correlation [23]. The Wooldridge test for autocorrelation in panel data has a test statistic of F (1, 24) that equals to 35.434 with a prob. value of 0.000, which is found to be statistically significant at 1% significance level, thereby denoting existence of autocorrelation in the panel model.

Due to the existence of heteroskedasticity and autocorrelation problems in the fixed effect panel model, the acquired fixed effect model results may offer biased results. Therefore, the feasible generalized least square (GLS), which allows the estimations of panel data model under heteroskedasticity across panels and autocorrelation presence, is employed so as to conclude the results of the model [21, 24].[5] The feasible GSL estimators are obtained as in Eq. (7).

$$\widehat{\beta_{FGLS}} = \left(X'\widehat{\Omega}^{-1}X^{-1}\right)^{-1} X'\widehat{\Omega}^{-1}y \qquad (7)$$

where $\Omega = \sum_{n \times n} \otimes I$, which is the error variance matrix and obtained as in Eq. (8).

$$\widehat{\sum}_{i,j} = \frac{\widehat{\epsilon_i}'\widehat{\epsilon_j}}{T} \qquad (8)$$

The estimated test results from the Feasible GLS for both two models are suggested in **Table 5**.

As observed in the estimation results of model 1, the impact of economic growth on the domestic investment is positive and significant at 1% significance level. This result is anticipated, since growing economy such as emerging markets and developing economies may offer valuable prospects for private investors to obtain profitable returns, when they invest in these countries. Similarly, the studies of Bahmani-Oskooee and Hajile [12] and Safradi and

Variables	INV (Model 1)	INV (Model 2)
GDP_G	0.376* (0.049)	0.319* (0.062)
RIR	−0.017 (0.027)	−0.015 (0.027)
VOL	0.118* (0.045)	0.118** (0.456)
CRI	–	−0.856*** (0.500)
Constant	20.073* (0.735)	20.377 (0.755)
Observations	275	276
Number of country	25	25
Wald chi-squared	60.29*	62.29*

Notes: Robust standard errors are given in square parentheses.
*,**,*** denote the significance level at 1%, 5% and 10% respectively.

Table 5. The feasible GLS estimation results.

[5] See also http://www.stata.com/manuals13/xtxtgls.pdf.

Soleymani [11] also prove positive association between GDP and domestic investment. As for real interest rate, the impact of real interest rate on the domestic investment is found to be negative; however, this impact is statistically insignificant. When considering the real interest rate and investment linkage, it is inevitable to observe that increases in real interest rates lead to declines in domestic investment due to the increasing cost of capital stock. Finally, it is observed that an increase in the exchange rate uncertainty leads to an increase in domestic investment in these EMDEs. The result is found to be statistically significant at 1% significance level. In general, it is expected that heightened uncertainty in exchange rates may constrain the investors from involving in domestic investments, if the investors hold the position of "wait and see." But, if the investors are risk-neutral or risk appetent, they may perceive the volatile environments in terms of exchange rates as lucrative opportunities to engage in investments. Likewise, Bahmani-Oskooee and Hajile [12] find the impact of exchange rate uncertainty on the domestic investment as positive for Colombia, Italy, Singapore, Sweden, and US in the long run. For the positive linkage, they suggest that some investors may tend to invest more in order not to be exposed to the future price volatility arising from exchange rate uncertainty. When considering model 2, the effect of exchange rate uncertainty, economic growth, and real interest rate on domestic investment is found similar to the results of model 1. The impact of GFC on domestic investment of these countries is negative and statistically significant at 10% level.

4. Conclusion

Although the effects of exchange rate uncertainty on the macroeconomic variables such as economic growth, capital flows, and international trade are examined vastly in the literature, the number of studies associated with the impact of exchange rate uncertainty on the domestic investment is rather sparse to our knowledge. The evidence on the effects of exchange rate uncertainty on the domestic investment is inconclusive. Hence, this study attempts to provide some new evidence on this topic for 25 EMDEs under a panel data model for the time span of 2004 and 2014 by regarding the economic growth, real interest rate, and GFC as controlling variables. Rather than examining the countries individually, this study gives a broad scanning about the impact of exchange rate uncertainty on the domestic investment in EMDEs by employing feasible generalized least square panel data method, which offers more robust result compared to fixed effect panel data method. Exchange rate uncertainties for the selected countries are modeled by GARCH(1, 1), EGARCH(1, 1), or GJR-GARCH(1, 1) model, depending on the individual exchange rate patterns. This study finds that the impact of exchange rate uncertainty on domestic investment for EMDEs is found to be positive and statistically significant. This may imply that domestic investors in these countries are risk neutral and insensitive to adjustment costs related to the exchange rate fluctuations and the irreversibility of the investments in case the conditions worsen. Furthermore, exchange rate volatility could potentially provide a profitable opportunity for risk-appetent investors. In some cases, movements in the exchange rate could be beneficial for the domestic investors, particularly for the sophisticated ones.

A. Appendix A

See **Tables A1–A5.**

Country	Chile	Georgia	Kenya	Philippines	Thailand	Uganda	Uruguay
Mean equation							
(C)	0.0051 (0.5834)	0.0162 (0.1499)	−0.0196 (0.0441)	0.0057 (0.3218)	0.0063 (0.2287)	−0.0202 (0.0066)	−0.0001 (0.9936)
Variance equation							
ω	0.0024* (0.0001)	0.0819* (0.0000)	0.0221* (0.0000)	0.0012* (0.0000)	0.0032* (0.0000)	0.0192* (0.0000)	0.0475* (0.0000)
α	0.0530* (0.0000)	0.2107* (0.0000)	0.1501* (0.0000)	0.0770* (0.0000)	0.1374* (0.0000)	0.2088* (0.0000)	0.0670* (0.0000)
β	0.9419* (0.0000)	0.4500* (0.0000)	0.8273* (0.0000)	0.9175* (0.0000)	0.8488* (0.0000)	0.7705* (0.0000)	0.8841* (0.0000)
$Q^2(1)$	1.395 (0.237)	0.000 0.993	1.382 (0.240)	3.339 (0.068)	0.466 (0.495)	0.708 (0.400)	1.081 (0.298)
$Q^2(10)$	2.613 (0.989)	0.022 1.000	2.245 (0.994)	11.623 (0.311)	6.568 (0.765)	7.545 (0.673)	1.127 (1.000)
ARCH_LM (2)	0.7363 (0.4790)	0.0007 (0.9993)	0.6929 (0.5002)	3.3374 (0.0678)	1.5956 (0.2030)	0.4433 (0.6419)	0.5434 (0.5808)

Notes: The p-values are given in parentheses.
*, **, *** denote 1%, 5% and 10% significance levels, respectively.

Table A1. Test results for GARCH(1, 1) model.

Country	Brazil	Hungary	Madagascar	Moldova	Papua New Guinea
Mean equation					
(C)	0.0064 (0.6120)	−0.0126 (0.4045)	−0.0154 (0.3655)	0.0087** (0.0328)	−0.0604** (0.0000)
Variance equation					
ω	−0.1718* (0.0000)	−0.0595* (0.0000)	−0.1870* (0.0000)	−0.4689* (0.0000)	−0.1867* (0.0000)
α	0.2108* (0.0000)	0.0751* (0.0000)	0.1925* (0.0000)	0.4394* (0.0000)	0.3360* (0.0000)
γ	−0.0737* (0.0000)	−0.0373* (0.0000)	−0.0588* (0.0000)	0.0177** (0.0482)	−0.0958* (0.0000)
β	0.9746* (0.0000)	0.9942* (0.0000)	0.7837* (0.0000)	0.9232* (0.0000)	0.9693* (0.0000)
$Q^2(1)$	0.157 (0.692)	0.1728 (0.678)	0.046 (0.829)	2.847 (0.092)	0.706 (0.401)
$Q^2(10)$	5.332 (0.868)	7.0918 (0.717)	0.332 (1.00)	7.372 (0.690)	2.979 (0.982)
ARCH_LM(2)	1.6679 (0.1888)	0.1832 (0.8326)	0.0254 (0.9749)	1.4528 (0.2341)	0.3683 (0.6919)

Notes: The p-values are given in parentheses.
*, **,*** denote 1%, 5% and 10% significance levels, respectively.

Table A2. Test results for EGARCH(1, 1) model.

http://dx.doi.org/10.5772/intechopen.71195

Country	Paraguay	Peru	South Africa	Tanzania
Mean equation				
(C)	−0.0258* (0.0000)	0.0062* (0.0082)	−0.0339*** (0.0527)	−0.0376* (0.0000)
Variance equation				
ω	−0.3817* (0.0000)	−0.5954* (0.0000)	−0.0874* (0.0000)	−0.2078* (0.0000)
α	0.3836* (0.0000)	0.5014* (0.0000)	0.1131* (0.0000)	0.2792* (0.0000)
γ	−0.0519* (0.0000)	0.0226** (0.0448)	−0.0555* (0.0000)	−0.0429* (0.0000)
β	0.8853* (0.0000)	0.9054* (0.0000)	0.9851* (0.0000)	0.9754* (0.0000)
$Q^2(1)$	0.171 (0.679)	0.003 (0.954)	1.197 (0.274)	2.494 (0.114)
$Q^2(10)$	4.736 (0.908)	0.842 (1.000)	14.378 (0.156)	3.991 (0.948)
ARCH_LM(2)	0.2964 (0.7434)	0.0334 (0.9671)	1.8915 (0.1510)	1.2477 (0.2873)

Notes: The p-values are given in parentheses.
*, **,*** denote 1%, 5% and 10% significance levels, respectively.

Table A3. Test results for EGARCH(1, 1) model.

Country	Colombia	India	Indonesia	Mexico	Mongolia
Mean equation					
(C)	0.0039 (0.6909)	0.0019 (0.7708)	−0.0090 (0.2340)	−0.0041 (0.6598)	−0.0045 (0.3579)
Variance equation					
ω	0.0053* (0.0000)	0.0019* (0.0000)	0.0044* (0.0000)	0.0047* (0.0000)	0.0004* (0.0000)
α	0.0777* (0.0000)	0.0796* (0.0000)	0.0804* (0.0000)	0.0303* (0.0003)	0.1756* (0.0000)
γ	0.0444* (0.0000)	0.0216** (0.0128)	0.1327* (0.0000)	0.0803* (0.0000)	0.1074* (0.0000)
β	0.8978* (0.0000)	0.9052* (0.0000)	0.8624* (0.0000)	0.9154* (0.0000)	0.9030* (0.0000)
$Q^2(1)$	3.2730 (0.070)	1.324 (0.250)	0.702 (0.402)	0.035 (0.851)	0.031 (0.859)
$Q^2(10)$	5.7863 (0.833)	7.439 (0.683)	2.599 (0.989)	14.292 (0.160)	0.327 (1.000)
ARCH_LM(2)	1.6470 (0.1928)	2.4714 (0.0846)	0.4738 (0.6227)	2.6023 0.0743	0.0390 (0.9617)

Notes: The p-values are given in parentheses.
*, **,*** denote 1%, 5% and 10% significance levels, respectively.

Table A4. Test results for GJR-GARCH(1, 1) model.

Country	Poland	Serbia	Seychelles	Turkey
Mean equation				
(C)	0.0096 (0.4946)	−0.0181 (0.1867)	0.0307 (0.5809)	−0.0152 (0.2477)
Variance equation				
ω	0.0041* (0.0004)	0.0072* (0.0000)	2.3273* (0.0000)	0.0126* (0.0000)
α	0.0315* (0.0001)	0.0162* (0.0001)	0.3578* (0.0000)	0.0541* (0.0000)

Country	Poland	Serbia	Seychelles	Turkey
γ	0.0361** (0.0001)	4.3485* (0.0000)	−0.2691* (0.0002)	0.0681** (0.0000)
β	0.9456* (0.0000)	0.9564* (0.0000)	0.1587* (0.0001)	0.8923* (0.0000)
$Q^2(1)$	3.350 (0.067)	0.506 (0.477)	0.000 (0.982)	0.066 (0.796)
$Q^2(10)$	11.476 (0.322)	3.330 (0.973)	0.012 (1.000)	11.973 (0.287)
ARCH_LM(2)	1.6651 (0.1894)	0.3007 (0.7403)	0.0005 (0.9994)	0.8228 (0.4393)

Notes: The p-values are given in parentheses.
*, **,*** denote 1, 5 and 10% significance levels, respectively.

Table A5. Test results for GJR-GARCH(1, 1) model.

Author details

Bilge Canbaloglu[1]* and Gozde Gurgun[2]

*Address all correspondence to: bbakin@ybu.edu.tr

1 Department of International Trade and Business, Ankara Yıldırım Beyazıt University, Ankara, Turkey

2 Communications and Foreign Relations Department, Central Bank of the Republic of Turkey, Ankara, Turkey

References

[1] Hartman R. The effects of price and cost uncertainty on investment. Journal of Economic Theory. 1972;**5**(10):258-266

[2] Abel AB. Optimal investment under uncertainty. American Economic Review. 1983;**73**(3): 228-223

[3] Dixit A, Pindyck R. Investment under uncertainty. New Jersey: Princeton University Press; 1994. 488 p

[4] Darby J, Hughes HA, Ireland J, Piscitelli L. The impact of exchange rate uncertainty on the level of investment. The Economic Journal. 1999;**109**:C55-C67

[5] Campa J, Goldberg LS. Investment in manufacturing, exchange rates and external exposure. Journal of International Economics. 1995;**38**(3–4):297-320

[6] Lafrance R, Tessier D. Exchange rate variability and Investment in Canada. In: Bank of Canada Conference on Revisiting the Case for Flexible Exchange Rates. Ottawa: Bank of Canada; Novermber 2000. p. 1-8

[7] Harchaoui T, Tarkhani F, Yuan T. The effects of the exchange rate on investment: Evidence from Canadian manufacturing industries. Bank of Canada, Working Paper. 2005;22

[8] Caglayan M, Torres RM. The effect of the exchange rates on investment in Mexican manufacturing industry. Open Economies Review. 2011;**22**(4):669-683

[9] Serven L. Real exchange rate uncertainty and private investment in LDCS. The Review of Economics and Statistics. 2003;**85**(1):212-218

[10] Soleymani M, Akbari A. The relationship between exchange rate uncertainty and investment in some of sub-Saharan African countries. International Journal of Business and Public Management. 2011;**1**(1):51-57

[11] Safradi M, Soleymani M. Exchange rate uncertainty and investment in some of Middle East and North African countries. Global Economy and Finance Journal. 2011;**4**(2):60-73

[12] Bahmani-Oskooee M, Hajilee M. Exchange rate volatility and its impact on domestic investment. Research in Economics. 2013;**67**:1-12

[13] Chowdhury AR, Wheeler M. The impact of output and exchange rate volatility on fixed private investment: Evidence from selected G7 countries. Applied Economics. 2015;**47**(25): 2628-2641

[14] Bollerslev T. Generalized Autoregressive conditional Heteroskedasticity. Journal of Econometrics. 1986;**31**:307-327

[15] Nelson DB. Conditional heteroscedasticity in asset returns: A new approach. Econometrica. 1991;**59**(2):347-370

[16] Dutta A. Modelling volatility: Symmetric or asymmetric Garch models? Journal of Statistics: Advances in Theory and Applications. 2014;**12**(2):99-108

[17] Glosten LR, Jagannathan R, Runkle DE. On the relation between the expected value and the volatility of the nominal excess return on stocks. Journal of Finance. 1993;**48**: 1779-1801

[18] Hull JC. Risk Management and Financial Institutions. 2nd ed. United States of America: Pearson Education Inc; 2010. 556 p

[19] Aktas R, Acikalin S, Bakin B, Celik G. The determinants of banks' capital adequacy ratio: Some evidence from south eastern European countries. Journal of Economics and Behavioral Studies. 2015;**7**(1):79-88

[20] Baltagi BH. Econometric Analysis of Panel Data. 3rd ed. England: John Wiley & Sons, 30 Ltd.; 2005;1-302

[21] Greene WH. Econometric Analysis. New Jersey: Pearson Education Inc; 2003

[22] Baum CF. Residual diagnostics for cross section time series regression models. The Stata Journal. 2001;**1**(1):101-104

[23] Drukker DM. Testing for serial correlation in linear panel-data models. The Stata Journal. 2003;**3**(2):168-177

[24] Cameron AC, Trivedi PK. Microeconometrics Using Stata. StataCorp LP: Texas; 2009;1-692

Chapter 13

Effects of Inflation Uncertainty on Economic Policies: Inflation-Targeting Regime

Mehmet Kenan Terzioğlu

Additional information is available at the end of the chapter

http://dx.doi.org/10.5772/intechopen.71625

Abstract

Inflation uncertainty maintains its importance in emerging economies as well as in others. Increases in the level of inflation uncertainty constitute an important risk factor by affecting macroeconomic variables in the markets that are sensitive to price changes. The stabilization programs implemented in Turkey during 1980–2003 could not reduce the sensitivity of economic structure to inflationary shocks. Between 2003 and 2015, changes occurred, switching from high inflation to the single-digit inflation rates, in Turkey with transition to the inflation-targeting regime. Within the scope of this study, the effect of inflation uncertainty on inflation, economic growth and selected monetary-fiscal policy variables was examined using multivariate generalized autoregressive conditional heteroscedasticity (MGARCH) models. The dynamic conditional covariance model is designed to reflect the strong time-dependent correlation structure. While the inflation-targeting regime studies in developing countries focus on either the adoption or nonadoption of such a regime and its feasibility, this study evaluates the success of the regime in Turkey as an emerging economy.

Keywords: inflation uncertainty, inflation targeting, monetary policy, fiscal policy, MGARCH models

1. Introduction

The phenomenon of high inflation arising from the 1970s oil crisis and the collapse of Bretton Woods's system has brought price stability to the base of the monetary policy. While inflation, growth, exchange rate and interest rate should be in harmony in order to prevent financial-based crises, to eliminate income distribution imbalances and to increase prosperity, the implicit relationship between monetary and fiscal policies should not be ignored in developing countries that are subject to the inflation-targeting regime.

Inflation uncertainty has an effect not only on monetary and fiscal policy variables but also on economic growth and indirectly on the real sector by affecting both real net revenues and price system efficiency in resource allocation. In emerging markets economies, interest rate and exchange rate, which are indicative variables, have a decisive influence on the real and nominal sectors for sustainable development and a stable economy. Changes in interest rates and exchange rates affect domestic and foreign investment decisions and consumer behaviors. High interest rates increase risk perception as they cause inflationary expectations. Moreover, volatility that may be experienced at interest rates creates exchange rate uncertainties. Thus, the exchange rate instability affects the real sector and it causes economic instability. In open economies, exchange rates are controlled through interest rates (usually short term) when it is necessary.

Tax revenues follow a fluctuating structure in emerging economies where the economies are not fully managed due to the influence of political structure. Tax revenues can be seen as a means of development by the direct or indirect effect of resource allocation in developing countries. Macroeconomic balances are realized at a lower cost in the shorter term as the tax revenues are directed toward the financing of the growth. The longer the average collection period of taxes, the greater the magnitude of the corrosive effect on tax revenues is related with inflation. Depending on inflation, inflation rate increases by increased risk premiums due to economic uncertainty and instability. Funds used in the financing of the growth by excluding investments shift to nontaxable areas. The economic contraction due to the diminishing of investments reduces the taxable potential.

Tax revenues create economic conditions for stability and growth by reducing the debt burden of the public sector and alleviate the pressure on interest and inflation. Therefore, public expenditures also have an effect on the relation between inflation and tax revenues. The change in public expenditure activates the multiplier mechanism and causes a change in income, consumption and tax revenues. The high public debt burden may affect inflation expectations and can constitute difficulties to meet the inflation target. Government revenues increase as total savings, and taxable potential increases in moderate inflation periods.

Imbalances between government revenues/expenditures, elimination of existing debts by borrowing, problems in banking system, deficiencies in risk management processes, monetary and fiscal policy approaches which are far from rationality and the environment where short-term capital movements for speculative purposes are widespread due to increasing globalization and economic liberalization movements make an inflation spiral in emerging economies as well as in Turkey.

The effectiveness of inflexible monetary policies has disappeared because of the fluctuations in the variables used as main or intermediate target. High inflation, floating growth rates, high public deficits and a dollarized economy emerged between 1989 and 2001 in Turkey because of not only the short-term capital movements started to be effective in the economic structure but also unrealizable financial and structural reforms. In this period, monetary policy approaches that target interest rate, foreign currency exchange rate and monetary aggregates had been used in the economic system. Interest-exchange rate targeting has been abandoned because of the changes in shocks in the economic structure and high-floating inflationary periods that make interest targeting difficult. The increase in capital movements and the decrease in flexibility against global shocks made the use of the exchange rate ineffective. Monetary aggregates could not be applied as intermediate targets owing to the structural changes and financial liberalization, and programs had resulted in disappearance of stability in the currency speed of money, the emergence of new financial instruments and the destabilization of the money demand caused by fast-growing financial sector. The exchange rate policy has been changed to the floating exchange rate regime because of the anticipation that it could be effective in closing the current account deficit and the monetary policy gained independence. Inflation had been adversely affected because the foreign exchange rate, which is sensitive to external shocks, exhibited a volatile structure and the perception that the interventions made on the interest rate were considered as interventions to the exchange rates.

In order to achieve price stability in the Turkish economic structure, it has been decided to implement the inflation-targeting regime, a monetary policy approach that targets directly inflation without using any intermediate targets. In Turkey, due to domestic debt stock and high interest rates, the transition to the inflation-targeting regime could not be possible immediately. With the transition to the inflation-targeting regime, which had been implemented in 2003, inflation and the level of dollarization had started to decrease. With the transition to the inflation-targeting regime in 2006, inflation reached single digits and the aim changed as price stabilization. Due to the difficulty of keeping inflation under control in emerging economies and the delayed/prolonged effects of the monetary-fiscal policy instruments on inflation, the long-term internal and external shocks experienced in Turkey between 2002 and 2009 created disruptions in the operation of the regime.

Since the relationship between uncertainty and macroeconomic variables is sensitive to various factors such as sampling period, model classification and uncertainty identifications, different results have been determined in studies among inflation, output growth, interest rate and inflation uncertainty. Almost none of the studies have been found within the scope of the developed economies or the developing economies on the interactions of inflation uncertainty with real effective exchange rate, tax revenues and government expenditures.

Cukierman et al., Azariadis et al., Friedman and Deveraux [1–4] argue that there is a positive relationship between inflation and inflation uncertainty. Baillie et al. [5] conclude that the Cukierman-Meltzer hypothesis is valid only in high inflationary countries. Pourgerami et al., Ungar et al. and Grier et al. [6–8] argue that there is an inverse relationship between inflation uncertainty and inflation rate. Bhar et al. [9] have concluded that inflation uncertainty has diminished inflation after inflation targeting. Holland [10] argues that higher inflation uncertainty may be associated with lower average inflation. While Dotsey and Sarte [15] find that inflation uncertainty has a positive effect on growth, Friedman, Pindyck, Beaudry et al.,Tommasi and Fountas et al. [1, 11–14] determine an inverse relationship between inflation uncertainty and output growth. Bhar et al. [9] point out that inflation uncertainty reduces the growth rate after inflation targeting. Chan [16] suggests that uncertainty reduces output growth by reducing consumption and investment spending with interest rates when there is a positive relationship between inflation uncertainty and interest rates. Berument et al. [17] show that inflation uncertainty increases 3-month deposit interest. Omay et al. [18] show that the effect of the inflation risk on the interest rates is regime dependent.

In case of uncertainty, determining the interaction of real and nominal economic variables with inflation uncertainty is important in shaping economic policies of countries experiencing problems with inflation. In this study, it is investigated whether the inflation-targeting regime causes a structural change in the economic system exposed to high- and low-inflation periods. It is aimed to contribute to the literature by focusing on the effect of inflation uncertainty on inflation, output growth and selected monetary-fiscal policy instruments under the inflation-targeting regime. Within the scope of the study, inflation-targeting period was accepted between 2003 and 2015 and preinflation-targeting period was between 1987 and 2003. The effect of inflation uncertainty on real and nominal economic indicators is examined using multivariate generalized autoregressive conditional heteroscedasticity (MGARCH) model. Because volatility is a quantitative measure of the risk that individual investors and financial institutions face, it is one of the noteworthy features of financial data. Because of the fact that financial changes move together over time, the ability to envision and forecast the dependency of second-degree moments of return is important in financial econometrics. The multivariate GARCH models, which are developed based on the fact that financial asset volatilities move together over time, provide efficiency gains. In order to handle all the possible interactions in a system equation, solutions are obtained by using full-information maximum-likelihood method.

In this way, with the help of an equations system that is stated in a multivariate structure, all the possible interactions are tackled together and solutions are obtained based on complete information. In addition, with the help of a slope dummy variable, which was defined to differentiate the periods before and after 2003, the effects of inflation and output uncertainty have been assessed for both high and low inflation periods. The study first takes a general look at the related literature about inflation uncertainty. It then moves on to defining the model and obtaining empirical findings which were established over the model. The study concludes with an assessment section in which the empirical findings obtained are evaluated.

2. Model structure

The generalized autoregressive conditional heteroscedasticity (GARCH) approach includes the time dependencies between conditional variances and covariances between various markets and assets. Although multivariate GARCH (MGARCH) models fundamentally resemble univariate GARCH models, the significant difference between the two is the definitions of the equations that show how the covariances of multivariate models move over time. To elicit these changes, performing analysis within the framework of multivariate modeling allows the researcher to obtain results that are more realistic. From the financial perspective, it facilitates taking better risk management decisions.

Expansion from the univariate GARCH model to a model with n variables requires that random variables (ε_t) with n dimensions and a zero average are dependent on elements in the information set of the conditional variance–covariance matrix. If H_t with respect to $\mathcal{F}_{t-1}$' (information set) can be measured, then the multivariate GARCH model is expressed as $\varepsilon_t | \mathcal{F}_{t-1} \sim N(0, H_t)$. Because H_t is a variance matrix, positive definiteness should be satisfied. MGARCH

http://dx.doi.org/10.5772/intechopen.71625

models allow the researcher to solve multivariate financial models requiring the variances, and covariances to be dependent on the vector ARMA-type information set require modeling the variances and covariances. To explain time dependency, Bollerslev et al. [19] expanded univariate ARCH/GARCH models with multivariate models under VEC parameterization. Because the VEC-GARCH model requires the estimation of too many parameters, and the positive definiteness of the covariance matrix cannot be satisfied always, it has some inherent applicability problems. Moreover, developing MGARCH models attempt to solve the dimension problem in financial modeling. Since it is difficult to secure the positive definiteness of H_t in VEC representation without bringing serious restrictions on parameters, it is focused on alternative MGARCH model constructions. From the perspective of applicability, structures in the form of factor or diagonal parameter matrix can be incorporated into the model.

This model class makes the theoretical structure of unconditional moment, ergodicity and stationarity conditions easier (He and Terasvirta, [20]). Since it is difficult to secure H_t's positive definiteness in VEC representation without bringing serious restrictions on parameters, the Baba-Engle-Kraft-Kroner (BEKK) model, which is a restricting version of the VEC-GARCH model, is used (Engle and Kroner, [21]). As in the VEC model, the parameters of the BEKK model do not show a direct effect of the different lag terms of H_t's elements. Structurally, the conditional covariance matrices of the BEKK-GARCH model satisfy positive definiteness. When C_0^*, A_{ik}^* and B_{ik}^* denote n x n parameter matrices, C_0^* denotes a triangle, C_{1k}^* denotes J x n parameter matrices and K determines generalization of summation limit process:

$$H_t = C_0^{*'} C_0^* + \sum_{k=1}^{K} C_{1k}^{*'} x_t x_t' C_{1k}^* + \sum_{k=1}^{K}\sum_{i=1}^{q} A_{ik}^{*'} \varepsilon_{t-i} \varepsilon_{t-i}' A_{ik}^* + \sum_{k=1}^{K}\sum_{i=1}^{p} B_{ik}^{*'} H_{t-i} B_{ik}^* \quad (1)$$

can be written as BEKK (1,1,K) model. Eq. (1) is positive definite under weak conditions. In addition, because the model contains all positive-definite diagonal representations and almost all positive-definite VEC representations, it is adequately general. The BEKK model directly concentrates on the model structure, notably as A and B matrices. The main advantage of this is that because there is no constraint requirement necessitating H_t to be positive definite, parameters can be easily estimated. One disadvantage, on the other hand, is that because parameters enter the model in the form of matrices, and are transposed, effects on H_t can easily be interpreted. While matrix A measures the ARCH effect in the model, each element of the matrix B (b_{ij}) represents continuity in conditional variance from the variable "i" to the variable "j".

Using conditional variance and correlation in direct modeling of conditional covariances is a relatively new approach. Conditional correlation models are much more convenient alternatives in the estimation and interpretation of parameters. These models, which are nonlinear combinations of univariate GARCH models, allow for separate determination of individual conditional variances on the one hand, and of a conditional correlation matrix between the individual series on the other, or of another dependency criterion. Time-dependent correlations are usually calculated by the cross product of returns and by multivariate GARCH models that are linear in their squares. The dynamic conditional correlation (DCC) model takes the change of conditional correlation over time into account. The multivariate models that are called DCC have the flexibility of parsimonious parametric models and relevant univariate GARCH models for correlations. In other words, the DCC estimators have the flexibility of univarate GARCH; however, they refrain from the complexity of multivariate GARCH. Despite being nonlinear, they can be calculated by two-step methods or single-variable methods that are based on probability function. These models, which directly parameterize the conditional correlations, can be estimated in two steps: the first being a series of univariate GARCH estimations and the second being correlation estimation. It is observed that under many circumstances they function well and provide reasonable empirical results.

When $\varepsilon_t = D_t^{-1} r_t$ and $D_t = \text{diag}\{\sqrt{h_{i,t}}\}$, $R = E_{t-1}(\varepsilon_t \varepsilon_t') = D_t^{-1} H_t D_t^{-1}$ represents a correlation matrix containing conditional correlations:

$$H_t = D_t R D_t \tag{2}$$

The dynamic conditional correlation model, which is a generalized form of the constant conditional correlation (CCC) estimator, is shown as follows:

$$H_t = D_t R_t D_t \tag{3}$$

The only difference in the dynamic conditional correlation model is that R changes over time (Engle, [22]). Parameterization of R requires that conditional variances are in integrity, and it has the same requirements as H.

The possible simplest and best method is exponential smoothing, which is expressed as a geometrical weighted average of normalized residuals. Another alternative is obtained using the GARCH (1,1) model. When the equation is written as

$$q_{i,j,t} = \bar{\rho}_{i,j} + \alpha(\varepsilon_{i,t-1}\varepsilon_{j,t-1} - \rho_{i,j}) + \beta(q_{i,j,t-1} - \bar{\rho}_{i,j}) \tag{4}$$

the below equation

$$q_{i,j,t} = \bar{\rho}_{i,j}\left(\frac{1-\alpha-\beta}{1-\beta}\right) + \alpha \sum_{s=1,\infty} \beta^s \varepsilon_{i,t-s}\varepsilon_{j,t-s} \tag{5}$$

is obtained. Assuming that the unconditional expectation of the cross product is $\bar{\rho}$, variances are $\bar{\rho}_{i,j} = 1$. Because the $Q_t = |q_{i,j,t}|$ covariance matrix is positive definite and the weighted average of the positive semi-definite matrix, the correlation estimator $\rho_{i,j,t} = \frac{q_{i,j,t}}{\sqrt{q_{i,i,t}\,q_{j,j,t}}}$ is positive definite.

When S is an unconditional correlation matrix of epsilons, the matrix forms of these estimators are written as

$$Q_t = (1-\lambda)(\varepsilon_{t-1}\varepsilon_{t-1}') + \lambda Q_{t-1} \tag{6}$$

$$Q_t = S(I-\alpha-\beta) + \alpha(\varepsilon_{t-1}\varepsilon_{t-1}') + \beta Q_{t-1} \tag{7}$$

http://dx.doi.org/10.5772/intechopen.71625

As long as unconditional moments are adapted to a simple correlation matrix, in order to parameterize the correlations, more complex positive-definite multivariate GARCH models can be used.

3. Effects of inflation uncertainty on economic policies

Quarterly data (1987:Q1–2015: Q3) were used to examine the effect of inflation uncertainty for Turkey on the variables of consumer price index, real gross domestic product, real effective exchange rate, 12-month deposit interest rate, government expenditures and tax revenues. The data set was taken from the Central Bank of the Republic of Turkey (CBRT) electronic data distribution system (EVDS). Different term dates for different base years are organized according to the 1987 base year. The seasonal structure in the real gross national product, government expenditures and tax revenue variables is eliminated by using the Tramo/Seat method. The government expenditures and tax revenues series are divided by the seasonally adjusted nominal gross national product and multiplied by 100. Growth measures expressed as percentage changes are obtained by taking the logarithmic first-order differences, multiplying by 100, of the consumer price index, real gross domestic product, 12-month deposit interest rate and real effective exchange rate.

MGARCH model structure by using inflation (π_t), output growth (b_t),exchange rate change (d_t), interest rate change (f_t), governmentexpenditures (kh_t), tax revenues (vg_t), dummy variable (D_k) and inflation uncertainty (h_{π_t})

$$\pi_t = a_0 + a_1 D_k + \sum_{i=1}^{p} a_{2i}\pi_{t-i} + \sum_{i=1}^{p} a_{3i} b_{t-i} + \sum_{i=1}^{p} a_{4i} d_{t-i} + \sum_{i=1}^{p} a_{5i} f_{t-i} + \sum_{i=1}^{p} a_{6i} kh_{t-i} + \sum_{i=1}^{p} a_{7i} vg_{t-i} + \delta_1\sqrt{h_{\pi_t}} + \gamma_1 D_k\sqrt{h_{\pi_t}} + \varepsilon_{1t} \quad (8)$$

$$b_t = b_0 + b_1 D_k + \sum_{i=1}^{p} b_{2i}\pi_{t-i} + \sum_{i=1}^{p} b_{3i} b_{t-i} + \sum_{i=1}^{p} b_{4i} d_{t-i} + \sum_{i=1}^{p} b_{5i} f_{t-i} + \sum_{i=1}^{p} b_{6i} kh_{t-i} + \sum_{i=1}^{p} b_{7i} vg_{t-i} + \delta_2\sqrt{h_{\pi_t}} + \gamma_2 D_k\sqrt{h_{\pi_t}} + \varepsilon_{2t} \quad (9)$$

$$d_t = d_0 + d_1 D_k + \sum_{i=1}^{p} d_{2i}\pi_{t-i} + \sum_{i=1}^{p} d_{3i} b_{t-i} + \sum_{i=1}^{p} d_{4i} d_{t-i} + \sum_{i=1}^{p} d_{5i} f_{t-i} + \sum_{i=1}^{p} d_{6i} kh_{t-i} + \sum_{i=1}^{p} d_{7i} vg_{t-i} + \delta_3\sqrt{h_{\pi_t}} + \gamma_3 D_k\sqrt{h_{\pi_t}} + \varepsilon_{3t} \quad (10)$$

$$f_t = f_0 + f_1 D_k + \sum_{i=1}^{p} f_{2i}\pi_{t-i} + \sum_{i=1}^{p} f_{3i} b_{t-i} + \sum_{i=1}^{p} f_{4i} d_{t-i} + \sum_{i=1}^{p} f_{5i} f_{t-i} + \sum_{i=1}^{p} f_{6i} kh_{t-i} + \sum_{i=1}^{p} f_{7i} vg_{t-i} + \delta_4\sqrt{h_{\pi_t}} + \gamma_4 D_k\sqrt{h_{\pi_t}} + \varepsilon_{4t} \quad (11)$$

$$kh_t = k_0 + k_1 D_k + \sum_{i=1}^{p} k_{2i}\pi_{t-i} + \sum_{i=1}^{p} k_{3i} b_{t-i} + \sum_{i=1}^{p} k_{4i} d_{t-i} + \sum_{i=1}^{p} k_{5i} f_{t-i} + \sum_{i=1}^{p} k_{6i} kh_{t-i} + \sum_{i=1}^{p} k_{7i} vg_{t-i} + \delta_5\sqrt{h_{\pi_t}} + \gamma_5 D_k\sqrt{h_{\pi_t}} + \varepsilon_{5t} \quad (12)$$

$$vg_t = v_0 + v_1 D_k + \sum_{i=1}^{p} v_{2i}\pi_{t-i} + \sum_{i=1}^{p} v_{3i} b_{t-i} + \sum_{i=1}^{p} v_{4i} d_{t-i} + \sum_{i=1}^{p} v_{5i} f_{t-i} + \sum_{i=1}^{p} v_{6i} kh_{t-i} + \sum_{i=1}^{p} v_{7i} vg_{t-i} + \delta_6\sqrt{h_{\pi_t}} + \gamma_6 D_k\sqrt{h_{\pi_t}} + \varepsilon_{6t} \quad (13)$$

$$\varepsilon_{1t} = \sqrt{h_{\pi_t}}^{*} z_{t.} \quad (14)$$

is performed. The mean-model structure consists of Eqs. (8)–(13). Agumented Dickey-Fuller (ADF), Kwiatkowski-Phillips-Schmidt-Shin (KPSS) and Phillips-Perron (PP) unit root tests were applied in **Table 1** to set out the stationarity of the variables. It is decided that all variables are stationary, generally, when the ADF, KPSS and PP stationarity test results are evaluated for all variables.

Figure 1 shows the tendencies of the series used in the model construction with respect to time. When the inflation series is examined, it is observed that there has been a fluctuation in the period of 2003 with the transition to the inflation-targeting regime. A dummy variable has been added to the model structure to reveal the effects of this period. Dummy variable(D_k) used in the model construction is defined as 1 for the quarter of 2003–2015 and 0 for the other periods.

In the one-dimensional case, the mean equation for the model should be decided. In addition, the first condition that must be satisfied before dealing with the general structure of the variance equation in the multivariate GARCH model is that the series should be a white noise vector process. Residuals should be serially uncorrelated to each other, as well as have zero correlation with the lags of other components. It is suggested to use low-order VAR models to get rid of nested autocorrelation structure. **Table 2** shows the optimal lag length calculated for the model structure.

Detection of autocorrelation in residuals and/or squared residuals within the framework of established VAR (1) model leads to the use of MGARCH models. A preliminary multivariate ARCH effect test was performed in order to question the existence of the ARCH effect on the model constructed. In **Table 3**, it is shown that the absence of the ARCH effect is strictly rejected. Since the null hypothesis, constant and all other lagged parameters are equal to zero and are rejected, it can be said that there is no constant correlation and a dynamic structure can be mentioned with strong time-dependency correlation between the selected variables.

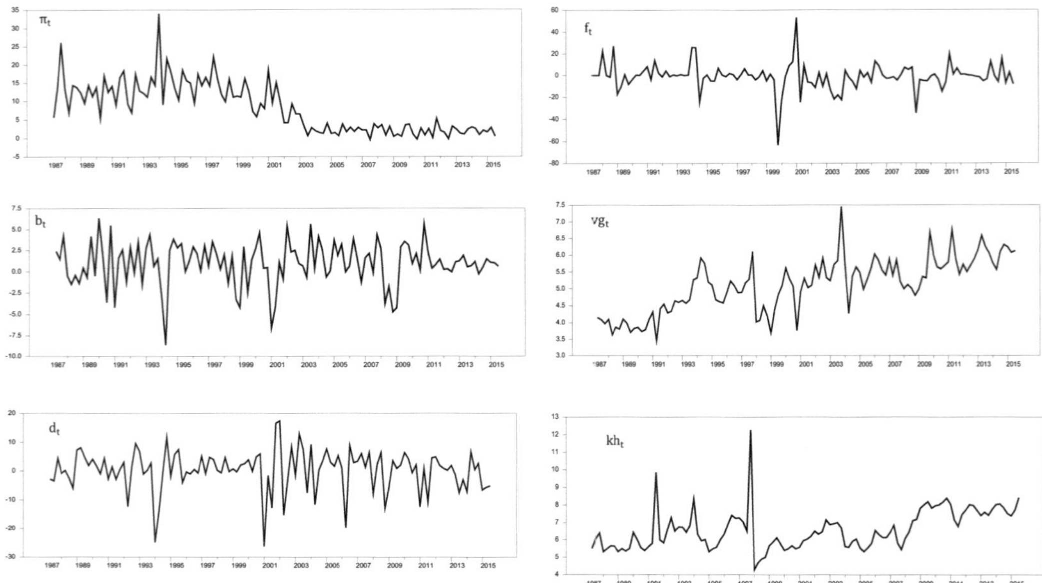

Figure 1. Graphical representation of the tendency of the series used in model construction over time.

http://dx.doi.org/10.5772/intechopen.71625

		ADF test statistics	KPSS test statistics	PP test statistics
π_t	Level	−2.199	0.159***	−9.539**
b_t	Level	−7.599**	0.087**	−12.743**
d_t	Level	−10.836**	0.141**	−12.830**
f_t	Level	−9.754**	0.095**	−9.717**
vg_t	Level	−6.332**	0.081**	−6.332**
kh_t	Level	−7.304**	0.157***	−7.654**

***0.01, **0.05 and *0.10 test critical values.

Table 1. Unit root test results.

	Lag length	SC	HQ	AIC	FPE
Model C	0	30.7841788	30.6922946	30.6311298	808155.7
	1	30.4943727*	29.8511831*	29.4757366*	239794.0
	2	31.3253894	30.1308945	29.5447431	219511.0*
	3	32.3555313	30.6097310	29.9389591	247924.9
	4	33.3434204	31.0463148	30.4465451	272942.8
	5	34.4803294	31.6319184	31.2983202	356934.9
	6	35.7085147	32.3087984	32.4907265	527368.6
	7	36.9301733	32.9791516	34.0022509	805829.9
	8	37.5814766	33.0791495	35.3800101	733320.2
	9	37.9362941	32.8826617	37.0656734	530976.8
	10	38.1716960	32.5667583	39.5027360	373253.0
	11	38.5220873	32.3658442	43.3755930	332466.6
	12	38.9348464	32.2272979	49.4561719	374125.8

*minimum value on each information criteria for model order selection.

Table 2. Lag-length selection for model structure.

Multidimensional ARCH effect test statistic	Significance level
1898.86	0.000

***0.01, **0.05 and *0.10 significance level is not statistically significant.

Table 3. The presence of a priori ARCH effect.

Panel A: Model parameter tahminleri											
π_t		b_t		d_t		f_t		kh_t		vg_t	
Constant	4.10*	Constant	0.65*	Constant	–0.750	Constant	–1.013*	Constant	2.001*	Constant	–1.327*
π_{t-1}	0.630*	π_{t-1}	–0.026	π_{t-1}	0.120	π_{t-1}	0.105*	π_{t-1}	–0.101	π_{t-1}	0.242
b_{t-1}	0.126	b_{t-1}	–0.042	b_{t-1}	0.114	b_{t-1}	0.526*	b_{t-1}	0.522	b_{t-1}	0.982**
d_{t-1}	–0.567	d_{t-1}	0.043*	d_{t-1}	0.092	d_{t-1}	–0.308**	d_{t-1}	0.092*	d_{t-1}	0.443*
f_{t-1}	0.033**	f_{t-1}	–0.028*	f_{t-1}	0.083*	f_{t-1}	0.190*	f_{t-1}	0.874*	f_{t-1}	–0.323*
kh_{t-1}	0.001	kh_{t-1}	–0.021	kh_{t-1}	0.314	kh_{t-1}	0.093*	kh_{t-1}	0.021	kh_{t-1}	0.084
Vg_{t-1}	0.074	Vg_{t-1}	0.013	Vg_{t-1}	0.053*	Vg_{t-1}	0.042	Vg_{t-1}	0.092*	Vg_{t-1}	0.463*
D_k	–0.48*	D_k	–0.095*	D_k	0.995	D_k	0.689*	D_k	–1.000*	D_k	0.154*
h_t	0.479*	h_t	0.155**	h_t	0.045	h_t	–0.093*	h_t	0.679**	h_t	–0.18*
$D_k^* h_t$	–0.12*	$D_k^* h_t$	–0.362*	$D_k^* h_t$	0.023	$D_k^* h_t$	0.102*	$D_k^* h_t$	–0.878*	$D_k^* h_t$	0.247*
Panel B: GARCH parameter estimates											
C(1)	3.019***	C(4)	4.620***	A(1)	0.546*	A(4)	0.409**	B(1)	0.245***	B(4)	0.480***
C(2)	2.009*	C(5)	8.372***	A(2)	0.365	A(5)	0.352***	B(2)	0.514***	B(5)	0.583***
C(3)	5.267**	C(6)	9.157***	A(3)	0.709***	A(6)	0.222***	B(3)	0.235*	B(6)	0.534

http://dx.doi.org/10.5772/intechopen.71625

Panel A: Model parameter tahminleri					
π_t	$\mathbf{b}_t$	$\mathbf{d}_t$	$\mathbf{f}_t$	$\mathbf{kh}_t$	$\mathbf{vg}_t$
Panel C: Correlation parameter estimates					
DCC(1)	0.120***		DCC(2)	0.672***	
Multivariate Q (10) statistic			390.851*		
Multivariate ARCH statistic			3416.55**		

***0.01, **0.05 and *0.10 test critical values.

Table 4. DCC model parameter estimation results.

Within the scope of the study, the model structure is examined as a dynamic conditional correlation model to determine the effect of inflation uncertainty on economic variables. For this reason, the volatilities of the involved variables are restricted within the DCC framework. The DCC model established in the study states that there are unstable interactions of the series concerned with conditional correlation and that this correlation affects the correlations with a one lag-period. The DCC model estimation results are shown in **Table 4**. According to the result of the multivariate Q statistic in **Table 4**, no residuals were found to be serially correlated, and the ARCH effect was no more observed in the model. It is found that there is no autocorrelation problem when considering the autocorrelation function of residuals and its squares. When these results are taken into consideration, the effect of uncertainty in the inflation can be evaluated using the DCC model. The DCC model provides more precisely the dynamic structure of the correlation between inflation uncertainty and macroeconomic variables.

The dummy variable used for inflation targeting was found to be statistically insignificant for exchange rate changes, while statistically significant for inflation, output growth, interest rate change, governmet expenditure and tax revenues. This result indicates the effect of inflation uncertainty on selected variables differs pre-2003 and post-2003 periods. In other words, the effects of inflation uncertainty on real and nominal economic indicators are not the same in high and low inflationary periods. Inflation uncertainty had a positive and statistically significant effect on inflation, a positive and statistically significant effect on output gowth, a positive and statistically insignificant effect on exchange rate change, a negative and statistically significant effect on interest rate change, a positive and statistically significant effect on government expenditures and negative and statistically significant effect on tax revenues pre-2003 period. In the post-2003, inflation uncertainty affects inflation positively and statistically, output growth negatively and statistically significant, exchange rate change positively and statistically insignificant, interest rate change positively and statistically significant, government expenditures negatively and statistically significant, and tax revenues positively and statistically significant.

4. Findings and remarks

As unexpected inflation increases with rising inflation uncertainty, the more inflation uncertainty increases inflation for the pre-2003 and post-2003. It is noteworthy that increases in the period after 2003 are less than the previous period. In the period before 2003, the more inflation uncertainty is an increasing effect on economic growth. In this period, as consumption expenditures were made for saving, the increase in inflation uncertainty has led to a shift in commodity markets. Since consumption expenditures are not made for saving, more inflation uncertainty makes the reducing effect on economic growth in the post-2003 period.

Inflation uncertainty increases domestic prices, and so nominal exchange rate is also increased for both of the periods. While an exchange rate regime system was based on the "devaluation as much as inflation" idea in the period before 2003 (excluding the period between December 1999 and February 2001), flexible exchange rate system was implemented under implicit and explicit inflation-targeting regime in the post-2003 period. Due to the fact that the adequate

http://dx.doi.org/10.5772/intechopen.71625

adjustment is provided in nominal exchange rate, inflation uncertainty has no effect on the reel exchange rates for the pre-2003 and post-2003 periods.

The increase in inflation uncertainty reduces the nominal interest rate in the period before 2003. Although the reduction of the nominal interest rate as inflation uncertainty increases, or the negative impact of inflation uncertainty on the nominal interest rate, seems contradictory at first glance, this result describes the features of the period before 2003. A severe increase in government borrowing needs is the basic phenomena that determine market interest rate for the pre-2003 period. In case that the state borrowing to repay the debt is a key factor in determining the market interest rates. The banks become main actors in financing the government. Given that deposits be a source of funding for banks, the decreasing effect of more inflation uncertainty on deposit interest rates is a reflection of the behavior of the banks' increasing profit margin, because bank is shrouded in a structure that they collect the deposits to the state as a debt in the period before 2003.

The increase in nominal interest rate as an impact of more inflation uncertainty is an expected result in the period after 2003. The most capital inflow to Turkey was experienced in the post-2003 period. It is a period in which it becomes very important that interior interest rates are too sensitive to outside interest rates and foreign interest rate is extremely high in the determination of domestic interest rates in Turkey. The supply of funds in the financial markets is largely shaped by a capital flow to Turkey. Capital flows to Turkey largely consist of hot money flows. In this sense, nominal interest rates are increasing due to the reduction in hot money flows as inflation uncertainty increases.

In addition, the inflation uncertainty and nominal interest rate relationship obtained from the study findings support the findings of inflation uncertainty and growth relationship. Consumption spending has become sensitive to interest rates due to the increase in financing consumption spending with credits (the most common example of a credit card) in the post-2003 period. If our findings are being analyzed, in the period after 2003, inflation uncertainty has an impact on nominal interest rate increase.

The fiscal policies implemented before the 2003 period and the conjunctural situation of the country caused the inflation rates to be considerably higher than the developed countries especially. Inflation uncertainty has led to the realization of the Tanzi effect, known as inflation cause to erode the real value of the tax revenues, in the pre-2003 period. In the same period, there was no inverse Tanzi effect, which means a decrease in the real value of public expenditures due to high inflation. When the post-2003 period was passed, the opposite effect was observed.

Author details

Mehmet Kenan Terzioğlu

Address all correspondence to: kenanterzioglu@trakya.edu.tr

Econometrics Department, Faculty of Economics & Administrative Sciences, Trakya University, Edirne, Turkey

References

[1] Friedman M. Nobel lecture: inflation and unemployment. The Journal of Political Economy. 1977;**85**:451-472

[2] Cukierman A, Meltzer AHA. Theory of ambiguity, credibility, and inflation under discretion and asymmetric information. Econometrica: Journal of the Econometric Society. 1986;**54**:1099-1128

[3] Azariadis C, Smith BD. Private information, money, and growth: Indeterminacy, fluctuations, and the Mundell-Tobin effect. Journal of Economic Growth. 1996;**1**(3):309-332

[4] Deveraux M. A positive theory of inflation and inflation variance. Economic Inquiry. 1989;**27**: 105-116

[5] Baillie RT, Chung CF, Tieslau MA. Analysing inflation by the fractionally integrated ARFIMA-GARCH model. Journal of Applied Econometrics. 1996;**11**(1):23-40

[6] Pourgerami A, Maskus KE. The effects of inflation on the predictability of price changes in Latin America: Some estimates and policy implications. World Development. 1987;**15**(2): 287-290

[7] Ungar M, Zilberfarb BZ. Inflation and its unpredictability—theory and empirical evidence. Journal of Money, Credit and Banking. 1993;**25**(4):709-720

[8] Grier KB, Henry ÓT, Olekalns N, Shields K. The asymmetric effects of uncertainty on inflation and output growth. Journal of Applied Econometrics. 2004;**19**(5):551-565

[9] Bhar R, Mallik G. Inflation uncertainty, growth uncertainty, oil prices, and output growth in the UK. Empirical Economics. 2013;**45**(3):1333-1350

[10] Holland S. Inflation and uncertainty: Tests for temporal ordering. Journal of Money, Credit, and Banking. 1995;**27**:827837

[11] Pindyck RS. Irreversibility, uncertainty, and investment. Journal of Economic Literature. 1990;**29**:1110-1148

[12] Beaudry P, Caglayan M, Schiantarelli F. Monetary instability, the predictability of prices, and the allocation of investment: An empirical investigation using UK panel data. University of British Columbia Discussion. 1996;**4**

[13] Tommasi M. The consequences of price instability on search markets: Toward understanding the effects of inflation. The American Economic Review. 1994;**84**:1385-1396

[14] Fountas S, Karanasos M, Kim J. Inflation and output growth uncertainty and their relationship with inflation and output growth. Economics Letters. 2002;**75**(3):293-301

[15] Dotsey M, Sarte PD. Inflation uncertainty and growth in cash-in-advance economy. Journal of Monetary Economics. 2000;**45**(3):631-655

[16] Chan LK. Consumption, inflation risk, and real interest rates: An empirical analysis. Journal of Business. 1994;**67**:69-96

[17] Berument H, Güner N. Interest rates, inflation and variability of of inflation: A case study for Turkey. METU studies in. Development. 1997;**24**:319-327

[18] Omay T, Hasanov M. The effects of inflation uncertainty on interest rates: A nonlinear approach. Applied Economics. 2010;**42**(23):2941-2955

[19] Bollerslev T, Engle RF, Wooldridge JM. A capital asset pricing model with time-varying covariances. J Polit Econ. 1988;**96**:116-131

[20] He C, Teräsvirta T. An application of the analogy between vector ARCH and vector random coefficient autoregressive models. SSE/EFI Working Paper Series in Economics and Finance. 2002;(516)

[21] Engle RF, Kroner KF. Multivariate simultaneous generalized ARCH. Economet Theor. 1995;**11**:122-150

[22] Engle RF. Dynamic conditional correlation: A simple class of multivariate generalized autoregressive conditional heteroskedasticity models. Journal of Business and Economic Statistics. 2002;**20**:339-350

Chapter 14

The Economics of Foreign Exchange in Emerging Markets

Okyay Ucan and Nizamettin Basaran

Additional information is available at the end of the chapter

http://dx.doi.org/10.5772/intechopen.71752

Abstract

This chapter is to clarify macro issues and suggest main policy tools for emerging countries. Furthermore, financial markets, capital mobility and monetary policy are theoretically discussed. The exchange rate management (that is contractionary devaluation and real exchange rate rules) via exchange rate regimes is the purposed subject of this chapter, that is, consideration of open macroeconomic development policies for emerging markets. We take up three issues related to exchange rates in emerging countries for discussion. The first one is the concept and measurement of real exchange rates as well as exchange rate misalignment and its impact upon economic growth. The second topic taken up is the factors that are important in deciding upon the exchange rate regime and the exchange rate determination for emerging markets. Finally the dilemma problem of policy, in the face of sustained capital inflows, is discussed. A key economic feature that differentiates developed and developing countries is the structure of their financial systems.

Keywords: open economies, exchange rates, international finance, macroeconomics, international policies

1. Introduction

In this chapter, we mainly examine the macroeconomic problems of emerging countries. To be a developed country means not only being a mirror image of an emerging country's future but also having more economic qualifications than the emerging ones. For both developed and emerging countries, foreign exchange market is the oldest and intense one among the financial markets because of the financial integration and exchange rate crisis after the 1960s. The foreign exchange market is the center of attention not only for the firms but also for the people on the street. Exchange rate that is the principal of foreign exchange market is the key source of this attention. Here, the important problem is the determination of the real exchange rate.

There are various points of view made by authors in the economics literature. Up to middle of the 1980s, international goods and service flow, individuals' portfolio choices, interest rate, inflation, economic growth and money supply have been widely used in the exchange rate determination models. With these variables, seven types of exchange rate determination models were introduced. They are purchasing power parity (PPP), Mundell-Fleming approach (MFA), sticky price monetary model (SPMM), flexible price monetary model (FPMM), hybrid model (HM) or real interest differential model (RIDM), portfolio balance model (PBM) and currency substitution model (CSM) [1–4].

The purchasing power parity is the oldest approach among the exchange rate determination models. In most general terms, nominal exchange rate between two currencies and price level differentials is defined as purchasing power parity. Gustav Cassel, during the World War I, wrote [6]:

"At every moment the real parity between two countries is represented by this quotient between the purchasing power of the money in the one country and the other. I propose to call this parity 'the purchasing power parity'."

After Cassel, the term was widely used in the economics literature. PPP theory has two main variants. They are absolute PPP and relative PPP. The concept that is told about in the previous paragraph is often termed as the "absolute PPP." The relative PPP hypothesis states that percentage changes in exchange rate are equal to the difference between the percentage changes of the prices of two countries.

Mundell-Fleming approach has been developed in the early 1960s. MF model has had a huge impact on the theory of determination of exchange rates. Original model assumed static expectations and fixed prices. Furthermore, regressive expectations or rational expectations are relatively easier. Mundell-Fleming approach totally analyses the effects of the exchange rate differences under various types of exchange rate regimes [7, 8].

Sticky price monetary model, which is also known as the Dornbusch model, was first introduced by Rudiger Dornbusch in 1976. The model fits into the Keynesian tradition, i.e. stickiness of prices in labor and product markets. Dornbusch's observation is that financial markets seem to adjust more rapidly while product market adjusts slowly. According to Dornbusch, this point makes the base for SPMM [9, 10].

Flexible price monetary model, also known as the Frenkel model, was first introduced by Jacob Aharon Frenkel in 1976. A simple assumption for FPMM is that all prices are flexible. That is to say, aggregate supply curve is vertical, and a shift in aggregate demand has no effect on output. The model also assumes that PPP holds continuously. That is, IS part of IS-LM analysis is irrelevant here. Therefore only a slight shift in aggregate supply results in a change in output [11, 12].

In Ref. [13] Frankel indicates that sticky price monetary model is effective and applicable for the countries with low and stable inflation. On the other hand, flexible price monetary model is effective and applicable for the countries with high inflation. Besides these two extremities, Frenkel asserts that neither SPMM nor FPMM is applicable for the economies with moderate inflation. Then, he introduces hybrid model or the so-called real-interest differential model that accommodates the flexible price and sticky price monetary models as special cases [4, 13, 14].

The important difference of portfolio balance model among the exchange rate determination models is the assumption of perfect substitution between the domestic and foreign assets. In this model, there is a long-run and a short-run differentiate. So, the exchange rate is evaluated in this concept. In the short run, exchange rate is determined by supply and demand of financial assets. However, in the long run, real factors are added to financial assets. Portfolio balance model is far more complex among the other models. The price of the complications is not only the problem. There exist some variables (such as wealth) that are difficult to measure in the model. Therefore, application of PBM is difficult in practice [4, 5, 9].

Individuals have more than one currency in their portfolio in currency substitution models. In other words, individuals' demand for money is defined not only for domestic currency but also for a group of currencies. There are two types of currency substitution models. The first type interprets either current account deficit or surplus as reflecting excess supply or demand of domestic currency relative to the foreign one. The second type of CSM considers money supply as being a worldwide object within the context of a highly integrated world capital market [18–20].

The plan of this chapter is as follows. The second section is titled "Capital mobility and IS-LM-BP model and effects on firms" and deals with types of capital mobility information and Mundell-Fleming approach that is one of the exchange rate determination models under different types of capital mobility. Thus, open macroeconomic policies will completely be examined for the emerging countries and firms of these countries. The exchange rate will play an important role for firms that export goods and import raw materials. Essentially, a depreciation (devaluation) will make exports cheaper, and exporting firms will benefit. However, firms importing raw materials will face higher costs of imports. An appreciation makes exports more expensive and reduces the competitiveness of exporting firms. However, at least raw materials (e.g., oil) will be cheaper following an appreciation. The final section will give the conclusions.

2. Capital mobility, IS-LM-BP model and effects on firms

There are three forms of foreign private capital flows to emerging countries. These are bond finance, commercial bank loans and foreign investment.

To increase capital inflow for investment, emerging countries can issue bonds to foreign investors. These bonds may be either in foreign or domestic currency. Of course there exist particular risks for the investors. There is an inflation risk when bonds are issued in the domestic currency, whereas they are also subject to default risk, in the sense that a poor country may not be able to reimburse the bond when bonds are issued in the foreign currency. If selling bond option does not work to raise capital, emerging countries may borrow from foreign commercial banks. Commercial bank loans may be either short term or long term. Also interest rates may be fixed or flexible by a group of banks or a single bank. The last form of capital mobility is foreign direct investment. This is another type of capital flow to emerging countries. A multinational company may establish a new enterprise or expand its existing one.

Direct investment is the most important one among the three forms explained above. Therefore, capital flow as the form of direct investment is the driving force of growth and raises the employment in emerging country (see [1]).

As described in the first section, there are seven exchange rate determination models. However three of them are the fundamentals. These are Mundell-Fleming model, flexible price monetary model and sticky price monetary model. Together with foreign private capital flow information and different types of restrictions on capital flows, the common point for these three is that IS-LM-BP model is an important phenomenon in the exchange rate determination literature.

Mundell-Fleming model has a wide usage area among the open economy macro models. This model consists of a Keynesian structure and is the expanded form of IS-LM model. The Mundell-Fleming model is based on the following assumptions:

- Nominal wages and prices are constant.
- Aggregate demand is positively related with government expenditure (G), foreign output (Y_f) and exchange rate (e) and negatively related with domestic interest rate (r_d).
- Money demand (M_d) is a function of domestic interest rate (negatively) and domestic income (Y_d) level (positively).
- Money supply (M_s) is negatively affected from the deviation of exchange rate's targeting level.
- Trade account is determined by domestic output level.
- Capital account is determined by domestic and foreign real-interest rate differentials (r_d-r_f).

Constant wage and price assumptions state the distinct part of the Keynesian model that has a perfect elastic supply curve, i.e. output is determined by aggregate demand curve. The degree of capital flow is determined by the sensitivity of real-interest rate differentials in the Mundell-Fleming model [1].

Mundell-Fleming model combines the assumption of net international capital flow that depends on domestic interest rates and the simple Keynesian model consisting of goods and money markets. In the analysis, model focuses on the domestic money supply and interest rates as a monetary policy agent, while foreign prices and interest rates are exogenous [3].

BP curve is the balance of payments, and the slope of BP curve indicates the degree of capital movements. If BP curve is vertical, capital movements are completely limited. On the other hand, if BP curve is horizontal, free movements of capital occur, i.e. perfect capital mobility.

The equilibrium condition for commodity, money and currency markets is given in **Figure 1**. Point E shows the simultaneous equilibrium of all three markets with the internal and external balances at the same time. Points on the left (right) side of the IS curve indicate goods supply (demand) surplus. Points on the left (right) side of the LM curve indicate money demand

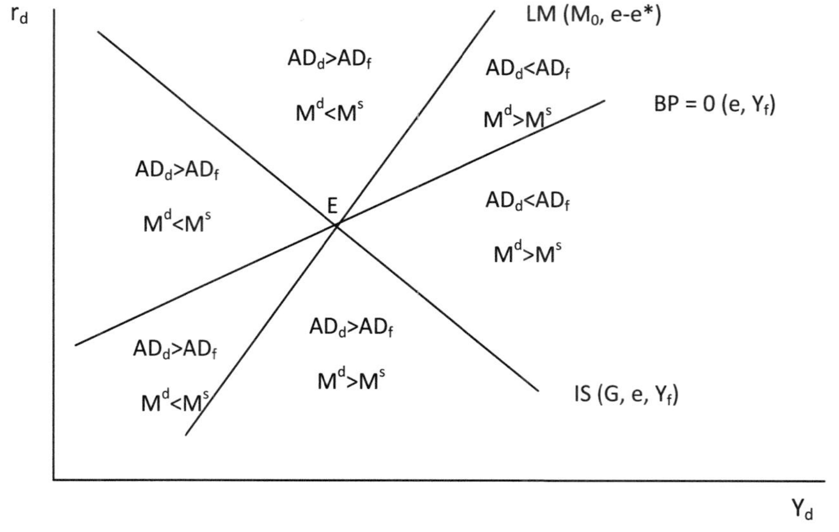

Figure 1. Internal and external balance under open economy.

(supply) surplus. If BP curve shifts to the right (left), this means the existence of a balance of payment deficit (surplus). This situation shows that capital flows are constant at a certain interest rate. However, more domestic income level means more trade deficit.

Three markets must be stable both inland and outland since unsterilized capital movements match up to perfectly elastic exchange rate regime at the fixed exchange rate regime. When the internal balance shifts to the left side of the balance of payments due to a shock, LM curve shifts to the left. Following this, if the exchange rate that gives rise in net exports is perfectly elastic, it will depreciate.

In an open economy, relative efficiency of monetary and fiscal policies depends on the degree of capital mobility and the applied exchange rate regime. Although most of the emerging economies are affiliated with international markets, there may be limitations in the capital movements. Therefore, it is difficult to say there exists a perfect liberalization. Interest rate does not have an important role in money demand since financial sector in emerging countries is not developed. Hence, LM curve is relatively vertical in emerging countries because of low sensitivity to interest rate.

According to the traditional approach of the Mundell-Fleming model, monetary devaluation has an expansionary effect on the output. Devaluation makes the cost of goods produced at home more expensive than the cost of goods produced from the rest of the world. This causes economic agents at home to consume more. The more the consumptions, the more the expansions in output become. This effect is known as the expenditure shift policy, and it is the fundamental expansionary channel of devaluation. On the other hand, devaluations in the 1990s, during the crisis in Asian economies, started to question this fundamental macroeconomic model. Living the economic collapses in the emerging countries makes the academicians and politicians deal with the expansionary and contractionary effects of devaluation.

2.1. Macroeconomics policy under the fixed exchange rate system

Central Bank can intervene at the currency through a fixed exchange rate regime by buying or selling bonds [8]. In this context, monetary and fiscal policies are examined particularly taking into account the capital mobility, whether perfect or not. Five successive equations below present the IS-LM-BP model by using I_0, S_0, Z_0, L_0 and K_0 constant terms. In these equations, investment, saving, import, net capital inflow, money demand, money supply (stock), interest rate and income are expressed with I, S, Z, K, L, M_s, r and y, respectively:

$$I = I_0 + I_r r \tag{1}$$

$$S = S_0 + S_y y \tag{2}$$

$$Z = Z_0 + Z_y y \tag{3}$$

$$M_s = L_0 + L_y y + L_r r \tag{4}$$

$$K = K_0 + K_r r \tag{5}$$

According to the five equations above, resulting IS-LM-BP equations and appropriate equilibrium points E_1 and E_2 are as follows:

$$\text{IS } (S_y + Z_y)y - I_r r = -S_0 - Z_0 + I_0 + G + X = E_1 \tag{6}$$

$$\text{LM } L_y y + L_r r = M_s - L_0 \tag{7}$$

$$\text{BP } -Z_y y + K_r r = -X + Z_0 - K_0 = E_2 \tag{8}$$

Government expenditure (G) and export level (X) variables are added. Equilibrium points can then be calculated using IS-LM-BP equations in matrix form:

$$\begin{pmatrix} S_y + Z_y & -I_r \\ -Z_y & K_r \end{pmatrix} \begin{bmatrix} y \\ r \end{bmatrix} = \begin{bmatrix} E_1 \\ E_2 \end{bmatrix} \tag{9}$$

$$\begin{bmatrix} y^e \\ r^e \end{bmatrix} = \begin{pmatrix} K_r/T & I_r/T \\ -Z_y/T & (S_y + Z_y)/T \end{pmatrix} \begin{bmatrix} E_1 \\ E_2 \end{bmatrix} \tag{10}$$

The result calculated in Eq. (10), while $T = K_r(S_y + Z_y) - I_r Z_y > 0$, gives the equilibrium for points y and r.

2.1.1. *Monetary policy*

The money supply Eq. (11) is found by putting the equilibrium points calculated in Eq. (10) to the LM equation:

$$M_s^e = L_0 + (L_y K_r + L_r Z_y)E_1 + [L_y I_r + L_r(S_y + Z_y)]E_2 \tag{11}$$

http://dx.doi.org/10.5772/intechopen.71752

Money supply is constant in the equilibrium. It determines to conserve the defined fixed exchange rate. Monetary policy is only used for adjusting the currency reserve level and causes an economic imbalance. This result is independent from the international capital mobility [15]. Because an expansionary domestic credit shock places pressure on interest rates to decrease it, capital outflow starts and currency depreciates. So the intervention of Central Bank will be inevitable. Only way for Central Bank is to sell foreign currency from the reserve equal to the domestic credit expansion to avoid the depreciation of the exchange rate. Policymaker has to maintain value of the national currency because of fix exchange rate. Therefore, Central Bank sells dollar at the current exchange rate which leads to the tightening of money supply. **Figure 2** shows that LM curve will come back the original level at each case. As a result, monetary policy is totally ineffective. As described before, this result is independent from the international capital mobility and valid for all four cases.

2.1.2. *Fiscal policy*

To see the effect of fiscal policy, government expenditure (G) is taken exogenous. The following multipliers are calculated by taking total differentials of Eqs. (10) and (11):

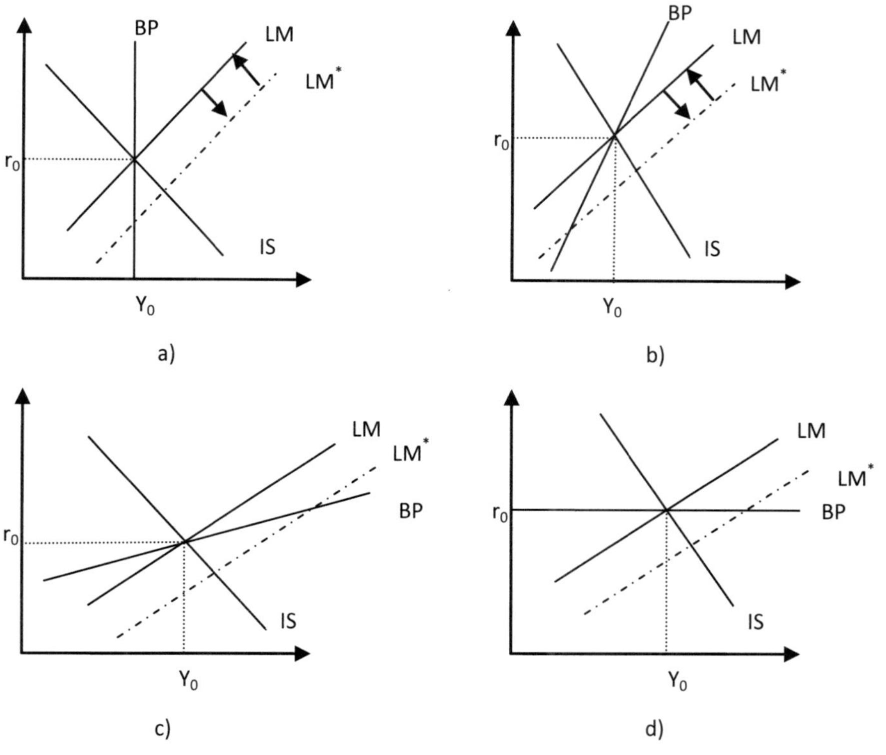

Figure 2. Monetary policy under fixed exchange rate. (a) Imperfect capital mobility, (b) low capital mobility, (c) high capital mobility and (d) perfect capital mobility.

$$\frac{dy^e}{dG} = \frac{K_r}{K_r(S_y + Z_y) - I_r Z_y} > 0 \tag{12}$$

$$\frac{dr^e}{dG} = \frac{Z_r}{K_r(S_y + Z_y) - I_r Z_y} > 0 \tag{13}$$

$$\frac{dM_s^e}{dG} = \frac{L_y K_r + L_r Z_y}{K_r(S_y + Z_y) - I_r Z_y} >< 0 \tag{14}$$

Fiscal policy effects under fixed exchange rate are examined in **Figure 3**. When capital mobility is perfect, $K_r \to \infty$ and multipliers Eqs. (12)–(14) are calculated as follows:

$$\frac{dy^e}{dG} = \frac{1}{S_y + Z_y} > 0 \tag{15}$$

$$\frac{dr^e}{dG} = 0 \tag{16}$$

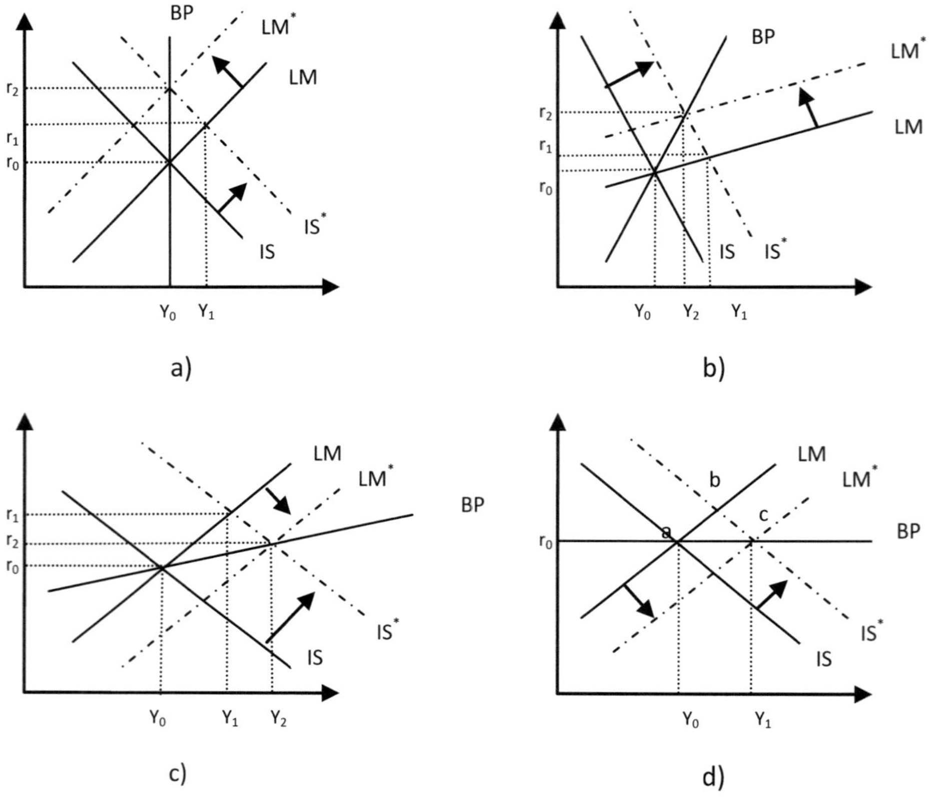

Figure 3. Fiscal policy under fixed exchange rate. (a) Imperfect capital mobility, (b) low capital mobility, (c) high capital mobility and (d) perfect capital mobility.

$$\frac{dM_s^e}{dG} = \frac{L_y}{S_y + Z_y} = L_y\left(\frac{dy^e}{dG}\right) > 0 \quad (17)$$

As shown in **Figure 3d**, when expansionary fiscal policy is applied at the point a with coordinates (r_0, Y_0), IS curve shifts to IS′. New equilibrium is now at point b. There is a balance of payment surplus at this point. This is the difference between expansionary fiscal policy and expansionary monetary policy. This surplus at point b means there exists a capital inflow. Thus, the monetary authority purchases dollar at the current currency to prevent the appreciation of the national currency. Then, the domestic money supply rises. Hence, LM curve shifts to LM′ and reaches the equilibrium at point c as shown in **Figure 3d**.

Under imperfect capital mobility is $K_r = 0$ (**Figure 3a**). After some manipulations the multipliers are as follows:

$$\frac{dy^e}{dG} = 0 \quad (18)$$

$$\frac{dr^e}{dG} = \frac{-1}{I_r} \quad (19)$$

$$\frac{dM_s^e}{dG} = \frac{-L_r}{I_r} \quad (20)$$

According to the calculated multipliers, after an expansionary fiscal policy, equilibrium money stock declines (Eq. (20)). This is because the higher interest rate induces liquidity choices. So currency reserves reduce at the same rate. At the last equilibrium while interest rate is increasing, income level can be as same as the beginning [15].

When capital mobility is high or imperfect, Eqs. (12)–(14) are used. As a response to fiscal mobility, both output and interest rates increase. By inspecting Eq. (14), the equilibrium money stock may rise or fall, depending on whether $L_yK_r + L_rZ_y$ are greater or less than zero. If $L_yK_r + L_rZ_y > 0$, the slope of the LM curve is greater than the slope of the BP curve (**Figure 3b**). In this case, $-L_y/L_r > Z_y/K_r$. The left side of inequality gives the slope of the LM curve, and the right side gives the slope of the BP curve. Economically, the equilibrium money stock rises as foreign exchange is accumulated by the monetary authority. However, if $L_yK_r + L_rZ_y < 0$, the slope of the BP curve is greater than the slope of the LM curve (**Figure 3c**). Monetary authority loses foreign exchange, LM shifts right, and equilibrium money stock declines.

2.2. Macroeconomics policy under the flexible exchange rate system

Flexible exchange rate is a system which allows the exchange rate to freely change within the market. These variations in the exchange rate demand/supply provide the equilibrium that pass through the nominal rate. Exchange rate changes that are part of the expenditure shift policies are used to provide the external balance in the exchange rate systems. Potential external surplus keeps decreasing the exchange rate, while potential external deficit gives a rise in the exchange rate. Both of them separately prevent a real external imbalance. Central Bank has no responsibility on the exchange rate and BP under the flexible exchange rate system. If there is an imbalance in the exchange rate or BP, it recovers automatically.

Governments cannot control exchange rate, interest rate and capital movements at the same time using flexible exchange rates. This is known as the impossible trinity, asserted by [16]. Two of them are chosen as policy instruments, and the other is determined by market dynamics. Under the perfect capital mobility with a flexible exchange rate system, the two policy instruments (interest rate and capital movements) can be effectively controlled since exchange rate is determined by market dynamics. However, it is asserted that exchange rates are not allowed to be determined by interest rates in many countries using flexible exchange rate systems [17].

Setting "e" as exchange rate, the IS-LM-BP equation system with a flexible exchange rate can be written as follows:

$$I(r) = S(y) - G + Z(y, e) - X(e) \tag{21}$$

$$M_s = L(y, r) \tag{22}$$

$$X(e) - Z(y, e) + K(r) = 0 \tag{23}$$

When we differentiate the equations above according to the endogenous variables y, r and e:

$$\begin{pmatrix} S_y + Z_y & -I_r & Z_e - X_e \\ L_y & L_r & 0 \\ Z_y & -K_r & Z_e - X_e \end{pmatrix} \begin{bmatrix} dy \\ dr \\ de \end{bmatrix} = \begin{bmatrix} dG \\ dM_s \\ 0 \end{bmatrix} \tag{24}$$

Using $T = (Z_e - X_e)(L_r S_y - L_y K_r + I_r L_y) > 0$, the result of the matrix system for dy, dr and de is as follows:

$$\begin{bmatrix} dy \\ dr \\ de \end{bmatrix} = \begin{pmatrix} L_r(Z_e - X_e)/T & (I_r - K_r)(Z_e - X_e)/T & -L_r(Z_e - X_e)/T \\ -L_y(Z_e - X_e)/T & S_y(Z_e - X_e)/T & L_y(Z_e - X_e)/T \\ -(L_y K_r + L_r Z_y)/T & [K_r(S_y + Z_y) - K_r Z_y]/T & [-L_r(S_y + Z_y) + L_y I_r]/T \end{pmatrix} \begin{bmatrix} dG \\ dM_s \\ 0 \end{bmatrix} \tag{25}$$

2.2.1. Monetary policy

We obtain the following multipliers, which can be used for observing the monetary policy functions after mathematical manipulations, in Eq. (25):

$$\frac{dy}{dM_s} = \frac{I_r - K_r}{L_r S_y - L_y K_r + I_r L_y} > 0 \tag{26}$$

$$\frac{dr}{dM_s} = \frac{S_y}{L_r S_y - L_y K_r + I_r L_y} < 0 \tag{27}$$

$$\frac{de}{dM_s} = \frac{K_r S_y}{(Z_e - X_e)(L_r S_y - L_y K_r + I_r L_y)} > 0 \tag{28}$$

The multipliers are as follows, under perfect capital mobility (**Figure 4d**), $K_r \to \infty$:

$$\frac{dy}{dM_s} = \frac{1}{L_y} > 0 \tag{29}$$

$$\frac{dr}{dM_s} = 0 \tag{30}$$

$$\frac{de}{dM_s} = \frac{S_y}{-(Z_e - X_e)L_y} > 0 \tag{31}$$

There is no difference in the interest rate with a perfect capital mobility as shown in Eq. (30). When we observe **Figure 4d**, LM shifts to LM′ after an expansionary monetary policy. Hence, the domestic interest rate will be lower than the world interest rate, and the national currency will depreciate due to the capital outflow. As a response, exports will rise and imports will fall.

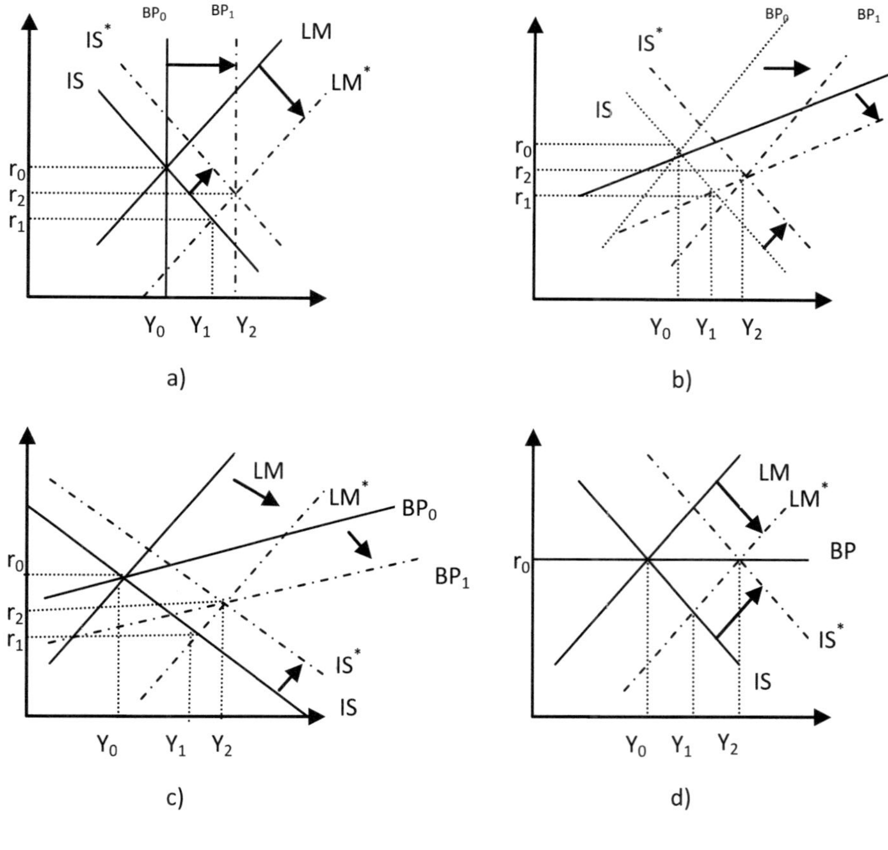

Figure 4. Monetary policy under flexible exchange rate. (a) Imperfect capital mobility, (b) low capital mobility, (c) high capital mobility and (d) perfect capital mobility.

This gives rise to an increase in the aggregate demand, and IS will shift to IS′. The last equilibrium point will be at Y_2. Finally, it is obviously and can be seen that monetary policy is really efficient under flexible exchange rate.

On the other hand, when $K_r \to 0$ with imperfect capital mobility, the multipliers for y, r and e will be as follows, respectively:

$$\frac{dy}{dM_s} = \frac{I_r}{L_r S_y + I_r L_y} > 0 \tag{32}$$

$$\frac{dr}{dM_s} = \frac{S_y}{L_r S_y + I_r L_y} < 0 \tag{33}$$

$$\frac{de}{dM_s} = 0 \tag{34}$$

IS-LM-BP curves move similarly in imperfect capital mobility, low capital mobility and high capital mobility (**Figure 4a–c**). As a result, income and interest rate efficiencies resemble each other for all cases in **Figure 4**.

2.2.2. *Fiscal policy*

Applying Cramer Rule on Eq. (25), the following multipliers are calculated to observe the fiscal policy functions:

$$\frac{dy}{dG} = \frac{L_r}{L_r S_y - L_y K_r + I_r L_y} > 0 \tag{35}$$

$$\frac{dr}{dG} = \frac{-L_y}{L_r S_y - L_y K_r + I_r L_y} > 0 \tag{36}$$

$$\frac{de}{dG} = \frac{-\left(L_y K_r + L_r Z_y\right)}{(Z_e - X_e)\left(L_r S_y - L_y K_r + I_r L_y\right)} >< 0 \tag{37}$$

The multipliers for y, r and e are as follows under perfect capital mobility (**Figure 5d**), $K_r \to \infty$:

$$\frac{dy}{dG} = 0 \tag{38}$$

$$\frac{dr}{dG} = 0 \tag{39}$$

$$\frac{de}{dG} = \frac{1}{(Z_e - X_e)} \leq 0 \tag{40}$$

According to Eqs. (38)–(40), the national currency depreciation is not possible since the capital account effect of fiscal policy is dominant. Because of this, fiscal policy is not efficient under flexible exchange rate. On the other hand, efficiency of fiscal policy may be observed from

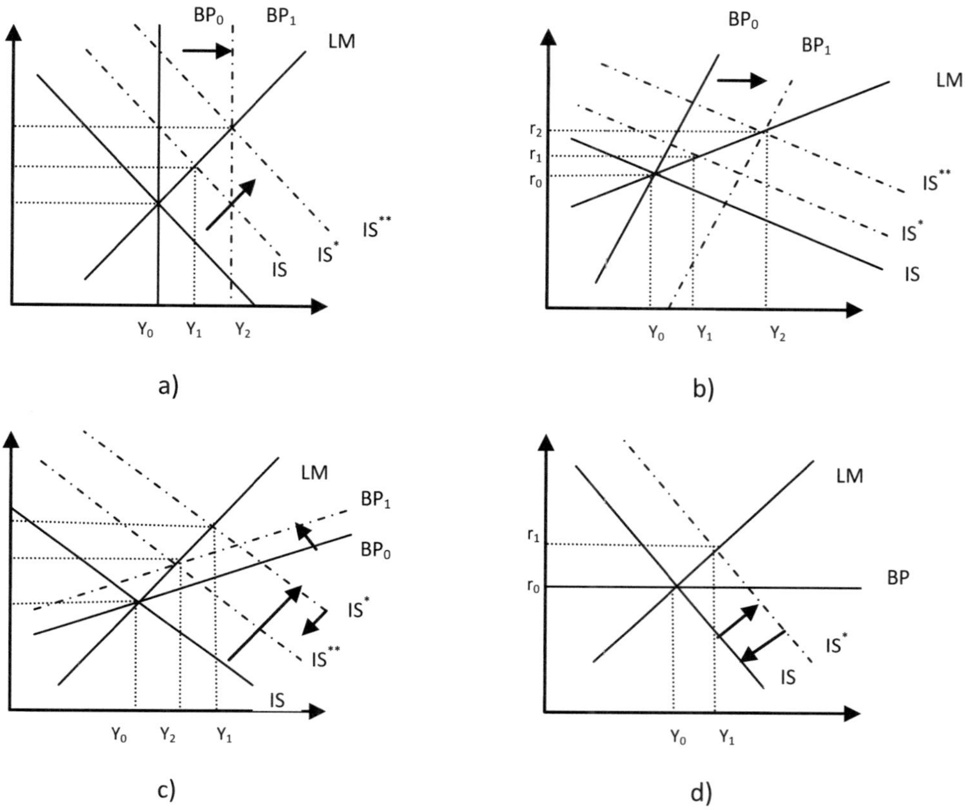

Figure 5. Fiscal policy under flexible exchange rate. (a) Imperfect capital mobility, (b) low capital mobility, (c) high capital mobilit and (d) perfect capital mobility.

different sights due to the degree of capital mobility. In this context, since the inequalities $L_yK_r>0$ and $L_rZ_y<0$, Eq. (37) may be positive or negative. As it is described before $Z_y/_{K_r}$ is the slope of the BP curve, and $-L_y/_{L_r}$ is the slope of the LM curve. We get the following Eq. (41) since $L_yK_r+L_rZ_y>0$:

$$Z_y/_{K_r} < -L_y/_{L_r} \tag{41}$$

It is obvious that the slope of the LM curve is larger than the slope of the BP curve. This indicates the low capital mobility case. The shifting of IS-LM-BP system is examined in **Figure 5b**. If $L_yK_r+L_rZ_y<0$, the slope of the LM curve will be lower than the slope of the BP curve. Hence, high capital mobility case occurs. The movements of IS-LM-BP of this case are given in **Figure 5c**.

At last, the multipliers are as follows under imperfect capital mobility, i.e. $K_r=0$:

$$\frac{dy}{dG} = \frac{L_r}{L_rS_y + I_rL_y} > 0 \tag{42}$$

$$\frac{dr}{dG} = \frac{-L_y}{L_r S_y + I_r L_y} > 0 \tag{43}$$

$$\frac{de}{dG} = \frac{-L_r Z_y}{(Z_e - X_e)\left(L_r S_y + I_r L_y\right)} > 0 \tag{44}$$

According to the three multipliers Eqs. (42)–(44), fiscal policy affects only current account so national currency depreciates, i.e. exchange rate rises.

2.3. Effects on firms

Firms are influenced by exchange rate changes due to the effects they have on the general economy and also because of the activities they carry out in foreign currency. Fluctuations in exchange rates affect firms either positively or negatively, which is defined as exposure to exchange rate or exchange rate risk in financial literature. The exchange rate sensitivity is the potential for changes in exchange rates, company cash flows and hence the market value. Exchange risk is not an issue if the change in the cash flows of a firm that is exposed to this exchange rate effects can be predicted in advance. In short, if there is no difference between expected cash flows and realized cash flows due to exchange rate changes, exchange rate risk is not a concern. Openness to exchange rate, in general, becomes clear in three ways: accounting, economic and transaction effects. The accounting effect, also called the translation exposure, is an effect that occurs when the financial statements of the subsidiary are converted into the central currency of the country during the consolidation of the financial statements, and it is the measurement of the change that this effect causes on the firm's equity. The main way of protecting from accounting effect is to increase liabilities by reducing assets from weaker currencies and reducing liabilities by holding assets from stronger (revalued) currencies. A position in the derivative markets can be taken to support this approach. The economic impact, defined as the effect of unexpected changes in the exchange rate on the future cash flows of firms, is important as much as the degree it affects company value. However, since future cash flows are not easy to predict, many researchers describe the effects of exchange rate changes on the firm value, which is assumed to be the present value of future cash flows, as an economic impact. Since the effects of exchange rate changes on the economic side are long term, the hedging methods in derivative currencies lose their validity in decreasing the economic effect; instead, firms can develop their own strategies and avoid the risks of economic vulnerability. The transaction effect is the effect of exchange rate changes on the sales and profitability plans together with the foreign currency denominated receivables and payables of firms. In order to be able to determine the presence of the transaction effect, the estimation of the net cash flows in foreign currency, and its potential effect should be measured. Since they are mostly short lived, it is possible to solve the problem with the help of derivatives (forward, future, option contracts) and money (hedge transactions) markets. Due to the growth strategy that Turkey has embraced, exporting companies have a critical prescription in the economic structure. For this reason, it is important for policymakers to determine the effect of the exchange rate variability on firms' performance. The effects of changes in exchange rates on firms can be listed as follows [23, 24]:

- Uncertainty: Since the exchange rate at the date of the commercial agreement differs from the exchange rate at the date of payment, there is uncertainty about the future profits of economic agents operating in foreign trade. As a result, foreign trade volume decreases. However, it is also argued that the degree of avoidance of risk plays an important role in determining the effects of exchange rate uncertainty on exports. For an exporter who does not like risk, for example, an increase in exchange rate variability would increase the marginal benefit of expected export revenue. This is because the exporter would prefer to do more production in order to avoid the decrease in export revenues.
- Effect on foreign trade: Rise in the real exchange rate is called real depreciation. The relative price (e/P) increases in the case of real depreciation, so that the goods produced domestically are cheaper than the goods produced abroad, whereas the goods produced abroad are more expensive than the goods produced domestically. As a result, the sales of firms abroad and total sales increase. On the other hand, the real value gain has the opposite effect. The magnitude of the effect of real depreciation and real value gain on firms' performance depends on the demand elasticities of export and import goods.
- Impact on investment decisions: In the event that the managers of the firms dealing with international trade are unable to make accurate predictions as to whether the exchange rate changes are permanent or temporary, investment decisions are postponed.
- Competitive impact: Changes in exchange rates can affect the competitiveness of companies in the face of their competitors. The effect of exchange rate changes on the competitiveness, and hence cash flows of companies according to their qualifications can be positive or negative. In addition, the change in the exchange rate affects the competitiveness of firms by changing the input prices used by firms.
- Economic impact: This refers to the effect of exchange rate changes on the income, expense or accumulated deficit or receivable of the company. In other words, the economic impact is the effect of exchange rate changes on the company's future cash flows. Exchange rate changes affect the value of the company by changing the current real value of the income streams [23, 24].

3. Conclusions

We can summarize the fiscal and monetary policies under fixed and flexible exchange rate with different types of capital movements as can be seen in **Table 1** [4]. We see that fiscal policy is efficient under fixed exchange rate regime with perfect capital mobility. In addition monetary policy is efficient under flexible exchange rate regime with perfect capital mobility.

By the early 1960s, macroeconomics had become firmly established as an approach to open economy questions. The standard analysis was one of the comparative statics in a model with income demand determined and with the exchange rate setting relative prices. The following years brought the highly influential work of Robert Mundell, who created models under fixed and flexible exchange rates [8, 21, 22].

Policy	Zero mobility	Low capital mobility	High capital mobility	Perfect mobility
Fixed exchange rate regime				
Expansionary monetary policy	0	0	0	0
Expansionary fiscal policy	0	Multipliers increases as the degree of capital mobility increases		$\frac{1}{S_y+Z_y}$
Flexible exchange rate regime				
Expansionary monetary policy	$\frac{I_r}{L_rS_y+I_rL_y}$	Multipliers increases as the degree of capital mobility increases		$\frac{1}{L_y}$
Expansionary fiscal policy	$\frac{L_r}{L_rS_y+I_rL_y}$	Multipliers decreases as the degree of capital mobility increases		0

Table 1. The effects of monetary and fiscal policies under various exchange rate regimes.

Toward the early 1970s, the field opened up in many directions. The formal orientation had led to interest in empirical work, and soon questions of capital mobility, or trade and payment adjustment, become popular areas of applied research.

There was a perception, almost up to the late 1980s, that the emerging countries were not different from the developed ones except for levels of per capita. The developed country represented to the developing country a mirror image of its future [15]. However, it is not like that. There are completely different problems in emerging countries because of the differences in social life, geography, that is, the location of the country and political problems. Emerging countries' lack of structural reforms and shallow financial markets curb economic growth. To overcome this obstacle, emerging countries must give priority to the reforms and financial markets.

The early 1990s have witnessed a large increase in capital inflows to emerging countries. These flows are characterized according to their magnitude, timing, regional and country destination, asset composition and sectoral destination. This chapter examines the nature of the capital inflows in a theoretical way. There may be various responses undertaken by the recipient countries against capital inflows. Capital inflows result in huge expansion of aggregate demand resulting in an increase in domestic inflation and an appreciation of the real exchange rate. Specifically, with a predetermined exchange rate, capital inflows generate an overall balance of payment surplus. This may cause appreciation of the nominal exchange rate. The Central Bank has to intervene in the foreign exchange market to buy the excess supply of foreign currency at the current rate to avoid an appreciation of the nominal exchange rate. Thus, monetary base expands. Base expansion would lead to growth in broader monetary aggregates, which results in an expansion of aggregate demand. This would increase domestic price level. Rising domestic prices with fixed nominal exchange rate would imply an appreciation of the real exchange rate. Policymakers can break this chain trough a policy intervention. These interventions are as follows [23]:

There exist policies, which:

- Limit the net capital inflow. This can be done in two ways: firstly, by limiting gross capital inflow and secondly by allowing more gross capital outflow. Inflow of capital usually faces administrative controls, whereas there is a reduction in limitations on the outflow of capital. Exchange rate bands can also be widened to increase the uncertainty.

- Limit the inflow of net foreign exchange. This can be done through an offset of the current account to achieve a surplus in the capital account. This effect can be seen in the trade liberalization and the nominal exchange rate appreciation.
- Accept the accumulation of reserve that has a relation with a balance of payment surplus. However, these policies try to correct this effect on the monetary base.
- Accept a base increase, but at the same time, try to limit its effect on the broader monetary aggregates. Examples include increase in the reserve requirements and quantitative credit restrictions.
- Accept monetary expansion; however, try to overcome their effects on aggregate demand as it can lead to inflation as well as appreciation in the real exchange rate.

Author details

Okyay Ucan* and Nizamettin Basaran

*Address all correspondence to: okyayu@hotmail.com

Nigde Omer Halisdemir University, Nigde, Turkey

References

[1] Hossain A, Chowdhury A. Open Economy Macroeconomics for Developing Countries. 1st ed. England: Edward Elgar; 1998. p. 252

[2] Macdonald R, Marsh I. Exchange Rate Modelling. 1st ed. England: Kluwer; 1999. p. 214

[3] Isard P. Exchange Rate Economics. 1st ed. Great Britain: Cambridge University; 1995. p. 275

[4] Ucan O. Döviz Kuru Dinamikleri. 1st ed. Ankara: Seçkin; 2013. p. 220

[5] Sarno L, Taylor MP. The Economics of Exchange Rates. 1st ed. United Kingdom: Cambridge University; 2002. p. 318

[6] Cassel G. Abnormal deviations in international exchanges. The Economic Journal. 1918; **28**(112):413-415

[7] Fleming JM. Domestic financial policies under fixed and floating exchange rates. IMF Staff Papers. 1962;**9**(1):369-380

[8] Mundell RA. Capital mobility and stabilization policy under fixed and flexible exchange rates. Canadian Journal of Economics and Political Science. 1963;**29**(4):474-485

[9] Copeland L. Exchange Rates and International Finance. 4th ed. Pearson: England; 2005. p. 500

[10] Dornbusch R. Exchange rate expectations and monetary policy. Journal of International Economics. 1976;**6**(1):231-244

[11] Frenkel JA. A monetary approach to the exchange rate: Doctrinal aspects and empirical evidence. Scandinavian Journal of Economics. 1976;**78**(1):200-224

[12] Wang P. The Economics of Foreign Exchange and Global Finance. 1st ed. Germany: Springer; 2005. p. 351

[13] Frenkel JA. On the mark: A theory of floating exchange rates based on real interest differentials. Journal of International Economics. 1979;**69**(4):610-622

[14] Pilbeam K. International Finance. 3rd ed. New York: Palgrave Mcmillan; 2006. p. 497

[15] Jha R. Macroeconomics for Developing Countries. 2nd ed. USA: Routledge; 2003. p. 496

[16] Frankel JA. No Single Currency Regime Is Right for all Countries or at all Times. NBER Working Paper 73381999; September. p. 49

[17] Calvo GA, Reinhart CM. Fear of floating. Quarterly Journal of Economics. 2002;**107**(2): 379-408

[18] Krueger AO. Exchange Rate Determination. 1st ed. New York: Cambridge University; 1983. p. 218

[19] Barro RJ. A stochastic equilibrium model of an open economy under flexible exchange rates. Quarterly Journal of Economics. 1978;**92**:149-164

[20] Calvo G, Rodriguez C. A model of exchange rate determination under currency substitution and rational expectations. Journal of Political Economy. 1977;**85**:617-625

[21] Dornbusch R. Open Economy Macroeconomics. 1st ed. USA: Basic Books; 1980. p. 293

[22] Agenor PR, Montiel PJ. Development Macroeconomics. 2nd ed. New Jersey: Princeton University; 1990. p. 871

[23] Mutluay AH, Turaboglu TT. The effects of exchange rate fluctuations on corporations and evidence from Turkey. BDDK. 2013;**2**(1):59-78

[24] Akalin G, Uzgoren E. The impact of reel exchange movements on firm performance: An empirical study on Turkish firms. Cankiri Karatekin Universitesi IIBF Dergisi;**6**(1):449-469

Chapter 15

Bitcoin and the World of Digital Currencies

Asma Salman and Muthanna G. Abdul Razzaq

Additional information is available at the end of the chapter

http://dx.doi.org/10.5772/intechopen.71294

Abstract

A peer-to-peer system of blockchain, originally started for a cryptocurrency Bitcoin, has caused major disruptions in the stock market. It has affected many businesses if not all, but its significance in the financial world is magnanimous. Historical data (daily rates) for the past 23 months are analyzed to understand the market size, market capitalization and price volatility for Bitcoin. Time series data and financial model are applied to realize the shocks. Monte Carlo simulation is applied to assess the dynamic structure of Bitcoin. With greater volume and activity, the banks and financial intermediaries may become outdated, and the middleman will have no place. It seems like a distant thought, but the facts are pointing toward its reality.

Keywords: finance, stock market, cryptocurrencies, Monte Carlo, ADF

1. Introduction

Change is the only *constant* the world witnesses, and it is certainly inevitable. Toward the end of the 1990s, the information technology phenomenon had the world tied together, and the Internet has surely revolutionized the world. Considering it is only 20 odd years old, here comes another paradigm shift in the form of Internet of ***value*** or data technology. The economies around the world are considering, what may be the end of the largest Financial Intermediaries, The Banks! It was a fearful thought but so were the palm tops, where the tech gurus predicted that everyone will be walking around with a computer in their hands. The thought was scrapped by many, but it became a reality sooner than it was predicted. Developed in 2008 by an anonymous under the name of Nakamoto [1], Bitcoin, a cryptocurrency, was introduced to the world. A 'virtual currency' [2], which is defined as any type of digital unit, used as a medium of exchange, a unit of account, or a form of stored value. The idea was close to the gold standard but with an alternative view. To

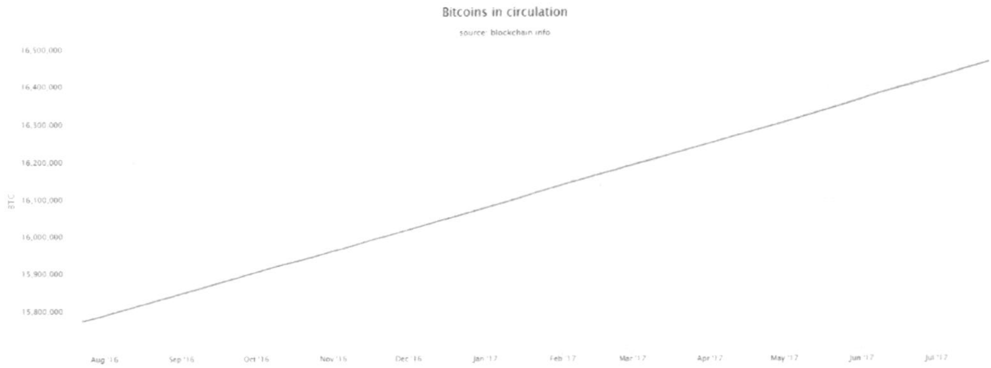

Figure 1. Bitcoin circulation: the mining map.

tackle inflation and its value, Bitcoins have a predetermined number of having 120 million Bitcoins in circulation around the world for the next 25 years. At the moment, 16.5 million Bitcoins [3] have already been mined. So, is this the currency of the world, without having any central authority?

Prominent Market Analysts [4] compare it to the "sharing" economy, which is expected to grow from $15 billion in 2015 to $335 billion by the year 2025, according to a report by PricewaterhouseCoopers. Airbnb, founded in 2008, is a notable player in the sharing economy. The company provides a platform for property owners and visitors to agree and transact short-term rental contracts. While it does not own rental properties, Airbnb today has over 2 million listings in 34,000 cities in 191 countries, generating annual revenue of over $1 billion with a market value of $24 billion.

The decentralized cryptocurrency, Bitcoin, relies on blockchain technology to record its transactions in a public ledger: a technology originally conceived for Bitcoin in 2008 and first implemented in 2009. The blockchain [5] is a distributed database that maintains a continuously growing list of records called blocks secured from tampering and revision. Each block contains a timestamp and a link to a previous block. It serves as the public ledger for all transactions. Every compatible client can connect to the network, send new transactions to it, verify them, and take part in the competition to create new blocks. The competition creating new blocks is known as mining. The Bitcoin design has been the inspiration for other applications and certainly for other cryptocurrencies. If blockchain technology is like metal, then Bitcoin is like gold (**Figure 1**).

2. Cryptocurrencies and the world economy

The last thing on every analyst's mind was Bitcoin surpassing the gold rate. Even the tech-gurus could not predict it, as gold is a league of its own. A lot was dependent upon the US inflation rates and China's trading opportunities, while political instability being a constant factor. A volatile asset witnessed the making of overnight billionaires in a matter of seconds, when the price jumped from $700 to $2100+. The youngsters, who were merely experimenting with it, became "accidental millionaires", and history was made. Dash, Doge, Litcoin, PlexCoin, Ethereum and many more cryptocurrencies made their way to the volatile market to leave a mark of their own. While the price of gold remained flat in the last year, there has been an eruption of the virtual currencies while bringing down the fiat currencies. With the market trends going anywhere with prediction, the shift is incorrigible, the facts are surprising and more shocks are due.

A closer look in the historical rates of Bitcoin raises the question about the future of cryptocurrencies. With a surge of supply and demand, analysts are marking the mining to be completed by the year 2041. What needs to be seen is the price volatility post mining. The world changes at the speed of light, they say, the world of technology is even faster, quicker, not only in terms of change but also in terms of implementation. **Figure 2** shows the price volatility in Bitcoin in the US Dollar since Sep 2015. The daily data for the Bitcoin Price Index have been derived from coindesk [6].

Tapscott [7], author of Blockchain Revolution and one of the top most influencers of the world, quoted: *"Ethereum* [8] *blockchain has some extraordinary capabilities. One of them is that you can build smart contracts. It's kind of what it sounds like. It's a contract that self-executes, and the contract handles the enforcement, the management, performance, and payment"*. **Figure 3** shows the price volatility in Ethereum in the US dollar since Sep 2015. The daily data for Ethereum have been derived from coindesk [6].

2.1. The stock market volume and the dollar value

Trading volume is generally reported not only in terms of number of shares but also in terms of the dollar value. These are the two most fundamental figures in the stock market,

Figure 2. Bitcoin price in USD from September 2015 to July 2017.

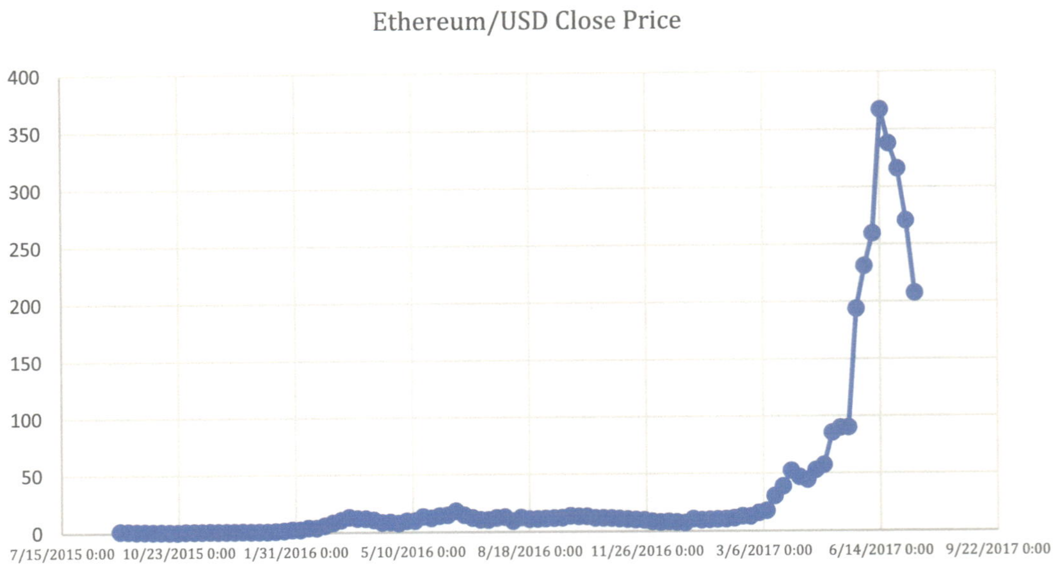

Figure 3. Ethereum price in USD from Sep 2015 to July 2017.

the price and the volume. In public stock exchanges, shares are publicly traded, transactions are recorded and the volumes are displayed. Hence, it becomes easy to calculate the trading volume for such stock exchanges. To better understand this trade volume, let us consider the following example:

EXAMPLE:

Suppose that Samsung only changes hands twice during the day. Let's assume that 20 million shares were bought at $10 a share; later 30 million shares were purchased at $10.5 a share.

The total trading volume = 20 +30 = 50 million shares

Dollar amount equals = (20X10) + (30X10.5) = $515 million

So, the total circulation of Samsung Shares is 515 million for that day.

3. Empirical analysis

There is a plethora of information about Bitcoin. The blockchain provides free information about every detail of the market on an hourly basis. To better understand the market size of Bitcoin, market capitalization [9] data are used. Further investigation is carried out to understand the price impact of Bitcoin as a currency against the US Dollar and the economic movement in terms of a commodity, and the following time series variables are analyzed. The sample is taken from Sep 2015 till July 2017 from coinmarketcap [10].

1. Total Bitcoins in circulation: market capitalization
2. Estimated output volume
3. Bitcoin price changes

3.1. Regression analysis

A regression analysis is used to explain the impact of the variables, market capitalization (CAP), output volume (VOL) and Bitcoin closing price (BTC), and then the relationship of the regression equation to the model is discussed. The best regression equation, based on the analysis of DW (Durbin-Watson), AIC (Akaike information criterion) and SC (Schwarz criterion), is fitted (**Table 1**).

From the resultant equation, the t-statistics, r-squared and adjusted r-squared show a strong positive relation and suggest that the regression equation fits well as indicated in **Figure 4**.

3.2. The augmented Dickey-Fuller (ADF) unit-root test

ADF is used under the three conditions for every time series. The random process includes intercept (c) and trend (t), second includes intercept (c) but no trend (0) and third includes no intercept (0) and trend (t). It was observed that each variable under the Augmented Dickey-Fuller test statistic has a unit root at various lag lengths. This augments the data and the model (**Figure 5**).

3.3. Objectives of the gradient function

Table 2 and **Figure 4** allow us to observe the gradients of the objective function for Bitcoin and to help us find a unit root before applying the cointegrating techniques. The result indicates that all the variables, Bitcoin price, market capitalization and volume have a unit root in their levels and are stationary in their first-order differences (**Figure 6** and **Table 3**).

Variable	Coefficient	Std. error	t-Statistic	Prob.
VOL	5.00E−08	1.00E−08	4.980007	0.0000
CAP	5.90E−08	3.99E−10	147.9187	0.0000
C	39.11393	3.673930	10.64635	0.0000
R-squared	0.994337	Mean dependent var	825.9079	
Adjusted R-squared	0.994320	S.D. dependent var	628.2927	
S.E. of regression	47.35140	Akaike info criterion	10.55743	
Sum squared resid	1,533,634	Schwarz criterion	10.57722	
Log likelihood	−3623.476	Hannan-Quinn criter.	10.56508	
F-statistic	60046.28	Durbin-Watson stat	2.019589	
Prob(F-statistic)	0.000000			

Table 1. Regression results.

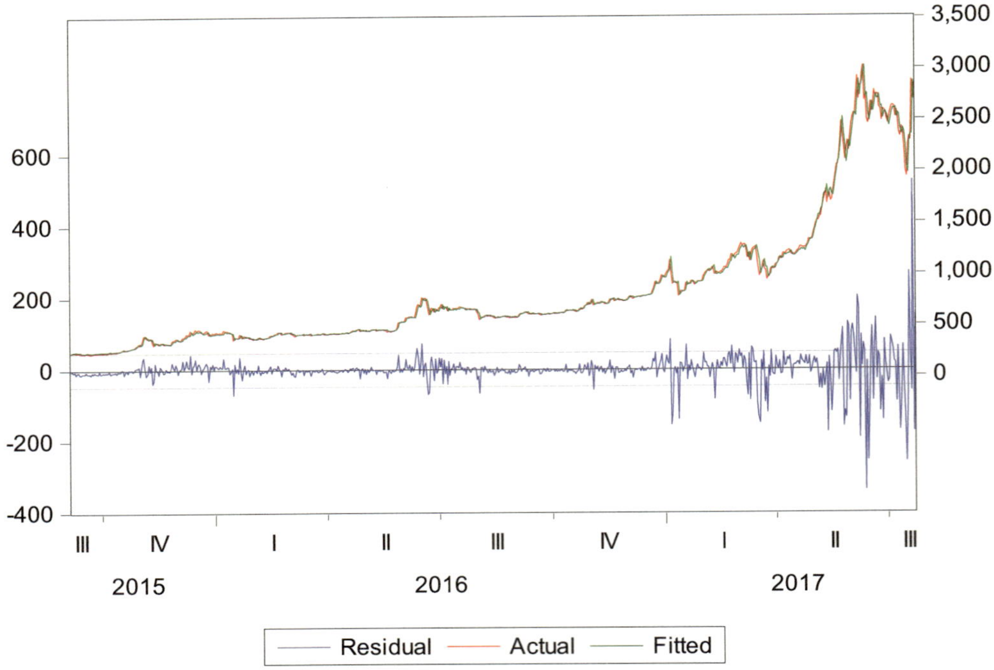

Figure 4. Residual, actual and fitted.

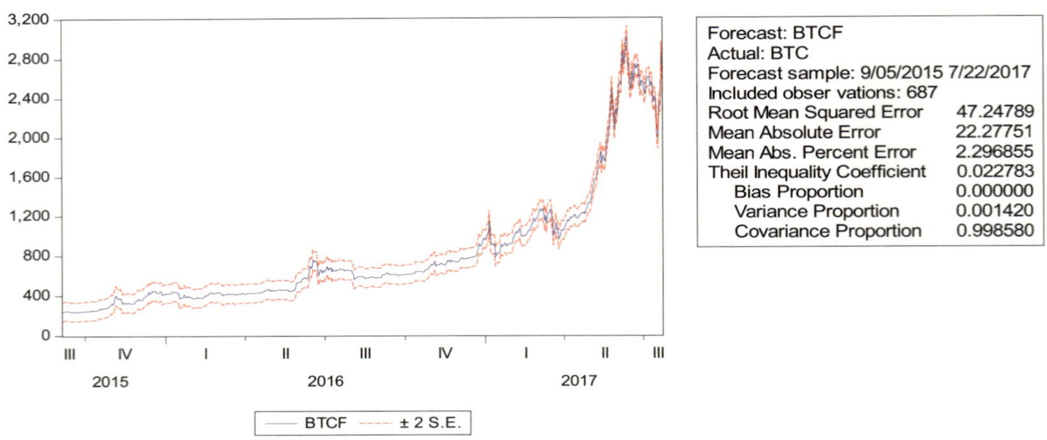

Figure 5. BTC estimated value, denoted as BTCF.

3.4. Var cointegration test statistic

The Johansen cointegration technique is used to check the behavior of the variables. The results obtained are presented in **Table 4**. The cointegration relationships are determined with lag intervals between 1 and 4 with 5% critical values. The unrestricted co-integration rank is applied.

http://dx.doi.org/10.5772/intechopen.71294

Null hypothesis: D(BTC) has a unit root			
Lag length: 0 (automatic-based on SIC, maxlag = 19)			
		t-Statistic	**Prob.***
Augmented Dickey-Fuller test statistic		−27.86005	0.0000
Test critical values:	1% level	−3.439668	
	5% level	−2.865542	
	10% level	−2.568958	
Null hypothesis: D(VOL) has a unit root			
Lag length: 4 (automatic-based on SIC, maxlag = 19)			
		t-Statistic	Prob.*
Augmented Dickey-Fuller test statistic		−17.96755	0.0000
Test critical values:	1% level	−3.439724	
	5% level	−2.865567	
	10% level	−2.568971	
Null hypothesis: D(CAP) has a unit root			
Lag length: 0 (automatic-based on SIC, maxlag = 19)			
		t-Statistic	Prob.*
Augmented Dickey-Fuller test statistic		−26.47374	0.0000
Test critical values:	1% level	−3.439668	
	5% level	−2.865542	
	10% level	−2.568958	

*MacKinnon (1996) one-sided *p*-values [11].

Table 2. The ADF test statistic.

3.5. Granger causality tests

The Granger causality test is used to analyze further the relationship between the three variables. Pairwise tests are carried out in Eviews, and results are shown in **Table 5**. When the lag is 2, the Granger-cause between the variables does not exist. Hence, this proves that the above cause-and-effect relationship is unidirectional and not bidirectional for BTC.

3.6. Impulse response function

To categorize the dynamic structure of Bitcoin, the Monte Carlo simulation is applied through the impulse response functions in the model. It shows how shocks to any one variable filter through the model can affect every other variable and eventually feed back to the original variable itself.

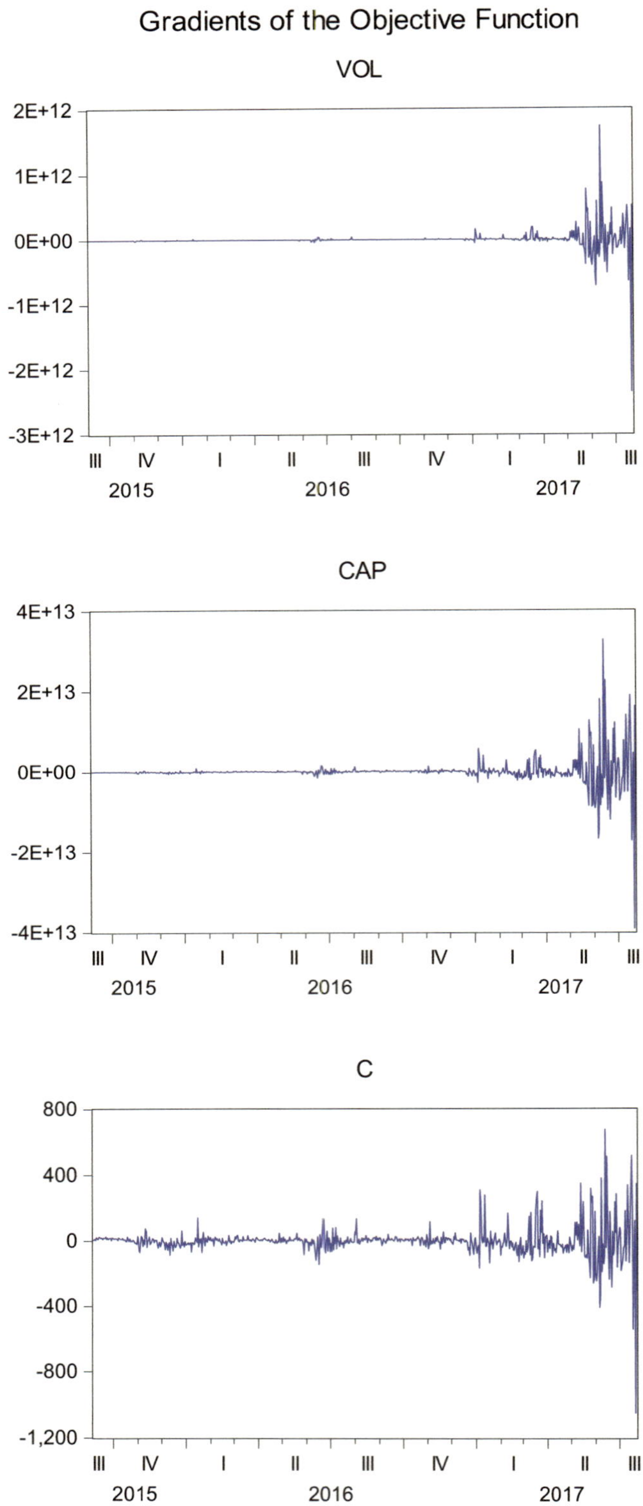

Figure 6. Gradients of the objective function.

Variable	Sum	Mean	Weighted grad.
VOL	0.063843	9.29E−05	2.35E−26
CAP	−1.869141	−0.002721	−3.00E−27
C	−8.16E−11	−1.19E−13	6.36E−17

Table 3. Gradients of the objective function.

Unrestricted Cointegration Rank Test (Trace)				
Hypothesized		**Trace**	**0.05**	
No. of CE(s)	**Eigenvalue**	**Statistic**	**Critical value**	**Prob.**[**]
None[*]	0.058289	68.77080	29.79707	0.0000
At most 1[*]	0.037385	27.81187	15.49471	0.0004
At most 2	0.002675	1.826302	3.841466	0.1765
Unrestricted Cointegration Rank Test (Maximum Eigenvalue)				
Hypothesized		**Max-Eigen**	**0.05**	
No. of CE(s)	**Eigenvalue**	**Statistic**	**Critical value**	**Prob.**[**]
None[*]	0.058289	40.95893	21.13162	0.0000
At most 1[*]	0.037385	25.98507	14.26460	0.0005
At most 2	0.002675	1.826302	3.841466	0.1765

Trace test indicates 2 cointegrating eqn(s) at the 0.05 level; Max-eigenvalue test indicates 2 cointegrating eqn(s) at the 0.05 level.

[*]Rejection of the hypothesis at the 0.05 level.

[**]MacKinnon-Haug-Michelis (1999) *p*-values [12].

Table 4. Johansen cointegration test.

Null hypothesis	Obs	F-statistic	Prob.
VOL does not Granger Cause BTC	685	3.49151	0.0310
BTC does not Granger Cause VOL		32.2346	4.E−14
CAP does not Granger Cause BTC	685	3.58576	0.0282
BTC does not Granger Cause CAP		10672.5	0.0000
CAP does not Granger Cause VOL	685	28.1865	2.E−12
VOL does not Granger Cause CAP		10.9612	2.E−05

Table 5. Pairwise Granger Causality Tests with lags 2.

Monte Carlo [13] simulation is best employed through possible random movements in the model. This perfectly fits the scenario of Bitcoin. There are two components to a stock's price movements: drift, which is a constant directional movement, and a random input, representing market volatility. By analyzing historical price data, the drift, standard deviation,

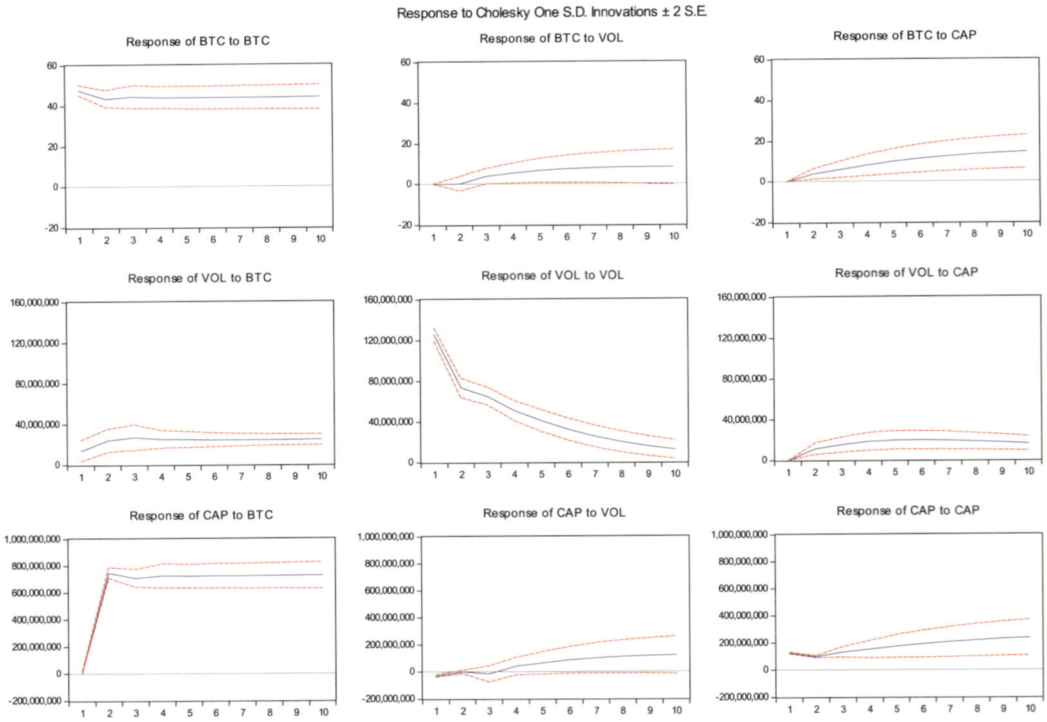

Figure 7. Impulse response functions—Monte Carlo simulation.

variance and average price movement for a security is determined. These are the building blocks of a Monte Carlo simulation. The horizontal spool in **Figure 7** delegates trace periods of the response function, and the vertical spool delegates responses of dependent variables to independent variables.

4. Bitcoin and the future economy

In an era where having a smart phone is highly more likely than having a Bank account, Bitcoin is here to stay. The architecture of money that we live in today brings the borrower and lender together through a financial intermediary, usually a Bank. One of the parties usually conforms to the rules and regulations put forth by the financial institution making it the most sought-after financial product the banks have to offer. People with limited education and a profile not matching to open a bank account can open a Bitcoin account in under 30 seconds.

Bitcoin is Gold 2.0 because Bitcoin is great as a store of value.

As of June 2017, the total value of all cryptocurrency in circulation is now [14] almost $100 bn.

http://dx.doi.org/10.5772/intechopen.71294

This is almost double of what was at the beginning of this year. The value of the fiat currency issued by the Federal Reserve Bank of $1.4 trillion cannot be undermined, but an alternative is underway albeit faster than predicted. Cryptocurrencies are borderless, decentralized, and capable of replacing money in just about any transaction. Without any physical infrastructure, Bitcoin has paved its way into the world economy because of ease of use. The "no-strings" attached idea has appealed to the masses. It is positively one of the most innovative inventions ever since the Internet came. It is Internet money and a digital currency; to stop this, we would have to stop the Internet. This is the power of Bitcoin.

From pizza to Porsche, hotel bookings and even goat, [15] you can buy just about anything by using Bitcoin.

5. Blockchain, Bitcoin and the UAE

Bitcoin and blockchain technology are currently being used by different businesses and organizations. A peer-to-peer system, without the middlemen, where the buyer pays less and the seller receives more is a phenomenon the world is witnessing currently. Countries are passing policies for its free trade, while other countries like UAE and especially Dubai are adopting it as a part of their Smart Dubai 2020 initiative. Taking the possibilities to another level, the future of Bitcoin is evident from the establishment of a Global Block Chain Council under Dubai Government. It quotes: "As part of its efforts to adopt the latest technologies and innovation practices at the global level, Dubai Future Foundation has announced the establishment of the Global Blockchain Council to explore, discuss current and future applications, and organize transactions through the Blockchain platform. Blockchain records every transaction made by the digital currency Bitcoin" [16]. Similarly, a UAE start-up has come out with a gold-backed cryptocurrency called one-gram, giving users, an asset-backed model of digital currencies. With the GCC accounting for a substantial proportion of global remittances, foreign exchange houses are big business, and many say incorporating Bitcoin-enabling technology would be commercially advantageous, as it would help them to cut costs and provide better services to customers [17]. The volatility of Bitcoin is yet to be seen, as some analysts claim it to be a bubble, while others are cashing in on the cryptocurrency. The future where money may be limited to exchange of Bitcoins, the circulation of the Bitcoins remains to be seen once all 120 million Bitcoins are mined and circulated.

Author details

Asma Salman* and Muthanna G. Abdul Razzaq

*Address all correspondence to: asma.salman@aue.ae

American University in the Emirates (AUE), Dubai, United Arab Emirates (UAE)

References

[1] Satoshi Nakamoto. Bitcoin: A Peer-to-Peer Electronic Cash System. 2008. https://bitcoin.org/bitcoin.pdf

[2] Gulf News. UAE Central Bank clarifies virtual currency ban [Internet]. 1st Feb, 2017 [Updated: 1st Feb, 2017]. Available from: http://gulfnews.com/business/sectors/banking/uae-central-bank-clarifies-virtual-currency-ban-1.1971802 [Accessed: 24th July 2017]

[3] Blockchain Luxembourg. Bitcoin Stats [Internet]. 23rd July 2017 [Updated: 23rd July 2017]. Available from: https://blockchain.info/charts/total-bitcoins [Accessed: 23rd July 2017]

[4] Amro Zakaria Abdu. Newsweek Middle East Business Outlook: Will "Share Economy" be Disrupted by Blockchain Technology? [Internet]. 9th November 2016 [Updated: 9th November 2016]. Available from: http://newsweekme.com/business-outlook-will-share-economy-disrupted-blockchain-technology/ [Accessed: 24th July 2017]

[5] Mark Hewitt, The Digital Transformation People. What is Blockchain? [Internet]. November 10, 2016 [Updated: November 10, 2016]. Available from: http://www.thedigitaltransformationpeople.com/channels/enabling-technologies/what-is-blockchain [Accessed: July 24th, 2017]

[6] Coin Desk. Coin Desk Prices [Internet]. 24th July 2017 [Updated: 24th July 2017]. Available from: https://www.coindesk.com/price/ [Accessed: 24th July 2017]

[7] Don Tapscott. Blockchain Revolution: How the Technology Behind Bitcoin is Changing Money, Business, and the World [Internet]. April 2016 [Updated: July 2017]. Available from: http://dontapscott.com/ [Accessed: 24th July 2017]

[8] Blockgeeks. [Internet]. Feb 2017 [Updated: July 2017]. Available from: https://blockgeeks.com/guides/what-is-ethereum/ [Accessed: 24th July2017]

[9] Kristoufek L. What are the main drivers of the Bitcoin price? Evidence from wavelet coherence analysis. PLoS One. 2015;**10**(4):e0123923. PMC4398561. DOI: 10.1371/journal.pone.0123923

[10] CryptoCurrency Market Capitalizations. Historical Data [Internet]. Hourly [Updated: 24th July 2017]. Available from: https://coinmarketcap.com/currencies/bitcoin/historical-data/?start=20150905&end=20170722 [Accessed: 24th July 2017]

[11] MacKinnon JG. Numerical distribution functions for unit root and cointegration tests. Journal of Applied Econometrics. 1996;**11**(16). DOI: 10.1002/(SICI)1099-1255(199611)11:6<601::AID-JAE417>3.0.CO;2-T

[12] MacKinnon JG, Haug AA, Michelis L. Numerical distribution functions of likelihood ratio tests for cointegration. Journal of Applied Econometrics. 1999;**14**(5). DOI: 10.1002/(SICI)1099-1255(199909/10)14:5<563::AID-JAE530>3.0.CO;2-R

[13] Investopedia. Monte Carlo Simulation [Internet]. [Updated: July 2017]. Available from: http://www.investopedia.com/terms/m/montecarlosimulation.asp [Accessed: 24th July 2017]

[14] Financial Times. The Consequences of Allowing a Cryptocurrency Takeover, or Trying to Head One Off [Internet]. June 8, 2017 [Updated: June 8, 2017]. Available from: https://ftalphaville.ft.com/2017/06/07/2189849/guest-post-the-consequences-of-allowing-a-cryptocurrency-takeover-or-trying-to-head-one-off/ [Accessed: Sep 22, 2017]

[15] Business Insider. 10 Real Things You Can Buy with Bitcoin [Internet]. April 10, 2013 [Updated: April 10, 2013]. Available from: http://www.businessinsider.com/what-can-i-buy-with-bitcoins-2013-4#want-to-start-at-the-beginning-11 [Accessed: Sep 22, 2017]

[16] Dubai Future Foundation. Global Blockchain Council [Internet]. 2016 [Updated: 2017]. Available from: http://www.dubaifuture.gov.ae/our-initiatives/global-blockchain-council/ [Accessed: Sep 22, 2017]

[17] Arabian Business. Banking on Bitcoin: Cryptocurrency's Growth in the Gulf [Internet]. Aug 31, 2017 [Updated: Aug 31, 2017]. Available from: http://www.arabianbusiness.com/interviews/banking-finance/377722-banking-on-bitcoin-cryptocurrencys-growth-in-the-gulf [Accessed: Sep 22, 2017]

Section 6

Real Estate and Health Finance

Chapter 16

Performance Stability of Turkish REITs

Sema Bayraktar

Additional information is available at the end of the chapter

http://dx.doi.org/10.5772/intechopen.71629

Abstract

The main purpose of this study is to analyse the performance stability of REIT Index and individual REITs over different sub-periods. The performance of the REITs is compared to mainly that of BIST 100 Index. For analysing the performance stability, three different risk-adjusted measures, namely Sharpe ratio, Treynor ratio and Jensen's alpha, are employed for four different periods. These periods are determined with respect to important regulatory changes in the Turkish REIT market and also to economic states of the country. The results show that Treynor and Sharpe ratios rank the REITs consistently for the high-growth periods. However, the rankings are not that consistent in low-growth periods and even they may contrast significantly. The results also show us that regulatory changes almost have no impact on the performances of the REITs. On the other hand, time-varying behaviour of betas also makes it difficult to attribute the changes in performances to states of economy

Keywords: REITs, performance, portfolio management, stock market, emerging market

1. Introduction

Turkish Real Estate Investment Trusts (T-REITs) have been legally established in 1995 long before many other developed countries [1] and started to be traded in Stock Exchange in 1997. Like in other markets, T-REITs are important investment vehicles, thus they are encouraged to grow by some favourable regulations [2].

Whether REITs perform better than the other financial assets has been one of the main research questions to be answered in the literature since they have started to be traded in the market. There are quite a number of studies on developed markets' REITs trying to answer this question. However, the studies on the investment performance of emerging markets' REITs are limited. Similarly, the number of studies on the performance of T-REITs can be counted on the fingers of two hands. One of the earliest studies on T-REITs is carried out by Kıyılar and

Hepşen [3]. This study compares the performance of the REIT sector with the ISE-100 index using the Sharpe and Jensen indices using monthly data for 2000–2008. Results of the study show that most of the T-REITs have higher monthly returns than those of ISE-100, but they also have higher variabilities. Thus, for most of them, Sharpe indices are lower than those of ISE-100. Although Jensen's indices are positive for most of the cases, it is not possible to claim that T-REITs perform better than common stocks since the indices are not statistically significant. Erol and Tırtıroğlu [4] compare hedging characteristics of T-REITs against inflation with stock indexes between December 1999 and December 2004. They show that REITs provide better hedge against both unexpected and expected inflation compared to stock indices and that property of T-REITs is more effective in high-inflation periods.

Erol and İleri [5] try to determine which macroeconomic factors influence BIST sector indices and individual REIT companies by analysing data between 2002 and 2011. The results show that Turkish REIT stocks act more like the stock market than the real estate sector. T-REITs, like the same BIST sectoral indices, provide negative protection against inflation, exhibit a positive correlation with real sector volatility and are heavily influenced by the ISE risk premium. The study by Aktan and Ozturk [6] investigates the risk-return relationship for T-REITs over the period 2002–2008 by using CAPM and Single Index Model (SIM) and shows that linearity assumption of these models are rejected. Altınsoy et al. [1] analyse whether the declining beta property of REITs observed in many markets also prevail for Turkey and the results show that it is true for 2002–2009. Their results show that T-REITs' betas – correlation between REITs and stock market – decreases over time. On the other hand, REIT returns more closely track stock market in high-growth economic states than low-growth economic states, unlike to the findings from other countries. Another study [2] examines the portfolio diversification and risk/return characteristics of T-REITs using monthly data between 2008 and 2015. The study shows that Fama-French model is better than CAPM in capturing the variation of T-REITs' returns. Additional macroeconomic factors also improve the explanatory power of the model.

All of these studies cover only short-term periods. Thus, the questions of how well the T-REITs have performed over a long period and how stable the performance of T-REITs remain unanswered. Previous research shows that different sampling periods may result in different performance results [7]. Thus, it is important to adapt a longer period and try to analyse whether there are significant differences in the investment performance of T-REITs.

The objective of this study is to investigate the performance of T-REITs with respect to stock market by using risk-adjusted measures. By using a relatively longer period over 2002–2017, the study is going to investigate the stability of performance of T-REITs. In this study, we analyse four periods: 2001–2005; 2006–2008; 2009–2013 and 2014–2017. This separation allows us to distinguish both pre- and post-crisis periods and also the effects of some important regulation changes in Turkey. For example, in 2007, the new regulations regarding mortgage loans were introduced. This change was expected to increase the demand for real estate and thus to have a positive effect on the future of REITs. At the beginning, T-REITs were supposed to invest at a minimum 75% of their portfolios in real estate and real-estate backed securities with the 1998 Communique, Article 27. Later, that ratio has been decreased to 50% in 2013, so the flexibility of T-REITs with respect to investment has increased. Also, with the amendment made in 2013, requirement to have a leader entrepreneur (partner or partners having a minimum of 25% of the company's capital) has been abolished, real estate investment companies started to be able to issue real estate certificates as an extra means of finance instrument and some procedural obligations have been reduced, all of these resulting in easing of management of T-REITs. So, if not in the third period due to the financial crisis, REIT performance may be expected to be increased in the fourth period. In addition, the frequency of the data that is used in this study may give us some additional information about the time-varying behaviour of T-REITs. The study by Altınsoy et al. [1] used both daily and weekly data in analysing the time-varying behaviour of T-REITs' betas and different frequency data led them to find different empirical results, namely, they observe declining beta for the weekly data but more stable beta for daily data. The data used in this study is monthly data. Thus, it is interesting to know how using monthly data is going to contribute to this observation in the study by Altınsoy et al. [1]. The period before 2008 has also been divided into two periods based on the results of [1]. This study has also shown that tracking behaviour of REIT returns of stock market change from high-growth economic states to low-growth economic states. Thus, following this study, in defining the periods, the author also paid attention to low-growth and high-growth states. Accordingly, 2001–2005 and 2009–2013 periods are accepted to be high-growth periods; on the other hand, 2006–2009 and 2014–2017 periods are taken to be low-growth periods[1]. The study ends up analysing four different periods with the aim of observing the changes in the performance of T-REITs of these important structural changes.

Section 2 describes the data and explains the methodology employed. In Section 3, preliminary results of performance comparison between T-REITs and some financial variables are given and also its findings are reported and discussed. Final section gives the summary of results and some concluding remarks.

2. Data and methodology

Turkey currently has 28 REITs, each of which is reflected by a certain weight in the constructed REIT index. **Table 1** shows their Ticker, Names, and their weights in the index. As shown in **Table 1**, 16 out of 28 REITs has a weight less than 1%. On the other hand, the other 12 REITs comprise 92.55% of the REIT index in total. For the sake of clarity and integrity of the chapter, the aim of the study would be to analyse the performance stability of these REITs that have larger weights in the REIT index. We also add Pera GYO (PEGYO) to the sample since it is the only REIT that survived throughout the whole period. The data used is the monthly prices of these REITs over more than 14-year period from January 2001 to July 2017. For each REIT, the monthly returns are calculated based on data gathered from the Bloomberg database by taking the log of difference between two subsequent observations[2]. Monthly return of BIST 100 which is also gathered from Bloomberg serves as a proxy for market return. The monthly interest rate values of 1-year Treasury bills are employed to proxy for risk-free rate. Interest rate values are obtained from Federal Reserve Bank of St. Louis for the period 2001–2004 and from investing.com website for the period 2005–2017.

[1]Average growth rates for the periods of 2001–2005, 2006–2008, 2009–2013 and 2014–2017 are 0.80, −0.05, 0.54 and 0.01, respectively.

[2]Interest rates are not transformed to their logarithms since data for interest rates were already obtained as percentages.

Ticker	Name	Weight
XGMYO index		
EKGYO TI Equity	Emlak Konut Gayrimenkul Yatirim Ortaklig	57.721044
YGGYO TI Equity	Yeni Gimat Gayrimenkul Ortakligi AS	9.283066
ISGYO TI Equity	Is Gayrimenkul Yatirim Ortakligi AS	5.904721
TRGYO TI Equity	Torunlar Gayrimenkul Yatirim Ortakligi A	5.315489
AKSGY TI Equity	AKIS Gayrimenkul Yatirimi AS	3.383685
ALGYO TI Equity	Alarko Gayrimenkul Yatirim Ortakligi AS	1.988418
HLGYO TI Equity	Halk Gayrimenkul Yatirim Ortakligi AS	1.87651
SNGYO TI Equity	Sinpas Gayrimenkul Yatirim Ortakligi AS	1.555767
KLGYO TI Equity	Kiler Gayrimenkul Yatirim Ortakligi AS	1.550455
VKGYO TI Equity	Vakif Gayrimenkul Yatirim Ortakligi AS	1.49898
AKMGY TI Equity	Akmerkez Gayrimenkul Yatirim Ortakligi A	1.373071
NUGYO TI Equity	Nurol Gayrimenkul Yatirim Ortakligi AS	1.100913
RYGYO TI Equity	Reysas Gayrimenkul Yatirim Ortakligi AS	0.948177
OZKGY TI Equity	Ozak Gayrimenkul Yatirim Ortakligi	0.855248
PAGYO TI Equity	Panora Gayrimenkul Yatirim Ortakligi	0.823887
AKFGY TI Equity	Akfen Gayrimenkul Yatirim Ortakligi AS	0.777751
YKGYO TI Equity	Yapi Kredi Koray Gayrimenkul Yatirim Ort	0.502913
DGGYO TI Equity	Dogus Gayrimenkul Yatirim Ortakligi A.S.	0.499015
YGYO TI Equity	Yesil Gayrimenkul Yatirim Ortakligi AS	0.489101
OZGYO TI Equity	Ozderici Gayrimenkul Yatirim Ortakligi A	0.456993
PEGYO TI Equity	Pera Gayrimenkul Yatirim Ortakligi AS	0.444152
AVGYO TI Equity	Avrasya Gayrimenkul Yatirim Ortakligi AS	0.4257
AGYO TI Equity	Atakule Gayrimenkul Yatirim Ortakligi	0.363115
MRGYO TI Equity	Marti Gayrimenkul Yatirim Ortakligi AS	0.282384
TSGYO TI Equity	TSKB Gayrimenkul Yatirim Ortakligi AS	0.239008
ATAGY TI Equity	Ata Gayrimenkul Yatirim Ortakligi AS	0.207019
SRVGY TI Equity	Servet Gayrimenkul Yatirim Ortakligi AS	0.092782
MSGYO TI Equity	Mistral Gayrimenkul Yatirim Ortakligi AS	0.040637

Table 1. REIT indices in Turkey.

Basically, there are three measures that are mostly used to assess the risk-adjusted performance of a portfolio: Sharpe ratio [8], Treynor ratio [9] and [10], and Jensen's alpha. Sharpe ratio is defined as follows:

$$Sj = \frac{\overline{Rj} - \overline{R_f}}{\vartheta j} \quad (1)$$

where $(\overline{Rj} - \overline{R_f})$ is the average excess return of REIT over risk-free rate, ϑj is the standard deviation of the same REIT. Thus, Sharpe ratio shows the average excess return per unit of risk. The higher the ratio, the better the performance is.

Treynor ratio is the ratio of average excess return of REIT to its systematic risk, that is, beta (β);

$$Tj = \frac{\overline{Rj} - \overline{R_f}}{\beta j} \quad (2)$$

where β is the beta coefficient of each REIT portfolio. It is calculated by using the following relationship:

$$R_{jt} - R_{ft} = \alpha_j + \beta_j\left(R_{mt} - R_{ft}\right) + \varepsilon_{jt} \quad (3)$$

where $R_{jt} - R_{ft}$ is the excess return of REIT portfolio over risk-free rate, $R_{mt} - R_{ft}$ is the excess return of market portfolio over risk-free rate, β_j is the regression coefficient standing for the systematic risk, α_j is Jensen's alpha for each REIT portfolio. As can be seen from this specific regression, the calculation of Treynor ratio and Jensen's alpha requires the selection of a reference market portfolio. In this study, BIST 100 is going to be employed as the reference portfolio. The main purpose of the study is to observe the performance stability of REIT portfolios over a relatively long period, that is, the trend of the risk and return performances of the portfolios is more important than the actual level of the performances. Thus, the selection of the reference portfolio is not critical for the present study. Indeed, study by Myer and Webb [11] shows that the performances of the real estate funds are not very much affected by the choice of real estate benchmarks employed. Whether the employed benchmark portfolio is satisfactory or not is decided by looking at the explanatory power of the regression measured by R-squared values.

As in the case of Sharpe ratio, the higher the positive ratio, the better the performance of REIT index is. A positive and significant alpha indicates a superior performance of the REIT index relative to reference portfolio, while a negative alpha indicates the fund's inferior performance.

3. Results

Table 2 presents the statistical summary between BIST REIT Index return and some important financial indicators for four different periods, namely 2001m5–2005m12, 2006m1–2009m1, 2009m1–2013m12 and 2014m1–2017m7. The indicators that are compared with BIST REIT index are BIST 100, 10-year Treasury bond, gold prices in USD, consumer price index and USD/TRY currency. It is clearly observed that REIT index is closely linked to BIST index both in terms of returns and volatilities for all periods. In the first period, that is high-growth period, average returns of BIST 100, REIT index and CPI have their highest values. But for the second period, that is low-growth period, index returns become negative and BIST 100 is

	BIST REIT	BIST 100	10Y T-Bond	GOLD/OUNCE (USD)	CPI	USD/TRY Currency
A. 2001m5–2005m12						
Mean	2.36	2.02	NA	1.15	1.48	0.26
Median	4.27	2.16	NA	0.81	0.98	–0.32
Maximum	26.03	32.03	NA	8.10	5.92	11.55
Minimum	–25.89	–26.98	NA	–6.09	–0.58	–9.67
Std. Dev.	11.95	12.92	NA	3.00	1.43	4.87
B. 2006m1–2009m1						
Mean	–1.16	–3.16	NA	1.44	0.73	0.53
Median	1.72	–0.31	NA	0.89	0.80	–0.49
Maximum	18.45	10.53	NA	10.33	2.57	19.47
Minimum	–26.29	–38.16	NA	–12.26	–0.73	–7.61
Std. Dev.	9.82	10.87	NA	5.53	0.76	5.55
C. 2009m1–2013m12						
Mean	1.54	1.58	0.75	0.72	0.69	0.59
Median	0.78	1.97	0.76	0.70	0.58	0.49
Maximum	20.58	23.90	0.91	1.22	11.40	3.22
Minimum	–14.39	–18.35	0.51	0.42	–6.88	–1.44
Std. Dev.	7.58	9.10	0.10	0.16	3.96	0.84
D. 2014m1–2017m7						
Mean	0.94	0.97	0.80	0.08	0.72	1.18
Median	1.24	1.10	0.80	0.16	0.57	0.84
Maximum	10.87	13.91	0.92	9.61	2.43	10.53
Minimum	–9.23	–10.76	0.58	–7.13	–0.52	–5.13
Std. Dev.	5.13	4.91	0.08	3.37	0.70	3.23

Table 2. Statistical summary for BIST 100 and REIT index returns and some important financial indicators.

affected more harshly than REIT index. On the other hand, apparently as alternative investments gold and USD/TRY currency seem to be positively affected from this state change. In the third period, post-financial crisis, while changes in CPI and USD/TRY currency are relatively stable and returns on gold price decreases compared to the previous period, index returns become positive and looks like catching up with the pre-crisis levels. This expectation, however, is not realised since the last period is also a low-growth period and what happens to index returns is only a dramatic fall again. Meanwhile, gold returns for final period also dramatically decreased. When a similar statistical analysis is done for individual REITs for the same periods, more or less, we observe similar changes. These results are not

http://dx.doi.org/10.5772/intechopen.71629

presented here for the sake of brevity. However, we present **Table 3**, where the statistical summary between BIST 100 and BIST REIT index and individual REITs are presented for the whole period. There are three REITs that perform better than BIST 100. Two of them are Vakıf GYO (VKGYO) with an average of 1.67 and Nurol GYO (NUGYO) with an average of 1.18 and they both have much higher volatilities compared to BIST 100. The third one is AKIŞ GYO (AKSGYO) with an average of 1.17 and a lower volatility than that of BIST 100. All other individual REITs and REIT index perform worse than BIST 100 and they also have high volatilities for the period.

The correlations between BIST 100 and REIT indices are shown in **Table 4**. The strongest relation is between BIST 100 and BIST REIT index. For all of the individual REITs except two, the correlation with BIST 100 is larger than 40%. For Akiş GYO (AKSGYO), the correlation is only 3% and for Yeni Gimat GYO (YGGYO), the correlation is even a negative number, −7%.

Table 5 reports the risk-adjusted performance results of Sharpe, Treynor and Jensen alpha measures alongside their respective performance rankings for different periods. However, as shown in all periods, there are some negative Sharpe ratio and Treynor ratio values. As the study by Israelsen [12] shows, these negative ratios can lead to incorrect rankings by making you choose the worse portfolio due to larger volatility. Craig Israelsen [12] has created modified Sharpe ratio where the denominator is adjusted as follows:

$$S_j = \frac{\overline{Rj} - \overline{R_f}}{\vartheta j^{ER/|ER|}} \tag{4}$$

	Mean	Median	Maximum	Minimum	Std. Dev.	Skewness	Kurtosis	Obser.
BIST 100	1.15	2.23	26.03	−26.29	9.11	−0.25	3.83	193
BIST REIT	0.67	1.11	32	−38.2	10.2	−0.27	4.57	194
AKMGY	0.27	0	45.4	−31.3	10.5	0.62	6.6	147
AKSGYO	1.17	0.46	31.4	−12	8.1	1.76	7.52	54
ALGYO	1.08	1.6	41.2	−48.8	12.5	−0.07	4.34	195
EKGYO	0.6	0	36.1	−22.9	8.7	0.51	5.27	79
HLGYO	0.04	0	12.8	−10.6	5.5	0.01	2.44	53
ISGYO	0.53	0.9	36	−42	11.4	−0.13	4.52	195
KLGYO	0.01	0.56	39	−29	11.9	0.45	4.76	75
NUGYO	1.18	−1.06	59	−46	15.4	0.44	5.01	195
SNGYO	−0.59	0	45.2	−43.4	13	−0.17	4.99	121
TRGYO	0.69	0	25.2	−29.3	10.2	−0.11	3.05	81
VKGYO	1.67	0.7	50.2	−45	15	0.3	4.43	195
YGGYO	1.11	0	20.9	−12.8	6.5	0.9	4.93	47
PEGYO	−0.22	−0.9	85.3	−74.8	18.1	0.24	7.05	195

Table 3. Statistical summary for REIT index and individual REIT portfolio returns (2001m5–2017m7).

	BIST 100	XGMYO	AKMGY	AKSGYO	ALGYO	EKGYO	HLGYO	ISGYO	KLGYO	NUGYO	SNGYO	TRGYO	VKGYO	YGGYO
BIST 100	1.00	0.86	0.50	0.03	0.63	0.65	0.53	0.77	0.44	0.57	0.76	0.66	0.45	–0.07
XGMYO	0.86	1.00	0.60	–0.06	0.73	0.95	0.53	0.88	0.53	0.60	0.81	0.75	0.51	0.10
AKMGY	0.50	0.60	1.00	0.00	0.48	0.42	0.22	0.36	0.33	0.37	0.45	0.36	0.19	0.28
AKSGYO	0.03	–0.06	0.00	1.00	–0.13	–0.10	0.14	0.01	–0.17	–0.03	0.04	–0.03	0.17	–0.08
ALGYO	0.63	0.73	0.48	–0.13	1.00	0.48	0.41	0.63	0.38	0.49	0.57	0.56	0.43	0.14
EKGYO	0.65	0.95	0.42	–0.10	0.48	1.00	0.47	0.63	0.44	0.37	0.61	0.67	0.16	0.00
HLGYO	0.53	0.53	0.22	0.14	0.41	0.47	1.00	0.55	0.40	0.35	0.48	0.36	0.31	–0.19
ISGYO	0.77	0.88	0.36	0.01	0.63	0.63	0.55	1.0	0.36	0.46	0.60	0.52	0.44	0.04
KLGYO	0.44	0.53	0.33	–0.17	0.38	0.44	0.40	0.36	1.00	0.49	0.54	0.58	0.18	–0.08
NUGYO	0.57	0.60	0.37	–0.03	0.49	0.37	0.35	0.46	0.49	1.00	0.49	0.50	0.45	0.09
SNGYO	0.76	0.81	0.45	0.04	0.57	0.61	0.48	0.6	0.54	0.49	1.00	0.66	0.25	–0.11
TRGYO	0.66	0.75	0.36	–0.03	0.56	0.67	0.36	0.52	0.58	0.50	0.66	1.00	0.19	–0.07
VKGYO	0.45	0.51	0.19	0.17	0.43	0.16	0.31	0.44	0.18	0.45	0.25	0.19	1.00	0.01
YGGYO	–0.07	0.10	0.28	–0.08	0.14	0.00	–0.19	0.04	–0.08	0.09	–0.11	–0.07	0.01	1.00
PEGYO	0.61	0.61	0.33	–0.04	0.47	0.39	0.34	0.5	0.46	0.38	0.50	0.47	0.33	–0.03

Table 4. Correlation matrix between REIT index and individual REIT portfolio returns (2001m5–2017m7).

	BIST REIT	AKMGY	AKSGYO	ALGYO	EKGYO	HLGYO	ISGYO	KLGYO	NUGYO	SNGYO	TRGYO	VKGYO	YGGYO	PEGYO
A. 2001m5–2005m12														
Sharpe ratio	−0.11			−0.05			−0.15		−0.10			0.00		−0.13
Modified Sharpe	−18.18			−11.80			−32.05		−26.16			0.00		−75.04
Ranking	**3**			**2**			**5**		**4**			**1**		**6**
Treynor ratio	−1.44			−0.99			−2.09		−1.67			0.07		−2.52
Modified Treynor	−1.38			−0.64			−2.24		−1.52			0.07		−3.81
Ranking	**3**			**2**			**5**		**4**			**1**		**6**
Jensen's alpha	−0.42			0.06			−0.86		−0.55			1.49		−0.63
Prob value (alpha)	0.63			0.97			0.46		0.72			0.40		0.82
Ranking	**3**			**2**			**6**		**4**			**1**		**5**
Obs.	55			56			56		56			56		56
B. 2006m1–2009m1														
Sharpe ratio	−0.43	−0.39		−0.43			−0.31		−0.36			−0.31		−0.26
Modified Sharpe ratio	−51.16	−29.46		−69.45			−56.56		−79.86			−53.93		−131.70
Ranking	**2**	**1**		**5**			**4**		**6**			**3**		**7**
Treynor ratio	−4.86	−5.62		−6.57			−3.84		−6.34			−5.05		−5.22
Modified Treynor	−4.56	−2.04		−4.55			−4.54		−4.57			−3.26		−6.46
Ranking	**5**	**1**		**4**			**3**		**6**			**2**		**7**
Jensen's alpha	−2.09	−1.76		−3.22			−1.24		−3.09			−1.89		−2.80
Prob value (alpha)	0.03	0.12		0.06			0.40		0.16			0.32		0.42
Ranking	**4**	**2**		**7**			**1**		**6**			**3**		**5**
Obser.	37	37		37			37		37			37		37

	BIST REIT	AKMGY	AKSGYO	ALGYO	EKGYO	HLGYO	ISGYO	KLGYO	NUGYO	SNGYO	TRGYO	VKGYO	YGGYO	PEGYO
C. 2009m1–2013m12														
Sharpe ratio	0.09	0.01		0.14	−0.05		0.11	−0.50	0.20	0.04	−0.09	0.28		−0.05
Modified Sharpe ratio	0.09	0.01		0.14	−5.98		0.11	−55.62	0.20	0.04	−10.64	0.28		−6.93
Ranking	**5**	**7**		**3**	**8**		**4**	**11**	**2**	**6**	**10**	**1**		**9**
Treynor ratio	0.90	0.18		2.06	−0.58		1.20	−5.04	3.16	0.31	−0.78	10.08		−0.55
Modified Treynor ratio	0.90	0.18		2.06	−0.53		1.20	−5.49	3.16	0.31	−1.18	10.08		−0.69
Ranking	**5**	**7**		**3**	**8**		**4**	**11**	**2**	**6**	**10**	**1**		**9**
Jensen's alpha	0.07	−0.62		1.02	0.06		0.31	−4.44	2.59	−0.79	−0.04	4.28		−1.54
Prob value (alpha)	0.92	0.70		0.45	0.96		0.72	0.00	0.21	0.40	0.98	0.05		0.12
Ranking	**5**	**8**		**3**	**6**		**4**	**11**	**2**	**9**	**7**	**1**		**10**
Obs.	60	60		60	36		60	32	60	60	38	60		60
D. 2014m1–2017m7														
Sharpe ratio	0.03	0.01	−0.05	0.13	0.02	−0.11	0.03	0.22	−0.01	−0.15	0.07	−0.25	0.08	0.12
Modified Sharpe ratio	0.03	0.01	−2.84	0.13	0.02	−3.16	0.03	0.22	−1.14	−5.97	0.07	−30.92	0.08	0.12
Ranking	**6**	**9**	**11**	**2**	**8**	**12**	**7**	**1**	**10**	**13**	**5**	**14**	**4**	**3**
Treynor ratio	0.24	0.17	64.65	1.86	0.17	−1.09	0.36	7.41	−1.72	−1.27	0.76	−18.55	−4.75	1.21
Modified Treynor ratio	0.24	0.17	0.002	1.86	0.17	−0.33	0.36	7.41	−0.01	−0.72	0.76	−0.42	−4.75	1.21
Ranking	**6**	**7**	**14**	**2**	**8**	**10**	**5**	**1**	**9**	**12**	**4**	**11**	**13**	**3**
Jensen's alpha	−0.05	−0.02	−0.46	1.08	−0.12	−0.86	0.11	1.83	−0.25	−1.28	0.45	−3.20	0.63	1.07
Prob value (alpha)	0.93	0.97	0.69	0.42	0.87	0.22	0.90	0.29	0.86	0.09	0.73	0.07	0.56	0.47
Ranking	**8**	**7**	**11**	**2**	**9**	**12**	**6**	**1**	**10**	**13**	**5**	**14**	**4**	**3**
Obser.	43	43	43	43	43	43	43	43	43	43	43	43	43	43

Table 5. Performance comparison of REITs with BIST 100 for different sub-periods.

The Sharpe ratio is adjusted by adding an exponent to the denominator, standard deviation of excess return. The exponent is excess return divided by the absolute value of excess return, $\overline{Rj} - \overline{R_f}$. This modification does not have any impact on positive ratios. But by modifying the negative ones, modified Sharpe ratio leads to correct rankings. Since the time period is quite a long one, negative Treynor ratios are also observed. By using the same logic, to prevent counterintuitive results, Treynor ratios are also modified in the same way:

$$T_j = \frac{\overline{Rj} - \overline{R_f}}{\beta j^{ER/|ER|}} \quad (5)$$

Table 5 reports both Sharpe and Treynor ratios and their modified versions.

The performance rankings by Sharpe ratio (whether modified or not) theoretically can differ from those of Treynor ratio and Jensen's alpha since Sharpe ratio depends on volatility of return, while Treynor ratio and Jensen's alpha depend on systematic risk, beta, as the relevant risk factor. For the first period (Panel A of **Table 5**), there is no significant difference in the ranking orders of REIT performances. Even though none of the Jensen's alpha values are significant (probability values are quite large), the rankings for all of three measures are almost the same. Similarly, the observed rankings by Treynor ratio and Sharpe ratio are fairly consistent with each other in Panel C, for the second high-growth period. Jensen performance measures, though not significant, are not really far away from those rankings, either. Some minor differences can be observed in the rankings in Panel B between Treynor and Sharpe ratios. However, the last period, presented in Panel D of the **Table 5** has some real contrasts in ranking orders of Treynor and Sharpe. The most important one is the Yeni Gimat REIT (YGGYO). While it is ranked as fourth by Sharpe ratio, it is only the second from the last (13th) in ranking by Treynor. Such differences of course can be attributed to the differences in risk measure employed, that is, standard deviation of return versus beta. Given that the reported R-squared values for REITs are high (see **Table 6**), it can be assumed that beta coefficients are quite reliable and thus, Treynor ratios that uses beta can be thought to be giving more convincing performance rankings than Sharpe.

When the performance ratings are compared over the periods, between first and second periods, there is not much difference. In the third period for AKMGY, VKGYO and NUGYO some changes are observed. AKMGY ranking as first before the crisis (Panel B) becomes only the seventh after the crisis period (Panel C). On the other hand, NUGYO improves by four rankings (from six to two) and VKGYO improves by at least one ranking for the same periods. However, the last period is witness to much more important changes in the rankings for most of the REITs, namely, for KLGYO, NUGYO, SNGYO, TRGYO, VKGYO, YGGYO and PEGYO. It can be even stated that the rankings are shuffled around for the last period so that VKGYO, which has the first ranking in the third period becomes the last one in the last period. In contrast, KLGYO, which has the 11th ranking in the high-growth period, becomes first one in the last period for all of the performance measures. The others also experience radical changes in their rankings. These results basically show us that regulatory changes almost have no impact on the performances of the REITs. Otherwise, we would observe stable improvements in the performances of the REITs throughout the

REIT	BIST REIT	AKMGY	AKSGYO	ALGYO	EKGYO	HLGYO	ISGYO	KLGYO	NUGYO	SNGYO	TRGYO	VKGYO	YGGYO	PEGYO
A. 2001m5–2017m7														
Beta	0.97***	0.70***	0.04	0.83***	0.93***	0.49***	0.98***	0.81***	0.94***	1.25***	1.12***	0.70***	−0.08	1.18***
R-squared	0.73	0.26	0.00	0.38	0.42	0.28	0.61	0.19	0.31	0.58	0.43	0.18	0.01	0.35
Prob value (beta)	0.00	0.00	0.82	0.00	0.00	0.00	0.00	0.00	0.00	0.00	0.00	0.00	0.64	0.00
B. 2001m5–2005m12														
Beta	0.98***			0.80***			1.04***		0.95***			0.78***		1.23***
R-squared	0.79			0.49			0.70		0.52			0.36		0.38
Prob value (beta)	0.00			0.00			0.00		0.00			0.00		0.00
C. 2006m1–2009m1														
Beta	0.97***	0.60***		0.83***			1.09***		0.85***			0.80***		1.11***
R-squared	0.77	0.46		0.41			0.62		0.32			0.35		0.23
Prob value (beta)	0.00	0.00		0.00			0.00		0.00			0.00		0.00
D. 2009m1–2013m12														
Beta	0.96***	0.96***		0.83***	0.96***		0.83***	1.04***	1.11***	1.56***	1.23***	0.46*		1.12***
R-squared	0.64	0.26		0.28	0.40		0.49	0.52	0.23	0.73	0.60	0.05		0.57
Prob value (beta)	0.00	0.00		0.00	0.00		0.00	0.00	0.00	0.00	0.00	0.10		0.00
E. 2014m1–2017m7														
Beta	0.68***	0.32**	−0.01	0.62**	0.90***	0.55***	0.50***	0.35	0.07	0.75***	0.91***	0.15	−0.12	1.05***
R-squared	0.50	0.12	0.00	0.12	0.47	0.29	0.18	0.03	0.00	0.40	0.24	0.00	0.01	0.25
Prob value (beta)	0.00	0.03	0.98	0.02	0.00	0.00	0.01	0.30	0.79	0.00	0.00	0.66	0.57	0.00

***Shows that beta coefficient is significant at 1% level, **shows beta coefficient is significant at 5% level, *shows the significance at 10% level.

Table 6. Comparison of beta values for different sub-periods.

years. In consistent with the previous literature, it is possible that state of the economy (whether it is a low-growth or high-growth state) is more important in terms of the performances of REITs.

So far, the risk-adjusted returns of the REITs have been analysed for different periods. It may be interesting to look at the systematic risk behaviour of REITs for the same sub-periods. Indeed, a study by Altınsoy et al. [1] shows systematic risks of REITs, betas, decline over time for the period of 2002–2009. They also show that REIT returns more closely track stock market in high-growth economic states than low-growth economic states, unlike to the findings from other countries. **Table 6** compares the beta values of REITs for the sub-periods of the study and aims to investigate whether we can observe similar facts of the mentioned study. Panel A of the **Table 6** shows the CAPM results for the whole period. Panels B, C, D and E show the regression results for periods of 2001–2005, 2006–2008, 2009–2013 and 2014–2017, respectively. Results show that except for five REITs in the last period, AKSGYO, KLGYO, NUGYO, VKGYO and YGGYO, all beta coefficients are significant and mostly at 1% significance level. Respectively, high R-squared values are observed for most of the REITs. On the other hand, the results with respect to beta behaviour over the sub-periods are different than the results of Altınsoy et al. [1][3]. The betas do not decrease from the high-growth (Panel B) to low-growth period (Panel C). For 2009–2013, which is also a high-growth period, different effects are observed, REIT index beta is relatively stable, some betas decrease and some increase. Finally, betas decrease in the last period (low-growth period) substantially. Thus, it is not possible to easily relate decreasing betas in total to economic states as it is done in the previous studies[4]. There may be other important reasons for time-varying betas. Another important thing to notice is the fact that most of the REITs have lower risks than the market portfolio, that is, beta values are lower than one. It shows that although REITs have lower risks, they do not perform better than market index (alphas are not significant but betas are significant).

4. Conclusions

The main purpose of the study is to analyse the performance stability of REIT index and individual REITs over different sub-periods. The sample for the study contains 12 individual REITs that have weights larger than 1% in the REIT index and the REIT index that survived for the whole REIT history in Turkish stock market, thus, in total, 13 individual REITs and REIT index itself. The performance of the REITs is compared to mainly that of BIST 100 Index which is

[3]The present study differs at many aspects from the study by Altınsoy et al. [1]. This study uses monthly returns of both REIT index and individual REITs and uses simple CAPM over a longer period. The study carried out by Altınsoy et al. [1] uses weekly and daily returns for only REIT index for the period 2002–2009 and calculates time varying betas by using three different methods. It does not analyses the individual REITs.

[4]The author has also run regressions with several macroeconomic factors including GDP. Only for the second period, the financial crisis period, 50% of the REIT returns has significant negative relation with GDP. For all other periods, the relationship between REIT returns and GDP is not consistently significant. The best can be said about the relationship is being unclear. These multifactor regressions are also consistent with the declared conclusions on alpha and beta behaviour. The results are not presented here for the sake of brevity and integrity.

accepted to be the reference portfolio in the study. Data employed in this study is the monthly returns for a 14-year period and Treasury bill rates are used as a proxy for the risk-free rate.

For analysing the performance stability, three different risk-adjusted measures, namely, Sharpe ratio, Treynor ratio and Jensen's alpha, are employed for four different periods. These periods are determined with respect to important regulatory changes in the REIT market and also to economic states of the country. The results show that although Treynor and Sharpe ratios use different risk measures, volatility and beta, they rank the REITs consistently for the high-growth periods. However, the rankings are not that consistent in low-growth periods and even they may contrast significantly. In terms of stability, whether the performance of the REITs changes over time, it is observed that the rankings of the REITs in the last period virtually are shuffled up with respect to the previous period. These results basically show us that regulatory changes almost have no impact on the performances of the REITs. Otherwise, we would observe stable improvements in the performances of the REITs throughout the years. In consistent with the previous literature, it is possible that state of the economy (whether it is a low-growth or high-growth state) is more important in terms of the performances of REITs. However, time-varying behaviour of betas does not tell us the same story. The betas do not consistently decrease from the high-growth to low-growth period. Thus, it is not possible to easily relate decreasing betas to economic states as it is done in the previous studies. There may be other important reasons for time varying betas. As a future study, it looks important to analyse why the betas of REITs are decreasing over time.

Author details

Sema Bayraktar

Address all correspondence to: sema.bayraktar@gmail.com

Department of Banking and Finance, School of Applied Sciences, Istanbul Bilgi University, Istanbul, Turkey

References

[1] Altınsoy G, Erol I, Yıldırak K. Time varying beta risk of Turkish Real EState Investment Trusts . METU Studies in Development. 2010;**37**:83-114 (August)

[2] Çoşkun Y, Selçuk-Kestel S, Yılmaz B. Diversification benefit and return performance of REITs using CAPM and Fama-french: Evidence from Turkey. Borsa Istanbul Review. 2017. https://ac.els-cdn.com/S221484501630179X/1-s2.0-S221484501630179X-main.pdf?_tid=904eb3e6-c45b-11e7-8dd6-00000aab0f01&acdnat=1510128500_07262f7b0da532b6df55bf4f3967c83f. DOI: 10.1016/j.bir.2017.08.003

[3] Kıyılar M, Hepşen A. Performance Appraisal of Real Estate Investment Trusts (REITs): A practice in İstanbul Stock Exchange. Yönetim Journal. February 2010;**21**(65):11-23

[4] Erol I, Tırtıroğlu D. The inflation-hedging properties of turkish REITs. Applied Economics. 2008;**40**:2671-2696. DOI: 10.1080/00036840600970237

[5] Erol I, İleri A. What determines REIT returns in Turkey? An application of time-varying arbitrage pricing model in an emerging REIT market. İktisat İşletme ve Finans. 2013;**28**(331): 9-32. DOI: 10.3848/iif.2013.331.3781

[6] Aktan B, Ozturk M. Empirical examination of REITs in Turkey: An emerging market perspective. Journal of Property Investment & Finance. 2009;**27**(4):373-403. DOI: 10.1108/14635 780910972297

[7] Han J, Liang Y. Historical performance of real estate investment trusts. Journal of Real Estate Research. 1995;**10**(3):235-262

[8] Sharpe WF. Mutual fund performance. Journal of Business. 1966;**39**(1):119-138

[9] Treynor JL. How to rate management of investment funds. Harvard Business Review. 1965;**43**:63-75

[10] Jensen M. The performance of mutual funds in the period 1945-1964. Journal of Finance. 1968;**23**(2):389-416

[11] Myer FCN, Webb JR. The effect of benchmark choice on risk-adjusted performance measures for commingled real estate funds. Journal of Real Estate Research. 1993;**8**(2):189-203

[12] Israelsen CL. Refining the Sharpe Ratio. Journal of Performance Measurement. Spring 2009;**13**(3):23-27. DOI: doi.org/10.2469/dig.v40.n1.26

Chapter 17

Analysis of Financial Losses due to Poor Adherence of Patients with Chronic Diseases and Their Impact on Health Economics

Adina Turcu-Stiolica, Mihaela-Simona Subtirelu, Adriana-Elena Taerel, Anamaria Bobcia and Anca Berbecaru-Iovan

Additional information is available at the end of the chapter

http://dx.doi.org/10.5772/intechopen.70320

Abstract

Pharmaceutical drugs—prescription drugs, not over-the-counter drugs—have prices that are negotiated between pharmaceutical companies and National Ministry of Health or national agency for medicines or national health insurers in every country. Prescription drug expenditures have increased every country's healthcare costs. Medication adherence (defined as not obtained refills of prescriptions or suboptimal dosing of prescribed drugs) is a growing concern to physicians and healthcare systems because of the multiple evidence of noncompliance among patients and correlated adverse outcomes. A patient is considered adherent if he/she takes 80% of his/her prescribed medicine(s). Different studies showed that patients do not take their prescribed medicines about half the time. Financial losses due to poor adherence are the result of unnecessary time-consuming work and costs for potential harm to patients. Hospitalization rates are reduced at higher levels of medication adherence. There are two types of financial losses due to poor treatment adherence: medical costs (measured by hospitalization risk) and drugs costs (without patient copayments). This financial loss analysis underlines the promotion of medication adherence by the patients.

Keywords: adherence, drugs, costs, persistence, concordance, compliance

1. Introduction

Chronic diseases such as diabetes, stroke, arthritis, and heart diseases are the main cause of disability and death throughout the world. More than 40% of the people suffer in their adult life from a chronic disease, and approximately 20% are hospitalized because of it. Another perspective is that they are costly, but in many cases preventable. The main cause is usually lifestyle choices that are hard to change; eating foods that are low in fats, becoming more physically active, and avoiding tobacco can help from developing high-risk conditions and diseases.

Patients with multiple chronic diseases struggle with great challenges on their daily lives; also, they experience poor health outcomes and will tend to use health national services more than patients with single chronic disease. Not respecting treatment prescriptions have both personal health impact and health economics consequences. These people are regarded as the highest cost patient populations in the healthcare system [1], with a poor adherence to treatment and medical advices. Worldwide, experts are examining the situation in which health care can be better organized to meet the needs of every patient. It was demonstrated that every dollar spent for improving adherence saves seven dollars in total healthcare costs [2, 3].

The absence of appropriate clinical practice guidelines for patients with multiple chronic diseases is a huge problem, which healthcare providers contend. Furthermore, patient-centered care needs to be supported through the transition of a more oriented approach to help patients prioritize their condition.

Moreover, not taking the required medication prescribed can have both personal health impact and health economics consequences. Recently, patients have shown increased interest in their own healthcare possibilities, raising the overall rate of adherence to treatment. However, the cost-effectiveness is still a parameter that is often ignored when a medical expert chooses to treat different kinds of conditions. Adherence is defined as "persistence in a practice," so this definition emphasizes the routine that people with chronic disease ideally engage in when taking prescription medication [4].

The term first used was "compliance." Charavel et al. [5] described this concept like physician alone makes the treatment decision, while the passive and dependent patient is obliged to comply with it. But the patient is not so silent and the term "adherence" is more used, the patient is more engaged in taking prescription medication.

Adherence cannot be defined as an "all or nothing" response in which the patient either follows the prescriber's instruction to the letter (adherence) or deviates from it in some way (nonadherence) [6]. A patient is considered adherent if he/she takes 80% of his/her prescribed medicine(s). In the current era of free and easy access to information, with a higher educational level across the population, the concept of "concordance" seems to win for some diseases, when the patient want to defer decisions entirely to their health professionals or family members. Some patients prefer a collaborative role, whereas others prefer a passive role.

The most common chronic diseases that have a low adherence rate to treatment are asthma, diabetes, heart disease, obesity, rheumatic diseases, eating disorders, chronic obstructive pulmonary disease (COPD), and psychotic disorders.

The estimated rate of adherence is only half of the percentage of the patients with chronic diseases. Ten days after a new prescription has been filled [7], another quarter of the patients have missed one dose of the medication (intentionally or unintentionally). This kind of behavior causes concern among the medical experts, so they have to make strong decisions in order to make the treatment more functional for every patient.

The top three therapy classes used for chronic diseases are inflammatory conditions, multiple sclerosis, and cancer. These three account more than a half of the total spend for all specialty medications. The new trend is that patients often shift from using brand medications to lower cost generics; as they do this, the copayments decline and also the adherence drops significantly.

The medications used to treat diabetes, high blood cholesterol and high blood pressure, ulcer, and asthma were the most expensive traditional therapy class. Also these classes had the minimum nonadherence rate (between 20 and 35%). In the case of ulcer disease, it is more likely for aged people to be more adherent to the treatment. Asthma is another case of strong nonadherence cases for the pediatric patients.

Correct understanding of barriers for adherence and strategies used can help physicians educate their patients more appropriately, reducing the risk of nonadherence and achieving an improvement of the healthcare system [8].

A lot of studies were done to estimate the costs related to nonadherence to drug therapy in developed countries, making distinctions between primary nonadherence (prescriptions not being filled by the patient) and secondary nonadherence (medication not being taken as prescribed). World Health Organization (WHO) published in 2003 a report of poor adherence to treatment of chronic diseases in which developing countries were found to have a higher rate of nonadherence than the 50% average of nonadherence to long-term therapy for chronic diseases in developed countries [9].

Mills et al. [10] examined both developed and developing nations in a systematic review of adherence and reported the same important barriers (fear of disclosure, substance abuse, forgetfulness, suspicions of treatment, too complicated regimens, too many pills, and decreased quality of life), with some facilitators reported by patients in developed nation (having a sense of self-worth, accepting their disease, understanding the need for strict adherence, making use of reminder tools, and having a simple regimen).

2. Pharmacoeconomic tools

An economic evaluation of adherence consists in assessing the outcomes and costs of intervention designed to improve health. It is like we evaluate a new intervention when the new one is not compared with usual health care, for example the standard intervention, but with no intervention at all. The incremental cost-effectiveness ratio (ICR) is the difference in costs (C) between the drug and no drug divided by the difference in effects (E) between the drug and no drug.

$$\text{ICR} = \frac{C_{\text{drug}} - C_{\text{no drug}}}{E_{\text{drug}} - E_{\text{no drug}}} \tag{1}$$

There are four form of economic evaluation of interventions:

- Cost-effectiveness analysis
- Cost-utility analysis
- Cost-benefit analysis
- Cost-minimization analysis

A summary of the characteristics of these types of economic evaluation is described in **Table 1**.

The most used techniques are cost-effectiveness analysis (CEA) and cost-utility analysis (CUA). A budget impact analysis (BIA) might be added to the economic evaluation.

2.1. Cost-effectiveness analysis

A cost-effectiveness analysis of adherence shows effects in naturally occurring units, such as death, illnesses or burns prevented, and the costs in monetary units (Euros, Dollars, etc.). We can use this type of analysis because it provides information about the relative efficiency of alternative interventions that serve the same goal, what happened if the adherence is smaller comparative with a higher value. A cost-effective analysis must contain effect outcomes and the costs for the different values of adherence and should compare them. Cost-effectiveness analysis is the simplest type of economic evaluation to explain the differences in outcomes.

Measuring benefits in natural units is the main advantage and focusing on a single outcome—adherence—could be considered a disadvantage.

2.2. Cost-utility analysis

Cost-utility analysis evaluates the difference in costs relative to the difference in quality adjusted life years (QALYs). Both types of effects—on the life expectancy and on quality of life—are used to justify the costs. QALYs are represented by the number of gained life

Methods	Costs	Effects	Evaluation question
Cost-effectiveness analysis (CEA)	Monetary units	Natural units (life-years gained, burns prevented, etc.)	Comparisons of interventions with same objective
Cost-utility analysis (CUA)	Monetary units	Utility and QALY (quality-adjusted life-year) or DALY (disability-adjusted life-year)	Comparison of interventions with different objectives
Cost-benefits analysis (CBA)	Monetary units	Monetary units	Are the benefits worth the costs?
Cost-minimization analysis (CMA)	Monetary units	The effects are not measured, since they are considered to be equal	Least-cost comparisons of programs with the same outcome

Table 1. Characteristics of the four types of pharmacoeconomic evaluations [11].

years corrected for quality of life. The QALY is the standard outcome measure existed in health economic evaluations, but there are some countries (Germany, Spain, and USA) that decided to ban the use of QALY in Health Technologies Assessment (HTA), after considering that QALY is methodologically and ethically not robust for health decision making. It is based on the use of subjective parameters, which are less robust than the chemical and biochemical parameters.

QALYs are determined with the aid of generic measurement instruments like EQ-5D [12], SF-6D (Short Form 6D), DCE (discrete-choice experiment), or MCDA (multi-criteria decision analysis). Another examples of generic instruments are Nottingham Health Profile (NHP), quality of well-being scale (QWB), sickness impact profile (SIP), and Health Utilities Index (HUI) Mark III.

EQ-5D is one of the most commonly used questionnaires to measure health-related quality of life (HRQOL). It consists of a questionnaire about five directions of current health (mobility, self-care, usual activities, pain/discomfort, and anxiety/depression) and a visual analogue scale (EQ-VAS). It was developed for adults, but a new version has been recently developed for children aged 8–18 years old (EQ-5D-Y) and the five dimensions are: walking about, look-after myself, doing usual activities, having pain or discomfort, feeling worried, sad or unhappy.

Nottingham Health Profile (NHP) [13] includes two parts: Part I about distress within the following domains: emotions, sleep, social isolation, energy, pain, and mobility and Part II about health-related problems within the domains: occupation, housework, social life, home life, sex life, hobbies, and holidays.

Quality of Well-Being Scale (QWB) [14] includes questions about symptoms/problems, mobility, physical activity, and social activity.

Sickness impact profile (SIP) [15] includes questions about sleep/rest, eating, work, ambulation, mobility, communication, home management, recreation and pastimes, body care and movement, alertness behavior, emotional behavior, and social interaction.

Health Utilities Index (HUI) Mark III [16] includes questions about vision, hearing, speech, ambulation, dexterity, cognition, pain and discomfort, and emotion (**Figure 1**).

The complexity of assessing outcomes in cost-utility analysis is a disadvantage, even if this analysis can decide the best way of spending a given treatment budget or the healthcare budget as a whole.

2.3. Cost-benefit analysis

Cost-benefit analysis evaluates the difference in costs relative to the difference in benefits, with the benefits expressed in monetary units. This is the only pharmacoeconomic analysis that could determine how much more or less of society's resources could be allocated to pursuing increasing patient adherence.

Mobility
I have no problems in walking about ☐

I have some problems in walking about ☐

I am confined to bed ☐

Self-Care
I have no problems with self-care ☐
I have some problems with washing or dressing myself ☐
I am unable to wash or dress myself ☐

Usual Activities (*e.g. work, study, housework, family or leisure activities*)
I have no problems with performing my usual activities ☐
I have some problems with performing my usual activities ☐
I am unable to perform my usual activities ☐

Pain / Discomfort
I have no pain or discomfort ☐
I have moderate pain or discomfort ☐
I have extreme pain or discomfort ☐

Anxiety / Depression
I am not anxious or depressed ☐
I am moderately anxious or depressed ☐
I am extremely anxious or depressed ☐

Best imaginable health state

Visual Analogue Scale

Please indicate on this scale how good or bad your own health state is today.

The best health state you can imagine is marked 100 and the worst health state you can imagine is marked 0.

Please draw a line from the box to the point on the scale that indicates how good or bad your health state is today.

Your own health state today

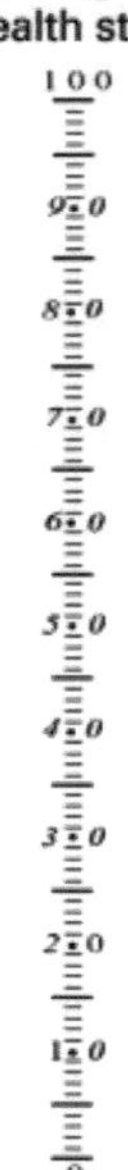

Worst imaginable health state

Figure 1. EQ-5D health questionnaire.

Measuring benefits in monetary units is a disadvantage because it is a problem to valuate benefits, including death and disease, in money units.

2.4. Cost-minimization analysis

This analysis is performed when two health alternatives are equal, but few interventions are actually equally effective. Some evidence must support the assertion that outcomes are the same.

Cost-minimization analysis is not an appropriate method of analysis adherence costs.

In order to estimate costs, studies must include costs for hospitalization, outpatient services, hospital stays, emergency care, clinical visits, laboratory tests, professional services, pharmaceuticals, and medical devices. Patients' copayments and deductibles must not be included in costs assessment. Indirect costs (cost to society due to illness) and direct nonmedical costs (costs to the patient such as travel) could have a significant impact on total costs.

3. Adherence measuring

The concept of adherence or compliance can be measured in many different ways, including multi-item questionnaire scales, individual questionnaire, independent observations from patients and physicians, electronic monitoring devices, etc.

Many methods have been utilized to collect data for measuring medication adherence. Some data collection techniques include directly observing patients consuming medications, monitoring through electronic pill dispensers, and measuring clinical outcomes, such as, serum drug concentration levels. Other methods include clinical data from clinical trials, administrative claims data, electronic pharmacy databases, registries, patient and provider surveys, and paper medical records. There are several methods for measuring medication adherence using data obtained from these techniques that measure the time a patient has access to medication, including the medication possession ratio (MPR = number of days of medication supplied within the refill interval/number of days in refill interval), proportion of days covered (PDC=total days all drugs available/days in follow-up period), missing days, time to discontinuation, persistence rate, medication gaps, or self-reported questionnaires like Composite Adherence Score (CAS), Morisky Medication Adherence Scale (MMAS) with 4/8/9 questions, and Compliance Questionnaire for Rheumatology (CQR) with 5/19 questions.

3.1. Rheumatic diseases

In rheumatology clinics, Berry et al. [17] found nonadherence patients who were answering 'no' to the question "Have you taken medicine regularly as prescribed or directed?", more common among new (28%) than follow-up patients (1%). Overall, the patients were more on nonsteroidal anti-inflammatory drug (NSAIDs) than on disease-modifying antirheumatic drug (DMARDs), also the adherence was better for them, according to the symptoms and directed dose. Another difference measured in adherence is the cultural one, especially because of the economic impact of the treatment, that can lead to big cost problems. The follow-up adherence among patients with lupus depends on the medications prescribed. McElhone et al. [18] discussed that the perfect adherence rate is between 100% for treatment with azathioprine, 94% for oral steroids, and 68% for NSAIDs.

In the case of rheumatoid arthritis (RA), adherence is estimated at similar values. Researchers such as Neame and Hammond [19] found that 90% of the patients with RA are in fact taking their medication according to doctors' recommendations. Adherence rate is also correlated with the type of medication that is prescribed. The overall adherence is approximately 70% for NSAIDs, 50% for sulfasalazine and 80% for methotrexate, according to Klerk et al. [20]. Viewing the results, the weekly treatment with methotrexate may facilitate the enhanced adherence rate. In addition, patients' result are not as dependent on NSAIDs as it is thought, and this can be a good thing for the recent concerns about the cardiovascular risk associated with continuous usage of the high-dose drug.

3.2. Diabetes

The healthcare costs and the nonadherence to treatment for diabetes are both problems that need to be resolved. The information that is available at this moment regarding patient's adherence in diabetes is very poor. Studies have shown that adherence in diabetes is related more often to insulin (from 19 to 46%) [21], than to oral agents. The complications and the cost-effectiveness of antidiabetic drugs are a serious problem, according to the American Diabetes Association [22]. Inadequate use or poor adherence to insulin results in ketoacidosis that often requires hospitalization and more costs.

For people with diabetes, all-cause medical costs decrease as hypoglycemic drugs' adherence increases.

Sokol et al. [2] demonstrated that costs and hospitalization risk for people with diabetes monotonically decreased as adherence to drug treatment increased (**Table 2**).

Even if drug cost is bigger and medical cost is smaller in the case of adherent patients (adherence level>80), the total cost is the smallest. These savings probably reflect the effects of

Adherence level	Medical cost ($)	Drug cost ($)	Total cost ($)	Hospitalization risk (%)
1–19	8812	55	8867	30
20–39	6959	165	7124	26
40–59	6237	285	6522	25
60–79	5887	404	6291	20
80–100	3808	763	4570	13

Table 2. Costs for people with diabetes.

http://dx.doi.org/10.5772/intechopen.70320

improved glycemic level on related diseases like microvascular disease or neuropathy, reducing the need for medical services.

Balkrishnan et al. [23] found that a 10% increase in medication possession ratios (MPRs) for an antidiabetic medication was associated with an 8.6% reduction in total annual healthcare costs.

Cobden et al. [36] used MPR to assess diabetic patients and found that MPR of 80% or greater was associated with significant reduction in all-cause healthcare costs. MPR of 68% was associated with total mean costs of $8056, whereas an MPR of 59% had total mean costs of $8699.

Gilmer et al. [24] estimated that medical care costs increased significantly for each 1% increase in HbA1c (glycosylated hemoglobin) above 7%. For a person with an HbA1c value of 6%, successive 1% increases in HbA1c resulted in cumulative increases in charges of almost 4, 10, 20, and 30%. For adults with diabetes and other diseases the costs are also increased. The most substantial cost increments occurred in individuals who had diabetes in combination with heart disease and hypertension: a 1% improvement in HbA1c level from 10 to 9% was associated with increasing in costs of $4116. The differences in costs are lower if the HbA1c value is smaller. If the patient isn't adherent to the antidiabetic medicines, the increased HbA1c will rise the costs for healthcare system (**Table 3**).

Nonadherence to oral hypoglycemic medications may partly explain why only 43% of patients with diabetes mellitus have HbA1c below 7% level [21].

3.3. Pulmonary diseases (chronic obstructive pulmonary disease)

Chronic obstructive pulmonary disease (COPD) is a chronic limitation hat is usually progressive and not reversible. The main treatment for this condition aims to reduce symptoms, prevent exacerbations and delay the progression of the disease. Although medication has not been shown to modify the long-term of lung disease, various medications are available to prevent and control patients' symptoms, and improve health. Patient adherence to medication for COPD is very poor compared with rates for medicines and other long-terms conditions. Nonadherence to medication is a risk factor for morbidity, hospital admission and increased mortality.

Zaniolo et al. [27] made a budget impact study to demonstrate the implications of the adherence to patients with chronic obstructive pulmonary diseases. The target population that they

	Changes in HbA1c levels			
	10–9%	9–8%	8–7%	7–6%
Patients with diabetes, heart disease, and hypertension	$4116	$3090	$2237	$1504
Patients with diabetes and heart disease	$2796	$2088	$1503	$1002
Patients with diabetes and hypertension	$1703	$1260	$897	$588
Patients with diabetes	$1205	$869	$601	$378

Table 3. Costs for patients with diabetes and other diseases.

examined corresponds to the entire sick population. They simulated that the same target population is managed under the same strategies of medical purpose. The current strategy is defined in order to reproduce the actual pattern of healthcare resource consumption and related costs for COPD management.

Toy et al. [28] had examined in their study the adherence level among patients with inhaled COPD medications. They used the data from real-world clinical practice, as well as the national healthcare database. As a conclusion, it was emphasized that a correct management of COPD can be aided by the frequency which the patient is using the drug. Drugs with fewer daily doses are associated with improved adherence, and as well with lower healthcare resource use and cost. For 1000 COPD patients, a 5% increase in proportion of days covered (PDC) reduced the annual number of inpatient visits with 2.5% and emergency room visits with 1.8%, with a slightly increased outpatient visits (+0.2%) and a net reduction in annual cost of approximately $300,000. This study suggests that dosing frequency should be an important method in increasing adherence of COPD patients because patients with once-daily dosing frequency had highest adherence levels relative to patients with twice-daily, three times daily and four times daily dosing frequency.

Simoni-Wastila et al. [25] used administrative data with COPD patients, medication continuity and proportion of days covered (PDC) for assessing adherence. COPD patients with higher adherence to prescribed treatments experienced fewer hospitalizations and lower medicare costs than those who presented lower adherence behaviors. Both lack of interruption in drug dispensing and higher adherence were associated with better clinical outcomes.

3.4. Heart diseases

The costs for heart diseases are creating a burden on the patients' finances. Most commonly they experience acute myocardial infarction, known as heart attack. The costs include ambulance rides, diagnostic test, hospital stays, and also surgery if needed. Employees suffering from heart disease require additional days off, so they are less productive at work, so it is not cost-effective for the economy. Additionally, the premature deaths caused by heart diseases are growing in the United States. In 2010, according to George and Hong [26], $41.7 billion was lost in potential productivity due to cardiovascular diseases.

To lower the high costs of this condition, patients must make small changes in their lifestyle. These preventive changes include weight lost, exercising, avoiding smoking, eating healthy, also they can monitor their blood pressure and cholesterol levels every month, for lowering the rate of mortality.

Sokol et al. [2] demonstrated that hospitalization risk for people with hypertension monotonically decreased as adherence to drug treatment increased. Differences were significantly higher than the outcome for adherence >80% in the case of low adherence (<60%). We observe higher costs only for adherence in the interval [20].

In the case of congenitive heart failure, the differences in costs were not so obvious like in the case of hypertension. The total costs are the highest in the case of adherent patients (adherence level >80%). Hospitalization risk is significant higher than the outcome for adherent patients with congenitive heart failure in the case of patients with adherence in the interval (**Tables 4** and **5**) [20].

http://dx.doi.org/10.5772/intechopen.70320

Adherence level	Medical cost ($)	Drug cost ($)	Total cost ($)	Hospitalization risk (%)
1–19	4847	31	4878	28
20–39	5973	89	6062	24
40–59	5113	184	5297	24
60–79	4977	285	5262	20
80–100	4383	489	4871	19

Table 4. Healthcare costs and hospitalization risk at different levels of adherence for patients with hypertension.

Adherence level	Medical cost ($)	Drug cost ($)	Total cost ($)	Hospitalization risk (%)
1–19	9826	15	9841	58
20–39	7643	90	7733	63
40–59	11244	134	11378	65
60–79	13766	158	13924	64
80–100	12261	437	12698	57

Table 5. Healthcare costs and hospitalization risk at different levels of adherence for patients with congenitive heart failure.

Similarly, for hypertensive patients, the total costs are the smallest even if the drug cost is higher. These values reflect the impact of related conditions like, for example, renal disease.

Levine et al. [29] estimated for cardiology patients in USA that 125,000 deaths per year lead to a societal cost of 20 million lost work days and $1.5 billion lost earnings.

McCombs et al. [30] used individual patient inpatient and outpatient claims data to identify increased health service costs associated with interruptions in therapy. The medicines costs were lower with $281, but the healthcare costs were higher with $873 ($637 due to increased hospitalization).

3.5. Barriers to chronic disease treatment and management

Morbidity from nonadherence to medications is a major public health problem in many therapeutic areas [31]. About one in four people do not adhere well to prescribe drug therapy. Poor adherence is considered a critical barrier to treatment success and remains one of the challenges to healthcare professionals [32]. Combining adherence to drug therapy with adherence to other interventions limits the ability to examine the relation between adherence to drug therapy and health outcomes. The effect of adherence should be measured on an objective health outcome, such as mortality. Individual studies have reported that good adherence was associated with a lower risk of mortality. The association between adherence to harmful therapy and mortality is a very important subject in the light of recent issues of the safety of patients and postmarket drug surveillance.

The correlations between the mortality/morbidity rates for most chronic diseases are shown in **Table 6**.

Most nonadherence is intentional. Patients make the decision to not take their medicines based on some reasons:

- Fear: Patients may be scared of potential side effects or side effects they had previously with the same or similar medication.
- Cost: The prices of medicine can be a barrier to adherence.
- Misunderstanding: Patients do not understand the need for medicine, the side effects or the expected time it will take to see some results.
- Too many medications: The greater the number of different medicines prescribed and the higher the dosing frequency, the more likely a patient is nonadherent.
- Lack of symptoms: Patients who do not feel any differences when they start or stop to take their medicines may see no reason to take it.
- Worry: Concerns about becoming dependent on a medicine leads to nonadherence.
- Depression: Patients who are depressed are less likely to take their medications as prescribed.
- Mistrust: Patients may be suspicious of their doctor's motives for prescribing certain medications, for example because of the marketing efforts of pharmaceutical companies to influence some prescribing patterns.

The costs of new drugs often exceed the costs of existing drugs. Such increased costs can be compensated by savings in other areas of health system (costs-offsets). For example, a new drug has fewer side effects and fewer costs to cure them. But, the first step is the patient to be adherent and to respect the prescription.

We cannot say that nonadherence always leads to financial losses. Nonadherence is not always bad for the patient. Nonadherence is protective if the prescription is inappropriate or has adverse reactions. It is not useful to pay for an inefficient drug. New undesired costs will appear if side effects occur. Savings associated with undercompliance with overprescribed medications are positive economic effects. We must highlight the fact that the doctor, the pharmacist and the patient carry mutual responsibility for the outcome of the treatment. Further work is needed to develop optimal adherence patterns for individual patients and treatments. Important policy decisions need to be made about increasing nonadherence.

Physicians play a key role in medication adherence. Trust and communication are two elements critical in optimizing adherence. Various studies have shown that physicians trust is more important than treatment satisfaction in predicting adherence to prescribed therapy. In consequence, physicians trust correlates positively with the acceptance of new medication, and improves the self-reported health status. A recent meta-analysis of physician communication and patient adherence to treatment found that there is a 19% higher risk of

http://dx.doi.org/10.5772/intechopen.70320

nonadherence among patients whose physician communicates poorly than among patients whose physician communicates well [34].

Healthcare providers play an unique role in assisting patients to carry out healthy behaviors and also to change patient's beliefs about the risks and benefits of new medication. Another factor is concordance, in which patients and their providers (and physicians) agree whether

Chronic noncommunicable diseases	Percentage mortality	Percentage morbidity
Cardiovascular disease		
Rheumatic heart disease, hypertensive heart disease, ischemic heart disease, cerebrovascular disease, inflammatory heart disease	49.90	21.23
Malignant neoplasms		
Mouth and oropharynx cancers; esophagus cancer; stomach cancer; colon and rectum cancers; liver cancer; pancreas cancer; trachea, bronchus, lung cancers; melanoma and other skin cancers; breast cancer, cervix uteri cancer; corpus uteri cancer; ovary cancer; prostate cancer; bladder cancer; lymphomas; multiple myeloma; leukemia	21.23	10.83
Respiratory diseases		
Chronic obstructive pulmonary disease, asthma	11.04	7.90
Digestive diseases		
Peptic ulcer disease, cirrhosis of the liver, appendicitis	5.87	6.66
Neuropsychiatric conditions		
Unipolar depressive disorders, bipolar disorder, schizophrenia, epilepsy, alcohol use disorders, Alzheimer's and other dementias, Parkinson disease, multiple sclerosis, drug use disorders, post-traumatic stress disorder, obsessive-compulsive disorder, panic disorder, insomnia, migraine, lead-caused mental retardation	3.32	27.70
Diabetes mellitus	2.95	2.32
Genitourinary diseases		
Nephritis and nephrosis, benign prostatic hypertrophy	2.53	2.18
Endocrine disorders	0.72	1.14
Other neoplasms	0.44	0.25
Musculoskeletal diseases		
Rheumatoid arthritis, osteoarthritis, gout, low back pain	0.32	4.32
Skin diseases	0.21	0.54
Congenital anomalies		
Abdominal wall defect, anencephaly, anorectal atresia, cleft lip, cleft palate, esophageal atresia, renal agenesis, Down syndrome, congenital heart anomalies, spina bifida	0.15	3.92
Sense organ diseases		
Glaucoma, cataracts, age-related vision disorders, adult-onset hearing loss	0.01	9.94
Oral conditions		
Dental caries, periodontal disease, edentulism	0.01	1.06

Table 6. Morbidity and mortality rates for chronic diseases [33].

and how a medication should be taken. Adherence requires the patient to believe there is a benefit to the medicine being prescribed and agree with the instructions on how to take it. Building trust and developing skills for successful communication between the patients and their provider, demands time, effort, knowledge, and practice.

Even those patients who fill and refill their prescriptions appropriately may have lapses in the continuity of their doses. One in five patients who receives a prescription medication cannot read the label.

Elliot et al. [35] concluded there is not possible to make definitive conclusions about the cost-effectiveness of Adherence-Enhancing Interventions (AEIs) due to the heterogeneity of the reported studies: unclear reported adherence and outcomes, poorer quality of costs data, and omitted some cost elements.

4. Conclusions

The assessment of pharmaceutical drugs and healthcare programs has been in recent years expanded beyond efficacy and safety to cover economic implications and other consequences. The incorporation of an economic perspective into the decision making process as to which therapies will be reimbursed by the national healthcare system and not only that, has made the subject of debate and discussion. National programs combining patient education with behavioral intervention strategies could decrease the financial losses due to poor adherence. The intention of this chapter was to highlight a very important problem of adherence in direct symbiosis with the economic situation. To ascertain the true extent of financial losses due to low adherence in emerging countries, more studies are urgently required. The absence of national policies grows the financial losses due to poor adherence. The answer, in our opinion, is not to spend more money on drugs and expensive treatment costs, but to work towards the patient in general. As individuals we are constantly making choices as to how we use our time and money, but we do not always think about our well-being regarding the health.

Author details

Adina Turcu-Stiolica[1*], Mihaela-Simona Subtirelu[1], Adriana-Elena Taerel[2], Anamaria Boboia[3] and Anca Berbecaru-Iovan[1]

*Address all correspondence to: adina.turcu@gmail.com

1 University of Medicine and Pharmacy of Craiova, Craiova, Romania

2 University of Medicine and Pharmacy Carol Davila, Bucharest, Romania

3 University of Medicine and Medicine Iuliu Hatieganu, Cluj-Napoca, Romania

References

[1] DiMatteo MR. Variations in patients' adherence to medical recommendations: a quantitative review of 50 years of research. Medical Care. 2004;**42**:200-209

[2] Sokol MC, McGuigan KA, Verbrugge RR, Epstein RS. Impact of medication adherence on hospitalization risk and healthcare cost. Medical Care. 2005;**43**(6):521-530

[3] Zolnierek KB, Dimatteo MR. Physician communication and patient adherence to treatment: a meta-analysis. Medical Care. 2009;**47**(8):826-834

[4] The Oxford English Dictionary. Adherence. OED Online. 2nd ed. Oxford: Oxford University Press; 1989. Available from: http://dictionary.oed.com/cgi/entry/50002621. [Accessed October 14 2005]

[5] Charavel M, Bremond A, Moumjid-Ferdjaoui N, Mignotte H, Carrere MO. Shared decision-making in question. Psycho-Oncology. 2001;**10**:93-102

[6] Horne R, Weinman J, Barber N, Elliott R. Concordance, adherence and compliance in medicine taking. Report for the National Co-ordinating Centre for NHS Service Delivery and Organization R&D (NCCSDO); December 2005

[7] Barber N, Parsons J, Clifford S, Darracott R, Horne R. Patients' problems with new medication for chronic conditions. Quality and Safety in Health Care. 2004;**13**:172-5

[8] Osterberg L, Blaschke T. Adherence to medication. The New England Journal of Medicine. 2005;**353**:487-97

[9] Adherence to Long-Term Therapies: Evidence for Action. World Health Organization; Published by World Health Organization (2003) ISBN 10: 9241545992 ISBN 13: 9789241 545990

[10] Mills E, Nachega J, Bangsberg D, Singh S, Rachlis B, Wu P, Wilson K, Buchan I, Gill C, Cooper C. Adherence to HAART: A systematic review of developed and developing nation patient-reported barriers and facilitators. PLoS Medicine. 2006;**3**(11):e438

[11] WHO Regional Office for Europe. Methodological Approaches for Cost-effectiveness and Cost-utility Analysis of Injury Prevention Measures. Europe: WHO, 2003

[12] Rabin R, de Charro F. EQ-5D: A measure of health status from the EuroQol Group. Annals of Medicine 2001;**33**:337-343

[13] Hunt SM, McKewan J, McKenna SP. Measuring health status: A new tool for clinicians and epidemiologists. The Journal of the Royal College of General Practitioners. 1985;**35**:185-188

[14] Kaplan RM, Anderson JP. The general health policy model: An integrated approach. In: Spilker B, editor. Quality of Life and Pharmacoeconomics in Clinical Trials. 2nd ed. Philadelphia: Lippincott-Raven; 1996. pp. 309-322

[15] Bergner M, Bobbitt RA, Carter WB, Gilson BS. The Sickness Impact Profile: Development and final revisions of a health status measure. Medical Care. 1976;**14**:57-67

[16] Furlong WJ, Feeny DH, Torrance GW, Barr RD. The Health Utilities Index (HUI®) system for assessing health-related quality of life in clinical studies. Annals of Medicines. 2001;**33**:375-384

[17] Berry D, Bradlow A, Bersellini E. Perceptions of the risks and benefits of medicines in patients with rheumatoid arthritis and other painful musculoskeletal conditions. Rheumatology. 2004;**43**:901-905

[18] McElhone K, Teh L-S, Walker J, Abbott J. Treatment adherence in systemic lupus erythematosus (SLE). Rheumatology. 2005;**44**(Suppl.):i141

[19] Neame R, Hammond A. Beliefs about medications: A questionnaire survey of people with rheumatoid arthritis. Rheumatology. 2005;**44**:762-767

[20] Klerk E, van der Heijde D, Landewé R, van der Tempel H, Urquhart J, van der Linden S. Patient compliance in rheumatoid arthritis, polymyalgia rheumatica, and gout. Journal of Rheumatology. 2003;**30**:44-54

[21] Kerr EA, Gerzoff RB, Krein SL, et al. Diabetes care quality in the Veterans Affairs Health Care System and commercial managed care: The TRIAD study. Annals of Internal Medicine. 2004;**141**:272-281

[22] American Diabetes Association. Standards of medical care in diabetes—2007. Diabetes Care. 2007;**30**:S4-S41

[23] Balkrishnan R, Rajagopalan R, Camacho FT, et al. Predictors of medication adherence and associated health care costs in an older population with type 2 diabetes mellitus: A longitudinal cohort study. Clinical Therapeutics. 2003;**25**:2958-2971

[24] Gilmer TP, O'Connor PJ, Manning WG, Rush WA. The cost to health plans of poor glycemic control. Diabetes Care. 1997;**20**(12):1847-1853

[25] Simoni-Wastila L, Wei YJ, Qian J, Zuckerman I, Stuart B, Shaffer T, Dalal A, Bryant-Comstock L. Association of Chronic Obstructive Pulmonary Disease maintenance medication adherence with all-cause hospitalization and spending in a population. The American Journal of Geriatric Pharmacotherapy. 2012;**10**(3):201-210

[26] George M., & Hong, Y. Aspirin therapy for primary prevention of cardiovascular disease. National Business Group on Health, April 2011

[27] Zaniolo O, Bettoncelli G, Bosio G, et al. Ricerca assistenza e programmazione: dall'audit clinic al modello di impatto sul budget nella BPCO. Farmacoeconomia e percorsi terapeutici. 2010;**11**:121-135

[28] Toy EL, Beaulieu NU, et al. Treatment of COPD: Relationships between daily dosing frequency, adherence, resource use, and costs. Respiratory Medicine. 2011;**105**:435-411

[29] Levine DM. Improving patient compliance. Paper presented at the 33rd Pharmacy Conference. Rutgers University; 1984

[30] McCombs JS, Nichol MB, Newman CM, Sclar DA. The costs of interrupting antihypertensive drug therapy in a Medicaid population. Medical Care. 1994;**32**(3):214-226

[31] Lewis A. Noncompliance: A $100 billion problem. Remington Rep. 1997;**5**(4):14-15

[32] Simpson SH, Eurich DT, et al. A meta-analysis of the association between adherence to drug therapy and mortality. British Medical Journal. 2006. DOI: 10.1136/bmj.38875.675486.55

[33] Stuckler D. World Health Report 2004 and Global Burden of Disease Statistics, World Health Organization. Population causes and consequences of leading chronic diseases: A comparative analysis of prevailing explanations. Milbank Quarterly. 2008;**86**(2):273-326. DOI: 10.1111/j.1468-0009.2008.00522.x

[34] Haskard Zolnierek KB, DiMatteo. Physician communication and patient adherence to treatment: A meta-analysis. Medical Care. 2009;**47**(8):826-834

[35] Elliot RA, Barber N, Horne R. Cost-effectiveness of adherence-enhancing interventions: A quality assessment of the evidence. Annals of Pharmacotherapy. 2005;**39**(3):508-515

[36] Cobden D, Lee WC, Balu S, et al. Health outcomes and economic impact of therapy conversion to a biphasic insulin analog pen among privately insured patients with type 2 diabetes mellitus. Pharmacotherapy 2007;**27**:948-62